Oxford Studies in Social History
General Editor: Keith Thomas

Sport and the British

Sport and the British

A Modern History

RICHARD HOLT

CLARENDON PRESS · OXFORD

1989

Oxford University Press, Walton Street, Oxford OX2 6DP

Oxford New York Toronto
Delhi Bombay Calcutta Madras Karachi
Petaling Jaya Singapore Hong Kong Tokyo
Nairobi Dar es Salaam Cape Town
Melbourne Auckland
and associated companies in
Berlin Ibadan

Oxford is a trade mark of Oxford University Press

Published in the United States
by Oxford University Press, New York

British Library Cataloguing in Publication Data
Holt, Richard, 1948 Apr. 19-
Sport and the British: a modern history.
1. Great Britain. Sports, history
I. Title
796'.0941
ISBN 0-19-822586-5

Library of Congress Cataloging in Publication Data
Holt, Richard, 1948-
Sport and the British: a modern history/Richard Holt.
(Oxford studies in social history)
Bibliography: p.   Includes index.
1. Sports—Great Britain—History. 2. Sports—Social aspects—
Great Britain. I. Title. II. Series.
GV605.H65   1988   796'.0941--dc19   88-21675
ISBN 0-19-822586-5

Set by Dobbie Typesetting Limited, Plymouth, Devon
Printed in Great Britain by
the Alden Press, Oxford

For Liz and Alice

ACKNOWLEDGEMENTS

THIS book tries to explain the nature of sport in modern Britain in terms of changes in society, politics, and culture since the late eighteenth century. Even ten or fifteen years ago this would have been an almost impossible task. It is only as a result of the appearance of a substantial body of new research in the history of sport itself and in the wider realm of social history that such a survey can be attempted at all. Rather than list the many individuals whose research I have used, I prefer simply to express my general gratitude to all those whose names crop up again and again in the footnotes. I am especially indebted to members of the British Society for Sports History and to the contributors to the *British Journal of Sports History* (now The *International Journal of the History of Sport*). Those working this area owe a special debt to Tony Mangan, who helped to set up the Society and the *Journal* as well as making a major scholarly contribution on athleticism and the nineteenth-century public schools. I also feel Tony Mason's *Association Football and English Society*—a model of how to write a scholarly and enjoyable study of a single sport—deserves a special mention. However, I have kept the manuscript to myself and I alone must take the blame for errors of fact or other shortcomings in the text.

Apart from specifically academic debts there are several others who have helped me to write this book. I must first thank Ivon Asquith of Oxford University Press who asked me to write a 'short' history of British sport and waited with great patience for seven years while I produced a rather longer one. Stirling University granted me several periods of leave—paid and unpaid—and colleagues had to cover my frequent absences. Neil Tranter shared his research on the social structure of sport with me and gave warm encouragement. Peter Bilsborough was helpful and Robin Law put some interesting references my way. Mike Hopkinson not only provided hospitality but put his prodigious memory for all things sporting at my disposal. Another friend, Alistair Grimes, was also very supportive and always seemed to know far more about sport as an 'amateur' than I did as a 'professional'. This, I fear, is the fate of those who venture into the study of an area that gives so many people so much pleasure.

No one should write about sport without having at least tried to play something themselves. I have sampled many sports and never succeeded more than very modestly at any. In this connection I have to place on record my appearances in the lower reaches of the Edinburgh Amateur Football League with an assorted bunch of teachers, social workers, and students. If sociability is an important theme in this book then my 'field-work' with the 'Middle Meadows Strollers' is partly to blame. Like so many other boys I grew up kicking a ball and could never quite give up the habit. Here I must mention my uncle Jack Scott, who loves sport. From him I learned to enjoy the banter as much as the game. From my father I got some fascinating memories of sport between the wars and as much uncritical enthusiasm as anyone could ask for.

Without Margaret Hendry to goad me on and to type seemingly endless sets of corrections and additions I would have been quite at a loss. I appreciate very much the trouble she has taken, which goes far beyond the secretarial assistance normally available to an author. Her help has been invaluable.

Finally, I must thank my wife, who has never liked sport and never will. Putting up with someone who first spent nearly ten years writing about French sports and then another seven on *Sport and the British* requires a peculiar kind of stoicism. She also financed much of the research and read through parts of the text. All I can do in return is promise to put a moratorium on another 'big' book on sport.

R.H.

CONTENTS

LIST OF PLATES

ABBREVIATIONS

BJSH	*British Journal of Sports History*
BSSH	British Society for Sports History
HISPA	International Association for the History of Sport and Physical Education
IJHS	*International Journal of the History of Sport*
JSH	*Journal of Sport History*
SSRC	Social Science Research Council

Introduction

'ALL peoples have their play, but none of the great modern nations has built it up in quite the same way into a rule of life and a national code.' This was the verdict of a German visitor to Britain in the 1920s. 'It is this natural evolution of the play-spirit', he continued, 'which has given the English character its most interesting features and from the political, cultural and broadly human point of view, its most important aspect.' Sport was responsible for that 'peculiarly cheerful and naïve philosophy, so elusive and incomprehensible to the foreign observer' that set the British apart. A young French nobleman, the Baron de Coubertin, who was to found the modern Olympic Games, had come to a similar conclusion almost forty years earlier in 1886. Standing 'in the twilight, alone in the great Gothic chapel of Rugby, my eyes fixed on the funeral slab on which, without epitaph, the great name of Thomas Arnold was inscribed, I dreamed that I saw before me the corner-stone of the British Empire'. Sport, he felt, was the source of our imperial dynamism; moreover, it created a solidarity amongst the middle and upper classes, which assured political stability in an era of economic and social upheaval. 'The role played by sport', observed de Coubertin, 'is what appears most worthy of notice in English education.' Whether such claims were true is probably less important than the fact that they were widely believed to be so. To foreigners, cricket in particular was a uniquely English and imperial thing quite beyond ordinary understanding. No doubt the robustly ethnocentric British sportsman would have been inclined to agree: let the French have their cycle races, the Germans their gymnastics, and leave the Americans to get on with their puerile game of baseball—an offensively commercialized form of an English girls' game. Such was the British view of other sports on the rare occasion they gave any thought to what passed for sport beyond the confines of the British Isles and the British

Empire. Anglo-Saxon sports were an integral part of the image that the British presented to the world, and which outsiders came to associate with Britain.[1]

Foreign visitors, of course, were usually well-off and were more concerned with the social élite than with the British nation as a whole. Public-school sport rightly has an important role in this study, but it tells only one part of the story. More compelling to most of the population were the Saturday afternoon matches of the Football League, the most popular and highly organized programme of spectator sport in existence. Beyond this world of clanking turnstiles and vast stadia with thousands of working men in caps and mufflers were the generations of young boys, who kicked their rag and string footballs around the back lanes or used the lamp-post at the street corner as a wicket; then there were all the humble club players, who would never play well but still with gusto and delight, enjoying a few pints and a chat with 'the lads'. The ordinary participant has been overlooked in the history of sport, which often has been little more than the book of Chronicles or the book of Numbers. Praising a few famous men and compiling records is not enough. The cult of statistical success, so pronounced this century, has obscured motives, pleasures, and values enshrined in the daily round of play. A social history of sport in modern Britain not only has to ask 'What has changed and why?' but 'How did people feel about the changing place of sport in their lives?' How do we differ from our forebears who baited cocks, bobbed for apples, fought 'singlestick', or cheerfully piled into the parish battles that passed for football? Only recently has sport become the subject of serious study rather than just existing as a thing apart, in isolation from the mainstream of history. The games we have played and our ways of playing them can be properly understood only in terms of the development of British society and the British Empire. The object of this study is to place sport in the widest possible historical context.

The standard 'theory' which explains how sport has changed can be stated simply: it is that the formal codification and national administration of sport are at the heart of the gulf between

---

[1] R. Kirchner, *Fair Play* (1928), pp. 5–6; J. J. MacAloon, *This Great Symbol* (1981), pp. 59, 80.

'traditional' and 'modern' sports. Violent, disorderly, and disorganized sports gave way to more carefully regulated ones adapted to the constraints of time and space imposed by the industrial city, embodying the Victorian spirit of self-control and energetic competition as well as taking advantage of the development of the railways and the mass press. Yet behind this apparently simple model of the 'modernization' of sport, there lie a whole series of subtle influences and interesting problems. Whilst a good deal of space has been devoted to the transformation of sport, the half-hidden continuities between generations are just as significant. To understand how far things did *not* change is just as important as understanding the extent to which they did. This is especially true of popular attitudes. Sport is cultural as well as physical, and what we do with our bodies is very much a product of what we think we ought to do with them. The prevailing conditions of life—forms and rhythms of labour, disposable income, housing, health, and communications—certainly help to determine new forms of leisure and place constraints upon existing ones. The economic base sets limits in terms of space, time, and resources, but what men chose to do within such limits may be strongly influenced by traditions, shifting patterns of behaviour, and taste that cannot be easily explained by material factors alone. As the anthropologist Clifford Geertz remarked, sports are a kind of 'deep play' in which the innermost values of a culture may be expressed. Sport is not just a gratuitous expenditure of energy determined by the immediate physical environment; sports have a heroic and mythical dimension; they are, in a sense, 'a story we tell ourselves about ourselves', the nature of which may differ markedly between countries with broadly similar levels of economic development.[2]

So writing the history of sport in modern Britain is a cultural and political as well as a social and economic enterprise; it involves maintaining a creative tension between the straightforward changes in the circumstances of most people—shorter hours, higher wages, new kinds of work—as well as the values that ordinary people brought to their play and 'their betters' sought to impose upon it. Until the third quarter of the

---

[2] C. Geertz, 'Deep Play', *Daedalus*, Winter 1972, p. 26.

nineteenth century the changes in methods of manufacturing and the concentration of the population in large industrial centres had been confined to a fairly small number of towns in Lancashire and West Yorkshire; and even in the 'industrial north' a good deal of manufacturing took place in relatively small centres of population and modest factories. Agriculture was the single largest employer of labour according to the 1851 census, and the country town was still typical of urban life in mid-Victorian Britain. Hence the opening section of the book deals with the gradual shift in cultural attitudes towards popular recreation which began to take shape in the eighteenth century rather than stressing the sudden changes or discontinuities brought about by the onset of industrialization. The first half of the nineteenth century has sometimes been portrayed as a time when popular recreation was under attack. But to what extent was this true? What sort of forces were aligned against traditional sports? How did they survive and how far were new ones already taking shape? These are the problems which are examined in Chapter 1.

Before looking at the emergence of a mature working-class culture, the impact on sport of the ever larger numbers of aspirants to gentility, or at least to the liberal professions and business, needs to be considered. A dramatic enlargement and transformation of private secondary education provides the best way of understanding the peculiar importance attached to the regulation and promotion of sports by Victorian élites. It was public school men who founded, amongst many other national governing bodies, the Football Association in 1863, the Rugby Union in 1871, and the Amateur Athletic Association in 1881. Young men who increasingly had to commute by rail to sedentary occupations had more need of exercise than ever before and less opportunity to enjoy country sports than their predecessors. Carefully regulated sports which were economical both in terms of time and space were the obvious answer. Well-fed, relatively affluent young men with energy to spare needed games to play, especially when so much importance was attached to sport at school. Equestrian pursuits that had taken up much of the time of young gentlemen previously were unsuited to urban life and the practice of arms was hardly appropriate for the sons of engineers and doctors.

However, there was far more to Victorian sport than finding games to play that were suited to suburban life. Increasingly a sense of personal moral worth and a new kind of patriotism and imperial fervour became embedded in the middle-class attitude to sport. *Cassell's Complete Book of Sports and Pastimes*, published in 1893 and aimed at a mainly middle-class audience, remarked on 'the unanimity that now exists among parents and guardians as to the desirability of encouraging a reasonable pursuit of games and sports'; the Preface to this encyclopaedia of sport quoted approvingly the words of the Hon. Edward Lyttelton, Etonian, head of Haileybury and future headmaster of Eton:

A boy is disciplined by athletics in two ways: by being forced to put the welfare of the common cause before selfish interests, to obey implicitly the word of command and act in concert with the heterogeneous elements of the company he belongs to; and, secondly, should it so turn out, he is disciplined by being raised to a post of command, where he feels the gravity of the responsible office and the difficulty of making prompt decisions and securing obedience.

What might loosely be called 'ideological' pressures on sport were closely bound up with the more obvious effects of changes in the social structure and the economy. The middle classes, for example, were most anxious to distance themselves from manual workers taking similar forms of exercise. Disentangling morality from snobbery, high-sounding rhetoric from subtle class prejudice is the subject of Chapter 2, which takes as its central theme the theory and practice of 'amateurism'.[3]

It was from the middle years of the nineteenth century onwards that changes in transport, urban life, and factory labour began to have a major impact on popular sport. The consolidation of the rail network permitted the creation of a truly national sporting life. Teams and spectators could travel easily and relatively cheaply to games, newspapers with match reports and results could be quickly and widely distributed. Whilst there had been little significant improvement in living standards in the first half of the century, from the 1850s onwards an expanding world economy and falling food prices both strengthened the bargaining powers of workers and cut living costs. As a result real wages

---

[3] *Cassell's Complete Book of Sports and Pastimes* (1893), p. iii.

rose considerably, first for skilled workers but increasingly from the 1880s for the unskilled as well, perhaps by as much as two-thirds between 1850 and 1914. Obviously groups of workers differed substantially in the benefits they enjoyed but the point here is simply to note that for the first time the majority of the population had small weekly surpluses to spend perhaps on a trip to the music-hall or on professional football. A working week with an average of around fifty-four hours and half-day working on Saturday spread from the skilled workers in the 1860s and 1870s to become a distinctive feature of British life in the late nineteenth century; 'la semaine anglaise' was the envy of European workers. During the final quarter of the century there was a decisive shift in the scale of urban life and factory work. By the turn of the century about a fifth of the population lived in cities of over 200,000 and another fifth lived in Greater London. Britain was becoming a land of conurbations. The population of Wales was largely crammed into the mining valleys of the south and most Scots lived in the west-central industrial belt around Glasgow by the turn of the century. The population of Tyneside almost trebled between 1871 and 1911 with the Armstrong naval yards and munitions manufacture alone employing 20,000 men. Britain had become a nation of city-dwellers and the crucial role of sport in creating and sustaining a new popular culture and new kinds of urban identity is examined in Chapter 3.[4]

Sport was never seen as purely playful; it was a national institution and beneficial for Britain. Team games, in particular, were 'a good thing'. The thrust of much of the sports propaganda of the later nineteenth century proceeded along predictably patriotic lines, becoming ever more fervent as the British Empire spread through Africa and Asia. Wherever the British went, the gospel of sport went with them. 'The Englishman carries his cricket bat with him as naturally as his gun-case and his india-rubber bath,' remarked *Blackwood's Magazine* in 1892. The French and Germans did not colonize in this fashion and the importance given by British imperialists to games both for the rulers and the ruled provides another distinctive feature of sport

---

[4] E. Hobsbawm, 'The Making of the Working Class, 1870–1914', in *Worlds of Labour* (1984), pp. 196–7.

and the British. The remnants of this cult of imperial play live on in the form of the Commonwealth Games, now thoroughly emancipated from their colonial past. This special relationship between sport and imperialism in British history is examined in Chapter 4 alongside the various reactions to it within the Colonies, the Dominions, and in Great Britain and Ireland. For closer to home sporting patriotism was not so much a matter of 'Britishness' as of the reaction against English dominance. The rise of a new kind of popular 'Welshness' and 'Scottishness' and its expression through rugby and football make British sport unique—in certain events Britain and Northern Ireland compete as a united nation, in others the United Kingdom is a federation of four nations each with its own teams; it is as if the French sent representatives from the Languedoc, Brittany, and Provence alongside a team from 'France' on the basis that these 'countries' had once been self-governing states. Being first in the field has given us special privileges as well as special problems; in football, for example, since England won the World Cup at home in 1966 'English' First Division teams, especially Liverpool, composed of an assortment of Scots, English, Irish, and Welsh, have enjoyed extraordinary success whilst all the national sides have faltered at the highest level.[5]

These are just some of the ways which Britain has diverged from other countries in its sports; but looking particularly at the second half of this century there has also been a marked swing towards convergence and an 'internationalizing' of sport. We are less distinctive than we once were. The role of commercialization and of the media in spectator sport in Britain and elsewhere has increased greatly. Yet is it legitimate to talk of a 'sports industry' or of sport as another form of 'commercial entertainment'? And if so, when did this come about? The final part of this book looks at sport, money, and the emergence of professional sportsmen as a distinct occupational group. The press has been a prime mover in the growth of professional sport but since the advent of television popular reporting of sport has changed greatly. Now that live sport can be watched world-wide, gossip and backroom chat have become the accepted currency of popular reporting—

---

[5] *Blackwood's Magazine*, cited in W. F. Mandle, 'W. G. Grace as a Victorian Hero', *Historical Studies*, Apr. 1980, p. 355.

'Big Ron Hits Out', 'Seb Slams Steve', and so on. Television marks a sharp discontinuity with the past. New habits of spectating have been formed; dying sports like snooker have been revitalized; the Olympics and the World Cup are now global visual events watched by about two-thirds of the world's population. Yet standardization is still a long way off. Cricket is still a mystery to the French and few Britons can follow the subtleties of the Tour de France. Sport is not yet a uniform international component of mass culture. Even in the era of high technology and expensive admission charges, football violence reminds us that sport is more than a 'leisure product' to be 'consumed' in the same way as a film or a magazine. Hooliganism, therefore, rounds off the study not so much as a result of current public concern but rather as a striking example of the mingling of ancient and modern attitudes, of the riotous traditions of youth, which have always had a place in games, and the specific forms of contemporary violence that strike at the heart of sport as wholesome televised family entertainment. Old customs live on and are adapted in ways we do not always understand.

The kinds of meanings that are attached to sport vary enormously according to age, class, or simply by virtue of being male or female. A special word about gender and ethnicity is required at this point. The history of sport in modern Britain is a history of men. Social divisions and, to a lesser extent, age differences crop up continually but women figure only fleetingly in this study; this is not from any unwillingness to give them their due but because sport has been so thoroughly identified with masculinity. Give or take hunting with its gentry ladies and leaving aside mixed doubles in tennis as a ritual of polite courtship, mixed sport has frankly been considered unnatural; moreover segregated female sport itself has been a frail and pallid growth in the shade of men's sport. Sport has always been a male preserve with its own language, its initiation rites, and models of true masculinity, its clubbable, jokey cosiness. Building male friendships and sustaining large and small communities of men have been the prime purpose of sport. Women have been banished to the sidelines both literally and metaphorically, except for a minority of public schoolgirls. This division has been as natural to past generations as it may seem strange to future ones. Women's sport deserves a full study in its own right which goes beyond the brief account of bourgeois education, suburban bicycling, and tennis offered here. The remarkable upsurge, for example, in female athletics, so striking in the last decade, marks a new stage in women's sport. The emergence of black sportsmen and sportswomen of late is another aspect which requires fuller discussion. Their recent impact on British athletics has been profound and their success extraordinary; and black boxers now dominate the sport in Britain. They point the way ahead.[6] Their absence from this history is unfortunate but it arises solely from my concern to portray the growth and decline of a distinct historical moment in British sport; for this is essentially a book about our imperial and industrial heyday and treatment of the third quarter of this century is highly restricted and selective.

There are several ways to write a social history of British sport. Each major sport could have been examined chapter by chapter; or the story might have been told decade by decade. Neither approach would have brought out the interconnections between different sports which enable the historian to point out their wider significance more easily. And, after all, few sportsmen ever confined themselves to a single activity. A strictly chronological approach would have involved constantly switching from sport to sport and from one social class to another. The result would have been a thin and confusing narrative. But abandoning strict chronology does not mean giving up the general idea of sequence. The first five chapters of the book follow a broad progression from the early nineteenth century to the present, though the bulk of new research has been on the late Victorian and Edwardian periods. Hence the fifty years from the 1860s to the First World War, in which the basic pattern of contemporary sport was laid down, occupy the centre of the stage. For those who wish to know more about the underlying assumptions, definitions, and theories upon which this study is based, I have included an appendix. All I need say here is that I have adopted a catholic approach, which does not attempt to restrict artificially what is or is not 'sport' by employing an elaborate set of abstract criteria

---

[6] K. E. McCrone, *Sport and the Physical Emancipation of English Women, 1870–1914* (1988); Jenny Hargreaves is preparing a major history of women's sport in Britain; E. Cashmore, *Black Sportsmen* (1982), provides a good introduction to black involvement.

to define it. Sport is pleasurable physical activity, which is normally organized and competitive but need not be so. No firm lines between 'sport' and 'physical recreation' have been drawn because none is appropriate. After all, most activities can be played in very different ways and we commonly use the word 'sport' to refer both to casual play and to the highest levels of performance.

Many enthusiasts will complain that their favourite sport is either treated cursorily or not at all. It is impossible to give each sport the space it deserves, and John Arlott's admirable *Oxford Companion to Sports and Games* along with J. A. Cuddon's similarly extensive work of reference already provide many of the basic facts about the history of the full range of sports. Cricket, rugby, and football receive the lion's share here because they were popular both as participant and as spectator sports, though I am only too aware that those who know far more about them than I do will want to know why such and such a person or match does not get a mention. All I can say is that this study is deliberately interpretative, not encyclopaedic. Individuals or incidents have been included not so much because of their special place in the history of any single sport but because they help to make sense of the wider picture. There are some major omissions: water sports have come off badly here despite their success; swimming, which has become so popular as a recreation, is not discussed, and fishing is very cursorily treated; nor is there space to discuss the British love of 'messing about in boats'. I must also ask the forgiveness of those who went down to Weybridge to watch the Bugattis and Bentleys roar around Brooklands, and to the generations of British boys for whom AJS, Norton, and BSA were magical names. Skiers, too, and mountaineers will feel aggrieved. Yet brutal sports in the early nineteenth century are given a major place because of their general importance in the wider transformation of British society and the same is true of field sports, which hitherto have tended to be set apart and studied separately from other sporting activities. No history that left out as distinctively British a social institution as the fox-hunt would be worthy of the name. At the other end of the social scale the 'submerged' tradition of bowls, pigeons, darts, and billiards has to be at least briefly brought into the mainstream of popular culture. But in the end selection is inevitably personal and perhaps even idiosyncratic. Far more could have been said about golf and tennis, whilst boxing, which next to football and cricket was perhaps the most popular spectator sport, crops up only from time to time.

Finally, and emphatically, this is *not* a history of the role of the state in the definition and development of physical education. This is a subject in its own right, and until recently 'drill', as it used to be called, or 'gym' has not had much impact on the wider development of British sport. In fact, a key element in the distinctiveness of the British tradition in sport lies precisely in the lack of strong official backing for formal physical training and scientific measurement of average performance. Gym was for Germans. Britons *played* rather than exercised.

In making sense of sport as part of the general history of modern Britain much has had to be left by the wayside. I hope that what remains amounts at least to more than a dry summary and conveys something of the pleasure of games. Sport may have to be explained in terms of things beyond itself but it has also to be enjoyed for its own sake. Celebration and analysis can and should go hand in hand.

1
Old Ways of Playing

FAR more has been written about sport in the last hundred or so years than about the period from the early eighteenth to the mid-nineteenth century. 'Modern' sport according to received wisdom was invented in the mid-Victorian years—the 1850s to 1880s—and everything that preceded this 'revolution' was 'traditional'. Furthermore it has often been suggested that there was a gap, a 'vacuum', between the decline of ancient forms of play and the spread of new ones. The attack on cruel sports, interference in street games, and sabbatarianism have combined to create an image of a gloomy and work-dominated world of factory and slum. But is this a true picture? Without seeking to devalue the impact of either the public school system or the progress of industrialization, it is important to see that major changes were already underway before the Victorians. It is misleading to think of popular culture from the mid-eighteenth to the mid-nineteenth centuries solely in terms of a decline of ancient amusements. This perspective has been handed down to us via the folklorists of the late nineteenth century, who took an interest in traditional games along with folk-songs, old wives' tales, and herbal potions. Living as they did in the midst of an unprecedented upsurge of urban and industrial change, it is hardly surprising that they tended to see the pre-Victorian world as a haven of ancient custom. Yet the power of an orally transmitted popular culture has to be set alongside the distinct changes in regulation and commercial organization that were also taking place. The interplay of change and continuity, persistence in some things and innovation in others, is too complex to be slotted neatly into a simple 'modernization' model. As we shall see, the early nineteenth century was less unambiguously 'traditional' and the late nineteenth century less 'modern' than first appearances might suggest.

1. BEFORE THE VICTORIANS

A remarkable range of popular games and contests was played and enjoyed in Britain before the advent of modern sports. Each town or village had its ball games, running races, and varieties of fighting and animal sports. An observer of early eighteenth-century London noted that the 'more common sort divert themselves at football, wrestling, cudgels, ninepins, shovel-board, cricket, stow-ball, ringing of bells, quoits, pitching the bar, bull and bear baiting, throwing at cocks'; and even the most cursory glance at Strutt's classic survey of *The Sports and Pastimes of the People of England* (1801) would further extend the list. For the most part there were no national games in the modern sense, although the Cotswold Games, revived by Robert Dover in 1604, attracted huge crowds to watch contests of leaping, shin-kicking, wrestling as well as coursing and jousting. These games survived into the mid-nineteenth century on 'Dover's Hill' near Chipping Camden as a kind of proto-national event. Yet most people still played only amongst themselves or with a neighbouring parish and had no need of written codes of practice. The young grew up playing the game in the way their elders had done and in turn passed on these traditions to their children.[1]

It is often incorrectly assumed that traditional games were childish or primitive. Richard Carew's *Survey of Cornwall* in 1603 gives one of the most detailed descriptions we have of a game of football, or hurling as it was called in Cornwall, which reveals complex rules and strategies for deceiving the opposition. In the east of Cornwall 'hurling to goales' involved teams of 15, 20, or 30 in which each player paired himself with another from the opposing team and attempted to block his advance, as in American football today. 'The Hurlers are bound to the observation of many lawes, as that they must hurle man to man, and not two set upon one man at once: the Hurler against the ball, must not butt, nor handfast under the girdle: that he who hath the ball, must butt onely in the others brest.' There was even an offside rule: 'that he must deal no Fore-ball, viz. he may not

---

[1] R. W. Malcolmson, *Popular Recreations in English Society 1700–1850* (1979), p. 34; Malcolmson provides a concise and indispensable introduction to traditional forms of popular sport.

throw it to any of his mates, standinge nearer the goale than himselfe.' Similarly an early eighteenth-century account of the Norfolk variant of traditional football called 'camping' notes that 'if caught or held, or in imminent danger of being caught, he *throws* the ball—he must in no case *give* it—to a less beleaguered friend, who . . . catches it and hastens homeward, in like manner pursued, annoyed and aided—winning the notch [or snotch] if he contrives to *carry* it—not *throw*—it between his goales'. These games were not just the contests of brute strength and collective violence that they were assumed to have been by the inventors of 'new' games in the mid-nineteenth century. As the observer of the Norfolk game remarks, if the teams were well matched— and the idea of balancing up sides carefully in itself assumes a fairly sophisticated concept of play—the scoring of a goal 'is no easy achievement, and often requires much time, many doublings, detours and exertions'.[2]

Although traditional sports were not necessarily crude, they did differ in important respects from our contemporary forms of play. Sports tended to be considered not in isolation but as integral parts of a wider pattern of amusement. The 'wakes', annual holidays in honour of the patron saint of the parish, were very widely observed as a kind of English equivalent of the Catholic festivities before Lent, involving the election of captains of youth to lead the revels. There were also numerous Shrovetide games directly linked to the traditions of the European Carnival in which the bachelors of around fifteen to twenty-five would assert their right of 'misrule' against those with the right to procreate, and often against the wider social and spiritual hierarchy as well. The May Day revels in Lincolnshire in the late sixteenth century involved assembling the male youth of the parish and electing a 'Lord of Misrule', who was anointed and crowned in an explicit parody of kingship. 'Then march this heathen company towards the church and churchyard, their pipers piping, their drummers thundering, their stumps dancing, their bells jingling, their handkerchieves swinging about their heads like madman,' complained a Puritan critic of these customs.

---

[2] Carew cited in N. Elias and E. Dunning, 'Folk Football in Medieval and Early Modern Britain', in E. Dunning (ed.), *The Sociology of Sport* (1970), pp. 126–9; Malcolmson, *Popular Recreations*, pp. 35–6.

They distributed badges to those who donated money for the revels, but those who did not approve of their 'devilish cognizances' and 'would not be buxom to them' were 'mocked and flouted at not a little'.[3]

This conflict between the married and unmarried was a very important part of the festive life of a society where individual wishes in matrimony and sexual relationships generally were far more subject to parental and community sanction than they are today. This division between 'young' and 'old' was embedded in the structure of artisan employment with apprentices working for set periods of their lives regardless of their actual skill in the work and being unable to marry until they had served their time. Sports, especially football, often embodied these divisions. The Freemen Marblers of Corfe Castle initiated their apprentices on Shrove Tuesday. Those who had married in the previous year paid for the feast and arranged the football that customarily took place the following day, Ash Wednesday; the game was played over the land that the company claimed for their special use upon the payment of a pound of pepper to the lord of the manor. So the football match was firmly rooted in the deeper structure of that small society, linking the work and rights of the guild with the relationships between masters and men, and those between the married and the unmarried. The game not only confirmed the customary rights of way by playing over the land itself, it helped to denote how that community of quarrymen was itself to be ordered. Sport, of course, is among other things an ancient display of prowess, and no doubt the young men of Corfe hoped to make themselves more attractive to the limited pool of marriageable girls by the display of bodily vigour. Certain sports had a similar significance for girls, and popular festivities often included races for women as well as for men. 'Nothing is more usual than for a nimble-footed wench to get a husband at the same time as she wins a smock,' observed Addison of the wakes at Bath in the early eighteenth century.[4]

Traditional sports were rooted in the territorial as well as in the conjugal order. During the seasonal pattern of amusements

---

[3] J. R. Gillis, *Youth and History* (1981), p. 27.
[4] Elias and Dunning, 'Folk Football', p. 124; P. Lovesey, *The Official Centenary History of the Amateur Athletic Association* (1979), p. 14.

that reached their height between spring sowing and summer harvesting and in the dead months of midwinter, the young not only organized themselves for mating and for work, they asserted the identity of each generation of village inhabitants. Deep attachment to the land and a fierce local patriotism were part and parcel of popular recreations. Inter-parish fights were commonplace throughout early modern Europe and were usually carefully regulated by custom. Football was often a good way of permitting the youth their violent rituals; the ancient match between the parishes of Saint Peter's and All Saints in Derby at Shrove-tide is a case in point. Solidarity may have existed within villages but peace rarely prevailed between them. A writer to the *Spectator* in the early eighteenth century, remarking upon the ferocity of these local antagonisms, claimed 'my tenant in the country is verily persuaded that the parish of the enemy hath not one honest man in it'. George Owen's *Description of Pembrokeshire* (1603) noted that those who played village football (*cnappen* in Welsh) 'contend not for any wager or valuable thing but strive to the death for glory and fame which they esteem dearer than any worldly wealth'. In the old traditions of carnival there would also be mummers dressing up and putting on farces to mock the pretensions of the clergy or unpopular local bigwigs. Amid the fighting and mockery, the eating and drinking, there would be weird and wonderful events often revealing humanity at its most hilarious and absurd. At the Halshaw Wakes near Bolton eager contestants were stripping the wicks from a pound of candles with their teeth and eating scalding porridge with their fingers well into the nineteenth century. There were greasy poles, greasy pigs, goose-rides, grinning or grimacing ('gurning') matches, and dozens more of what 'rational' or puritan critics considered to be daft or demeaning amusements.[5]

There were also numerous contests involving the killing or baiting of animals. These were a particular feature of the sports associated with major seasonal festivities. In the country they were occasional treats rather than regular weekly events because of the expense involved. Throwing at cocks was a favourite sport

---

[5] R. W. Malcolmson, 'Sports in Society', *BJSH*, May 1984, p. 63; D. Smith and G. Williams, *Fields of Praise* (1980), p. 18; P. Bailey, *Leisure and Class in Victorian England* (1978), pp. 21–2.

on Shrove Tuesday. The bird was tethered by a string a few feet long and passers-by paid to throw stones or sticks at what was a living coconut shy. The bird would dodge as best it could until its legs were broken and it was finally killed. The creature was then carried off in triumph by the thrower that had finished it off. Cock-fighting was even more popular. Schoolboys traditionally brought their cocks to school on Shrove Tuesday to match them. All large towns had cockpits, and here contests were more regular. Pepys went to one in London in 1663 and found 'the poorest prentices, bakers, brewers, butchers, draymen and whatnot . . . all fellows one with another swearing, cursing and betting'. In eighteenth-century Newcastle, in spite of the high admission charges cockfights were always crowded by 'eager and interested pitmen', and there were at least seven cockpits in the city in 1800. Cock-fights were a great feature of the wakes. Arnold Bennett described the Burslem Wake in the early nineteenth-century Potteries as a 'wild and naïve orgy . . . towards the end of the Wakes, by way of a last ecstasy, the cock-fighters would carry their birds, which had been called off, perhaps half a dozen times, to the town field and there match them to a finish.'[6]

Bull-baiting was very common too. There was a general belief that a bull needed to be baited to improve the meat before slaughter and certain by-laws actually required this to be done. The bulldog, thick set with short legs and powerful jaws, would try to crawl under the bull 'to seize him by the muzzle, the dewlap or the pendant glands'. The bull would try to toss the dogs with his horns while the owners ran round trying to break their fall with a pole or even catch them on their own backs. If the dog succeeded in getting a hold it clung on to the rearing and kicking bull and 'to all appearance put him to great pain. In the end either the dog tears out the piece he has laid hold on, and falls, or else remains fixed to him, with an obstinacy that would never end, if they did not pull him off'. Flour was used to stop the nostrils of the dogs and force them to let go. Enthusiasm for the characteristics of the bulldog were such that it became a national symbol. Bulls were not only baited, they were also let loose in

[6] K. Thomas, *Man and the Natural World* (1983); S. K. Phillips, 'Primitive Methodist Confrontation with Popular Sports', in R. Cashman and M. McKernan, *Sport: Money, Morality and the Media* (1982), p. 292.

the streets of a town and goaded with sticks in a frantic mêlée
of chasing and dodging. The more famous of these ceremonies
like the Tutbury or the Stamford bull-running often finished on
the town bridge where the 'bullards' would try to heave the
wildly threshing creature over the parapet and into the water.
If a bull could not be 'brigged' he was spared, while the rest were
chased and baited a little longer before slaughter. Bull-running
was popular in London. The vicar of Bethnal Green complained
in 1816 that the sabbath was disturbed by hundreds of men who
would 'enter into subscriptions to fee drovers for a bullock . . .
Monday is the principal day: one or two thousand men will leave
their looms and join in the pursuit'. So what tended to be a
relatively rare occurrence in the country, usually restricted to a
special festival, was more frequent in what was already a city of
over a million inhabitants by 1800. Distinctions between urban
and rural sports were not particularly great, and it is misleading
to see urbanization in itself as an agent of change. Traditional
sports can be played in modern circumstances, just as old wine can
be poured into new bottles. The persistence of ancient animal contests in early nineteenth-century London underlines the point that
attitudes are perhaps more important than the physical environment
in determining what is and what is not permissible in play.[7]

By the standards of our day the level of violence tolerated in
sports was remarkable. This is true whether we look at contests
between beasts or between men. Fighting was probably the single
most popular individual sport. 'Amongst the pit lads, boxing was
considered a manly exercise and a favourite amusement, and
I believed I counted no less than seventeen battles which I
reluctantly had to fight before I was able to attain a position
calculated to ensure respect', recalled William Fairbairn of North
Shields in 1803. In Lancashire there was evidence of

parties mutually agreeing to fight 'up and down', which includes the
right of kicking on every part of the body and in all possible situations,
and of squeezing the throat or 'throttling' to the verge of death. At races,
fairs and on other public occasions contests of this nature are watched
by crowds of persons who take part on each side . . . that death often
occurs in such battles will not be thought extraordinary.

[7] Malcolmson, *Popular Recreations*, pp. 45–6; H. Cunningham, *Leisure in the Industrial Revolution* (1980), p. 23.

At Pudsey in West Yorkshire in the 1820s men would fight 'until almost exhausted and sometimes women might be seen helping to form rings, and shouting encouraging words to the combatants'. Women were also willing to fight. A German visitor to London in the early eighteenth century met a woman who told him 'that two years ago she had fought another female in this place without stays and in nothing but a shift. They had both fought stoutly and drawn blood, which was apparently no new sight in England,'whilst William Hickey observed two women 'engaged in a scratching and boxing match, their faces entirely covered with blood, bosoms bare and the clothes nearly torn from their bodies' at Wetherby's near Drury Lane in the eighteenth century.[8]

Cudgelling matches were very popular and often played in teams for quite high stakes. Sometimes pugilism, wrestling, and cudgelling would be promiscuously mixed together in a single contest. A favourite form of sport involved a player holding a heavy stick in one hand to brain his opponent, while defending himself with a wicker shield. 'No head be deemed broke until the blood run an inch' specified an advertisement for a contest. Around 1800 the Govan 'rowdy' mob in Glasgow habitually spent part of New Year's Day 'throwing the cudgel for gingerbread cakes' and fighting with 'single sticks', in which the combatants often had one hand tied behind their back. Stone fights were popular too. On a small island in the Clyde a boy was killed at the end of the eighteenth century in just such a fight between the weaver lads of the Gorbals and their enemies from the other side of the Clyde. Stone-throwing was not confined to the lower orders. Up until the middle years of the nineteenth century Harrovians were inveterate throwers of stones. 'No dog', it was said, 'could live on Harrow Hill', and 'ponies frequently lost their eyes if they had to pull their owners' carts near the school'. Fighting in its various forms was part of the everyday life of male youth whether done casually or according to the rites and competitive traditions of village or trade corporation.[9]

---

[8] S. Shipley, 'Tom Causer of Bermondsey', *History Workshop Journal*, Spring 1983, p. 35; R. Rees, 'The Development of Physical Recreation in Liverpool during the Nineteenth Century', MA thesis (Liverpool Univ., 1968), p. 30; Cunningham, *Leisure in the Industrial Revolution*, pp. 26–7; A. Guttman, 'English Sports Spectators', *JSH*, Summer 1985, p. 116.

[9] P. Bilsborough, 'The Development of Sport in Glasgow', 1850–1914, M.Litt. thesis (Stirling Univ., 1983), p. 3; J. A. Mangan, *Athleticism in the Victorian and Edwardian Public School* (1981), p. 32.

However, it is misleading to think of fighting merely as primitive or atavistic. The realm of physical combat witnessed some of the first moves towards organized and commercialized sport. It is quite wrong to assume that sport was held fast by the dead hand of tradition until the nineteenth century. As Plumb and others have stressed there was a distinct 'commercialization' of leisure in the eighteenth century. 'Theatre, music, dancing, sport—these were the cultural pastimes for which the prosperous gentry and the new leisured middle class hungered', and which the recent availability of cheaper newspapers and books helped to enhance. Horse-racing and cricket were the main beneficiaries of the changing climate, but fist-fighting or 'pugilism', though lacking middle-class appeal, was one of the first sports to have a written code of rules and a rudimentary kind of national championship informally run by a coterie of sporting aristocrats, London publicans, and patrons of Figg's Emporium, a boxing-hall opened in 1719. Rules were laid down in 1743 by Jack Broughton after an opponent of his had died as a result of a fight. With revisions the Broughton rules regulated the practice of prize-fighting until the last great prize-fight held in England in 1860 between Sayers and Heenan, of which a prominent journalist said 'everything was conducted according to superstitiously observed rules' with 'almost as many ceremonies as at the Coronation'. The regulations against 'hitting a man when he is down', the right to half a minute's rest after going down, and the ban on 'hitting below the belt' were only loosely enforced—a great deal of what we would now call wrestling went on in pugilism—and designed less to protect the combatant and preserve 'civilized' standards than to prevent corruption. Huge sums were wagered on such contests. In 1750 the Duke of Cumberland backed Jack Broughton for £10,000. After getting several blows to the eye he called out pitifully to his angry backer, 'I can't see my man your Highness, I am blind but not beat. Only place me before him and he shall not gain the day yet.' Broughton's emporium was closed in 1750 after this fight, probably on the orders of the angry 'Butcher' Cumberland rather than as a result of the piteousness of the spectacle.[10]

[10] J. H. Plumb, *The Commercialisation of Leisure* (1973), p. 17; J. Arlott (ed.), *Oxford Companion to Sports and Games* (1976), pp. 96–8; A. Lloyd, *The Great Prize Fight* (1977), p. 134; D. Brailsford, 'Morals and Maulers', *JSH*, Summer 1985, esp. p. 133; see also Guttman, 'English Sports Spectators'.

Prize-fighting was patronized by the highest in the land. In 1786 it was said that there were wagers of up to £40,000, with the Duke of York and the Prince of Wales among the biggest gamblers. The nobility often provided private ground safe from the magistrates. The law regarded the sport primarily as a disorderly assembly. In London many of the prize-fights of the late eighteenth century were organized on private estates; amongst the favourite venues were Molesey Hurst and Coombe Warren under the royal protection of the Duke of Clarence. Although there was still intense localism in pugilism, the leading fighters were becoming national and sometimes legendary figures. Jack Broughton himself lived into old age, died a wealthy man, and was buried in Westminster Abbey. The Jewish boxer Mendoza followed him, then 'Gentleman' Jackson took the title after grabbing Mendoza's long hair with one hand and pummelling his face with the other. The exploits of Tom Cribb, the great Regency pugilist, were widely reported in new weekly papers such as the *Sporting Magazine* (from 1793), *Bell's Weekly Messenger* (from 1796), and the *Weekly Dispatch* (from 1801), selections from which were collected first in Oxberry's *Pancratia* and then Pierce Egan's famous five volumes of *Boxiana* in 1828–9. Prize-fighting employed a more or less professional core of men who fought regularly in a kind of circuit based mainly in London. Dennis Brailsford has studied the geographical and social origins of these sportsmen between 1780 and 1824. Of those whose origins were known, 36 came from London, 20 from Bristol, 10 from Birmingham and 6 from Bath with 40 others scattered widely across the country. Pugilism may have been southern-dominated on account of the wintering habits of the aristocracy around London and Bath and because London and Bristol were still the two major ports with dockside fighting traditions. The occupations of pugilists before entering the ring confirm the urban bias of the sport. There were, needless to say, no 'gentlemen' or middle-class persons directly involved as combatants. The age-old link between one form of slaughter and another was evident with twelve butchers heading a list that included four of each of the following: bakers, brewers, colliers, sailors, and shoemakers, and three carpenters, gardeners, greengrocers, metal workers, and navvies. A successful pugilist had but one ambition it seems—to become a publican. Brailsford traces at least a dozen who like the famous Tom Cribb, landlord of the Union Arms in London's Haymarket, moved from the ring to the bar. Such were the modest but tangible rewards for which men were willing to risk and occasionally to give their lives. Death in the ring was not uncommon despite the attempt to enforce rules, which required a break when a man went down. These 'rounds' were of indeterminate length and fights sometimes lasted several hours. Two contests on one day both ended in death in a field near Birmingham in 1787. Yet this seemed only to enhance the appeal. Crowds of up to 10,000 would trek long distances to see a fight.[11]

Another spectacle that attracted a good deal of popular support and élite patronage was rowing. The demise of professional rowing came as a result of the prestige of the public school, Varsity, and Henley events, and the declining economic importance of the watermen themselves; this had led to rowing being overlooked, although it was a major sporting amusement, especially on the Thames and the Tyne from the early eighteenth century until the mid-nineteenth century. Rowing can claim the oldest surviving fixture in the sporting calendar named after an Irish actor and impresario, Thomas Doggett, whose Coat and Badge became the leading event for young watermen just out of their apprenticeship. As if to underline the links between two sports dominated by large ports, Jack Broughton himself was a winner of this event. Doggett's Coat and Badge was only one of a number of challenge events eagerly watched from the river banks by crowds that often ran into thousands. The earliest record of a festival of rowing or 'regatta' is 1768 at Walton and it seems as if these may have attracted some 'amateurs' in the sense of men who did not earn their living as watermen. By the end of the century there were at least three 'amateur' clubs, the Star, the Arrow, and the Shark, which may have combined to form the oldest and most exclusive of modern rowing-clubs, the Leander, in the early nineteenth century. The adoption of rowing by Eton, Shrewsbury, Westminster, and in the Oxford and Cambridge colleges dates from around 1800 and culminated in

[11] D. Brailsford, 'Notes on the Geography of Regency Pugilism', private communication; also D. Brailsford, 'The Locations of Eighteenth Century Spectator Sport', in *Proc. Conference 'Geographical Perspectives on Sport', University of Birmingham, 7 July 1983.*

the institution of the Boat Race from 1829 onwards. These developments will be examined elsewhere in relation to the emergence of amateurism. The point at issue here is the existence and growth of loosely organized spectator sport before the later nineteenth century. The success of rowing on Tyneside was quite phenomenal. Great Geordie rowers like Harry Clasper were idolized around Tyneside by miners and keelmen alike. Crowds were estimated to run into many tens of thousands for big challenge matches on popular holidays. When Clasper died in 1870 'his funeral was held on a Sunday "to meet the convenience of numerous bodies of working men" and crowds of between 100,000 and 130,000 lined the street to witness the largest funeral yet held in Newcastle'. Purses were raised or held by riverside publicans or from the early nineteenth century in London by groups of enthusiasts who formed 'subscription rooms'. These gentlemen displayed none of that scrupulous disdain for money which was later to mark off amateur oarsmen. They backed themselves in races and wagered on others just as patrons of pugilists or owners of horses would do.[12]

If the popular success of rowing has been forgotten, there is no mistaking the triumph of horse-racing. Horse-racing was transformed from a casual competition between noblemen to perhaps the most highly organized of all sports, regulated by Wetherby's *Calendar* listing a wide range of meetings well in advance. Until the early eighteenth century racing had normally been for a wager between two owners, who usually rode their horses themselves. However, the introduction of Arabian bloodstock, the publication of a *Racing Calendar* from 1727, the laying out of courses near prosperous towns and the formation of the Jockey Club in 1752 combined to strike a new commercial and bureaucratic note albeit under strict aristocratic control. The establishment of the classic races—the St Leger in 1776, the Oaks in 1779, and the Derby in 1780—provided the framework for modern racing, although it is important to remember courses were not enclosed and gate-money could not be charged. Moreover until the railway permitted horses to be moved from

---

[12] *Oxford Companion*, pp. 759–60; J. A. Cuddon, *The Macmillan Dictionary of Sports and Games* (1980), pp. 652–4; A. Metcalfe, 'Organised Sport in the Mining Communities of South Northumberland, 1880–1889', *Victorian Studies*, Summer 1982, p. 24.

meeting to meeting easily, most events were quite small, annual occasions held in mid-week and dominated by the gentry. As late as 1840 only seventeen out of 137 racecourses held more than one meeting a year.[13]

The Derby provides the single most intriguing mixture of ancient festivity and sporting innovation. Despite the efforts of the Jockey Club to regulate the event, it soon became the excuse for a mass exodus from London. Derby Day saw up to a hundred thousand congregate on the Downs. 'The road to Epsom was crowded with all descriptions of people hurrying to the races', remarked *The Times* in 1793, 'some to plunder and some to be plundered. Horses, gigs, curricles, coaches, chaises, carts and pedestrians covered with dust crowded the Downs, the people running down and jostling each other as they met in contact.' Stories of trips to Epsom and drunken return journeys were part of cockney folklore, polished and elaborated in the telling into a kind of Londoner's *Tam o'Shanter*. In fact, the mass of the 'punters' did not bet on the race at all. They knew little or nothing about the form of the horses, which in any case were often impeded by dogs or spectators during the race itself as there was no properly fenced-off course. So the Derby was partly a 'fair' of the ancient kind and partly a modern spectacle. A corpus of professional jockeys had come into being as part of the new division of labour between owners, trainers, riders, and officials. The most famous of these jockeys was Sam Chiffney, who rode for the Prince of Wales, and was eventually warned off for allegedly holding back a royal mount in order to lengthen the odds, with the strong presumption of connivance by the heir to the throne himself. This happened in 1791 at Newmarket, which came to be established as the centre of the new racing world holding seven meetings a year each lasting several days and attracting the élite of owners and racegoers to the Two Thousand Guineas from 1809 and the One Thousand Guineas for fillies from 1814. Flat racing was now a sprint for highly bred young horses, normally two-year-olds, over a mile or so instead of longer races of four miles or more as had formerly been the fashion. Younger horses and shorter distances made for a less predictable result

[13] W. Vamplew, *The Turf* (1976), p. 25.

and better gambling. Alongside flat racing a vigorous winter programme of steeple-chasing grew up as huntsmen bred ever faster hunters to follow the fox. In 1836 a Grand Liverpool Steeplechase was held at Aintree, and this race, re-named the Grand National in 1847, with its terrifying jumps soon became a new national institution. A Steeplechase Calendar was published by the National Hunt Committee, from 1867 and these events were supplemented by races run by individual Hunts from the 1870's onwards called 'Point-to-Points', of which there were around fifty by 1900 including races for the Stock Exchange and the Bar members who kept hunters.[14]

The first regular references to cricket matches appear after the Restoration. As with pugilism and horse-racing, cricket seems to have been dominated by the nobility who organized teams to play for wagers that sometimes were very large indeed. While hunting and shooting remained the single most important of aristocratic pursuits, this 'leisure class' increasingly had the chance to indulge other sporting interests. Cricket was the first team-game in which the upper classes were expected to exert themselves without the aid of a horse. The landed classes generally confined themselves to the patronage of football and other popular sports but there are numerous references to cricket matches in which famous aristocrats took part alongside commoners. A French nobleman of the eighteenth century would not have considered such a thing possible without losing caste. The English aristocracy was perhaps not only more detached from 'feudal' preoccupations but also so formidably entrenched, so rich, so restricted in numbers that the democratic implications of sharing their play with commoners either never occurred to them or was never a problem. Moreover, their fellow players were often servants whose deference was unquestioned or very substantial tenant farmers—the yeomen of England—rather than agricultural labourers.

The first written rules of cricket were drawn up by the Duke of Richmond in 1727 for the purpose of determining the conduct and outcome of country-house games where a good deal of money might be at stake. These games stimulated the formation of more permanent teams and thus we see the emergence of the

---

[14] M. Wynn Jones, *The Derby* (1979), pp. 36-7; M. Seth-Smith *et al.*, *The History of Steeplechasing* (London, 1966).

'club' composed of similarly inclined individuals. The early pattern seems to have been for a great lord to act as patron to a village side, which mixed gentlemen and talented locals. The team from the village of Slindon run by the Duke of Richmond may have been the first such club, and drew large crowds for its games against the 'Gentlemen of London' in the 1740s. Although the ball was rolled underarm and the range of strokes played was restricted, there is no doubting the popularity of cricket as an early spectator sport. About 10,000 were thought to have attended the Artillery Ground, Finsbury, for a match in 1743. The most famous of these country cricket clubs was the Hambledon Club in Hampshire, which was founded around the middle of the century by the third son of the Duke of Bolton, and dominated cricket until the formation of the Marylebone Cricket Club in 1787. The home of the Hambledon Club was the Bat and Ball Inn overlooking 'Broad Halfpenny', the village green where the game was played. Hambledon took on the best sides in the country and the lack of modern transport does not seem to have stopped large crowds from assembling. Spectator sport certainly existed before the railway. During the second half of the century there were at one time or another at least 127 members, including 18 nobles, 4 clergymen, 6 Members of Parliament, and 27 officers, with the remainder being made up mostly of tenant farmers as John Nyren recalled in his memoir of his father Richard Nyren, landlord of the Bat and Ball and lifelong stalwart of the club. Some, however, had more humble origins such as Lambert, 'The Little Farmer', who had learned how to spin the ball while tending his father's sheep. On one occasion when his 'jerker' shaved the Duke of Dorset's left stump he bawled out in a broad Hampshire accent, 'Ah, that were *tedious* near you, Sir!', much to the amusement of the crowd. But such breaches of decorum were rare. Although some thought it 'highly unseemly that lords and gentlemen, clergymen and lawyers should associate themselves with butchers and cobblers', John Nyren was at pains to stress 'the style with which we were accustomed to impress our aristocratical playmates with our acknowledgement of their rank and station'.[15]

---

[15] A useful account of eighteenth-century cricket is C. Brookes, *English Cricket* (1978), esp. ch. 5; also J. Nyren, 'The Cricketers of My Time', in A. Ross (ed.), *The Penguin Cricketer's Companion* (1981), p. 337.

Beneath this highly competitive level, there seems to have existed a surprisingly dense network of village clubs, especially in the south and east of England, about which we know relatively little. Village cricket is the oldest team-sport to have survived and adapted, still just about recognizable despite rolled wickets, overarm bowling, whites, pads, and a host of complex rules. It is this sense of a continuous tradition, of ancient links, and English pastoral that tugs at the heart of so many devotees today. Using Buckley's gazetteers of cricket references before 1836, Bale has pointed out the southern dominance of cricket with 159 clubs in Kent alone, 109 in Sussex, 88 in Hampshire, and 86 in Essex out of a total of around a thousand in England and Wales. Alongside William Lillywhite of Sussex (the 'Nonpareil'), who stood 5 ft. 4 in. and bowled in a top hat and Gladstone collar, was Alfred Mynn of Kent, born the son of a farmer from Goudhurst in 1807. Mynn competed as a 'Gentleman' in the Gentlemen and Players match, the only representative national fixture, which was held annually from 1819; however, he took money from wealthy patrons and from leading 'village' clubs sponsored by the aristocracy such as West Kent at Chislehurst, Benenden, Leeds Park, Penshurst, and Sevenoaks. Gambling was rife and periodic purges had to be carried out to prevent professionals and gentlemen 'selling' a match. No one ever suggested the 'kind and manly Alfred Mynn' did such a thing, but doubts were raised more than once over the probity of the fourth son of the fifth Duke of St Albans, the Revd. Lord Frederick Beauclerk, who dominated the cricketing establishment in the first half of the nineteenth century; his 'tantrums on the field, unscrupulous wagers and utter lack of what would [later] be regarded as sportsmanship' were a byword. County cricket slowly emerged out of impromptu selections of teams by major patrons where 'gentlemen of the county' supplemented by professionals would take on an 'England' eleven or gentlemen of another county. Mynn's 125 not out in the North vs. South match in 1836, during which he sustained a leg injury that almost led to amputation, made him a popular hero, at least south of the Trent. North of that line cricket was also played with Nottinghamshire's William Clarke the most famous northern cricketer of the age. 'The original and unrivalled Mosslake Field Cricket Society' was formed in Liverpool in 1807 but apart from a few other prominent clubs the early history of the game in the Roses counties awaits proper research.[16]

Such was the pattern of sport before the Victorians. By way of conclusion two broad themes deserve emphasis. Firstly, the importance of sports as an element in a festive culture that was orally transmitted and had a high customary tolerance for violent behaviour of all kinds along with a good deal of gambling, eating, and drinking. This, if you like, was 'traditional' sport in the sense that the seasons, the 'holy days' of the Church, the rites of apprenticeship, the patronage of the landed, and the customs of the locality were the determining factors of play. However, there was a second level too. This was the more organized world of pugilism, rowing, racing, and cricket where written rules were established, challenges were issued and advertised in the press, and large crowds gathered to watch and to wager. Aristocratic patronage was shifting from traditional revels to 'modern' sports. Certain clubs—the Jockey Club, the MCC, and one might add the Royal and Ancient at St Andrews—emerged as regulatory bodies before the formal creation of national governing bodies by the Victorians. Over-concentration on football, which was perhaps untypical in its relatively late regulation and division into its Association and rugby forms, tends to obscure the degree to which sport was already evolving along more complex and commercial lines between the mid-eighteenth and mid-nineteenth centuries.

2. CRUELTY AND SLOTH: THE ABOLITIONISTS

Popular sports of various kinds had been subject to periodic interference from medieval times. Football was banned from time to time to encourage archery practice and maintain public order. Bowling was discouraged 'among the meaner sort of people' in the sixteenth century because of the time that was wasted at it when labourers were supposed to be working. Such examples could be multiplied, although it is very doubtful if these prohibitions had much effect. Monarchs simply did not have the

---

[16] J. Bale, *Sport and Place* (1982), pp. 70–2; P. Morrah, *Alfred Mynn and the Cricketers of His Time* (1986), pp. 30, 42–3, 74–5.

means to impose their will in such matters where communications were poor and enforcement difficult. However, from the sixteenth century onwards a new element was evident in the attitude of the educated classes to the amusements of the people. Puritanism took issue with the cruelty of some animal sports, and with the idleness, drinking, and profanity generally associated with sport and the alehouse. 'Time might better be bestowed and besides we see sin acted' was a common kind of criticism. In his Declaration of Sports for Lancashire in 1617, which came to be more widely known as the Book of Sports, James I took issue with 'some Puritans and precise people', who had interfered with the playing of sports after church on Sundays and authorized a range of amusements including dancing, piping, 'archery for men, leaping, vaulting or any other such harmless recreation'. Macaulay's famous jibe about Puritans being more affronted by the pleasure cruel sports gave to spectators than the pain inflicted on the animals was the culmination of a long tradition of attacking Non-conformity for imposing 'a gloomy godliness on a merry England'. Charles II was keen to be seen to be on the side of sport and helped foster the myth that Puritans were hostile to all sports. It suited the Crown and the country squires to see criticism of sports purely in terms of religious and political fanaticism. Unfortunately, this has tended to obscure the wider issues. New research has stressed that Protestant zealots were by no means always hostile to sport in itself; it was specifically the issue of the playing of games on Sundays that concerned most of them. Nor did they condemn the pleasure that games gave but rather the cruelty involved in some of them. To understand the critique of popular sports we have to look beyond the stereotype of the Puritan killjoy and consider long-term changes in values and behaviour. The 'fanaticism' of the seventeenth century was to become the 'respectability' of the nineteenth.[17]

We are dealing here with what Norbert Elias has called 'the civilizing process', that is, a long-term shift in the threshold of shame and embarrassment. Elias links a sensitivity to pain and criticism of cruelty to a far wider change in manners which began in the later Middle Ages spreading first among the social élite and

[17] J. K. Rühl, 'Religion and Amusements in Sixteenth and Seventeenth Century England', *BJSH*, Sept. 1984, pp. 140–1.

then slowly throughout society. He notes that medieval warriors positively relished the gore of battle and that the French king, for example, felt no compunction about attending a famous ceremony in Paris on Midsummer's Day when a dozen or so cats were ritually placed in a bag and burned alive. Likewise it was considered perfectly normal for Queen Elizabeth I to enjoy bear-baiting. In 1575 she watched dogs let loose on thirteen bears. As one of those present remarked it was 'very pleasant to see the bear . . . shake his ears twice or thrice with the blood and the slaver about his physiognomy as a matter of goodly relief'. Victorians might well have contrasted such cruelties unfavourably with the 'home life of their own dear Queen', and yet her illustrious predecessor clearly thought these things quite normal. Hunting was a casually brutal affair. Gentlemen might tear a wing off a live pigeon for their hawks or chop off the foot of a captured deer to blood young hounds on easy prey. 'When James I hunted the stag he would personally cut its throat and daub the faces of his courtiers with blood, which they were not permitted to wash off.' Sports were caught up in a subtle and diffuse cultural shift that spanned several centuries, encompassing such diverse phenomena as eating tidily and quietly with knives and forks, keeping clean and changing clothes, not urinating or picking your nose in front of others, and a host of other changes in manners that underpin what we now call 'decent' behaviour.[18]

Elias argues that the growing central power of the state and the gradual demilitarization of the aristocracy imposed new social standards and constraints on the European nobility. England with its early political unification and its reliance on protection by the navy rather than by a military aristocracy was particularly receptive to codes defining what was and what was not civilized behaviour. These codes were not so much enforced by law as more insidiously spread by the sanction of ridicule between peers and by the force of social emulation amongst those below. What begins as social constraint is slowly transformed into individual restraint, as the wide range of personal controls on behaviour, which people learn nowadays from childhood, came to be seen as the precondition for 'civilized' life. Fighting is a good example

[18] N. Elias, *The Civilising Process* (1978), esp. pp. 202–3; Thomas, *Man and the Natural World*, pp. 29 and 147.

of this. First the nobility were prohibited from duelling and gradually an educated rejection of all kinds of public fighting became widespread. Obviously duels still sometimes took place. But the norms of violence as a whole, of what is socially tolerable, have shifted so that behaviour that would once have seemed normal is now considered peculiar or problematic. Elias puts it like this: 'in modern times cruelty and joy in the destruction and torment of others, like the proof of physical superiority, are placed under increasingly strong social control anchored in the state organization. All these forms of pleasure, limited by threats of displeasure, gradually come to express themselves only indirectly, and in "refined" form.'[19]

The sharpest and most sustained attack on traditional sports was focused on activities involving the baiting or killing of tethered animals. The sport of 'throwing at cocks' was widely condemned from the early eighteenth century onwards. The *Gentleman's Magazine* called it an 'infamous and iniquitous custom' in 1751. At about this time another critic could only compare it to 'the behaviour of that silly fellow, who boasted of his activity, because he had tripped up a beggar who had a pair of wooden legs'. This was no way for 'a rational soul' to behave. It was both cruel and unfair. Although 'throwing at cocks' was largely suppressed in the eighteenth century, bull-baiting and bull-running continued to be popular despite the efforts to outlaw it in eleven bills presented to Parliament between 1800 and 1835. Most of those who denounced these and other forms of animal baiting also attacked cock-fighting even though some admitted the contest was fair in the sense that cocks were naturally aggressive and each had a more or less equal chance of victory.[20]

It was the inherent cruelty of the spectacle that increasingly offended reformers. The indifference with which the spectators treated the suffering of the animals was a source of shock and dismay. When James Boswell looked around a London cockpit in 1762 to see if anyone shared his pity for the 'mangled and torn' creatures he 'could not observe the smallest relenting sign in any countenance'. Attempts to impose direct controls on popular animal sports lapsed with the political decline of the puritans after

[19] Elias, *The Civilising Process*, p. 192.
[20] Malcolmson, *Popular Recreations*, pp. 120-2.

the Restoration, but it seems some of their objections to the ill-treatment of animals not only survived but became steadily more widespread. Why did this happen? How was the idea of 'the civilizing process' explained and expressed? The rise of a powerful, literate, and expanding élite of commercial, industrial, and professional men is central to the process. A combination of strong intellectual currents, which Keith Thomas has collectively labelled 'the dethronement of man', became more influential in educated attitudes to the natural world. From the sixteenth century through to the late eighteenth century the ancient notion that animals existed only for their usefulness to man or for the pleasure they might afford was increasingly called into question. Scientists began to investigate the natural world in its own right and to consider how animal biology differed from human biology. From the theological and philosophical viewpoint it became less acceptable to view the world as made purely for man. All species had an equal right to exist. Their place in the scheme of things was not determined solely according to human convenience, as medieval cosmologists had tended to think. All of divine creation deserved proper respect; 'Love God, love his creatures', as one early seventeenth-century divine succinctly put it. Philosophers and scientists fascinated by an apparently infinite and complex universe were more cautious in their assertions of human supremacy than their confidently anthropomorphic predecessors. Kant saw this hesitancy through to its logical conclusion when he denied that there was 'any being capable of laying claim to the distinction of being the final end of creation'. An enlightened shift from a purely man-centred view of the world began to seep into public discourse. This lent force to the views of tender-hearted individuals who had always expressed a concern for animal suffering. 'Pain is pain whether it be inflicted on man or beast,' wrote one critic in 1776. Bentham in 1789 stated the matter thus: the question was not whether animals could reason or use language, the real question was 'can they suffer?' 'Growing concern about the treatment of animals', Keith Thomas concludes, 'was one of the most distinctive features of late eighteenth-century English middle-class culture.'[21]

---

[21] Thomas, *Man and the Natural World*, pp. 53, 159, 168, 170, 176, and ch. iv *passim*. This work has revealed new and important intellectual influences on the decline of animal sports.

Methodists were among the strongest opponents of animal sports in the eighteenth century. The commitment of Dissenters to vital religion, though not always to the political radicalism of their puritan forebears, was a marked feature of late Hanoverian England. Methodists were particularly concerned with the reform of popular manners which they saw as inherently sinful. To save the souls of the living from torment in hell, the abuse of the sabbath for drinking and sports had to be stopped. Addressing a Whit Monday crowd at the huge Moorfields fair, the veteran preacher George Whitfield warned that 'there is never a horse course or a cockpit all over heaven'. Such things were 'the devil's entertainments'. Cock-fights with their furious gaming and drinking were peculiarly detested by the Methodists. James Crawfoot, the first Primitive Methodist travelling preacher, dreamed he attended a cock-fight, where he heard horrendous shrieks and groans, and was chased by 'the devil with chains'. Zealots would bravely tackle sporting malefactors on their own grounds, though their dire predictions of eternal damnation were not always taken as seriously as the Methodists might have wished. Reformers ran the risk of becoming an unintentional part of the entertainment. All the same they claimed some successes, although the renunciation of vice could itself take violent forms. After a sermon at Darlaston wake in 1832, a zealous convert 'was so affected that he cut off a cock's head which he had trained for fighting and drowned a bulldog he had trained for baiting'. Generally Methodists tried to provide alternative religious activities which embodied the vigour of the wake in a spiritual cause and eased the pain of crossing from the ranks of the damned to the saved. A few Primitive Methodists were particularly clamorous. William Clowes recalled that he was told to 'cease my noise in the love-feasts, or by my shouts of glory I made the chapel like a cockpit'.[22]

Other activists against animal sports tended to be drawn from the urban professional classes. The success in banning bull-baiting, cock-fighting, and other sports involving domestic animals is partly a reflection of the increasing wealth and influence of such

---

[22] Phillips, 'Primitive Methodist Confrontation', pp. 289–301; J. G. Rule, 'Methodism, Popular Beliefs and Village Culture in Cornwall, 1800–1850', in R. D. Storch (ed.), *Popular Culture and Custom in Nineteenth Century England* (1982), ch. 3.

groups inside and outside Parliament, especially after the extension of the franchise in 1832. The crucial piece of legislation in this respect was the Cruelty to Animals Act of 1835. This reform was pressed strongly by the Society for the Prevention of Cruelty to Animals, formed in 1824 mostly by evangelical humanitarians but with significant additional support from some sporting gentry who believed as strongly in the fair treatment of horses as they did in the right to hunt foxes—an issue that has divided and embarrassed the membership ever since. Their concern was not just to stop animal sports but to improve the treatment of working animals and the methods and conditions of slaughter. Several other societies with similar aims were set up at this time, but all were short-lived and several suspected of preying on the charity of credulous animal-lovers. Only the South Staffordshire Association for the Suppression of Bull-baiting (1824) was specifically concerned with animal sports.[23]

The efforts of the SPCA were certainly crucial in the history of bull-running in Stamford. They regarded it as a test case and devoted a large amount of time and money in the late 1830s to stopping the Stamford 'bullards'. The local magistrates were unenthusiastic, especially after earlier failures to outlaw this ancient custom that took place early each November and attracted large crowds from the surrounding countryside. A serious effort at prohibition was made in 1837 with charges brought by the Society against eight men for their part in the previous year's event. Vigorous petitioning of the Home Office to apply pressure to the magistrates was a further tactic of the abolitionists. Three hundred special constables were sworn in, but these were local men who, as it turned out, were prepared only to protect property and not to stop the bull-running. As a distressed agent of the Society observed, the constables themselves were soon joining in 'shouting and yelling "Bull for Ever! Yahoo Yahoo"'. The following year a number of police and soldiers from outside the town were brought in but a bull still found its way into the town and was pursued in the traditional manner. The same thing happened the following year despite the presence of 20 metropolitan police, 43 dragoons, and 90 local constables. The

---

[23] B. Harrison, 'Animals and the State in Nineteenth Century England', *English Historical Review*, Oct. 1973.

cost of this operation had led to an increase of sixpence in the pound on the rates and galvanized the town's property-owners to agree personally to suppress the custom. Outside forces were withdrawn to avoid antagonizing the locals and a letter from the Home Secretary put in every window. Apart from a few minor scuffles the ratepayers successfully imposed the ban and the custom died out. The manner of this prohibition is most significant. The SPCA sharply raised the cost of the sport. Without the external agitation of the Society, the forces of inertia would have been much too strong to permit change; but equally the case reveals the tenuousness of tradition and a willingness to abolish the custom as soon as the cost of it became too great. The shopkeepers, traders, and minor professionals of provincial England were not attached to the past in the way that country people or the urban apprentices were. As soon as it became more trouble to maintain tradition than to end it, the ratepayers of Stamford stopped the running of bulls and relinquished their ancient sport.[24]

The SPCA considered this a 'great triumph' and their success probably gave their campaign against cock-fighting a boost. Before the 1835 Act there had been occasional efforts to stamp out cock-fighting. In 1830 in Birmingham, forty spectators at a cock-fight had been seized, roped together, and marched in procession through the streets of the town as an example, and then brought before the magistrates. But it was the SPCA that took the lead after 1835 bringing over a dozen prosecutions between 1838 and 1841. One of the Society's inspectors was killed in a brawl after attempting to stop a cock-fight in 1839. Prosecutions continued through the 1840s with the result that the sport survived only in remote rural strongholds or on an infrequent secretive basis in cities. 'An Anglican parson in the Black Country told a factory inspector in 1850 that whereas twenty years earlier he used to see bulls, bears, badgers, dogs and cocks being brought in for baiting and fighting, he had almost put an end to such exhibitions in his parish.' The new legislation was restricted to 'domestic' animals and therefore the hunting of wild animals by the upper classes whether on horseback or by gun was unaffected by

[24] Malcolmson, *Popular Recreations*, pp. 126–33, provides a splendidly detailed account.

change. In fact, many of the titled members of the SPCA were huntsmen themselves. When Lord Dudley Stuart was criticized at a meeting of the society for keeping horses for hunting he brushed aside allegations of cruelty. 'I think these objections to our national sports may be carried too far', he replied dismissively, 'and, so long as unnecessary cruelty is avoided, I see no reason to cry them down on the score of humanity.' Radicals denounced the game laws as part of a wider attack on the Corn Laws, but with their repeal in 1846 the issue of hunting became less contentious.[25]

So much for the vociferous campaign against animal sports. However, the critique of popular sport did not end here. Many of those who opposed the use of animals for sport were also strong critics of other traditional sports. Part of the reason for this was the age-old concern that violent sports created violent men who would abuse their families and assault the public. Whether they were engaged in fighting cocks or in fighting one another, the result was alleged to be the same: a depraved, brutalized, and rowdy mob. Opposition to sports such as cudgelling, pugilism, wrestling, and football clearly did not reside in the question of consent to suffering but in the time-wasting, mayhem, and violence associated with them. It is important to be clear at this point that such complaints had as long a history as the sports themselves. Medieval kings, lords, and burgesses periodically denounced disorderly games, especially street or village football. Dunning cites twenty-three different edicts against the game in both England and Scotland between the fourteenth and the early seventeenth centuries. And there were no doubt far more local prosecutions of the kind recorded at Middlesex in 1576 when seven men 'with unknown malefactors to the number of one hundred assembled themselves unlawfully and played a certain unlawful game called football, by means of which there was amongst them a great affray, likely to result in homicides and serious accident'. Landlords and other employers were concerned not only about the damage and danger of such games, but more generally about their popularity with the common people. Fears that the people were idle, that they

---

[25] Harrison, 'Animals and the State', p. 789; Malcolmson, *Popular Recreations*, p. 154; N. Gash, *Aristocracy and People* (1979), p. 345.

preferred play to work, and that they would irresponsibly break off work to go to a wake, a fight, or a football match went back a long way.[26]

The problem of labour discipline preceded the development of large-scale mechanized manufacturing. The preference of traditional workers for free time rather than increased income was not simply a reaction against industrial forms of production. However, new eighteenth-century entrepreneurs were especially intolerant of such 'irrational' foibles. Those who invested large sums in capital equipment for the textile industry, for example, were anxious to get the most out of their machinery and this in turn meant instilling regular habits of work into their employees. The well-documented and strenuous efforts that were made in the creation of a new work discipline by certain employers have been seen as a major cause of the decline of traditional forms of recreation. At first sight the imposition of an unchanging routine for 'six days shalt thou labour' for twelve hours a day or more would indeed appear to have been decisive in the breaking of an integrated pattern of pleasure that was seasonal and customary. The clock and the factory hooter were after all no respecters of ancient amusements. Eighteenth-century manufacturers like Josiah Wedgwood complained that 'our men have been at play four days this week . . . for wakes must be observed though the world was to end with them'. The habit of following the hunt near Ashton-under-Lyne was attacked by local employers including a hat manufacturer who 'made a rule that we would not employ any person who wished to be off his two days'. Football was a particular nuisance to those who both required a regular injury-free labour force and depended on free public access for deliveries of raw materials or the sending out of orders. The concerted attack in the late 1840s on the Shrove Tuesday football match in Derby, and the rumbustious collections of beer money that went along with it, provide a classic instance of the business community making common cause with evangelical critics of the game. The council, which comprised both religious advocates of more rational recreation and prominent local business men, denounced the football match as 'the assembly of a lawless rabble, suspending business to the loss of the industrious,

---

[26] Middlesex County Records, cited in Elias and Dunning, 'Folk Football', p. 118.

creating terror and alarm to the timid and peaceable, committing violence on the person and damage to the properties of the defenceless poor'.[27]

Hostility to street football went beyond the ranks of the industrialists and was shared more widely in the business community, especially by shopkeepers who found themselves in the front line of play. Kingston upon Thames town council urged that Shrove Tuesday football be moved away from the city centre in 1840 complaining that 'it is not a trifling consideration that a suspension of business for nearly two days should be created to the inhabitants for the mere gratification of a sport at once so useless and barbarous'. After 1835 those who opposed street football strongly had a new legal weapon in their hands in the form of the Highways Act, which explicitly banned the game on penalty of a fine of up to forty shillings. Just as opponents of animal sports could use the nascent police force to enforce the prohibition of cock-fighting or bull-baiting, so more general critics of popular manners could urge the police to regulate street games. The Derby council had to get the support of the army in a three-year battle between 1846 and 1849 to outlaw their infamous match, but the more routine regulation of the highway increasingly became a matter for the police. Constables were required to enforce 'a sometimes subtle proliferation of tightening constraints of all kinds', ranging from licensing to Sunday trading to street sports. 'Where are the police?' was the new cry of the reformers, as Bailey points out in his study of Bolton. Those writing to the local press in the 1840s often demanded that the police, who were an expensive item on the rates, take action against all sorts of street games ranging from pitch-and-toss to crowds gathering to watch and gamble on running races in the streets.[28]

Traditional football, however, was not simply destroyed by action from above; it was already ailing when the police moved in to impose new regulations on the use of the public highway. Strutt, the most eminent chronicler of traditional sports, writing

[27] Cunningham, *Leisure in the Industrial Revolution*, pp. 45, 61; A. Delves, 'Popular Recreation and Social Conflict in Derby 1800–1850', in S. and E. Yeo (eds.), *Popular Culture and Class Conflict, 1590–1914* (1981), p. 90.

[28] Malcolmson, *Popular Recreations*, p. 143; Storch (ed.), *Popular Culture and Custom*, p. 12; Bailey, *Leisure and Class*, p. 21.

around 1800, claimed that football 'was formerly in vogue amongst the common people of England, though of late years it seems to have fallen into disrepute and is but little practised'. There is plenty of evidence of the continued popularity of Shrove Tuesday football despite the threat of prosecution, but we know much less about the more informal playing of the game in the manner of Elizabethan and Stuart apprentices or farm-labourers. The casual playing of football does seem to have been on the wane in comparison with the seventeenth and early eighteenth centuries. John Parker of Maldon observed in the Interregnum that on Sundays 'the people did usually go out of the church to play at football and to the alehouse'. Thomas Robinson, the early eighteenth-century rector of Ousby in Cumberland, used to 'set the younger sort to play at football (of which he was a great promoter) and other rustical diversions' after Sunday service, and Sunday football was apparently still well known in the West Country in the later eighteenth century. At harvest festival in the upper Wye valley, Francis Kilvert observed what sounds like traditional football in 1871: 'After dinner all the men played or rather kicked football at each other and then it grew dark, when the game ended in a general royal scuffle or scrummage.' Interrogating an old resident of Langley Burrell in Wiltshire, Kilvert discovered football had survived the sabbatarian efforts of the Revd. Samuel Ashe, a previous incumbent of Kilvert's father's parish, who 'used to come round quietly under the trees and bide his time till the football came near him when he would catch up the ball and pierce the bladder with a pin. But some of the young fellows would be even with the parson for they would bring a spare bladder, blow it, and soon have the football flying again.' 'Football, and hockey and other games', it appears, 'went on all over the common . . . on Sunday afternoons.' Victorian 'realist' painting certainly features traditional village football matches as an occasional subject, though this may be a species of pastoral nostalgia. The *Oswestry Observer* in 1887, quoting 'a man over eighty, now an inmate of the Lampeter Workhouse', noted that in 'South Cardiganshire it seems that about eighty years ago the population, rich and poor, male and female, of opposing parishes, turned out on Christmas Day and indulged in the game of football with such vigour that it became little short of a serious fight', with the implication that such goings-on were no longer common or tolerated. Proper primary research into the casual sports of the poor is required and it is hazardous to draw firm conclusions from the slight evidence available at present. Examining references to sport in the statistical accounts of Scottish parishes, Neil Tranter has recently concluded that sports were 'in all probability more, not less, prevalent in the 1830/40s than in the 1790s'. Whatever may have been the case elsewhere, for Scotland it is difficult to substantiate the claim that recreations like curling, football, and quoiting significantly declined in popularity during the period of early industrialization. Whether traditional football was still played regularly but in a less rumbustious fashion and on a smaller scale or whether it was increasingly confined to an annual festival is not clear. The relative silence of otherwise noisy and vituperative critics of popular culture seems to suggest that the game survived primarily as a casual rural pastime which had been in slow decline over a long period.[29]

Even where football survived as a festive event, it tended to lose much of its spontaneous violence and became increasingly confined to safe places. If part of the significance of the old games of football had been to assert the rights of the people to the fields or streets regardless of the claims of the legal title-holders, then nineteenth-century play was certainly a pale imitation of the past. Instead of banning the game, prominent local residents often preferred to relocate it out of harm's way. In Alnwick the Duke of Northumberland provided open space outside the town when there was an attempt to ban the annual free-for-all from the town centre in 1827–8. A local brewer offered to do the same in Twickenham in 1840 and this seems to have become a fairly general practice in the mid-Victorian period. Even the famous game played at Ashbourne, which still survives, was moved out of the centre of the town after an attempt to ban it in 1861. In Wales *cnappen* was played in the streets into the late nineteenth century, and as late as 1884 in Neath 'all shutters are put up and the principal thoroughfare is given over to the players'. But this

[29] J. Strutt, *The Sports and Pastimes of the People of England* (1903); Malcolmson, 'Sports in Society', p. 70, and *Popular Recreations*, p. 162; W. Plomer (ed.), *Kilvert's Diary* (1964), pp. 149, 211; V. Scannell, *Sporting Literature* (1987), pp. 193–9; N. L. Tranter, 'Popular Sports and the Industrial Revolution in Scotland', *IJHS*, May 1987, p. 3.

was the last time the game was played in the town where three years earlier the Welsh Rugby Union had been formed. In remoter areas, like Workington or Chester-le-Street in Durham, or Jedburgh in the Scottish borders, the game did survive as a folkloric oddity into the twentieth century. Even in Cornwall there was a distinct decline in traditional sports during the first half of the nineteenth century, especially in the incidence of Cornish hurling.[30]

This process of decline and regulation applied to summer sports as well. In Oxfordshire the Whitsun holiday was 'tamed' during the second quarter of the nineteenth century not simply because of the suppression of bull-baiting and cock-fighting, but also because of the decline in bare-fist fighting and in morris dancing. The drunken carousing and collections of beer money by the morris men were less readily tolerated by the Church and by the Friendly Societies, which were taking over the running of the festivities in the mid-nineteenth century. Obviously the preaching of Methodists and the enforcement of prohibitions against cruel sports by zealous private bodies played a part in the overall decline. But they were pushing against a door that was half open. This point was made clearly by Edmund Hyde Hall in his description of Caernarfonshire in about 1810. 'Of these folleries and pastimes of old,' he concluded, 'the greater part now lie buried in the grave dug for them partly perhaps by the growing intelligence of the people, but certainly with a more immediate effect by the sour spirit of Methodism.' Blaming the Methodists was especially popular in Wales, where the harpist to George IV, Edward Jones, bewailed 'the sudden decline of the national Minstrelsy', which he attributed to 'the fanatick impostors, or illiterate plebeian preachers, who have been suffered to overrun the country . . . dissuading [the common people] from their innocent amusements, such as Singing, Dancing and other rural Sports and Games, which heretofore they had been accustomed to delight in'. This, of course, exaggerates the impact of religious revival and begs the question why common people were receptive not only to change in religion but also in culture. 'The growing intelligence of the people' was indeed a force. As in the case of

[30] Malcolmson, *Popular Recreations*, pp. 142–3; Smith and Williams, *Fields of Praise*, p. 19.

the Stamford bull-running, it required the tacit consent of those who had in earlier generations opposed the regulation of customary recreations before the reformers could make much headway.[31]

The culture of respectability, which took so firm a hold of the skilled 'labour aristocracy' of the mid-nineteenth century, condemned the unbridled excess of the old festivals. This group was neither sufficiently deferential to tolerate noble patronage, nor were they still in the thrall of 'rough' traditions. In Birmingham the banning of brutal sports met with the approval of many of the more respectable and skilled workers. Such 'men saved up their cash', noted the *Morning Chronicle* in 1851, 'rather than spend it as they used to do on bull-baiting and cock-fighting at the wakes', although this was sometimes just to afford to take the train to other fairs and amusements. The paper had to admit that 'the uneducated portion of workmen', who formed the numerical majority, were still keen on the old sports, but the moral and intellectual leaders of the working class were distinctly less so. Radical artisans added their voice to the call for the suppression of Shrove Tuesday football in Derby in the late 1840s. They saw the game as part and parcel of an ancient culture of cruelty and ignorance which kept the working classes in their place by encouraging their worst instincts. 'Your "Betters" have been foremost in this Fête, hallooing you like brute dogs to the strife,' complained an artisan enemy of the game, in what may have been a jibe at Joseph Strutt, who had used his power as a major local employer to protect the game until his death in 1844. Although it involved only a small minority of the whole work-force, the denunciation of 'bread and circuses' by the radicals was more important than it might seem. For this group not only tended to be opinion-formers within their locality but also were frequently the instigators of trade unions and mutual aid societies. The feasts and festivals they organized tended to be as short on traditional sports as they were on strong ale. The aristocracy of labour crossed the threshold of shame and embarrassment, leaving behind crude joviality and exertion for the quieter and more

---

[31] A. Howkins, 'The Taming of Whitsun', in S. and E. Yeo (eds.), *Popular Culture and Class Conflict*, esp. pp. 202–3; P. Morgan, 'From a Death to a View', in E. Hobsbawm and T. Ranger, *The Invention of Tradition* (1983), pp. 44, 53.

respectable pleasures of the reading-room, the park, and the private club. Skilled artisans in Victorian Edinburgh preferred growing flowers and playing golf to fighting and playing the fool. In the south of England respectable workmen no longer engaged so readily even in well-established customs like 'guying' on 5 November. Douglas Reid's meticulous study of popular culture in nineteenth-century Birmingham notes that 'by mid century Saint Monday was well on the way to being internally transformed'. Cricket, for example, was the favourite sport amongst 120 'heavy steel toy' workers who possessed 'bats, wickets and balls . . . in common' and 'in summer turn out to play two or three times a week'. The Birmingham Athenic Institution was set up by Christian Chartists in 1842 to combine intellectual improvement, radical agitation, and rational recreation. In addition to classes for 'reading, writing, arithmetic, elocution and literature' there were also 'physical pleasures, dancing, cricket, quoits, football, ropes, horizontal-bar, running, wrestling, jumping, etc.' Before the phrase had become a public-school cliché these sober working men had adopted as their motto 'mens sana in corpore sano'.[32]

So popular manners were themselves changing 'from below'. Whatever else historians may say about the 'labour aristocracy', there is no doubt that they were a distinct and influential cultural force. The decline of traditional sports, especially those which involved fighting, was not simply a question of pressure from well-organized groups of evangelicals and business men; in addition to the agitation from abolitionists there was evidence of a gradual shift in public taste especially amongst the literate and more highly skilled élite of working people themselves. To complete the picture, however, we now need to look more closely at those who traditionally had regulated the affairs of early modern Britain: the gentry, the 'natural' rulers of what was still a predominantly rural society.

[32] D. Reid, 'Interpreting the Festival Calendar', in Storch (ed.), *Popular Culture and Custom*, p. 132; Delves, 'Popular Recreation in Derby', p. 104; R. D. Storch, 'Please to Remember the 5th of November', in Storch (ed.), *Popular Culture and Custom*, ch. 3. D. Reid, 'Labour, Leisure and Politics in Birmingham, c.1800–1875', Ph.D. thesis (Birmingham Univ., 1985), pp. 12, 183.

3. FIELD SPORTS AND THE DECLINE OF PATERNALISM

'That which distinguished life in the country was what was called our county life under which a body of gentlemen possessed of property and, having the interests of the people at heart, took part in sports and directed local affairs in the district, thus showing they were of use and influence in the world.' This classic exposition of the role of the country squire was given in rueful vein in 1880 by the Earl Percy. The nostalgic cast of mind was much in evidence amongst the late nineteenth-century aristocracy. The historian of the Brocklesby Hunt in 1902 had similar regrets at the passing of 'Old England': 'Gone are the landlords of the old school, the backbone of England, the fox-hunting squires are few and far between; gone are the sport loving farmers of fifty years ago, gone that charming country life that made so many great Englishmen.' Maudlin declamation and a melancholy, carefully savoured sense of the past have long provided a recurring theme in upper-class thought. Similarly the world before 1914 with its stable currency and plentiful servants now seems like an aristocratic golden age. All the same there had clearly been changes in the landed classes and in their relationship with their tenants, which had a major impact on the nature of traditional country sports between the eighteenth and late nineteenth centuries. It is as well to remember that the landed interest dominated Parliament at least until the repeal of the Corn Laws in 1846 and landed power continued to be over-represented in the Commons after the Second Reform Bill of 1867. The prosecution of cruel sports, which we have just examined, was sanctioned by a parliament of lords and squires. Richard Martin ('Humanity Dick'), who introduced the 1822 bill to prevent cruelty to domestic animals, cheerfully hunted foxes over his 2,000-acre estate in Connemara. How was it that 'sporting gentlemen' failed to defend cock-fighting and traditional football when at the same time they took up fox-hunting with such enthusiasm? What had happened to the Squire Westerns who loved sports and loathed puritans? Two broad and related changes were underway. The first involved a shift in the general standards of good behaviour amongst the gentry themselves—what we might call the application to landowners of the 'civilizing process' already mentioned; the second concerned changes in the economic organization of rural life and the social relationships that depended upon it.[33]

Over a wide area of eighteenth-century Europe there seems to have been a withdrawal of upper-class patronage of popular recreation. Instead of possessing both an élite culture *and* an interest in popular speech and customs, the privileged began to cultivate national languages, courtly dances, more sophisticated and complex kinds of music as an exclusive 'polite' culture. In Britain, where the aristocracy and gentry had been demilitarized for longer than in the rest of Europe and where profits from trade and agriculture were greatest, there was enormous scope for the creation of a more refined domestic way of life. The upper classes with their fine furniture and *objets d'art*, their classical houses and parks, their grand tours, and wider reading were increasingly coming to form a culturally as well as a socially distinctive group. On the Celtic fringe mutual incomprehension was aggravated as even limited familiarity with the Scots and the Welsh languages became unfashionable and gave way to the robust 'good English' of Addison, Steele, and Dr Johnson. The Welsh gentry of the post-Restoration period abandoned their native tongue for English and withheld much of their patronage of Welsh culture. Their houses were no longer organized around a central hall where the bards could sing and recite. Former gentry patrons withdrew into the more private spaces of English country-house architecture. Nor were Scottish gentlemen touched by the enlightened influence of David Hume or Adam Smith likely to support grinning contests or goose-riding. By the early eighteenth century gentry in the Lothians were coming to believe that the old customs were absurd. 'As their rhymes were mere unmeaning gibberish, and their demeanour exceedingly boisterous, the custom [of mumming] became intolerable; so that . . . they were generally hooted at and forbid in every decent family, and in the end they dwindled away into nothing.' Even amongst the less rigorously educated English gentry a similar reaction set in. In Lincolnshire 'rude jollity and merriment of country feasts' was becoming less common in the early nineteenth century. Obelkevich has shown in a painstaking local study how communal village culture was

---

[33] R. Carr, *English Fox Hunting* (1976), pp. 149–51, 198. This work provides a serious and entertaining introduction to a neglected and important topic.

first undermined by the withdrawal of the gentry and further
weakened in the mid-nineteenth century by the larger farmers,
who left the labourers to soldier on as bearers of the old customs
as best they could. 'The discontinuance in frequency of such
sports [football and wrestling] among the common people is
chiefly attributable to a change in the habits and manners of their
superiors,' noted a Cornish magistrate at the end of the eighteenth
century. 'Hospitality is now vanished from us', he concluded,
'and so are its attendant sports.'[34]

The Established Church, which was largely run by the younger
sons of the gentry, also tended to withdraw its patronage of
traditional sports. In 1765 a clergyman writing to his family
complained that 'wrestling, singlestick, or even football, are never
considered as diversions by the common people, but as attended
with danger, mischief or bloodshed'. Churches became more
reluctant to permit their property to be used for sports. St
Sepulchre's in London enclosed its yard in 1787 to stop 'idle
fellows and boys who meet there daily . . . tossing up and playing
other games', and parish accounts in Somerset in 1802 record
the spending of three shillings 'replacing the stones to prevent
fives playing against the church'. This process was continued by
the Victorians even in relatively remote areas. In the Vale of
Clywd, for example, 'church restoration removed stairways
connecting the chancels to local taverns, removed niches kept
in the churches for the prize ale given by the parson to winners
in Sunday sports, removed ball courts from churchyards, and
placed huge marble graves in churchyards formerly laid out for
dances and sports meetings.' The late eighteenth-century Church
of England was becoming more concerned with sabbatarianism
than before. Brailsford has shown that eighteenth-century boxing,
cricket, and horse-racing were restricted to weekdays, especially
Mondays and Tuesdays. Older sports seem to have been
increasingly rare on Sundays too. According to the *Gentleman's
Magazine* of 1783 'in order to avoid unseemly noise on a day
of holiness, the sports and diversions are now in many villages
prudently deferred until the Monday after'. In the eighteenth

---

[34] P. Burke, *Popular Culture in Early Modern Europe* (1979), p. 179; J.
Obelkevich, *Religion and Rural Society* (1976); Rule, 'Methodism, Popular Beliefs
and Village Culture in Cornwall', pp. 53–4.

century hunting parsons like the Revd. Billy Butler, who 'only married "the labouring classes" on non-hunting days', were commonplace. But the influence of evangelicalism combined with a decline in both income and social status meant that the rural clergy in the nineteenth century became a relative rarity in the Field. 'Bishop Pepys of Worcester could say with pride in 1854 that "the sporting clergyman, so common a character in former years, is now rarely to be met with".' With the collapse of the political dominance of Anglicanism in the 1830s after the achievement of Catholic Emancipation and the repeal of the Test and Corporation Acts against Dissenters, the Church of England was no longer the natural refuge of younger sons of the gentry. The number of Oxbridge graduates who were ordained was halved between 1842 and 1862. The new Victorian vicar preferred a cricket match to a cudgelling.[35]

The plain country gentleman who liked to join in village games, ritually throwing in the pig's bladder to start the football match and providing cakes and ale afterwards, had become a figure from the rural past. There were, of course, prominent exceptions to this rule in the shape of men like William Windham, a Tory diehard, who saw off several bills to ban bull-baiting at the beginning of the nineteenth century and stoutly defended the old sports as part of a common patriotic heritage threatened by weak-kneed evangelicals and the sinister forces of Jacobinism. But such uncompromising traditionalism became increasingly rare, and he was regarded as something of a curiosity even in his own time. Duelling, the ultimate expression of the established aristocratic code of honour, which had been widespread amongst the landed élite of the eighteenth century, came to be regarded as 'incongruous and foolish' during the first half of the nineteenth century and declined sharply in the 1830s and 1840s. 'To the old-fashioned sort of gentleman' adept with sword and pistol, there was 'opposed a new type of gentleman, the good citizen' who invoked the newly effective laws of slander and libel along with the police force to settle disputes. The 'civilizing process' worked to reform the gentry from within, and it was this shift

---

[35] Malcolmson, *Popular Recreations*, p. 163; D. Brailsford, 'Religion and Sport in Eighteenth Century England', *BJSH*, Sept. 1984, pp. 166-83; Carr, *English Fox Hunting*, pp. 176-7. Morgan, 'From a Death to a View', p. 54; Gash, *Aristocracy and People*, p. 337.

in the norms of polite society, which in turn permitted a hitherto ineffective humanitarian lobby to have its way. Tory paternalism was taking new directions both more relevant to the upsurge of economic activity and less atavistic or rude in their associations. Tory and Whig alike were sheepish, to say the least, about customary sports apart from field sports. It was the victims of middle-class 'progress' that Lord Shaftesbury was concerned about. There was more than enough to do to moralize and regulate the new industrial communities without protecting ancient and often barbarous activities.[36]

The eclipse of the country gentleman, who to some extent shared the recreations of the common people, by those who positively cultivated more refined manners provides one element in the explanation, but it does not tell the whole story. Changing social relations within the countryside as a result of enclosure and high capitalist farming was the other factor in the sporting equation. Obviously such developments often antagonized local people and interfered with traditional places for play. From the later eighteenth century farm-servants more often 'lived out' where they had formerly 'lived in', sharing a roof and a domestic routine with their masters. There was also a wider disruption of social relationships through the abandonment of a whole range of paternalist legislation that had been devised to enforce both the responsibilities of men to their masters and of masters to their men. The early nineteenth century witnessed the abolition of government mechanisms for the local regulation of wages and prices, the removal of apprenticeship statutes, and eventually the destruction of the system of support for the poor which had given prominent landowners a crucial role in the daily lives of the communities they lived in. The weakening of customary bonds and duties which tended to accompany the agricultural revolution was reflected in the pattern of sports that expressed the solidarity of the local community. Gentry involvement in popular sports depended very much upon an absolute and unquestioned acceptance of the social hierarchy. If the squire could often dispense with formalities and share games with his tenants, it was because he was sure of his own position. Social confidence encouraged expressions of fraternity, though a tendency to

[36] J. C. D. Clark, *English Society 1688–1832* (1985), pp. 115–16.

idealize a harmonious and close-knit pre-industrial past should be resisted. Broadly speaking the ties of deference held fast; however, gentry fears were greatly, and perhaps unduly, exaggerated by the course of the French Revolution. It was not so much that the bonds of deference had in fact been severed— the mid-Victorian countryside was a pretty stable and hierarchical place after all—but that the gentry were no longer so confident of their position. While their social pre-eminence was still a fact, it was increasingly being called into question.

It was not only a vocal minority of radicals who threatened the calm life of the countryside. Perhaps more important and more insidious was the penetration of new wealth into the ordered universe of landlord and tenant. At its crudest this involved shoddy barons and nabobs buying up ancient estates, although recent research has stressed the degree to which the most important aristocratic families were able to resist intermarriage until the later nineteenth century. From the early nineteenth century onwards demand amongst the rapidly expanding professional, commercial, and industrial élites for land was becoming stronger. Land was like no other commodity. 'It has a dignity and a set of duties attached to it which are peculiar to itself,' wrote William Marshall in 1804. It was this 'dignity', if not these 'duties' that the rising bourgeois sought, prompting Cobden to despair of the British as 'a servile, aristocrat-loving people who regard the land with as much reverence . . . as the peerage'. This, of course, was not the way the gentry viewed things. While radical urban liberals like Cobden and Bright feared the absorption of the most successful of the middle classes by the old landed interest, to country gentlemen new money spelled the destruction of ancient families and customs. It was the influence rather than the existence of the hereditary ruler which was at stake. In the mid-Victorian years the rail network aggravated such fears as it was henceforth possible to combine a job in the city with a life in the country.[37]

While agricultural rents were buoyant and large tenant farmers could still get good prices for their grain, it was possible to hold the pretensions of the bourgeois 'squire' in check. This was the situation in the third quarter of the century when the demand

[37] Carr, *English Fox Hunting*, pp. 47, 152.

for grain from the rising population of the industrial cities combined with high international transport costs to hold down foreign imports and keep the landed interest profitable. It was from the 1870s onwards that the true effect of the ending of agricultural protection was felt. A flood of cheap food brought to the exporting ports by rail led to a collapse in prices and a sharp decline in the value of farming land. In the last quarter of the century 'the new vulgarians' or the 'plutocrats', whose incomes came from banking and commercial services for the expanding Empire or from brewing and urban retailing, bought their way into the bastion of land. To make matters worse agrarian depression was combined with the opening up of rural politics to more democratic procedures. The creation of county councils in 1884 further undermined the position of the squire. As Wilde's Lady Bracknell remarked to her prospective son-in-law, land 'gives one position and prevents one from keeping it up'.[38]

These changes not only undermined the patronage of traditional country sports, they had a fundamental impact on what had been the most important leisure activity of the landed since the Middle Ages. Until the eighteenth century the deer had been the aristocratic huntsman's favoured prey. Hares were hunted too but there was relatively little interest in the fox. However, large-scale land clearance and drainage increasingly interfered with the woodland habitat while at the same time creating a new landscape of hedged fields which were usually part of landed estates rented out in large units to substantial tenant farmers. It was a wealthy Leicestershire squire, Hugo Meynell, who found the method of hunting most appropriate to a revolutionary agriculture and perfected it as Master of the Quorn from 1753 to 1800. Meynell was above all a great breeder of hounds. By inbreeding his dogs he produced a blend of speed, endurance, and good scenting powers that could keep track of a fast and wily fox over a long run. The 'field' followed them, mounted on 'hunters' some of which were highly prized possessions and like the best hounds the product of careful breeding. The emphasis on producing pedigree dogs and thoroughbred horses, which spilled over into horse-racing and

[38] J. Camplin, *The Rise of the Plutocrats* (1978).

hare-coursing too, was peculiarly appropriate to a group whose own breeding was also the subject of meticulous genealogical calculation. Fox-hunting was not just a hard ride through the landscape of the agricultural revolution; it combined the 'science' of breeding with the 'art' of hunting; it was less bloody and more highly organized than older forms of hunting; it brought together landlords and the larger tenants into a community 'with a growing body of conventions and etiquette' and 'a mystique and cohesion of its own'. 'The Field' made a regular public display of the power structure of the countryside. Fox-hunting became the new social institution of provincial upper-class life, uniting the age-old enthusiasm for the chase within a rudimentary national framework that was distinctively modern. By the early nineteenth century fox-hunting took place throughout England, which was divided up informally into 'countries' and ruled by that most admired of Englishmen—the Master of Foxhounds.[39]

Although fox-hunting began as a country sport enjoyed not only by larger landowners but often followed on foot by local people, it became increasingly fashionable and exclusive in the course of the nineteenth century. The smart Midland packs like the Quorn and the Pytchley attracted a large number of rich young men who wanted to do some hard and dangerous riding and had thousands to spend on horses and servants. This was the world of 'Regency bucks' and madcap runs, the world of 'Nimrod' who published what became a classic series of 'Hunting Tours' in the 1820s. 'Nimrod' was in real life Charles Apperley, the son of a parson, and friend of the high-born including the infamous John Mytton, a vastly rich Shropshire fox-hunter, who 'fought dogs and bears with his teeth, put horses' feet in his pocket, drove gigs over tall gates, shot ducks in winter in his night shirt, rode at impossible fences, hunted rats on skates . . . and died of drink in a debtors' prison'. Closer to the provincial realities was the prince of hunting writers, R. S. Surtees. He was the creator of the immortal Jorrocks, the hunting grocer who dropped his 'aitches' and of the plausible Mr Sponge, whose 'dexterity in getting into people's houses was only equalled by the difficulty in getting him out again'. Surtees admired the small hunt, run

---

[39] F. M. L. Thompson, *English Landed Society in the Nineteenth Century* (1963), p. 144; also D. C. Itzkowitz, *Peculiar Privilege* (1977).

without great expense and bringing together a few keen huntsmen rather than a crowd of flashy 'thrusters'. Men like 'old Sloc, a hard-riding, hard-bitten, hold-harding sort of sportsman, whose whole heart was in the thing, and who would have ridden over his best friend in the ardour of the chase' was the kind of unsentimental traditionalist who appealed to the taciturn Surtees, who became squire of Hamsterley and eventually High Sheriff of County Durham in 1856.[40]

Surtees was writing at a time when the early 'feudal' packs, which provided free sport for the friends and associates of a large landowner, were giving way to 'subscription' packs where members of the hunt would contribute significantly towards the Master's expenses. Rising costs were partly to blame. It cost around £2,000 a year to run a fox-hunt, and the big Midland packs cost much more. Only the greatest families could afford such sums and increasingly costs were shared by enthusiasts. There were only twenty-four subscription packs in 1810 but over a hundred by 1854. Trollope, writing in the 1860s, remarked that 'men now prefer . . . to pay their own proportion of the expenditure, and feel they may follow their amusement without any debt to the Master of the hunt other than that which is always due to zeal and success in high position'. The railway greatly increased the possibilities of hunting for the affluent urbanite and this lay behind the success of hunting by subscription. But the railway also opened the way for interlopers like Mr Sponge or for the unscrupulous Facey Romford, another of Surtees's creations, who hired himself out to run a hunt for subscribers. Flourishing as the mid-Victorian hunt may have been, it could no longer be accounted a straightforward country sport. The railways brought not only new wealth but a greater emphasis on smartness. Money became more important as newcomers competed with one another to appear the best dressed. Hunting pink with precisely the correct buttons and tight-fitting leather boots with immaculately polished boot-tops were what the smart huntsman wore. Surtees satirized the new sportsman in the person of Mr Waffles, who was 'all things by turns and nothing long', an endless talker and 'most enterprising youth, just on the verge of

[40] R. S. Surtees, *Mr Sponge's Sporting Tour* (1982), pp. 3, 21; on Mytton see Carr, *English Fox Hunting*, p. 95.

arriving of age, and into the possession of a very considerable amount of charming ready money'. The old world of hunt balls and intimate dinners between neighbours, which it was argued kept the large landowners on the land, was changing. 'There were blooming widows in every stage of grief and woe, from the becoming cap to the fashionable corset,' remarked Surtees of a Victorian hunting-town in the season.[41]

Despite the intrusions of parvenus, hunting did help to maintain the solidarity of the rural élite for most of the nineteenth century. New wealth was drawn in by the social prestige of the hunt and kept the sport going after the collapse of the agricultural economy in the 1870s. Retired imperial administrators and traders bought up broad acres and subsidized the sport of those whose income was less ample than before. The Quorn, for example, was revitalized by a Liverpool shipbroker who had hunted in India. In the great wheat-growing areas of the south and east it became much harder for landlords to pay for the damage that horses and hounds did to crops without giving up their masterships to outsiders, who sometimes failed to foster good relations with tenants by scrupulously fair compensation. Farmers tended to complain that subscription packs lacked a settled territorial interest and failed to pay up promptly and in full. When times were good in the age of 'high farming' in the 1850s and 1860s farmers might have ridden to hounds themselves and consequently been willing to bear some of the costs for damage out of their own pocket. But when earnings fell and there was little competition for tenancies, their sympathy for the hunt and for the increasing numbers of outsiders it attracted dried up.

The lure of mixing with the landed remained strong and agricultural decline did not affect all areas equally. In grasslands or the remoter border areas fox-hunting carried on much as before. The hunt still exerted a powerful fascination over those minority of leisured youths who were not sent off to row at public school. The young Siegfried Sassoon was one such devotee whose 'first reaction to the "field" was one of mute astonishment. I had taken it for granted that there would be people "in pink", but these enormous confident strangers overwhelmed my mind with

---

[41] Carr, *English Fox Hunting*, pp. 114–16; Surtees, *Mr Sponge's Sporting Tour*, pp. 22, 29.

the visible authenticity of their brick-red coats. It all felt quite different to reading Surtees by the schoolroom fire.' There were still a fair number of splenetic MFHs in the Edwardian era like Sassoon's Lord Dumborough in the Kentish backwoods or squires like Lord Willoughby de Broke, who hunted four times a week and knew his 'country' like the back of his hand. But they were a dying breed. The 'country life' of the hunt, which had been of real importance in the nineteenth century, became *Country Life* in the twentieth—a matter of 'horsiness' and nice houses.[42]

By and large the rich came to prefer shooting to hunting in the later nineteenth century. If the golden age of fox-hunting was the first half of the nineteenth century, the shooting of large numbers of carefully preserved game-birds such as grouse, pheasant, and partridge with ever more accurate and powerful firearms was the passion of late Victorian and Edwardian England. The game laws imposed ferocious penalties on poachers, which the game-preserving landlords enforced at the magistrate's bench. Game-shooting not only led to the resentment of farmers, who until 1881 were not even allowed to shoot rabbits and hares straying on to their land without the purchase of an expensive permit, it also was the cause of some sharp exchanges between huntsmen and marksmen. Owners of large shooting-estates investing up to two or three thousand a year in game-birds were understandably unwilling to tolerate large numbers of foxes on their land. The number of gamekeepers in England and Wales rose from 9,000 in 1851 to 23,000 in 1911. Separate game-departments were set up within the managerial structure of the estate and the Great Depression lent added importance to income derived from shooting-rents.[43]

Shooting was the sport of the plutocracy *par excellence*. Shooting was essentially private whereas hunting was part of the public life of the landed. Huntsmen were losing the long battle with game-preserving landlords over the shooting of foxes and the putting up of fences. Access to shooting came through intimate networks of friendship and influence or through great riches. The mania for counting the bag seems distinctively modern

---

[42] Itzkowitz, *Peculiar Privilege*, pp. 177–80; J. Lowerson, 'English Middle Class Sport', in Proceedings of the Inaugural Conference of the BSSH, 1982, p. 10; S. Sassoon, *Memoirs of a Fox-hunting Man* (1960), p. 32.

[43] Thompson, *English Landed Society*, pp. 137–41.

and only possible because of improvements in firearms and the large-scale rearing and conservation of birds. Edward VII was too fat to hunt and favoured country-house weekends with plenty of game-birds, good dinners, and pretty women. Men like Sir Edward Guinness bought their way into royal favour and into the House of Lords by giving lavish shooting-parties. In 1908 the King was welcomed by the former Sir Edward now Lord Iveagh with a torchlit procession plus '70 men catering for the game, a hundred beaters for perhaps 8 guns, 2 loaders, a cartridge boy and a detective for the King alone. Even the coverts were connected by telephone so that the latest information could be obtained on where the sport was best.' Not to be outdone, Harmsworth hired Sutton Place in Surrey for £1,750 a year even though he did not care much for shooting (though this may have seemed something of a bargain to a man who built a golf-course that he only ever used on one occasion). Edward set the exclusive social and sporting tone of the early twentieth century. He passed this passion, if no other, to the stolid George V, who, 'though tearful at a dead bird in a garden, in India shot among other game 21 tigers, 8 rhinos and a bear, and with six others at Sandringham dispatched 10,000 birds in four days'. The Highlands of Scotland were particularly favoured after the railway opened up vast tracts of hitherto inaccessible land and the visits of Queen Victoria gave the royal seal of approval. The grouse and the Glorious Twelfth lined many a laird's pocket and opened social doors to English and expatriate Scottish industrial magnates. Andrew Carnegie thought sporting-rents were becoming absurdly inflated. In 1885 alone the Guinness, Bass, and Whitbread families bought estates in the Highlands and a little later Cecil Rhodes paid £2,000 for two months on Rannoch Moor. Wealth courted birth from the Highland lodge to the big-game hunts of the African bush.[44]

Game-fishing too became caught up in the drive for exclusivity and the intrusion of market forces into élite amusements. The more successful and ruminative members of the liberal professions—judges and barristers, consultants and professors—were particularly fond of escaping the urban pressures for a few

[44] Camplin, *Rise of the Plutocrats*, pp. 222, 234; G. Jarvie, 'Dependency, Cultural Identity and Sporting Landlords', in Proceedings of the Third Annual Conference of the BSSH, 1985, pp. 93–4.

days or more of good fishing on a landed estate. Salmon and trout fishing were turned into a complex art in the late nineteenth century and the cost of renting good stretches of water rose astronomically. The peaceful world of the country angler, who like Francis Kilvert's clergyman father cast a good fly at little expense in the middle years of the century, was coming under pressure. By the 1890s it was costing a hundred pounds or more to fish the classic chalk-streams like the Itchen or the Test. As with shooting, the desire for beautiful and expensive equipment was strong, and the leading firm of fine rod makers in Alnwick saw the demand for their product rise from around 250 cane rods a year to 3,500. By 1905 there were 56,000 registered trout-anglers in Britain, who increasingly banded into syndicates to capture the best fishing rights in what was coming to be a fiercely competitive market.[45]

It was not so much that huntin', shootin', and fishin' had declined as that they had ceased to be the preserve of the landed. The gentry had detached themselves from popular traditions through agrarian change and cultural refinement only to find that they now faced infiltration from the cities by those who wanted the pleasures of the country life without the pain of a sore backside from a day in the saddle. Killing birds with guns at a safe distance or tempting a trout with a brightly coloured fly was more appealing than careering over fences in pursuit of baying hounds intent on tearing a fox to bits. Even fox-hunting was hardly brutal measured by earlier standards of sport. The killing of the fox was not the first consideration of the hunt, which was primarily an excuse to assemble for an exciting ride and for the real enthusiast to have a chance to watch the hounds at work. Although field sports remained popular amongst the shifting social élite, they lost the virtual monopoly they had formerly enjoyed. Young men learned the new team-games of rugby and football at public school. They played cricket and went rowing far more seriously than before; field sports came to be more closely associated with the middle-aged than was formerly the case, and even in this age-group the growth of golf could offer a walk round a manicured country estate without requiring the destruction of anything but one's self-esteem. To the upper classes the term 'sport' was no longer synonymous with the killing of animals.

---

[45] Lowerson, 'English Middle Class Sport', pp. 9–10.

4. SURVIVAL AND ADAPTATION

The degree to which a wide range of old-established sports continued to be practised into the late nineteenth century and beyond has tended to be overlooked. This is hardly surprising in the light of the enormous impact of organized team-games in the last quarter of the century. Until recently sports history has tended to be written by middle-class amateurs, who did not consider traditional pursuits to be 'sport' in their own amateur sense. The impression of decay was reinforced by the 'pessimistic' school of social history, which saw the Industrial Revolution as a cultural catastrophe, destroying old ways of playing through the imposition of grim industrial rhythms, urban dislocation, and middle-class interference. Hence the idea that there was a 'leisure vacuum', a hiatus between 'the good old days' and the emergence of new standardized and commercial forms of sport, has taken hold. However, cultural change is far more complex than this. Deeply held attitudes and habits do not die out overnight. During the second half of the nineteenth century and even into this century a wide range of old-established sports continued to be popular. To get a better understanding of the tension between change and continuity in sport we have to look at the limitations of the reform movement, even amongst employers, and at the relatively slow decline of the fighting and gambling traditions of roughs and young rakes who made up the 'Fancy'. And this confines continuity to urban Britain. Not surprisingly in certain well-defined rural areas the vigour of old sports was almost undiminished.

Although cock-fighting and bull-baiting had been prohibited and officials of the RSPCA endeavoured to enforce the ban, there is no doubt that cruel animal sports persisted. Alan Metcalfe has shown how cock-fighting was carried on in the mining communities of south Northumberland into the 1870s. Four men were prosecuted in Liverpool for cock-fighting in 1871 and in 1875 police broke up a cock-fight at the Aintree racecourse. The *Day's Doings* of 1871 reported a visit to a three-row cockpit with sixty or so spectators in a northern industrial town at which there were merchants and labourers present. The magazine was especially shocked by the presence of a small girl sitting happily on her father's knee. A few members of the nobility continued to take an interest in the sport. The Marquis of Hastings was prosecuted for organizing a cock-fight at his ancestral home of Donnington Hall in 1863. As late as 1895 *Cocking and Its Votaries* was privately published in handsome binding and with coloured plates making 'it quite plain that not a few wealthy Englishmen still follow up this sport—stealthily but with much zeal'. In the Lake District the holding of cock-fights in farms was an open secret up until the Second World War. It was still going on in the 1950s when a social anthropologist noted that cock-fighting was 'handed down within the family, deriving a high value from its mode of transmission'. 'Its appeal', he added, 'is undoubtedly strengthened by the fact that it is done surreptitiously in defiance of laws to which the community has never given its assent.' 'Game-cock fights,' recalled Bill Lightfoot of Wigton between the wars, 'we used to go to a lot of them. We used to have them at Islekirk, at Redhall.' On one occasion, while calling in at a pub, 'a bit of a row struck up over these cocks . . . so they went in that stable there and clipped two out, and there was an old body called Mrs Watson in the Sun there, and they just pushed all the chairs and they had a fight in the kitchen. Forty-four or forty-five years ago. I liked a cock-fight.' This was in the 1970s, but he added 'there's a fair bit of it goes on still. I'll tell you who has a full set of spurs'.[46]

Obviously it is very difficult to assess the extent to which such activities survived in the cities. A careful study of Leicester suggests that from the 1870s the power of the licensing authorities made it too dangerous for publicans to permit their premises to be used for cock-fights. However, dog-fights certainly continued, especially in their traditional stronghold in the Black Country. In the 1850s 'dogs were still bred for fighting; but to avoid the police, contests were held secretly at night'. Dog-fighting was specifically banned under an act of 1911 but an authoritative source on the sporting traditions of the area interviewed by the BBC in 1985 claimed that matching Staffordshire bull-terriers was widely and more or less openly done until the 1930s. Men would bring their dogs to certain well-known pubs and agree to match

---

[46] Metcalfe, 'Organised Sport', p. 475; Rees, 'Development of Physical Recreation in Liverpool', MA. thesis (Liverpool Univ., 1968) p. 175; for *Cocking and its Votaries* see Strutt, *Sports and Pastimes*, p. 226; W. M. Williams, *Gosforth: The Sociology of an English Village* (1956), p. 134; M. Bragg, *Speak for England* (1976), p. 394.

them, and at least one prominent nobleman was involved. That this tradition lingers on was made abundantly clear in the successful prosecution of seven men for organizing and filming such a fight in July 1985. It took several years of undercover work to penetrate this secretive and violent subculture. There was a strong suspicion on the part of the investigators that they had only revealed the tip of an iceberg. Dog-fights, alleged the RSPCA, were held in the emptied swimming-pool of a large house in the stockbroker belt, where tell-tale blood and hair could be quickly hosed away. Badgers too are still baited occasionally. Bill Lightfoot, the Cumbrian cock-fighter, also admitted a fondness for badger-baiting between the wars. 'On Sundays Mott and me went for badgers . . . [around] an old pipe there at Aikbank, once got four badgers out of it. Fletcher Gale was with us that day. Terriers would bait them then we would club them.' Although there is no doubt that such formerly widespread activities are now the province of a very small minority, it is highly probable that the enthusiasm for such contests has always outstripped the ability of the police and the animal protection lobby to prevent them from taking place more often than might be imagined. A covert tradition of cruel sports survived in the countryside, the full extent of which is still unknown.[47]

What can we say of the efforts of employers to transform the work discipline of the labour force through the reformation of their play? To what extent was the campaign against established patterns of sport widespread and successful? We have seen how a substantial number of industrialists backed up by evangelicals, middle-class humanitarians, and artisan radicals attacked the prevailing pattern of sports in the second quarter of the nineteenth century, but we should be cautious about crediting them with a full transformation of popular behaviour. There is an important difference between what certain groups of employers *wished* to happen on the one hand, and the actual process of cultural change on the other. Certainly in those areas where there was a high concentration of large-scale factory manufacturing, new rhythms of work and municipal regulations

[47] J. Crump, 'Amusements of the People', Ph.D. thesis (Warwick Univ., 1985), p. 325; *Guardian*, 1 Aug. 1985, p. 17; Gash, *Aristocracy and People*, p. 345; Bragg, *Speak for England*, p. 394.

brought about major changes in the way in which holidays were spent and games were played. But this came about gradually and was rarely the product of specific interventions on the part of employers. A recent study of the life of the factory-workers in mid-Victorian Lancashire shows clearly that old sports were in part preserved within the new system of production. In fact, some important employers like James Briggs, known to his men as 'Eawr Billy', was a great supporter of hare-coursing as were other industrialists like Rank, Pilkington, and Dennis—all members of the National Coursing Club founded in 1858 by a mixture of landowners and business men who clearly had no compunction about the adoption and promotion of country sports. Coursing has remained popular. Around 10,000 spectators still attend the Waterloo Cup at Altcar and there are an estimated 3,000 owners of coursing greyhounds. Despite vociferous protests by the League Against Cruel Sports, around 3,000 hares are coursed each year of which about 300 are caught and killed by the dogs. Sir Harry Hornby was another Victorian 'industrial squire' who cultivated a fondness for old sports alongside a devotion to Church and king. He was even known as 'th'owd 'Gam Cock' because of the cock-fighting tradition in his family, which interestingly also produced some fine Lancashire cricketers. 'Old' and 'new' sports were sometimes less far apart than we imagine. Ratting, wrestling, and 'purring' (a ferocious shin-kicking contest fought between pairs of men in heavy clogs) were all widely practised in what was one of the most economically advanced areas in the British Isles. The rush-bearing festival, which traditionally formed the main Lancashire holiday in the third week of August, involved the young gathering rushes for the floor of their parish church and transporting these on carts pulled by the local youth, who would collect money from passers-by and fight with their rival rush-bearers. Despite the fact that the carts tended to become more elaborate and organized, the young continued to fight until the 1880s at least. It was mainly cheap alternative amusements, especially rail excursions to the seaside, that weakened the rush-bearing rites rather than clumsy efforts at social control by godly or greedy factory-owners.[48]

---

[48] For the labour discipline thesis see E. P. Thompson, 'Time, Work Discipline and Industrial Capitalism', *Past and Present*, Dec. 1967; for 'industrial squires' in Lancashire see, P. Joyce, *Work, Society and Politics* (1980); J. K. Walton and R. Poole, 'The Lancashire Wakes in the Nineteenth Century', in Storch, *Popular Culture and Custom*, esp. p. 113.

In the Black Country artisan forms of manufacturing and smallish workshops were only slowly displaced by much larger units. Here the ancient habit of working hard towards the end of the week and observing 'Saint Monday' was strongly established and continued in force until the late nineteenth century. The attack on the traditional blood sports of the area that was mounted in the first half of the century came not in the main from employers but from outsiders with specific moral objections to cruelty. By the time the labour process was concentrated and the intensity of work increased, there were already statutory limits to permissible hours of work. Factory discipline came only a little earlier in the city of Birmingham itself. But now there was a new incentive to co-operation. With the introduction of steam-powered machines in engineering in the 1850s and 1860s large employers increasingly offered workers a half-day on Saturday in return for regular work at the beginning of the week; this arrangement had a fairly swift and significant effect on the work practices of big firms, but the large numbers employed in small workshops continued to take Monday off and to vary their hours of work, for example, arriving very early in the summer mornings and leaving early for an afternoon's amusement. Of course, there is no denying that labour discipline and Saturday half-day slowly suffocated Saint Monday, but for most of the nineteenth century rumours of its demise were greatly exaggerated. In fact, absenteeism continued to be a problem into the twentieth century, albeit of a more arbitrary and less serious kind. The traditions of Saint Monday lingered on into mid-week Edwardian football. In Bolton in 1908 'local workshops stopped for the afternoon, and in many cases work-people took "French leave" ' to watch an important game, while in Burnley 20,000 looms were stopped by a Burnley–Tottenham match in 1909. In Sheffield in 1893 'when managers refused permission [to go to a big game], the men "went all the same, and now the masters simply accept the inevitable and close the works" '.[49]

---

[49] For a careful survey of the Black Country see E. Hopkins, 'Working Hours and Conditions during the Industrial Revolution', *Economic History Review*, Feb. 1982; for Birmingham, see D. A. Reid, 'The Decline of Saint Monday, 1766–1876', *Past and Present*, May 1976; S. Tischler, *Footballers and Businessmen* (1981), pp. 126–7 for absenteeism to watch football.

Sport played a central part in the survival of Saint Monday. Writing in 1867, Thomas Wright, 'a journeyman engineer', noted that when work was plentiful even those with a Saturday half-day would take Monday too. Horse-races were mulled over and intricate bets worked out. Foot-racing organized on a casual local basis was particularly popular. Running-grounds were found in most of the suburbs of the large towns, often owned by a publican. Workmen would back the swiftest of their mates in all sorts of races that frequently ended in a full-scale brawl. These fights were almost part of the entertainment and a powerful reminder of the bonds between nineteenth-century sports and the pre-industrial world. 'When fights commence under these circumstances [arguments over the result of a race], the friends of the combatants immediately interfere . . . by forming a ring and encouraging the man of their choice to "wire in".' In the Black Country ratting-matches and dog-fights still sometimes led to what were known colloquially as 'up-and-down' fights where the men fought standing up and on the ground 'like beasts rather than like men, kicking and biting each other, when on the ground, with the utmost ferocity'. Prize-fighting predictably had an avid Saint Monday following despite its illegality. It had a language all of its own 'according to which the nose is the beak or conk, the eyes the ogles or peepers, the teeth ivories and the mouth the kisser or tater-trap'. Shrewd old workmen, 'knowing cards', would watch a new fighter like a new horse and make a few bob out of their superior grasp of the sport. The line between street fights, of which there continued to be any number on a Friday or Saturday night, and prize-fights was hazy. Consider the case of Samuel Fowkes, a twenty-seven-year-old dyer, who mortally injured Arthur Taylor, a plasterer of thirty-four in Leicester in 1887. The two were sworn enemies and arranged to fight it out after the pub was shut on a summer evening. A crowd followed them and formed a makeshift ring. Rounds and a 'no-kicking' rule were agreed just as in small-time 'professional' bouts. The judge determined that Taylor's death arose from 'a fair, stand-up fight' and gave Fowkes only two weeks' imprisonment. Fights like this apparently went on all the time in the 1870s off Shoreditch High Street, where Arthur Morrison's young Dick Perrot, in *A Child of the Jago*, saw his father win a fiver for a stand-up fight in his own close surrounded by the local criminal fraternity—'the swell mob'. These fighting traditions lived on, especially amongst Irish immigrants such as the notorious Hooligan family whose inveterate brawling added a new word to the language in the 1890s.[50]

The persistence of popular traditions is most evident in the enclosed world of the mining communities. In the pit villages of South Northumberland there were bowling matches, quoits, rabbit-coursing, dog-racing, pigeon-flying. Here cock-fighting was carried on after the legal ban, and there were seven prosecutions in 1850 alone. However, mine-owners and the Northumbrian gentry generally left the miners alone to get on with their sports, their drinking, and the gaming that went with it. The pub was the focus of this mining culture and publicans were their makeshift sponsors. The English alehouse survived the Industrial Revolution and continued to adapt to the recreational needs of its regulars. Pubs often ran bowling matches which involved covering an agreed distance in the fewest throws of a heavy iron ball. These were very popular. Each pit had its own champion and there were informally acknowledged champions for the whole coalfield. Whatever the sport, miners tended to play only with miners and even then rarely with miners from other coalfields. Despite the spread of the railways and the speed of communication miners remained happily locked into a fiercely masculine and introverted sociability based on pit pubs like the Astley Arms at Seton Delaval, which in 1879 had a bowling-track, a quoit-alley, and seating for 700. Even in Newcastle itself there was clear evidence of the continuity of country sports into the 1880s in the suburbs of Byker and Elswick among the shipyard and heavy industrial workers. The inner city pubs no longer ran workers' sports, but no fewer than twenty-five pubs outside the old city walls organized bowling, coursing, quoits, and other similar activities at the end of the New Year holiday in 1885. Much of this carried on into the Edwardian and inter-war years alongside the new world of professional football, which drew the miners into Newcastle and Sunderland on Saturday afternoons. Alan Metcalfe, who has opened up this submerged tradition for us, maintains that the exploits and anecdotes of the

---

[50] T. Wright, *Some Habits and Customs of the Working Classes* (1867), pp. 123–5; Crump, *Amusements of the People*, p. 328.

great bowlers were still remembered and personally recounted to him in the working-men's clubs of the pit villages in the 1970s.[51]

So it seems clear that any general attempt to root out traditional sports as a whole was a failure. The only instance of a successful policy of outright suppression was the banning of popular animal sports, and even these may have survived to a rather greater extent than we realize. Employer hostility was patchy, and in Lancashire there was a powerful current of traditionalism built up around factory communities where bosses and workers shared stubborn and clannish loyalties. This brings us to the world of the 'Fancy', of sporting aristocrats who slummed with fighters and publicans. To what extent did the gambling and pugilistic traditions of the sporting gentleman and his rough cronies remain an important component of sport? The connection between gambling on horses and on fist-fights was well established. But as racing became a major preoccupation of the late nineteenth-century aristocracy, the link with fighting declined sharply. The police arrested two prize-fighters at Aintree in 1875 and the fights that were customary at the Derby were stamped out by the Jockey Club and the police. The old hurly-burly of the open meeting with its side-shows and prize-fights was tamed, although it remained a pretty boozy and rumbustious day out. Regulated short contests with gloves in fairground 'boxing-booths' were introduced. Public displays of violence declined. Scenes such as that described by James Greenwood in 1868, where a bookie who welshed on his bets was set upon by an angry mob until 'ghastly, white and streaming with blood, [he] was hauled out and dragged away insensible', became much rarer. The old antics and excesses of the 'Fancy' were submerged in what became an organized social season moving from Newmarket and the Two Thousand Guineas in May to Epsom in June and Ascot in July finishing in the private park of the Duke of Richmond at 'Glorious' Goodwood near Chichester.[52]

The last great figure of the nineteenth-century 'Fancy', a real black sheep and uninhibited throw-back to the world of the Regency buck, was George Alexander Baird. He insisted on being

---

[51] P. Clark, *The English Alehouse* (1983); Metcalfe, 'Organised Sport'; also A. Metcalfe, 'Sport in Nineteenth Century England. An Interpretation', presented at the Second World Symposium on the History of Sport and Physical Education, note 10, and personal communication.

[52] K. Chesney, *The Victorian Underworld*, p. 340.

called 'the Squire', although his enormous fortune—he inherited nearly three million pounds—was the product of Scottish industry and bourgeois piety. He longed to achieve the notoriety of his hero, the famous hunting and racing Squire Osbaldeston, who had once won a thousand guineas by riding 200 miles in less than ten hours and died in celebrated poverty in 1865 having won and lost several fortunes. Baird was certainly the finest amateur jockey in Britain in the later nineteenth century and spent an enormous amount on acquiring the best horses to ride. 'The Squire' may technically have been an amateur but he was no 'gentleman' in late Victorian terms. He bought a country house near Newmarket and surrounded himself with tipsters and toughs. Emulating what he took to be the traditions of the squirearchy, he put on cock-fights in his country house and matched his ferocious bull-terrier 'Donald' against any dog in the neighbourhood, capping the proceedings with huge boozy dinners where half of the food would end up sticking to the walls. He once let a bag of rats loose in Lillie Langtry's theatre after her greed had got the better of her judgement and she had become his mistress. Baird is chiefly interesting because he was such an oddity by the end of the nineteenth century. Formerly there had been no shortage of young gentlemen who liked fighting and drinking. Squire Osbaldeston as an undergraduate in early nineteenth-century Oxford had cheerfully poured gravy over the heads of two poor scholars—'the act of a drayman or coal-heaver in a low coffee shop' as the Principal of Brasenose called it. But by the end of the century public-school mores were exercising some kind of restraint on the upper classes, who increasingly confined themselves to the occasional boozy boat-club dinner.[53]

Bare-knuckle boxing finally declined in the 1890s. In August 1889 the *Southwark Recorder* described a fight for £200 between George Camp of Bermondsey and 'Click' Soles of Nottingham. They fought to a standstill and after fifty rounds, with Soles 'considerably disfigured from his opponent's left-handed deliveries', his backers conceded. Surveying the decade following the fight, a sporting journalist concluded that 'prize-fights had been like angels' visits, few and far between'. Boxing definitively supplanted prize-fighting with the first gloved heavyweight

---

[53] R. Onslow, *The Squire* (1980); also Carr, *English Fox Hunting*, p. 93.

championship between Sullivan and Corbett in America in 1892. Sullivan, who had dominated the prize-ring of the 1880s, much preferred boxing to the bare-knuckle contests with 'such mean tricks as spiking, biting, gouging, strangling, butting with the head, falling down without being struck, scratching with the nails, kicking, and falling on an antagonist with the knees'. What became of the 'Fancy' in the new era? The National Sporting Club, founded in 1891 to put on professional contests under rules that had been drafted in 1867 in the name of the Marquess of Queensberry, was a kind of reformed and institutionalized successor to the 'Fancy'. It was a private club under the presidency of the Earl of Lonsdale composed of wealthy city merchants, some theatrical people, well-to-do bookmakers, and sporting aristocrats, who invited selected professional boxers to fight in front of them as an after-dinner entertainment.[54]

The National Sporting Club slowly tightened its grip on professional boxing. In 1909 the Lonsdale Belt was introduced to give official recognition to their men as national champions. Club members always wore dinner-jackets and were expected to remain silent during fights. This was in sharp contrast to the antics of men like 'the Squire', who had caused a scandal at a fight in 1891 between his own man and Frank Paddy Slavin (the Sydney Cornstalk) when he lurched into the ring shouting 'Do in the Australian bastard!' and was driven off by Lord Mandeville at knife-point. The criminal and the rakish aristocratic worlds were pulling apart. Lord Lonsdale expelled Baird from the Pelican Club after this incident, which became notorious as the 'Affair at Bruges' (the fight had taken place in the back garden of a retired army officer living in Belgium). The Pelican Club was in fact a forerunner of the National Sporting Club. It had been formed in 1887 by William Goldberg, who gave racing tips under the name 'The Shifter', and Ernest Wells known as 'Swears' through his association with the firm of Swears and Wells. Members included the aforementioned Lord Mandeville (later Duke of Manchester), the Duke of Hamilton, Lord Rossmore, and Lord Beresford. Henceforth such men tended to avoid the rougher end of the market and some patronized the Amateur Boxing Association that

---

[54] Shipley, 'Tom Causer of Bermondsey', pp. 38, 45–7; *Oxford Companion*, p. 98.

had been set up in 1880 to encourage schoolboy contests with the maxim 'box, don't fight'.[55]

The shady or overtly criminal elements tended increasingly to patronize what came to be known as the 'small halls'. Evening contests would be put on for small purses amongst the several thousand professional fighters, who worked this circuit. As a former patron recalled of the fights held until recently in Shoreditch Town Hall:

there was always 'nobbins' [coins thrown into the ring after a good fight]. You would always see a great fight. The word got round. This was the place to go if you wanna see a real scrap. It was like a *cockpit* [my italics] . . . You'd get people come out of the West End. Showbusiness people, they've always been closely involved with boxing . . . The villains? They were definitely at the ringside, no doubt about that, and everyone seemed to know it . . . In the 1960s the Krays come down with their entourage. It was about twenty or thirty of 'em. The heavy mob . . . Gambling, it used to go on all the time. Between people, and you used to get bookies round the ringside taking bets off East End business men. I'll have 4–1 on that one.

Shorn of some of its swells and subject to regulation by the British Boxing Board of Control, formed in 1929, elements of the 'Fancy' survived, especially in London, long after the term had ceased to be used.[56]

The tension between the forces of continuity and the 'otherness' of what we call 'modern' sport is the central theme of this book. So links between old and new ways of playing will occur and recur. Cricket and horse-racing, for instance, derived part of their appeal from the sense of the pastoral they evoked. Similarly hunting and shooting were steeped in affection or nostalgia for the countryside, the glory of 'getting away from it all', getting out of town and into the carefully preserved woods and well-tended fields that comprised the 'natural' world. Working men, who bred pigeons or greyhounds, were obscurely celebrating another aspect of traditional country sports. Such themes are woven into the wider argument of what is to come. For the moment we will confine ourselves to two examples of

[55] Onslow, *The Squire*, ch. 15.
[56] D. Robbins, 'Sport and Youth Culture', in J. Hargreaves (ed.), *Sport, Culture and Ideology* (1982), pp. 143–4.

explicit survival. These were not ancient sports that were enjoyed as self-conscious folkloric displays like the 'traditional' football match at Jedburgh or Ashbourne, but sports that were part of a customary life that was still vital and popular. For a few old games survived even in economically advanced areas, though obviously they were more important and tenacious in remoter places like the Highlands of Scotland and the west of Ireland.

Knur-and-spell is perhaps one of the most remarkable examples of survival. The name comes from *knorr*, a Teutonic term meaning a knot of wood; 'spell' probably derives from the Old Norse *spill*, meaning a game; and Norsemen apparently played a game called *nurspel*. Strutt attests to its popularity in the north of England. The game involved a player hitting the 'knur', a small ball rather like a large marble, with a special bat. In Lancashire the ball was suspended from a gallows-like contraption, while in Yorkshire it was flipped into the air from a spring-loaded trap. In each case the object was the same: to hit the object as far as possible. Contests of twenty-five or so 'wallops' or 'rises' were held between two players or 'laikers', who would often wager on the outcome. The sport always attracted spectators. In 1826 on Woodhouse Moor in Yorkshire a match for 40 guineas was held over forty rises and large crowds continued to flock to the moors around Sheffield, Barnsley, Colne, and Rotherham. There were all kinds of little tricks to help drive the spell distances of 200 yards or more but the essence of the thing was simple enough—'tha clouts it as far down t'meader as tha can, 'cause foithest wins, tha' sees. And if it come to a moutch [dispute], then tha' measures from t' pin wi' a squeer chain.' New and old sports sometimes happily coexisted—a point that can all too easily be overlooked by those who wish to set up a rigid and precise distinction between traditional and modern forms. Jerry Dawson, who was born in 1888 near Burnley, combined playing football as goalkeeper for Burnley from 1906 to 1929, winning a cup-winner's medal and an England cap, with being a champion at knur-and-spell. At this time the game had a significant regional following which continued into the 1930s. Champions like Billy Baxter, who became 'world champion' at Colne in 1937, was a kind of folk-hero in many a northern household along with others like the Machin brothers, Willie Lamb, Joe Edon, Tom Ellis, and Arthur Cooper. As late as 1970 a crowd of 3,000 gathered on

Easter Tuesday on the moors at the Spring Rock Inn near Elland in Yorkshire to see the annual championship. The sport had survived and even acquired a little modest sponsorship.[57]

In the Highlands and in the west of Ireland the Celtic sport of hurling, a stick-and-ball team-game that is the ancestor of modern field hockey, remained very popular. In Scotland the Gaelic name for it was 'camanachd' but the game was commonly known as 'shinty'. It had been played for centuries as an integral part of the dancing, piping, and whisky-drinking festivities of the clans. An early nineteenth-century source noted that 'the field has much the appearance of a battle scene; there are banners flying, bagpipes playing, and a keen *mêlée* around the ball'. When the Campbells played the Macleans on Calgary Sands near Oban in 1821 an account in the *Highland Home Journal* noted that the losing Campbells 'would have liked to have used their camans [sticks] on the Macleans instead of on the ball; but to resort to a fight with the Macs at this stage would have proved a worse match than the first, so they left the field completely vanquished and crestfallen'. Although rules were written down and an official association was formed in 1893, much of the older communal spirit lived on. Early this century in and around Oban 'people would gather in backshops and street corners to discuss the shinty match to be played on Saturday . . . When the team bus set off to travel to, say, Inverary [a journey of about thirty-six miles] it would leave the town deserted of people and would pass them by on the road, riding horses, carts, bicycles—anything they could lay their hands on which would enable them to reach Inverary in time for the match.' From the early nineteenth century the summer running and throwing events became more elaborately organized into 'Highland Games'. A semi-professional circuit of athletes emerged in what was an interesting adaptation of clan sports around a new sense of 'Scottishness', partly promoted by the presence of Victoria and Albert at the Braemar Gathering. The relationship between traditional sports and nationalism is an important subject in its own right which goes beyond mere continuity and into the realm of 'invented tradition'—a theme which is examined more fully in Chapter 4.[58]

[57] *Oxford Companion*, pp. 510–13.
[58] D. Whitson, 'Factors in the Survival of Local Games against the Inroads of Metropolitan Culture' in *Proc. 5th Canadian Symposium on the History of Sport, Toronto, Sept. 1982*, pp. 412–23.

In Ireland hurling has been particularly successful precisely because it has been able to play the 'national' card; for the moment, however, we need only note the continued vitality of ancient games in Ireland into the late nineteenth century. Thomas O'Crohan's account of his life as a fisherman on Blasket Island off the Dingle Peninsula, which first appeared in 1929 in Irish, offers a rare glimpse into a world still governed by ancient oral tradition in the late nineteenth century. 'Hurley' was played on the island's beach, the 'White Strand', at Christmas and New Year without shoes or socks. Players often had to wade up to their necks in water for the ball. Thomas's two uncles, Dairmid and Tom, were elected captains one year and a ferocious battle began. 'We didn't do much after the great match on Christmas Day,' recalled the author, 'but everyone was pretty well lamed.' At New Year another game was played involving the two brothers. 'I happened to be on the outer edge of the game', recalled the fisherman, 'and I swiped the ball as hard as I could, and who should be in the way but my Uncle Tom, and where should the ball hit him but on the knee-cap? It put his knee-cap out of joint. "Good for your arm," says Dairmid, the first voice I heard.' Dairmid delighted in revenge on a brother who after an earlier game had given him 'a blow in the ear-hole that sent him down on to the strand a cold corpse or nearly'. Regulated and managed under the auspices of the Gaelic Athletic Association hurling along with 'an caid' or Gaelic football prospered mightily, providing the single most dramatic example of the powers of survival and adaptation of ancient sports.[59]

The paradox, of course, was that in order to survive these ancient games had to take on the organizational forms of modern sports. Hence the line between what is 'traditional' and what is 'modern' is more difficult to determine than many imagine. Take the sport of curling, for example. The sliding of stones over ice had been played on the Scottish lochs since at least the sixteenth century. Walter Scott and James Hogg both claimed it as part of the Scottish cultural heritage. Burns even wrote an elegy to a famous curler, Tam Samson, who 'was the king o' a' the core, to guard or draw, or wick a bore, or up the rink like Jehu roar in time o' need'. In the nineteenth century curling went from

[59] Thomas O'Crohan, *The Islandman* (1978), pp. 133–5.

strength to strength, spreading to Canada with the waves of Scots emigrants whilst retaining a powerful hold on Scotland itself. Recent research in the Stirling area has revealed a thriving world of organized competition, sophisticated rules, and cups donated by enthusiastic local lairds. Gentlemen of the cloth were prominent in the early clubs, the first of which was the Duddingston Curling Society which forgathered at Duddingston Loch beneath Arthur's Seat in Edinburgh. In 1838 the bureaucratic process was consolidated with the formation of the Royal Caledonian Curling Club which quickly established the kind of control over the game that the Royal and Ancient at St Andrews established over golf.[60]

Like curling, golf was largely confined to Scotland until the second half of the nineteenth century and it evolved in similar fashion from an ancient and casual game to a more highly organized and competitive sport. The key factor here seems to have been the adoption of both games by new and powerful middle-class elements. This is particularly evident in golf. The game in its modern form developed at Edinburgh and St Andrews at the historical moment when clan power had been decisively broken and a distinctive administrative, academic, and mercantile élite took the reins of power in Scotland. So golf as the 'good walk spoiled', gentle exercise for the harassed business or professional man, goes back further than expected. This association is well illustrated in the records of the Glasgow Golf Club, which was formed in 1787 and by 1789 had twenty-five members, all of whom were merchants with the exception of two surgeons and four army officers. These were mostly the 'tobacco lords', the Virginia and West Indies traders who dominated the government of the growing city. Of forty members joining the club between 1810 and 1831 whose occupations have been traced, twenty-six were merchants and most of the rest engaged in associated employment such as insurance broking and warehousing. The west of Scotland business connection has been overlooked in the history of a game that tends to be commonly associated with St Andrews to the detriment of Prestwick, Troon,

---

[60] *Oxford Companion*, pp. 199–201; personal communication from Dr N. L. Tranter of Stirling University, who is doing research into sport in central Scotland *c*.1780–1850.

and Turnberry. The wider point to consider here is the way in which an old activity had adapted *before* the Victorian period. What at first sight might appear to be little more than a casual ancient game—James I is said to have played 'golf' on Blackheath—was taken up by the new wealth of trade in clear distinction to the clan sports of the Highland Games. Scotsmen like to reflect upon the robust popular heritage of golf, disparaging the effete and élitist tendencies of their English counterparts. But such enclaves of City money as Wentworth or Sunningdale have more than a little in common with the early merchants' clubs of central Scotland in terms of social composition. After all, continuity can take many forms.[61]

Let us conclude by taking a look at the games people played in a mid-Victorian county town before the arrival of Association football. Lancaster was at the heart of an agricultural community with a relatively large professional and commercial élite. Careful recent work has revealed an archery club composed of gentry, clergymen, surgeons, and merchants, and a rowing club which was similarly exclusive requiring the wearing of special dress and the holding of dinners. These clubs were for the small town élite and maintained their social pre-eminence by a black-ball system. In 1841 a cricket club was formed by eight middle-class men, some of whom were already in the archery and rowing fraternity. Sixty-eight of the seventy-one members of the cricket club have been identified, all drawn from non-manual occupations as one might expect of members of a club who often played on a Tuesday, had their own insignia and wore straw hats. Skilled workers formed the majority of a new club set up in 1859. This group, along with shopkeepers, seems to have been active in the world of bowls, which tended to be organized at greens owned by innkeepers in accordance with the long-standing association of sport and drink. Significantly these private clubs, mostly for the better-off and the very skilled, were of recent origin and minority interest. Up to the 1870s popular sports were still being organized around a seasonal calendar of wrestling, racing, rowing matches, quoits, and athletics as well as such festive staples as

---

[61] P. Bilsborough, 'The Development of Sport in Glasgow', M.Litt. thesis. (Stirling Univ., 1983), pp. 14–20.

the 'gurning' or grimacing contests. Closeness to the Lake District where there was a long history of wrestling made this event especially popular and local champions included a joiner, a tin-worker, and a wheelwright. Lancaster nicely encapsulates the delicate balance between old and new ways of playing, between private clubs and popular traditions in the middle years of the nineteenth century.[62]

[62] M. Speake, 'The Social Anatomy of Participation in Sport in Lancaster in Early Victorian England', in *Proc. XI HISPA International Congress*, ed. J. A. Mangan (1987), pp. 91–100.

2
Amateurism and the Victorians

VISITORS to Victorian Britain were often surprised by the amount of time devoted to sport amongst the middle and upper classes. Despite their reputation as sober and pious capitalists, even the business élite often seemed to be more interested in play than in work. The innovative and organizing genius of the Victorians for games turned out to be more durable than the philosophy of self-help or the evangelical revival, and Oxford athletes may have had more influence than the Oxford Movement. The vigour and scope of Victorian sport was quite remarkable, ranging from the subtle infiltration of the Field and the reorganizing of established activities like racing, boxing, and cricket to the wholesale transformation of the ancient forms of football and tennis. The new codified kinds of play, devised for the most part in the third quarter of the century, have become so commonplace that we tend to take them for granted as somehow logical and necessary results of industrialization. But this is to miss the point. The new games were certainly well suited to the life of the large industrial city, requiring only limited amounts of time and space, and utilizing improved communications to create national organizations that came into being to regulate the sporting life of the nation. Yet these changes in social conditions cannot explain the style and spirit in which the new sports were played nor the cultural centrality they came to have. For this we must look to the growth of the public schools and the distinctive range of ideas brought to bear on secondary and higher education in the mid-nineteenth century. Understanding the rise of the 'gentleman-amateur' is the key to understanding the cult of athleticism.

1. PUBLIC SCHOOLS

Perhaps the most remarkable feature of élite education in the nineteenth century was the changing status of games. The sons of the landed and the wealthy had always played games at school, but until the middle years of the century their masters had taken little or no interest in such activities save for the occasional intervention to prevent a particularly brutal affray or to stop boys rampaging around the land which bordered the school. At some of the most famous schools the authorities actually attempted to forbid organized games. In a famous outburst, Samuel Butler, the head of Shrewsbury from 1798 to 1836, condemned football as 'more fit for farm boys and labourers than for young gentlemen', although he later gave up the struggle and provided a football pitch so as to keep the game within the school boundary. The head of Westminster was determined to put a stop to the rowing matches that had been organized by the boys from the late eighteenth century. After successfully preventing the annual race with Eton in 1834, he tried to stop another race between local boys and the scholars. Such measures were deeply unpopular. Despite the efforts of what one of his charges called this 'cowardly, snivelling, ungentlemanlike, treble damnable shit of a Headmaster', the boys rowed their race between Vauxhall Bridge and Putney. The Master of Balliol similarly tried to spike the guns of one of the members of the first Oxford Boat Race crew in 1829 by requiring Johnathon James Toogood to go to a logic lecture on the day of the race. But the oarsman lived up to his name and contrived both to attend to his academic duties and to row in a race at Henley that was the subject of much speculation in *Bell's Life* and wagering amongst the 20,000 spectators lining the banks. Even the great Thomas Arnold of Rugby, who was mistakenly idolized by subsequent advocates of public school sports, had no time for games himself. The public schools may have been decadent, but he intended to reform them in the classroom and the chapel, not on the games field.[1]

The contrast with late Victorian and Edwardian educators is quite striking. Jesus College, Cambridge, head of the river for eleven consecutive years from 1875, was said to be 'nothing but a boat club'. This was not quite fair as the college excelled at other sports too; it was only in academic matters that it lacked

[1] T. J. L. Chandler, 'The Emergence of Athleticism', in *Proc. XI HISPA International Congress*, ed. J. A. Mangan (1987), pp. 27–32; C. Dodd, *The Oxford and Cambridge Boat Race* (1983), ch. 1.

distinction. Of twenty-nine freshmen entering the college in 1895, seventeen went on to represent the university in rugby, soccer, cricket, or rowing. The official support for games at Oxford and Cambridge permitted 'rowing men' to spend 790 of the 800 or so days of their nine terms 'on the river', or so at least claimed an indulgently ironic Leslie Stephen, who combined academic achievement with a lifelong devotion to Cambridge rowing. In this, of course, the ancient universities were merely reflecting the public school devotion to games, which was perhaps their most outstanding characteristic in the second half of the century. Whereas boys who loved sports might have been pronounced 'idle' by earlier generations, Victorian schoolmasters were inclined to reserve that word for those who did not care for games. 'Any lower boy in this house who does not play football once a day and twice on half holiday will be fined half a crown and kicked', read a notice at Eton, whose headmaster from 1884 until 1905 was Edmond Warre, a former Fellow of All Souls whose enthusiasm for the classics was only surpassed by his dedication to the Eight. Nothing pleased him more than the sight of his crew all pulling strongly and smoothly together on the Thames. The long domination of the dark over the light blues in the Boat Races of the 1890s was put down to the fact that more Etonians went to Oxford than to Cambridge. Prospective intellectuals might go to King's, but rowing men preferred Christ Church and the Thames. Seven of the Oxford crew who set up a record time for the Boat Race in practice in 1897 were Etonians and so was the cox. The prestige of Eton and Harrow as the leading schools in the land was almost as much a matter of sporting prowess as of ancient lineage. Harrow had been on the point of collapse in the 1840s until a new regime of manly exercise was introduced under the headmastership of Charles Vaughan. By 1864 the public schools investigated by the Clarendon Commission were commended for 'their love of healthy sports and exercise' which despite the excesses of the fagging system and the brutality of punishments had helped to teach Englishmen 'to govern others and to control themselves'.[2]

---

[2] J. A. Mangan, ' "Oars and the Man" ', *BJSH*, Dec. 1984, pp. 249–53; J. Chandos, *Boys Together* (1984), pp. 336, 328.

This official worship of the 'all devouring gods' of sport would certainly have come as a surprise to the young Lord John Russell, who in 1803 went up to Westminster where he found 'the boys play at hoops, pegtops and pea-shooters'. Earlier at Eton the games in favour were 'hopscotch, headimy, peg-in-the-ring, conquering lobs [marbles], trap-ball, chucksteal baggage and puss in the corner'. In addition to such childish games, there was the Eton Wall Game itself, which was played between those who boarded in and those who boarded out (collegers and oppidans), and involved a ferocious scrimmage running the length of the wall with the Slough Road. The Wall Game was in fact banned by the headmaster, Dr Keate, from 1827 to 1836 because of the divisions and brutality it encouraged amongst the boys. Though an important ritual at Eton, the Wall Game was less significant than the other form of football played on a more regular basis and known as the Field Game, involving two sides of eleven players who were not permitted to handle the ball. At other schools similar forms of football emerged according to local traditions and the requirements of the terrain. At Winchester football was particularly violent and boys were regularly carried off to the hospital with broken bones. None of this deterred their fellows who waited to take the place of the injured.[3]

Endurance and courage were the qualities most admired by the boys. The hero of Winchester football was known as 'Pruff' because he was said to be 'proof against pain'. A furious *mêlée* known as the 'rouge' at Eton, the 'hot' at Winchester, and most ominously the 'squash' at Harrow was the main feature of such games. Old boys like Thomas Hughes and his friend Sir Arthur Arbuthnot were fond of reliving the scrimmages of half a century earlier and passing judgement upon individuals according to their performance. 'We could neither of us call to mind having seen him in the thick of the scrimmage. He was generally hovering outside, looking for a chance to run with the ball' was their puzzled, dismissive verdict on a former pupil who later distinguished himself for valour in the army. By the time these two were mulling over their schooldays, values that had then been mainly prized by the boys alone had come to be proclaimed as

[3] I. and P. Opie, *Children's Games in Street and Playground* (1984), p. 4; Chandos, *Boys Together*, Appendix, pp. 352–4.

the cultural property of the system itself. This was the paradox
of the nineteenth-century public school.[4]

What had been little more than a free-for-all between two sides,
where a boy could make a name for himself by his 'pluck',
gradually became the testing ground of 'character'. Good
scrimmagers had naturally tended to be good fighters, and fighting
had enjoyed pride of place in the life of the unreformed public
school. Boys at Harrow happily fought gangs of navvies building
the railways and Etonians had clashed regularly with the butcher-
boys of Windsor. George Boudier of the Upper Fifth successfully
took on a professional pugilist in 1838 and became a school hero.
So did a pupil named Wyvill, who thrashed a burly soldier. He
in turn complained to the school and was asked to identify the
boy. 'Boy!' the guardsman exclaimed. 'Why, that's the biggest
man in tuttens' (the twin towns of Eton and Windsor). From time
to time this love of combat went tragically wrong. The most
notorious instance involved the youngest son of Lord Shaftesbury,
who died in 1825 after a fight with another boy that lasted two
and a half hours. This match had been properly arranged as a
prize-fight might have been, each boy having a 'second'.
Significantly Shaftesbury refused to prosecute through the courts
in what had been a fair fight between equals. Aristocratic morality
required that what had been a duel by fists should be respected,
even when the participants were only thirteen and fourteen years
of age.[5]

Violence and pain were taken for granted not only between
the boys but as a means of discipline. Masters flogged boys and
older boys flogged younger ones. This was so much a part of
everyday school life that only exceptionally severe punishments
seemed worth recording. 'I got an uncommon flogging this
morning,' wrote a boy at Winchester in the early nineteenth
century, 'the blood ran through my shirt and into my breeches.'
Boys, of course, sometimes got their own back on masters by
throwing them in ponds or even by organizing a 'rebellion' against
the authorities. Schoolboy revolts were fairly frequent in the late
eighteenth and early nineteenth centuries. Troops had to be called
in on one or two notorious occasions in what one authority has
called 'an irregular but continuous warfare against adult

---

[4] Chandos, *Boys Together*, p. 77.   [5] Ibid., pp. 141–2.

government . . . part of an approved way of life, an educational
exercise and a display of independence prescriptive by honour
for all aspirants to the respect of their peers'. Nor was such
behaviour confined only to privileged youths who refused to
concede what they saw as 'the liberties' of the pupils to masters
of lesser birth whose duties were merely academic. Grammar
school boys had their own rites of violence often involving the
locking out of masters from the school until certain customary
rights had been reaffirmed. 'Barring out', as it was called, was
a ritual of reversal where the pupils occupied the buildings and
locked out the masters, who tried to force down doors and climb
in windows; naturally the boys resisted with great ingenuity and
ferocity. This was almost a form of sport. 'If it had not all the
pleasure of a real siege and battle except actual slaughter, I don't
know what pleasure is', reflected a former enthusiast of what was
a declining custom in the Victorian age. Similarly an article in
the Eton school magazine for 1847–8 regretted the passing of the
old order when 'there used to be rebellions and the school was
full of fun'.[6]

Alongside such antics there was the habitual campaign against
the wildlife of the neighbourhood. 'Toozling' was a special word
for the chasing and killing of small birds, and the diary of a young
Harrovian added duck-hunting and beagling to the list of
schoolboy field sports. Boys were highly skilled in such things
and often noted down their kills, as their fathers might do in the
game-book of the estate. At Shrewsbury the boys organized their
own fox-hunt with eleven different 'runs'; all the parts, including
that of the fox, were played by the boys. Masters at the school
were instructed to stop the hunt partly because of complaints by
farmers, and partly because the 'hounds' were not averse to
shredding new copies of their Latin primer to lay a trail. Worse,
the text in question was written by a certain Dr Kennedy, the
headmaster of the school. 'Boar' hunts were another feature of
Shrewsbury which involved the chasing and killing of a common
pig. 'As disgraceful [an act] as ever schoolboy was guilty of', a
remorseful participant later confessed, though boys at Marlborough,

---

[6] J. Walvin, *A Child's World* (1982), p. 48; Chandos, *Boys Together*, pp. 167,
341; K. Thomas, *Rule and Misrule in the Schools of Early Modern England* (1975),
p. 26.

celebrating the founding of the school in 1843 with a frog-hunt around the grounds, might have contested this claim. They were also most adept at killing squirrels and rabbits with little canes topped with lead called 'squalers'.[7]

This brutal and disorderly dimension was one of the aspects of the public schools that Thomas Arnold and his followers set out to reform. Arnold himself had little use for games, but those whom he chose as his masters during his headship of Rugby from 1828 to 1842 saw the potential of sport as a source of discipline and morality more readily, especially in relation to the selecting of senior boys to impose discipline through the prefectorial system. From their earlier rejection of rough games, headmasters shifted their ground around the middle of the century, formally adopting and 'civilizing' what had long been part of the 'informal curriculum' of the boys. The 'scrum' became a prized institution of the public school. Cricket, which after all had been a popular game amongst the upper classes as well as the common people for long enough, began to be perceived as a way of imparting the values of team spirit and co-operation. 'The discipline and reliance on one another, which it teaches are so valuable . . . it merges the individual into the eleven; he doesn't play that he may win but that his side may win', muses the young master in a famous passage from *Tom Brown's Schooldays*; Thomas Hughes modelled this character on G. E. L. Cotton, who had been a master at Rugby and became head of Marlborough in 1853 after the last of the great pupil revolts had forced the previous occupant into resignation. Cotton believed that organized games would keep the boys together on the school's grounds and stop them roaming round the country poaching and causing havoc. 'New' sports would drive out the old. A trio of young games-playing masters were appointed to introduce the Rugby style of football into the school, joining in the games that were still played in ordinary clothes. One master at Marlborough used to throw himself into the scrum wearing a top hat. A. G. Butler, the rugger-mad head of Haileybury, could be seen pacing up and down the touchline roaring on encouragement, 'his figure presenting to view an immaculate shirt and a pair of red braces would be seen dashing into the fray, now emerging triumphant with the ball held aloft and at another moment bowled over in the mud like the humblest forward, eventually retiring from the field to the great detriment of his clothes but none to his dignity'.[8]

The 1850s was the crucial decade in public school sport. It was in 1852 that the Philathletic Club was formed at Harrow by senior boys but with behind-the-scenes prodding from Charles Vaughan, the headmaster, and the following year Cotton sent out the circular to parents that came to be regarded as a classic exposition of the new public school athletic system. Finally Edward Thring, whose brother had played a leading part in organizing football at Cambridge in the mid-1840s, took over Uppingham Grammar in 1853 and turned it into a great games-playing and most successful boarding-school in a matter of a few years. The encouragement of organized sports spread very quickly. The prize for the most athletic of all Victorian headmasters should perhaps go to a Scotsman, Hely Hutchison Almond, who went from Glasgow University to Balliol College, Oxford, and thence to Loretto School near Edinburgh, which he ruled for forty years from 1862. Every moment had to be filled with useful or energetic activity and there was a timetable that showed exactly how time was to be spent. There were compulsory games every day. Even the school uniform with its open shirts and long shorts looked rather like a football strip. If ever a man took Kipling's maxim of 'filling the unforgiving minute' it was Almond. Rugby was the main game and its virtues were extolled in the school song 'Go like blazes'. Running was another of Almond's enthusiasms and boys would be cheerfully chucked out into the depths of a bad Scottish winter when 'the roads were hedge high with snow' and 'every now and then they would fall into a drift'.[9]

Gradually sport ceased to be a means to a disciplinary end and became an end in itself. The culture of athleticism steadily came to dominate the whole system of élite education. Daily games created an ever more bizarre and elaborate hierarchy of athletic distinction. From playing in ordinary clothes boys soon moved

[8] Mangan, *Athleticism*, pp. 22–8; B. Haley, *The Healthy Body in Victorian Culture* (1978), p. 164.
[9] I. Thomson, 'The Acceptance of a National Policy for Physical Recreation in Scotland, 1872–1908', Ph.D. thesis (Stirling Univ., 1976), ch. 4; Mangan, *Athleticism*, pp. 48–58, 85.

on to shorts and flannels, and by the Edwardian period photographs of the first eleven reveal poised young men in striped blazers and special caps staring out at the world with supreme self-assurance. The athletic élite ran the school for the masters who delegated routine discipline to these 'bloods'. With their 'waistcoats flashing blues and reds' they would literally swagger round the school, lords of the young life they surveyed. The right to do up this button or undo that, to wear one kind of tie and not another, to show one inch of cuff or two, to carry a cane or wear a boater at a certain angle, were integral parts of what became primarily a hierarchy of physical achievement. For brains alone would not bring such rewards. Even Arnold had been wary of 'mere intellectual acuteness', though he would doubtless have been distressed at the contempt for the life of the mind displayed by some of his successors. 'Cleverness, what an aim!', fulminated Coterill of Fettes, 'Good God what an aim! Cleverness neither makes or keeps man or nation.' No wonder Kipling complained of 'flannelled fools at the wicket and muddied oafs at the goal'. Even the redoubtable Thring of Uppingham once had to warn his charges of the dangers as well as the joys of sport, taking as his text 'For he hath no pleasure in the strength of a horse, neither delighteth he in any man's legs.'[10]

But these were rare moments of self-doubt or criticism in what was otherwise a panegyric on the virtues of sport. Schools like Harrow spent vast sums on extending their playing-fields (from eight acres in 1845 to 146 in 1900). Charterhouse moved out of the City to Godalming in 1872 partly so that their pupils would have more room to develop their sporting skills. It seemed parents were less anxious about academic achievement than that their sons should be brought up in a sporting setting with broad acres and connotations of aristocratic grandeur. Most significantly this pattern was copied by the heads of ambitious grammar schools like Ripon, Bristol, and Worcester, who were increasingly drawn from the ranks of public school masters. Even where extensive playing-fields could not be purchased, the panoply of houses, teams, school colours, songs that surrounded the culture of athleticism were carefully reproduced and proved remarkably

---

[10] Mangan, *Athleticism*, ch. 7 and p. 109; P. McIntosh, *Physical Education in England since 1800* (1968), p. 63.

successful in attracting the fees of socially ambitious parents of modest means. Networks of influence spread out from the ancient schools via the movement of masters to and fro. The values of the public schools seeped into secondary schools through such men as A. B. Haslam, former captain of football and head boy of Rugby. As he told appreciative parents at Ripon Grammar School speech day in 1884, he 'believed in the old phrase "mens sana in corpore sano" and that Wellington was right when he said the battle of Waterloo was won on the playing-fields of Eton'.[11]

Going on to university, and that usually meant Oxford or Cambridge, was unlikely to be a difficult transition for the public school sportsman. The academic demands of the ancient universities were not particularly onerous and the college system fitted into the pattern of communal living and rivalries learned in school houses. Colleges became almost as serious about their prowess in sport as the public schools and furnished themselves with similarly splendid facilities. Fenner's in Cambridge and the University Parks in Oxford were the scene of first-class cricket. The two universities had a history of playing together since the first Varsity Boat Race in 1829 organized by Wordsworth's nephew, who also played in the first Oxford and Cambridge cricket match two years earlier. The Boat Race has become a British institution and annual cricket matches were played from 1839. However, despite the Boat Race varsity sport was desultory and restricted until the 1860s when contacts of all kinds grew very fast to include athletics, golf, football and rugby, cross-country, tennis, boxing, hockey, and swimming by the 1890s. The universities played an important part in establishing common rules for rugby and football as young men converged on them from different schools each of which in the early days had different ways of playing (several of the most ancient schools like Eton and Harrow have persisted in keeping their old games alongside the standardized rules that permitted them to play others). Boys from Rugby, where handling of the ball was permitted, could not agree on how to play with Etonians and Harrovians, who did not allow handling. Moreover the latter

[11] J. A. Mangan, 'Imitating their Betters and Disassociating from Their Inferiors', History of Education Society: Annual Conference (Dec. 1982), esp. p. 5.

resented the suggestion that they should bow down before the customs of another more recent, and as they saw it, inferior institution. In order to avoid games being confined to old boys of the same school two former pupils of Shrewsbury, de Winton and Thring, tried to act as honest brokers by drawing up common rules for football in 1846 mixing the handling and the kicking game. Rugby School published the rules of their own game in the same year and throughout the 1850s a number of different versions of football were played with the Cambridge compromise form being the most widespread, though this is by no means certain.[12]

As young men came down from university or left their public schools to join the professions or go into business they sought ways of continuing the games they had enjoyed. The Blackheath Club was founded in 1858 to play a handling and hacking game on the lines of Rugby School, while a year later the Forest Club was 'the creation of a few enthusiastic old Harrovians' advertising for games in *Bell's Life* in 1862 'on the rules of the University of Cambridge'. Meanwhile in Sheffield a club had been set up by old boys of Sheffield Collegiate School in 1858 who were mostly drawn from prominent manufacturing families with a few surgeons' and solicitors' sons as well. They were introduced to 'football' (probably the kicking game) by their public school-educated masters. This was also what happened in Wales with the arrival of a former undergraduate and fellow of King's College, Cambridge, the Revd. Rowland Williams, as the Vice-Principal of St David's College, Lampeter, in 1850. Games were played against Llandovery College, which had ambitions to become an English-style public school, after a rail link was established between the towns in 1857. In Scotland, Edinburgh Academicals were founded in 1857–8 by former members of Edinburgh Academy, whilst Merchiston and the Royal High School soon joined in as did Almond of Loretto, who turned his years at Balliol to good account and introduced the kind of handling game he had played at Oxford. Migrant members of the liberal professions brought the game to Glasgow and the core of what

---

[12] E. Hobsbawm, 'Mass-Producing Traditions: Europe, 1870–1914', in E. Hobsbawm and T. Ranger (eds.), *The Invention of Tradition* (1983), p. 298; E. Dunning and K. Sheard, *Barbarians, Gentlemen and Players* (1979), ch. 3; J. Arlott (ed.), *Oxford Companion to Sports and Games* (1976), pp. 294–6.

was later to become the Scottish (Rugby) Football Union was soon in place, playing friendly fixtures under rules laid out in 'the Green Book'. Thring, the energetic headmaster of Uppingham, who with his brother had earlier sought to bring some order into the game, tried again in 1862 when he drew up the ten basic rules of the 'simplest game' of football containing the modern essentials of the offside rule, permissible forms of tackling, goals (a ball thrown into the goal was not allowed), and goal-kicks. These rules stated that 'hands may be used only to stop a ball and place it on the ground before the feet'. The following year a committee of Cambridge men in which the main public schools were represented, revised the existing regulations more or less along the lines of Thring's proposals making no mention of running with the ball.[13]

At the same time in autumn 1863 a meeting was called of old-boy clubs recently founded in the London area to agree the basis upon which they could play each other. They decided to call themselves the Football Association and initially proposed draft rules that permitted both holding the ball and hacking (the kicking of opponents' shins). However, the deliberations at Cambridge along with a letter from the Sheffield Football Club urging that hacking be forbidden and that the hands ought not to be used convinced the bulk of the London group. There may have been an element of conflict between the old and the new public schools hidden within the argument over rules with the Clarendon schools insisting on their right to dictate to the rest and Rugby stubbornly refusing to abandon its tradition of handling. But, the distinctions were still fairly fluid at this stage and compromise might well have been possible had it not been for a sharp clash of personalities and the confusing issue of hacking. It was not until 1895 that a myth of origin was formally set out by Rugby School in the famous plaque in honour of William Webb Ellis, who, it was alleged, 'with a fine disregard for the rules of football as played in his time, first took the ball in his arms and ran with it, thus originating the distinctive feature of the Rugby game. AD 1823'. The claim to ownership of the game was based upon the most

[13] T. Mason, *Association Football and English Society* (1980), pp. 22–3; D. Smith and G. Williams, *Fields of Praise* (1980), p. 23; A. M. C. Thorburn, *The Scottish Rugby Union* (1985), p. 2.

flimsy evidence and designed primarily to counter the later pretensions of rival northern clubs. This schism will be discussed later; what matters here is to stress that no clear-cut distinctions were established before the 1860s and 1870s. Football or 'soccer' as it came to be known and rugby football had common roots in popular tradition. They were innovations rather than inventions. In the end football belonged to the people not to any public school. The new Football Association was even willing to permit a limited amount of handling at first and the real stumbling-block to agreement turned on the issue of hacking which the Blackheath representative called 'the true form of football'; 'if you do away with it,' he thundered, 'you will do away with all the courage and pluck of the game, and I will be bound to bring over a lot of Frenchmen who would beat you with a week's practice.' But Morley, the honorary secretary of the Football Association, was adamant that 'if we have hacking, no one who has arrived at the age of discretion will play at football, and it will be entirely left to schoolboys'. The practicality of a game for 'men in business' who had 'to take care of themselves' was the decisive factor. When the handling clubs formed the Rugby Football Union in 1871 one of their first decisions was to outlaw the old footballing maxim that 'you kick the ball if you can, and if you can't you kick the other man's shins', although rugby remained a more obviously physical and aggressive sport than football. Despite the success of soccer in most of the Clarendon schools, rugby was frequently advocated in the new public schools precisely because it was thought to require more courage. Courage shorn of cruelty, a civilized sort of simulated battle, that was what the country needed and the public schools set out to provide it.[14]

2. THE BODY IN VICTORIAN CULTURE

What underlay this obsession with sport amongst the rapidly swelling ranks of the middle classes as well as in the higher reaches of society? Only the sons of manual workers were thought not

[14] G. Green, *Soccer, the World Game* (1953), pp. 31–3, quoting FA minutes of Dec. 1863; Dunning and Sheard, *Barbarians*, ch. 5.

to require the experience of games, and at elementary school they generally had to make do with repetitive gymnastic drill if they were given any exercise at all. The fortunate few had all the space and the time they could want. They were an embryonic leisure class and no account of the brave new world of games should forget just how much those with resources in land or capital profited from the staggering expansion of the nineteenth-century economy. Many worked so that few could play. There were more affluent young people with more time on their hands than ever before, and in that sense it is hardly surprising that so much effort should have been spent having fun. Yet the study of urban conditions and of rising middle-class incomes cannot alone explain the character of Victorian sport and sportsmanship, which involved a shift away from gambling and spectating towards hard team-work, fair play, and physical exertion. The gratuitous expenditure of energy in organized groups according to carefully drafted laws is a very special way of having fun.

A wide range of cultural influences was evident in the character of amateur sport: the distinctiveness and significance of the new games was a product of the interplay of such diverse phenomena as changing attitudes to mental and physical health; the redefinition of masculinity and the new concept of 'manliness'; divisions within the Church of England and the desire to promote active religion; the influence of the biological and evolutionary theories of Spencer and Darwin; the powerful ethic of commercial competition and imperial endeavour linked to the equally strong traditions of élite solidarity and the assimilation of new wealth. The idea of the healthy mind and body merged into a garbled Darwinism that was itself often intermingled with notions of Christian and imperial duty. All this was contained within a framework where the fierce individualism that was required for economic success had to be balanced against the need for social cohesion and political stability.

The Victorians were much preoccupied with matters of health. The medical profession grew enormously in the first half of the nineteenth century producing over eight thousand university-trained doctors (more than in the whole preceding history of the profession) and building seventy new hospitals by 1860. Student doctors were often keen sportsmen and the honour of founding the first rugby club goes to Guy's Hospital in 1843. The rapid growth of industrial cities led to increased anxiety about pollution and dirt. Public health in the new cities became a big issue and Chadwick led a campaign to cut down the appalling inner-city mortality rates and to wipe out contagious diseases, especially cholera, that threatened the middle classes as well as the poor. Seaside resorts grew up in the first instance because sea bathing was thought not only pleasant but beneficial for general health. Likewise the spa towns that flourished claimed to offer not only civilized society and entertainment for the married and the marriageable but to cure or relieve all sorts of ailments as well. There was a general sense of concern about the health of those who had to work in industrial urban society, though it was the nervous strain on the leaders rather than the physical condition of the poor that engaged most of the early advocates of sport. If gainful activity was to be the first law of life, then proper exercise was needed to counteract the enfeebling effects of long hours at the office.[15]

The eighteenth-century ideal of cultivated leisure was giving way to the gospel of energetic outdoor pursuits. Dons like Leslie Stephen took the lead here, whether down by the river urging on his college eight or up in the Alps climbing new peaks with the Alpine Club, the foundation of which in 1857 led to a vogue for mountaineering especially among intellectuals. In the decade before 1865, when the death of four of the leading British climbers on the Matterhorn gave the new sport a tragic prominence, all but one of the Alpine peaks had been conquered in what came to be called the 'golden age' of British climbing. What had begun as little more than energetic and adventurous tourism came to be a competitive activity surrounded by an aura of quiet heroism and patriotic endeavour. For the Victorian view of health went deeper than a simple appreciation of the value of fresh air and exercise. There was a very widespread belief that problems of the mind had their origin in defects of the body. Such ideas were summed up in the overworked phrase 'mens sana in corpore sano', although its specific medical meaning in what was called 'psychophysiology' is less well known. This was the field of the President of the Royal Society, Benjamin Brodie, who claimed in 1854 that 'mental alienation is generally the result of

---

[15] Haley, *The Healthy Body*, ch. 1.

some wrong condition of the body'. Sir Leslie Stephen put it like this: 'no man would deny that a thoroughly healthy state of the body is the normal and most essential condition of athletic excellence. And just the same thing may be said of spiritual and intellectual health.' No wonder eminent Victorians were fond of Wordsworth. His physical vigour, his love of rivers and mountains, and his sense of the interdependence of the outer world of Nature and the inner life of man were in perfect keeping with the high culture of the age.[16]

Of course, public school masters, who led the athletic revolution, did not spend their time poring over medical textbooks, and their poetical interests tended to be divided between Latin verse and patriotic doggerel. High culture and science simply made athleticism more respectable. Schoolmasters, after all, were in the practical business of producing healthy boys. This was not just a matter of being sound of wind and limb. A healthy boy was also a good boy. Character formation was the principal reason for the quasi-monastic segregation of the sexes and the 'slow growth' philosophy of education. The stages between the complete dependence of early childhood and full adulthood became noticeably longer in the nineteenth century. This enforced lengthening of the youthful period in the life cycle amongst the swelling numbers of middle-class boys coincided with a lowering of the age of sexual maturity and better all-round physical development. Hence the public school had to cope with the 'problem' of puberty and of what later was called 'adolescence' on behalf of the parents. In this connection the most commonly used adjective in the public schoolmaster's vocabulary was 'manly'. Sport played a central role in the achievement of the kind of proper manliness that parents and teachers desired. Manliness was emphatically not to be confused with sexuality; manliness was to be an antidote to the precocious development of adult male sexuality by providing a new moral and physical definition of what masculinity was. True manliness was held to reside in the harmonious growth of the physique and the character side by side. A 'manly' boy was strong of body and pure of heart. The Victorian public school was the forcing-house of a new kind of masculinity in which the distinguishing characteristics

[16] Ibid., ch. 2 and p. 62.

of the male sex were not intellectual or genital but physical and moral. Man was neither a thinking machine nor was he governed by an unrestrained sexuality as animals were thought to be. He was loyal, brave, and active and as such the natural counterpart of woman who was spiritual, sensitive, and vulnerable. For this redefinition of gender comprised both sexes, establishing new standards of psychological and social normality based on the nuclear family and a firm division of roles between man the master and provider and woman as a kind of exclusively domestic creature whose life was regulated by her reproductive role and the caring duties it entailed.[17]

The construction of the masculine element of what was conceived as a 'natural' or even 'sacramental' family unit has received less attention than the female role. Because men were still sometimes permitted an element of sexual freedom which was rigorously forbidden to women, changes in what was considered to be proper male behaviour have been overlooked by feminist historians. A greater degree of self-control was expected from Victorian men than from their forebears; although their spartan upbringing did not exclude the notion of 'manly tears' and men might still take the arm of a friend in the street, in general the control of temper, desire, and affection was recommended. At precisely the moment when the new norms of maleness were coming into force, the incarnation of the opposite of 'manliness' was defined in the form of homosexuality, which for the first time was generally designated as a crime in 1885. The homosexual was not simply considered as a sexual pervert but was thought to have various other distinctive features with 'lusts written all over his face . . . pale, languid, scented, effeminate, oblique in expression'. An 'invert' was all that a sportsman was not. The legal battle between the Marquess of Queensberry, the man who had given his name to the modern rules of boxing, and Oscar Wilde in 1894 and 1895 over the issue of Wilde's homosexual relationship with the peer's son, Lord Alfred Douglas, offers an instructive sidelight on this tension between 'natural' and 'unnatural' physicality. The enormous publicity surrounding the trial, which juxtaposed aestheticism with true manliness and sportsmanship, presented the poet and

---

[17] J. Weeks, *Sex, Politics and Society* (1981), ch. 3, esp. pp. 38–40.

the upholder of the Queensberry rules in stark contrast. Ironically, of course, by cloistering boys together during puberty, public schools in some respects encouraged not manliness but vice. As J. A. Symonds alleged of Harrow in an unpublished autobiography, 'one could not avoid seeing acts of onanism, mutual masturbation and the sport of naked boys in bed together'. Symonds, a confessed homosexual, also revealed an illicit liaison between the headmaster, Charles Vaughan, and an ex-pupil, which led to Vaughan's resignation.[18]

None of these matters was openly discussed. At the official level homosexuality and masturbation, which was regarded as only slightly less heinous and a great deal more common, were the unspoken enemies of the new masculinity that the schools were there to spread. Games were the most powerful means by which such excesses were to be prevented. Instead of being the site of sexuality, the body was to be understood as the source of innocent vitality which required direction into appropriate channels. If boys were permitted to play sport each day then their bodies would be occupied in wholesome and useful purposes. Sports took raw energy and gave it meaning, turning boyish nature into manly culture. The sexual side of this transformation was carried out in an official silence that was far more eloquent than the loudest of public denunciations. But silence as a means of control broke down on the other side of the housemaster's door, erupting in occasional scandals which forced the headmaster to intervene. William Raymond of Lancing warned his boys of 'the enormous evil of unchastity' and Edward Thring denounced 'the devil work of impurity', but this kind of negative formulation was the nearest they came to a 'problem' that was somehow to be solved by a cold shower and a game of rugby. Montagu Butler, who followed Vaughan as head of Harrow, even insisted that the boys' pockets be sewn up, but this gave rise to such public amusement that the rule was hastily withdrawn. After a lifetime of avoiding the question, the creator of Tom Brown finally intervened to warn of 'souls hopelessly besmirched and befouled by this deadly habit'. 'More I dare not say,' he added darkly, 'this much I dare not suppress.' Edward Lyttelton, the Edwardian headmaster of Eton and a clergyman like so many other Victorian educationalists,

---

[18] Ibid., ch. 6 and p. 51.

probably summed up the feelings of his colleagues best when in a rare public airing of the subject in a letter to *The Times* he observed 'that in proportion as the adolescent mind gets absorbed in sex questions, wreckage of life ensues'. Premature interest in sex of any kind led to the destruction of 'sanity and upright manliness'; all the same he had to admit that 'athletes at public schools are never above the average standard of virtue, but often below it'—and this from a man of impeccable character who had made a hundred against Australia! Lyttelton was more honest than most heads, who cheerfully promoted sports for the moral qualities they were alleged to foster. Critics of the excessive athleticism of the public school were palmed off with the answer that at the very least games were good substitutes for something worse. 'You may think games occupy a disproportionate share of the boy's mind,' remarked the head of Clifton. 'You may be thankful this is so. What do you think French boys talk about?' Alec Waugh's *The Loom of Youth*, written in 1916 when he was only seventeen, was the first novel to break out of the *Boy's Own Paper* formula of good japes and hard-fought house matches and to refer in veiled terms to the sexual life of schoolboys. The fact that he described himself as 'the kind of boy who loved cricket and football' made his modest revelations seem all the worse.[19]

Games continued to be seen as important in preventing sexual promiscuity for undergraduates or during the long years of professional training before a man was considered to be in a proper position to maintain a wife. Charles Kingsley, writing to his fiancée, seemed to be obliquely making this point when he told her 'you cannot understand the excitement of animal exercise from the mere act of cutting wood or playing cricket to the manias of hunting, shooting or fishing . . . of these things more or less must young men live.' At least this was the case for serious young men taking holy orders who were expected to await marriage with due continence until they had a position. Sport was not just a source of bodily purification; it also came to be advocated more widely as part of a general programme of rational recreation and practical Christianity. These 'muscular Christians', as they came to be known (Kingsley personally disliked the philistine associations

---

[19] Mangan, *Athleticism*, pp. 38, 190; A. Waugh, *The Loom of Youth* (1955), preface, p. 9.

of what he called 'this painful term'), were a significant force in a mid-Victorian Church anxious both to reach the new industrial classes, whom the 1851 religious census had revealed were largely indifferent to organized religion, and to stop the drift into catholicism by High Church Anglicans. Kingsley in fact conducted a pamphlet war with Newman over his criticism of the excessive concern for bodily exercise in British schools and universities in the 1860s. Another well-known muscular Christian was Thomas Hughes, author of *Tom Brown's Schooldays* and pupil of Thomas Arnold's Rugby. Hughes was the son of a squire, whose Tory paternalism he had transformed into a kind of Christian Socialism. He threw himself into a wide range of improving schemes among London artisans in the 1860s ranging from the running of evening classes to the setting up of new model unions, though as he got older the Christian element in his thinking became much stronger than the socialist. For all his literary and spiritual activities it was as an ex-Rugby sportsman that he was most in demand, forever organizing athletics or boxing matches in the belief that 'the science of fisticuffs was a necessary prelude to the science of government, in London as much as at Rugby'. Dickens observed this too in the person of the Reverend Septimus Crisparkle whose 'radiant features teemed with innocence, and soft-hearted benevolence beamed from his boxing-gloves'. Upon seeing his mother while he was engaged in 'the noble art' he 'left off at this very moment and took the pretty old lady's entering face between his boxing-gloves and kissed it. Having done so with tenderness, the Reverend Septimus turned to again, countering with his left, and putting in his right in the most tremendous manner.' It was the Christian Charles Kingsley who produced a classic moral defence of modern sports. 'Through sport', he argued, 'boys acquire virtues which no books can give them; not merely daring and endurance, but, better still, temper, self-restraint, fairness, honour, unenvious approbation of another's success, and all that "give and take" of life which stand a man in good stead when he goes forth into the world, and without which, indeed, his success is always maimed and partial.'[20]

[20] Haley, *The Healthy Body*, ch. 5, pp. 109, 119; A. Briggs, *Victorian People* (1965), p. 171; J. E. Marlow, 'Popular Culture, Pugilism and Pickwick', *Journal of Popular Culture*, Spring 1982, p. 22.

What Kingsley called 'the divineness of the whole manhood' certainly offered an uplifting rationale for the reformed education of gentlemen. But it would be a mistake to assume that Christianity was the most important moral or intellectual force behind the spread of sport. The 'mind and body' analogy came to be increasingly applied in a collective national sense as the arguments of Spencer and of Darwin filtered into educated opinion in the later nineteenth century and as the needs of the Empire for men who could govern became more insistent. Herbert Spencer's grandiose theory of life as a quantum of energy evolving into ever more complex forms was blandly reduced to the famous dictum that 'to be a nation of good animals is the first condition of national prosperity'. Similarly Darwin's elaborate view of 'natural selection' was turned into a crude theory of the survival of the fittest which was widely misunderstood to mean 'the survival of the strongest'. Games were the most potent weapon in the armoury of public school stoicism, along with meagre rations and freezing dormitories that kept down overheads and inculcated a spartan contempt for comfort. The *Dublin Review* as early as 1860 complained that the real task of games was not so much to produce cheerful and practical Christians as 'a mere question of tissues and tendons—to bring out pluck, self-reliance, independence—the animal man'. Edward Thring thought that the most important gift a public school education could give was to make a boy tough, remarking of his own schooldays at Shrewsbury 'the more I suffered, the less I cared. The longer I stayed, the harder I grew.' After their defeat at the hands of Prussia in 1870, those concerned with the education of the French élite and the resurgence of the French nation began to take an interest in the public school system partly because they thought their own secondary schools had become too scholastic. Private colleges and state *lycées* were producing narrow-chested, round-shouldered aesthetes according to Baron Pierre de Coubertin, the founder of the modern Olympic Games.[21]

Of course, English sports had even more important virtues in the eyes of a liberal French aristocrat. The playing-fields of Eton

---

[21] J. A. Mangan, 'Social Darwinism, Sport and English Upper Class Education', in Proceedings of the Inaugural Conference of the BSSH, 1982, pp. 11–14; R. Holt, *Sport and Society in Modern France* (1981), pp. 62–4.

and Oxford, which he visited on several occasions, provided a perfect model of the solidarity of the privileged around robustly patriotic values, turning out, as A. C. Benson later put it, 'well-mannered, rational manly boys, all taking the same view of things, all doing the same things'. Coming from a country beset by the conflict between the hereditary nobility and middle-class constitutionalism, Frenchmen like Coubertin or the philosopher Hippolyte Taine were particularly well placed to appreciate the virtues of what Matthew Arnold called 'this beneficial, salutary intermixture of classes' where there were 'none of your absurd separations and seventy-two quarterings'. Although Matthew Arnold like his father thought sport produced 'a too exclusive worship of fire, strength, earnestness and action', he did appreciate that games were a possible source of cohesion between the sons of 'barbarian' aristocrats and 'philistine' factory-owners.[22]

The full importance of games and their distinctive social function cannot be grasped without some understanding of the changing relationship within and between the middle and upper classes in nineteenth-century Britain as a whole. In essence, the impact of middle-class economic power and political ambition on the traditional rulers was softened by the absorption of gentry values. By the end of the century Britain 'possessed a remarkably homogeneous and cohesive élite, sharing to a high degree a common education and a common outlook and set of values'. Owning a country house and broad acres was the ambition of many a successful business man, who might send his son to public school and then on to Oxford or Cambridge. For his part the son would often turn his back on the family firm and might venture into the law, medicine, the civil service, or become a schoolmaster, a don, or a clergyman. All of these occupations frequently gave greater status to the holder than could be obtained from the mere production of goods. City merchants and brokers were the only persons tainted with 'trade', who escaped the polite contempt for making money. The middle class was effectively split between gentrified occupations—the liberal professions expanded dramatically with the formation of special bodies to set standards and control admission—and the rank and file of factory managers or retailers. The process by which not only

[22] Briggs, *Victorian People*, pp. 152–3.

lawyers and doctors but architects, accountants, pharmacists, and others acquired grand buildings and a corporate identity implied the social elevation of such occupations. Those who had been educated alongside the old élite or even separately but under the same system tended to seek respect within the existing hierarchy. Those who played together stayed together.[23]

The public-school ideal spread far and wide. Even men who stayed in manufacturing might renounce the capitalist ethic, preferring leisure to work and spending to saving. Cobden, that bastion of pride and confidence in the bourgeois virtues, was appalled that 'merchants and manufacturers as a rule seem only to desire riches that they may be enabled to prostrate themselves at the feet of feudalism'. What would Cobden have thought of Marcus Samuel, who built up Shell into a major company from scratch only to sell out the majority shareholding to a Dutchman because amongst other things he preferred 'horses, gardens, angling and watching cricket in comfort'? His biographer called him an 'amateur'. 'Sport', which came increasingly to mean organized team-games rather than hunting or shooting, was something that the squire and the stockbroker could share, firing off a cricketing letter to *The Times* or enjoying the Boat Race, the Varsity rugger match, Henley, or Wimbledon. The industrious voice of the Protestant bourgeoisie was drowned by the din of gentlemen enjoying themselves. Small wonder that when a spectator at the Eton and Harrow match enquired 'playfully of a little Harrovian whether a bowler called F. C. Cobden was any relation to "the great Cobden", he was informed in reverent tones "he *is* the great Cobden" '.[24]

Team sports were of the essence here. Teams created a powerful focus for group loyalty which was duly celebrated in their songs. When they sang 'Swing, swing together', the boys of Eton were not only applauding the eight with their straight backs pulling on their oars in perfect time. They were also saying something about what it was like to be young and well-off enjoying the summer in an uncomplicated world of moral certainties and privileged solidarity. Sport became the true vehicle

---

[23] M. J. Wiener, *English Culture and the Decline of the Industrial Spirit* (1981), pp. 11, 112.

[24] Ibid., p. 14; Chandos, *Boys Together*, p. 335.

of school morality binding the simple joys of movement and fresh air—of running and throwing, pushing and shoving, hitting and catching a ball with grass underfoot and water and trees around—to the fortunes of the house, the school, and the nation. Although in principle sport was not supposed to be compulsory, in practice it was. Refusing to play took even more courage than participating. Games were the core of a kind of inclusive culture that sociologists nowadays identify with 'total institutions' like army barracks or prisons from which there is no escape and where an individual eats and sleeps, works and plays in collective isolation. A *Punch* cartoon of 1889 shows a headmaster in full academic garb addressing a new boy with the words 'Of course you needn't *work* Fitzmilksoppe: but *play* you must and shall.' No exceptions were made for the clumsy, the timid, or the brainy; weaklings just had to hang around the outfield or sneak away from the scrum as best they could.[25]

Held in a creative tension with this cohesiveness was the ideology of competition that ran strongly through the middle years of the nineteenth century as British goods conquered the world market and imperial power was extended far into Asia and Africa. Sport enshrined the ethic of competition, or more precisely the ethic of *fair* competition, by which Britons prospered. But it did not do so in a crude or simplistic way. The Victorians would never have subscribed to the contemporary orthodoxy that 'winning isn't the most important thing, it's the only thing'. Their philosophy of competition was altogether more subtle, emphasizing the value of victory much less than the utility of failure. The downgrading the mere 'winning' of games in favour of simply 'taking part' lay in the impetus this gave to widespread participation and to the idea of life as a constant struggle. By teaching boys how to lose as well as how to win with dignity, the wider competitive principle was strengthened. For to succeed in any competition—sporting, academic, or economic—the odds were very much that you would lose before you would win. It was vital that boys should not be discouraged by initial set-backs and that they should persevere until success finally came. There was no disgrace in losing so long as you 'did your best'. Dean Farrar, the head of Marlborough from 1871–6,

---

[25] Mangan, *Athleticism*, p. 90.

was by Victorian standards no great lover of sport but he still perceived its educational value, especially when it came 'to playing out tenaciously to the very last a losing game, ready to accept defeat but trying to the very end to turn it into victory'. So the idea of being a good loser was not just a matter of etiquette and upper-class style, it was also a device for encouraging a healthy as opposed to a Hobbesian competitiveness. Leisured youths were too prone to despair at the state of the world. A little learning could easily encourage the idea that success was either too sordid, too absurd, or just too exhausting to contemplate. Mid-nineteenth century moralists were much exercised by what they saw as vapid romanticism. Samuel Smiles had no time for the Byronic *Weltschmerz* of the well-off, which displayed itself 'in contempt for real life and disgust at the beaten tracks of men'. 'The only remedy for this green sickness of youth', he concluded, 'is physical exercise—action, work and bodily occupation.' Losing at games was infinitely preferable to refusing to 'play the game' at all.[26]

3. THE AGE OF THE 'GENTLEMAN AMATEUR'

So much for the broad cultural context of sport. But how did these influences operate in practice? To what extent was the ideal embodied in the reality? This general philosophy, which mixed group loyalty and group struggle with new attitudes to health, work, race, and religion can be summed up in two words: 'fair play'. Fair play was the watchword of the gentleman amateur. The term 'amateur' has come to mean anyone who does not play for pay, but the original meaning was more subtle. Amateurs were gentlemen of the middle and upper classes who played sports that were often also enjoyed by the common people—athletics, rowing, or cricket, for example—but who played these and other games in a special way. Fair play meant not only respecting the written rules of the game, but abiding by what was generally understood to be the spirit of the game. 'Not playing the game', which like so many other sporting expressions came quickly into general usage, referred not so much to the rules of play as to the

[26] P. McIntosh, *Fairplay* (1979), pp. 29–30.

manner in which the game was to be played. A true amateur should never seek to gain any advantage over an opponent that he would not expect his opponent to take over him. This code was not at first supposed to require much in the way of enforcement by an outside agency. Even when referees were introduced, the true amateur was still privately obliged to police himself. Corinthian Casuals, founded in 1882 to bring England's best public school footballers together for international matches, would withdraw their goalkeeper if a penalty was awarded against them, on the principle that it would be wrong not to accept the consequences of a foul, even if it had been accidental. The ethic of amateurism was to play in the spirit of fair competition. This did not mean 'the principle that as there is a penalty for cheating it is permissible to cheat at the risk of a penalty', as C. B. Fry neatly put it in 1911 in a side-swipe at declining moral standards in sport. Charles Burgess Fry ('C.B.') was, of course, the complete '*Boy's Own*' hero, captaining Oxford in the 1890s at cricket, soccer, and athletics and representing England in each, heading the first-class cricket averages for batting six times and holding the world long-jump record. He was also a fine rugby three-quarter and a fair classical scholar and writer. Fry inveighed against the existence of rules that assumed players would deliberately 'trip, hack and push their opponents and behave like cads of the most unscrupulous kidney', though he was forced to admit that by the early twentieth century, 'in football it is widely acknowledged that if both sides agree to cheat, cheating is fair'. F. G. J. Ford, whose record for the fastest hundred at Lords in 1897 remains unbroken, similarly upbraided batsmen who consistently used their pads to blunt the bowler's efforts. This Cambridge man fulminated against 'pad play' as 'the evil microbe'; 'the *fons et origo mali*'; 'this curse of modern cricket which has eaten into the very soul of the game and cast a slur upon the moral value of the very word "cricket" '.[27]

Sport had not only to be played in good spirit, it had to be played with style. 'Strife without anger, art without malice', as generations of Harrovians sang. The complete amateur was one

[27] Mason, *Association Football*, p. 233; E. Grayson, *Corinthian Casuals and Cricketers* (1983), pp. 63–4; *The Way to Lord's: Cricketing Letters to The Times*, sel. M. Williams (1984), p. 4.

who could play several games extremely well without giving the impression of strain. G. O. Smith, a slightly built figure for a great centre-forward, would casually saunter on to the pitch for a cup final just as he strolled to the wicket to score the odd century for Oxford. Hard training was bad form. 'The Corinthian of my day never trained', remarked Smith, 'and I can safely say the need of it was never felt.' Practising too much undermined natural grace and talent. For amateurs were above all gentlemen, and gentlemen were not supposed to toil and sweat for their laurels. The *Northern Athlete* remarked that Arthur Gould, one of the greatest of all Welsh three-quarters, would walk on to the field for an international in the 1890s 'thrusting his hands deeply in his pockets and surveying the cheering crowds with an equanimity born of supreme confidence'.[28]

Such men were sporting legends and clearly most middle-class sportsmen could neither emulate their achievements nor their sang-froid. The true amateur was an ideal type and the banal realities of play can rarely have taken on such a high moral tone. The ideologues of sport admitted as much when they criticized not only the fanaticism and violence of working-class sport but the seriousness and intensity with which it was taken by members of their own class. In the late nineteenth-century nostalgia for 'the good old days' was a refrain amongst the elderly just as the late Victorian and Edwardian years have since come to be thought of as 'the golden age' of sport. C. E. Green, who became president of the MCC, complained that county cricket had become too serious. 'There is very little sport in it now', he complained, significantly choosing the older usage synonymous with 'pleasure'. 'The feeling of *esprit de corps* . . . is fast disappearing' under the pressure of competition, he added. *Baily's Magazine* complained similarly of athletics that 'you now pass a policeman and show a season-ticket or pay for entrance into a ground furnished with a path of cinders, or fenced with grim barriers, in order to look at athletes who have been training systematically, instead of runners who take off their coats and go in with glorious uncertainty as to who's going to win what.' Far from promoting moral virtues, literary critics of sport like Wilkie Collins claimed

---

[28] Grayson, *Corinthian Casuals*, p. 31; Smith and Williams, *Fields of Praise*, p. 84.

that in practice it taught a man 'to take every advantage of another man that his superior strength and superior cunning can suggest'. Meredith's Richard Feverel wondered why 'silly mortals strive to the painful pinnacles of championship' and concluded that egoism was the only explanation. Amateur values were all well and good, but how far did they operate in ordinary competition?[29]

The greatest Victorian amateur of all fell notably short of the ideal. Only his prodigious talent earned 'the Doctor' the right to be different without dishonour. For W. G. Grace dominated what became the national summer game of England for forty years in a way which no player has done before or since. He started life as one of several cricketing brothers who were the children of a successful country doctor near Bristol, playing his first matches in the orchard guided by his Uncle Pocock, who 'took special pains with me, and helped me a great deal by insisting on my playing with an upright bat, even as a child'. Apart from their busy doctoring father, who also loved the game, the Grace family appear to have done little but play cricket; they had an *entrée* into the country-house matches of the time through their father's contacts with the Duke of Beaufort. W.G. was nurtured in the world of country hunts and touring cricket teams which supplemented the games organized by the village club founded by his father. From knocking around the countryside as a cricketing lad he shot to prominence as a fifteen-year-old in 1864 when he scored 170 and 56 not out against the Gentlemen of Sussex at Hove. He made his last century forty years later, by which time he had broken every record, including scoring over 54,000 first-class runs, a thousand of which were made in the month of May 1895 when he was already almost forty-seven.[30]

W.G. was not a product of the public school sporting system and never fulfilled the ideal of the gentleman amateur himself. 'He was probably the first sportsman to apply the work ethic to play . . . toiling long hours, practising, playing, travelling, propelled by immense stamina and a terrible will to win.' In a not particularly important match in 1876 he ran 168 singles in

[29] Dunning and Sheard, *Barbarians*, p. 179; Haley, *The Healthy Body*, p. 203 and ch. 11.

[30] W. G. Grace, *'W.G.': Cricketing Reminiscences and Personal Recollections* (1980), ch. 1.

an innings of 400 not out that took thirteen and a half hours. All his life he retained the marks of an older cricketing tradition in which a bit of gamesmanship and the odd wager were nothing to be ashamed of. He twice accepted large testimonials and organized his own paying-tours while remaining an amateur in name. He retained a furious youthful enthusiasm for each game he played and was not above hectoring an umpire or deliberately distracting an opponent. Those who came to expect spotless whites and smooth features in their cricketing heroes had a shock when they saw the Doctor with his spreading girth and great shaggy beard, his huge frame surmounted incongruously by a little cricketing-cap, striding around the field alternately bellowing or emitting a high-pitched giggle. Nor was he the cleanest or most sweet-smelling of men. Viscount Cobham said that he had the dirtiest neck he had ever kept wicket behind. Grace never grew up and this was his secret. He was the greatest of all the 'boy-men' of the age. Porrit, who took down the reminiscences of a man who hated writing and had very little time for learning of any sort, described him as a 'big, grown-up boy' who loved practical jokes. He took a good while to qualify as a doctor in the 1870s. He practised medicine in the winter but avoided it as much as possible in the cricketing months, when he is said to have dismissed the mother of young twins suffering from measles with the brusque advice 'put them to bed, and don't bother me unless they get to 208 for 2 before lunch'. Stories, apocryphal or otherwise, gathered around a man who undoubtedly was our first national sporting hero. He presided over cricket as it moved from a casual country game to an organized county championship. His own playing career spanned, as he recalled, the shift from 'open commons with rude tents as dressing-rooms' to 'the vast enclosure and palatial pavilion'; from 'the bumpy pitches to the smooth turf and billiard-table wickets' which led batsmen like himself to deal confidently with fast overarm bowling that would never have been thought playable by the early Victorian 'cracks'. Grace became a new kind of John Bull, a sporting Dr Johnson, popular amongst the lower classes as well as with the aristocracy and the professional élites. 'W.G. was almost as well known as W.E.G.', said a contemporary biographer and the sober *Dictionary of National Biography* unhesitatingly concurred that 'contemporary opinion would have singled him out as one of the best-known men in England'. Small boys scampered after souvenirs of his performances as if they were fragments of the True Cross. The fact that Grace transgressed most of the new norms of amateurism probably endeared him to those who saw through the code of fair play to the bedrock of privilege beneath it, even if his antics sometimes raised the odd eyebrow in the Long Room at Lord's. Perhaps these links with old country cricketing traditions and the lack of public school polish helps explain why, despite a press campaign led by *Punch*, he never received a knighthood. Grace was a splendid oddity, a supreme 'natural force', but to the inner sanctum of the MCC he was not quite a gentleman. Nor was the Queen disposed to grant to a cricketer the distinction she happily conferred on the actor Henry Irving.[31]

The new importance of '*how* you played the game', as the saying went, gave added significance to the vexed question of payment. The term 'professional' came into use in the 1850s and 'amateur' in the 1880s. Before the mid-nineteenth century the terms 'gentlemen' and 'players' were used mainly in cricket to denote those who were of independent means and those who were not. The distinction was purely one of social position and there was no dishonour attached to making money out of sport. Noblemen like the Duke of Richmond staked large sums on cricket matches in the eighteenth century, and the Revd. Lord Frederick Beauclerk was thought to make around £600 a year from cricket, though 'it was widely suspected that he owed a great deal of his financial success to backing his opponents in games in which he himself was playing'. This well-established tradition clashed with the new amateur ethic which saw sport as a moral end in itself rather than as a source of enrichment. Athletics at Oxford in the 1850s was organized on the same basis as horse-racing and the first Oxford meetings bring out the confusion that was felt by young men pulled between the old style of pedestrianism and new forms of uplifting exercise. In 1866 the Varsity meeting broke up in uproar after a dead-heat led to a fight between students, punters, and bookmakers, 'the sound of which, dinning into the

---

[31] P. Sutcliffe, *Times Literary Supplement*, 26 July 1981, p. 720, reviewing E. Midwinter, *W. G. Grace: His Life and Times*; Grace, '*W.G.*', p. xx; W. F. Mandle, 'W. G. Grace as a Victorian Hero', *Historical Studies*, Apr. 1980, pp. 357–8.

midnight, I can still hear' recalled Clement Jackson, an Oxford don, when he helped found the Amateur Athletic Association in 1880.[32]

Neither the Football Association set up in 1863 nor the Rugby Football Union formed in 1871 anticipated the problems that professionalism was to cause them. They assumed that their respective games would be played for pleasure and improvement but not for cash. The rapid popularity of both the handling- and kicking-codes beyond the confines of public school and old-boy teams inexorably set in motion a process of commercialization. The fact that large numbers of spectators were willing to pay to see good-quality play posed a serious threat to governing bodies established on firm amateur principles. This was not simply a question of money. Behind the issue of payment for play lay other considerations. Firstly there was the moral issue. If sport was commercialized then winning would become more important than taking part, and if this happened a game would no longer be a friendly encounter but a serious struggle for points in a league system. Teams would become the slaves of their supporters, who would be more interested in success than in fair play. The high priests of Victorian amateurism have so often been castigated— and rightly so—for their unsympathetic attitude towards working-class sportsmen that they ought at least to be given credit where it is due. Their vision of sport was a fine and proper one: What is wrong with their emphasis on restraint in victory and good humour in defeat, the conviction that rules should be freely accepted and the decision of a referee be respected, and their belief that the team was more important than the individual? What was *not* acceptable was the use to which these values were put, and the inflexibility of the rules through which they were applied.

The amateur code was in practice frequently a means of excluding working-class players from high-level competition. Moral arguments were a means of class exclusivity. The game of rugby is a case in point. The public school legislators simply could not come to terms with implications of the popular success of the sport in the north of England. By refusing to countenance 'broken-time' payments (compensation for loss of wages) they

[32] H. A. Harris, *Sport in Britain* (1975), p. 47; P. Lovesey, *The Official Centenary History of the Amateur Athletic Association* (1979), p. 41.

were effectively excluding manual workers from the better teams, who needed time to train and to travel. The split between the Rugby Football Union and the Northern Union in 1894 was not over professionalism *per se*; nor was it a matter of changes in the rules of the game. All that came later. The schism was rather the product of a refusal by the authorities to allow northern working-class players to have the leisure to compete on the same basis as the sons of the liberal professions and the landed. Clearly there were those who saw broken-time payments as the thin end of the wedge, the primrose path to full professionalism. This would lead to the intrusion of market forces into the realm of private life, buying and selling players to please the public. It would also place those who did not need or desire payment at a permanent disadvantage. But the northern clubs were not proposing this. Ironically, it was a requirement of what became the 'league' form of rugby that all players had proper employment. By legalizing broken-time payments they wanted to avoid the 'shamateurism' that inevitably arose where players of modest means played before paying spectators.[33]

In Wales, where the game established itself ahead of Association football, small payments to players were largely ignored by the Welsh Rugby Union, which even bought its star player, Arthur Gould, a house in recognition of his services. Provided players were discreet and sums were small, the Welsh officials were content with the occasional 'clean-up'. Too much of their national pride was tied up in rugby to take a high moral line in a small country where the pool of middle-class sportsmen was in any case restricted. So in Wales the league form of rugby never made much headway. Whereas the Welsh Rugby Union tried to maintain a popular base for the sport, in Scotland the opposite was true. Scotland went even further than England to enforce strict amateurism. Scottish rugby began as the preserve of the élite Edinburgh schools. Although it spread to the farming-towns of the borders with great success, it remained an exclusive game self-consciously distinct from Association football. By placing great stress on strict amateurism the large class of industrial workers in central Scotland would be discouraged from taking part.

---

[33] T. Delaney, *The Roots of Rugby League* (1984); Dunning and Sheard, *Barbarians*.

Scottish rugby's severity over expenses or payment was notorious. Internationals playing club rugby in Wales were required to hand back special commemorative watches and similar gifts. Even the numbering of players was felt to smack too much of professionalism. 'This is a rugby match not a cattle-sale', snapped a prominent Scottish official when George V protested that he could not identify players at the Calcutta Cup. The SFU reluctantly accepted this 'innovation' in 1932. English Rugby Union officials were similarly wary of pandering to the public, maintaining that rugby was essentially a game to be played rather than watched. However, even they did not go so far as the Scots, who bluntly declared themselves to be opposed to 'alterations designed to make the game faster, more interesting to spectators and, so, beneficial to gates'.[34]

The issue of professionalism was handled rather differently by the amateurs of the Football Association. The grandees of the Association game were even more privileged than their rugby counterparts, coming as they did from the most ancient of the public schools rather than the newer foundations. Perhaps this is the reason for their more paternalistic attitude to the needs of common people who wished to play 'their' game. 'Soccer' players—the term itself is Oxford undergraduate slang—were at first confident enough of their status to share their game with teams of mill-workers. When it became evident several northern teams were paying their players, there was certainly some strong criticism from purists and demands for the expulsion of the culprits. However, more cautious counsels prevailed and professionalism was permitted through the formation of the Football League in 1885. The administration of professional fixtures and players' terms and conditions were matters for the League whilst the Association remained custodians of the game itself. Despite these variations in response to the problem of payment, it would be wrong to stress the differences between the two codes too strongly. The FA was keen to keep professionalism at arm's length and introduced an amateur cup in 1893. Whereas the Rugby Union authorities made a formal distinction, the FA accepted professionalism in order to isolate

[34] Smith and Williams, *Fields of Praise*, ch. 4; Thorburn, *Scottish Rugby Union*, pp. 28–9.

it and to control it. How this was done will be examined elsewhere. What matters for the moment is that the government of the game remained in the hands of upper middle-class amateurs like C. W. Alcock, an old Harrovian JP, secretary of Surrey County Cricket Club and of the Football Association. Perhaps Alcock had learned something from cricket in his handling of the issue in soccer in the 1880s: professionalism was all right provided professionals knew their place.

In cricket, where there was a long tradition of professionalism, an elaborate code of conduct existed which distinguished carefully between gentlemen and players. There was a rough division of labour whereby the amateurs mainly batted and the professionals mainly bowled. Perhaps the onerous job of bowling permitted the continuation of mixed teams. Bowling was thought to be too much like hard work; and, besides, it was undignified for a gentleman's bowling to be struck nonchalantly round the ground by a social inferior. If this was not enough, professionals were also expected to look after the ground, clean the kit, serve the drinks, enter the ground by a separate entrance, and change in separate rooms. They even had their names set out differently on the score-card, with the gentleman's initials preceding his name in the normal fashion and the professional's placed after his surname. These curious distinctions permitted cricket to combine gentleman amateurs and lower-class professionals in the same team with the proviso that a professional should never lead a side when an amateur was available. In Lord Hawke's famous words, 'Pray God, that a professional should never captain England.' A professional never did until the early 1950s. As late as 1961 the following correction was broadcast at Lord's: 'Your cards show, at No. 8 for Middlesex, F. J. Titmus; that should read, of course, Titmus, F. J.' No letter from a professional cricketer was published in *The Times*, the established channel for influential discussion of the game, until 1962.[35]

The key issue was the shift in the definition of an amateur from a straightforward social distinction to a monetary one. This caused endless confusion and conflict. The various associations

---

[35] C. Brookes, *English Cricket* (1978), ch. 10; L. Allison, 'Batsman and Bowler', *JSH*, Summer 1980; A. Kuper, 'Gentlemen and Players', *New Society*, 9 Aug. 1984, p. 90.

that were set up to regulate the new sports in the 1860s and 1870s were often internally divided over the admission of manual workers to membership. On the one hand they wanted to maintain both the moral tone and the social exclusiveness of their sport; on the other hand they felt distinctly reluctant to erect open and explicit social barriers. Such reticence is instructive. Earlier generations of gentlemen would not have felt constrained in this way—either they would have cheerfully discriminated publicly against lower-class involvement, or they would have accepted professionalism when it suited them. As late as 1824 Brasenose College included a Thames waterman in its boat for a race against a Jesus four but this was the last occasion a college hired an oarsman. Excluding known 'professionals' in the sense of men who gained their living as watermen was perhaps understandable. What was much harder to justify in terms of the dominant ideology of moral improvement through play was the exclusion of all those who had to work with their hands for a living. The controversy surrounding the criteria of amateurism, which occupied several of the main governing bodies in sport, reflected the wider conflict between hierarchy and equality of opportunity in mid-Victorian England. Just as the skilled and literate worker was to be brought 'within the pale of the constitution' by the Second Reform Bill was he also to be excluded from athletics or rowing?

Amateur oarsmen could not hope to compete with the watermen of the Tyne or the Thames. They neither liked being beaten by social inferiors, nor could they mix socially. For sport was also a matter of getting on together after the event, a source of polite sociability between equals. Very few of the early amateur athletes would have been a match for pedestrians like the 'Gateshead Clipper', 'the North Star', or 'the Crowcatcher', who were named like horses and raced for purses on the sporting-grounds of the larger northern industrial towns. The first instinct of the Amateur Athletic Club, founded in 1866 by Oxford and Cambridge men to organize an athletics meeting to precede the Boat Race, was to exclude not only those who had competed in races for money but all manual workers. As athletic sports spread the new northern clubs pressed for a deletion of the 'artisan and mechanics' clause but there was strong resistance to change by men like Walter Rye, a London solicitor who had fought his way up the occupational ladder by his own efforts and insisted that an amateur must be 'a gentleman by position or education'. When tradesmen were admitted to the London Athletic Club in 1872, sixty members resigned. *The Times* agreed with segregation claiming that 'outsiders, artisans, mechanics and such like troublesome persons can have no place found for them. To keep them out is a thing desirable on every count. The status of the rest seems better assured and more clear from any doubt which might attach to it,' for 'loud would be the wail over a chased goblet or a pair of silver skulls which a mechanic had been lucky enough to carry off'.[36]

At the national level, however, it was the democratic principle that triumphed, although social distinctions remained of great importance at the club level. Only the Amateur Rowing Association (ARA), formed in 1882 by the Henley Stewards who had organized an exclusive regatta on the Thames since 1839, stubbornly clung to the formal exclusion of manual workers. Even in the rarefied world of amateur rowing there was a split between the Henley-based body and the National Amateur Rowing Association (NARA) set up in 1890 on the basis of open entry to all but professionals. NARA was inspired by ideals of muscular Christianity embodied in the formidable person of Dr F. J. Furnivall of Cambridge who dismissed the social exclusivity of the ARA. 'We feel', he wrote, 'that for a University to send its earnest intellectual men into an East End or other settlement to live with and help working-men in their studies and their sports, while it sends its rowing-men into the ARA to say to those working-men, "You're labourers; your work renders you unfit to associate and row with us" is a facing-both-ways, an inconsistency and contradiction which loyal sons of the University ought to avoid.' Likewise, amateur athletics had been reorganized on a theoretically non-discriminatory basis by three young Oxford men—Clement Jackson, Montague Sherman, and Bernard Wise. All three came from respectable professional families, had a public school education and distinguished careers. Why should they have bothered to ensure that athletics were open to the working classes? Why did the rugby and football

---

[36] Lovesey, *Centenary History of the AAA*, pp. 19–23. P. Bailey, *Leisure and Class in Victorian England* (1978), p. 135.

associations refuse to impose the straightforward segregation policy of the Henley stewards? It was certainly not that these men lacked a sense of their own status or desired to mingle with the lower orders. Their own clubs were composed of members of broadly similar social standing, and it was only in the north of England that there seems to have been any degree of social mixing at the team-level and even this was not very common.

What is at issue here is the nature and influence of Victorian liberalism. Before the setting up of the new regulatory bodies, the administration of sports was largely in the hands of private clubs—closed, self-perpetuating aristocratic cliques. Racing, cricket, and golf were dominated respectively by the Jockey Club, the Marylebone Cricket Club, and the Royal and Ancient Golf Club at St Andrews. The ex-public-school men who formed the new generation of administrators wished to create a more open élite rather than one dominated by noble patronage alone. Naked jobbery was not quite right. Here the administrative history of sports merges into the wider history of British institutions. For it was precisely at this period that landed control of the Church, the army, and the Civil Service was specifically called into question. The purchase of army commissions was phased out and the Northcote–Trevelyan report on the introduction of examinations for the Civil Service was implemented as part of a Gladstonian widening of opportunity for the professional and industrial élites. Just as the institutions of state were officially supposed to have been thrown open to the bracing winds of fair competition, so the new sports which themselves embodied most fully the concept of 'letting the best man win' could hardly have been set up on any other basis than that of open access.[37]

Of course, this openness of access was more apparent than real for most sportsmen, especially for officials. Just as the Civil Service was now open to all who had the classical education required to pass the entrance examination, so the running of sport was in practice confined to those with the necessary time, income, and organizational experience. Very few outside the ranks of the liberal professions had such qualifications and even

---

[37] E. Halladay, 'Of Pride and Prejudice', *IJHS*, May 1987, p. 50; G. Kitson Clark, *The Making of Victorian England* (1962), pp. 220, 260; P. C. McIntosh, 'The History of Sport and Other Disciplines', in Proceedings of the Inaugural Conference of the BSSH, 1982, pp. 5–6.

then a measure of social influence via the old-boy network was important. The new bureaucracy offered only a limited broadening of an upper-class system of rule as the social composition of the fifteen-man founding committee of the Rugby Football Union reveals: of the eleven whose schools have been traced, seven went to Rugby and the other four came from Marlborough, Tonbridge, Wellington, and Haileybury; six of the ten whose occupations are known were solicitors, the remaining four were made up of a doctor, a Civil Servant, a business man, and a lecturer at the Military College, Richmond. In Scotland rugby was also dominated by the liberal professions rather than from land or commerce, with recruitment further confined to a handful of exclusive Edinburgh schools. Two men, both of whom served in various official capacities from the 1890s to the 1930s, dominated Scottish rugby. A. S. Blair, Loretto and Oxford, was a Writer to the Signet (a solicitor) whilst James Aikman-Smith, Royal High and George Watson's College, qualified as a chartered accountant. No paid official was appointed until 1910 when another chartered accountant was brought in as secretary and treasurer.[38]

The new administrative élite did not so much seek to remove the nobility from organized sport as to share the management opportunities offered by the enormous expansion of activity. The hard edge of meritocracy was softened by the allure of social prestige. Everyone loved a lord, and no one more than the upper middle-class men who asked a succession of viscounts and earls to hold honorific office in their associations. The first president of the Amateur Athletic Association was the 7th Earl of Jersey, who also held the same office with the Welsh Rugby Union; the second president was Viscount Alverstone, who was Attorney-General when he took over the office and later became Lord Chief Justice. Baron Desborough managed to preside over five different national sporting bodies: the MCC, the Lawn Tennis Association, the Amateur Fencing Association, the Amateur Wrestling Association, and the Amateur Athletic Association. He is said to have been on one hundred and fifteen local government committees, and still managed to go big-game hunting and swim

[38] Dunning and Sheard, *Barbarians*, p. 123; Thorburn, *Scottish Rugby Union*, pp. 11–12.

the Niagara twice (once in a snowstorm). Clearly he was sufficiently occupied to leave the running of the sports he nominally governed to the various secretaries, treasurers, and other officials who no doubt preferred it that way. Although the Jockey Club did remain a fiercely noble preserve, the proportion of title-holding members of the MCC was halved in ten years falling from 14.7 per cent in 1877 to 6.4 per cent in 1887 as membership rose dramatically from a mere 650 in 1863 to over 5,000 in the mid-1880s when life memberships were being sold for £100. Instead of simply providing a forum for cricketing aristocrats, Lord's became a social and sporting institution of great importance. For a mere £3 (the subscription remained unchanged from 1856 to 1948) members of the liberal professions, City merchants, and country gentlemen could wear the distinctive MCC tie, slumber in the pavilion, and swing their legs from the tables of the Long Room. Members of county committees were often also members of the MCC, and this informal network of gentlemanly contact did much to preserve its influence and authority.

The Marylebone Cricket Club was able to head off potential challengers to its authority—the all-professional touring teams of the 1850s and 1860s—by making membership available on a broader basis. However, the old club structure was skilfully retained by keeping key positions of power for nominees. The President of the club was nominated annually by the outgoing holder. Of 111 Presidents of the MCC between 1825 and 1939 only sixteen were neither knights nor peers. The offices of secretary and treasurer were held for longer periods and it was here that true sovereignty lay. The MCC has had only eleven club secretaries in two centuries. One of the most famous was Francis Lacey whose term of office extended from 1898 to 1926. He ruled the MCC with the help of the Treasurer, Lord Harris, who had captained England and once remarked 'My whole life has pivoted on Lord's' as if his period as Governor of Bengal had been no more than a minor distraction from cricket. Sir Pelham Warner took over the mantle of authority from Harris. As a son of the Attorney-General of Trinidad, passing from Rugby to Oxford and then to test captaincy, the pedigree was perfect. He was as deeply English as Bertie Wooster, with whose creator he shared the nickname of 'Plum'. He wore a top hat to the Varsity match and insisted on calling professionals by their surname. Last in the line of succession has come 'Gubby' Allen whose Eton and Cambridge education belied the fact that he was born in Australia of a half-French mother. Family money and the fact he was 'something in the City', financed a long career as a Middlesex and England amateur. Significantly, both 'Plum' and 'Gubby' were very fine cricketers in their own right as well as being middle-class 'gentlemen'. Ambition alone could not win a place of influence at Lord's, whose luminaries were required to embody a uniquely British blend of talent, breeding, and affluence. Britain's national summer game remained in the hands of a small group who, in the best Whig traditions, had followed a policy of reforming to conserve.[39]

The MCC offers an excellent illustration of how the new moral philosophy of amateurism was mixed with social ambition. The rapidly growing cohorts of successful professional men along with bankers, City merchants, and industrialists did not just want to climb the social ladder; they wanted to pull it up behind them and set themselves apart from the massed ranks of the clerks, the managers, and the shopkeepers who made up the rest of the middle classes. Sport played a most important part in this process. The new definition of élite or gentlemanly status depended not so much on birth or on wealth alone as on education, which distinguished those who had only an elementary schooling from the sons of the upper middle classes; these young 'gentlemen' increasingly enjoyed what earlier generations would have considered an absurdly prolonged childhood leaving school at eighteen or nineteen and maybe going on to university after that. Just as the possession of the baccalaureate and the superior culture which came from a fee-paying secondary education was the major determinant of bourgeois status in France, so a less academic but equally lengthy period of secondary schooling was necessary to acquire an upper middle-class culture in Britain. New research is starting to uncover the transformation of the older forms of patronage in the later nineteenth century. Historians of the eighteenth century have long been aware of the central importance of 'connection' and influence but nineteenth-century

[39] Lovesey, *Centenary History of the AAA*, pp. 63, 91; Brookes, *English Cricket*, ch. 9; G. Moorhouse, *Lord's* (1983), pp. 42-9.

studies have put 'string-pulling' and jobbery into the margins of historical debate. Patronage changed its forms but kept its importance. As the older world of noble connections and county contacts broke down, a new system of favours based upon education replaced it. The true beneficiaries were not so much business men, especially northern ones, but southern members of the liberal professions—the non-industrial bourgeoisie who filled the swelling ranks of salaried state employees and recipients of official honours. Far from being uniformly run by 'the middle class' late-Victorian Britain split the middle classes into an educated élite that was merged with land, and a business class, which received little in the way of official approval. Perhaps this is why wealthy local business men were often willing to sink money into professional football clubs, or to become directors of that blot on the landscape of public school rugby, the Northern Union. If recognition was not forthcoming from the centre, it had to be nurtured in the localities. Here the mill-owner or merchant could achieve the prominence and respect he felt his wealth entitled him to within the municipality or the boardroom of 't' Rovers' or 'United'.[40]

The shared experience of public school offered a splendid excuse for a new kind of exclusive sociability later on. Hence the proliferation of old-boy dinners and associations from the 1870s onwards, the invention of the old school tie, and the habit of sending a boy to his father's 'old school'. The memory of shared sports and nostalgia for lost youth held men together 'twenty, thirty and forty years on'. Old-boy sports-teams offered just the right focus for such feelings. The early development of Association football was dominated by old-boy teams with the Old Etonians, Old Carthusians, and the Wanderers, which had an old Harrovian element, all winning the FA Championship in its first decade. Direct participation was only a part of a wider social network that involved watching the old school and cheering them on. The annual cricket matches between Marlborough and Rugby, Lancing and Brighton, Loretto and Fettes, and so on were significant social occasions. This was

---

[40] J. M. Bourne, *Patronage and Society in Ninetenth Century England* (1986), provides a new framework for the wider understanding of the split in rugby discussed by Dunning and Sheard, *Barbarians*, ch. 7, and confirms the emphasis of Wiener's *English Culture and the Decline of the Industrial Spirit*.

supremely true of the Eton versus Harrow match at Lord's, which attracted around 15,000 spectators at an entrance fee designed to keep out those who merely liked cricket and had no social reason to be there. A Harrovian described it as 'the supreme rite when one identified oneself with every member of the side, suffered in their failures, exalted in their triumphs'. The Etonians were no less fervent. In 1910 after an unexpected last-minute victory a prominent politician was seen 'weeping, laughing and dancing on a Harrovian flag' and 'portly citizens in Bond Street [were] yelling the news to strangers with the light-blue ribbon on them who had quited the ground in despair an hour before'. Loyalty to the old school assembled thousands of old boys together and attracted a fair share of ladies with marriageable daughters who 'do not go to Lord's to see the cricket'. Twelve hundred carriages were counted at the 1876 game. The Varsity match attracted almost as much prestige and even bigger attendances: 377,449 watched Oxford play Cambridge at cricket between 1871 and 1887.[41]

In this kind of society games might occasionally be played with social inferiors—the Old Etonians had several memorable confrontations with Lancashire mill-workers of Blackburn Olympic—but increasingly public schools were extremely careful about whom they would play and tended to avoid league arrangements that would force them into contact with their social inferiors. The Rugby Union had no formal fixture system and was run on a county basis leaving clubs free to choose whom they played—an arrangement which continued until very recently. As soccer became much more popular in the 1880s and northern professional teams began to dominate, the public school teams increasingly played either amongst themselves or on a casual invitation only basis. The Corinthian Casuals would never agree to an official fixture list, although their players did take on professional sides from time to time. The public school teams finally formalized their relationship in the creation of the Arthur Dunne Cup in 1902 in memory of a footballing Etonian, the founder of Ludgrove, a famous prep school, which boasted the

[41] Hobsbawm, 'Mass-Producing Traditions', pp. 293–8; Mangan, *Athleticism*, pp. 143–4; K. A. Sandiford, 'English Cricket Crowds during the Victorian Age', *JSH*, Winter 1982.

greatest Corinthian of all, G. O. Smith, among its masters. Rugby clubs were frequently based on old school loyalties with the leading London clubs like Richmond, Blackheath, and Harlequins (whose members were reputed to prefer sherry to beer after a game) having a privileged social standing as did the Civil Service, the teaching hospitals, and the universities that made up most of the early member clubs of the Rugby Football Union. Socializing between opposing teams became an important and much-prized feature of the game in the comfortable club-houses that the membership could afford. Whereas most football teams, who rarely had their own private facilities, would retreat to their own territory after a game (usually their local pub), rugby players regarded drinking together in the early evening as integral to the game, making and maintaining friendships with social equals.

Sumptuary distinctions were important in this world of amateur sport. Richard Usborne recalled how in the 1920s his mother had taken him to see Sussex play and given him the benefit of the sartorial education she had received as a 'gel' and younger sister of a keen Old Harrovian. She had learnt the meaning of all the best blazers. She thought the Harlequin the prettiest, but she knew and admired also the pale blue Etonian, the tri-coloured Eton Ramblers, the pink Carthusian and the prismatic Old Carthusian, the IZ [I Zingari or 'gypsies', a team of well-off itinerant country-house cricketers], the Free Foresters, which she also thought very pretty, the Harrow Wanderers and the Oxford Authentics. Such was the social and sporting network of one upper-class lady who claimed not to be much interested in cricket. Sartorially supreme were the Leander Club in their pink-cerise scarves and caps, who were the oldest rowing-club and composed mainly of Old Etonians and Oxbridge rowing-blues. From their splendid boat-house at Henley, they dominated both the social and the sporting life of the upper Thames winning thirty Henley trophies between 1891 and 1914 along with the Olympic Eights in 1908 and 1913.

This was the world of 'the gentleman amateur'. Amateurism was an important and distinctive element in the ideology of the British élite through which divisions between land and money were effectively bridged whilst manual workers and the lower middle class were informally excluded. This was done either through the social restrictions on club membership or the tight regulations on the acceptance of money for competition rather than by explicit class discrimination in the definition of an amateur. Rowing apart, there were plenty of working-class amateurs, but they rarely met the middle and upper classes outside the formal context of a game or an athletics meeting. Sport reflected and reinforced the ambiguities of an increasingly democratic society, which continued to be governed by a social élite. Amateurism was democratic in principle but not in practice.

4. FEMALE SPORT AND SUBURBIA

Belief in the virtues of amateur sport was not confined to men. Two powerful cultural forces collided head-on over the question of female sport: first there was the Victorian 'female stereotype' with its stress on the medical vunerability, emotional 'nature', and social limitations of women; set against this was the new culture of games, health, and fair play, which found energetic and articulate supporters amongst the most influential female educationalists. One orthodoxy was ranged against another. What was good for the brothers, was good for the sisters. This kind of 'me-too' feminism was particularly hard for most men to swallow when it came to sport, which, like the holding of a career, was considered an essentially masculine activity. Men developed the stamina, perseverance, and competitiveness in their play, which they used up in work and 're-created' again in their spare time. Work and sport were mutually reinforcing; 'man does, woman is'—the stereotypes were interdependent, each needing the other against which to define itself. Hence the fear of women taking up sport, and the derision and hostility it aroused. How could men be men if women adopted the very activities through which masculinity was defined? And yet, when couched in terms of the dominant values of Darwinism, patriotism, and 'character-building', the idea of sport for women was equally hard to resist. How could the sons be strong if their mothers were weak? In addition came the conflicting demand for greater freedom for women, especially young women, who often linked educational, professional, and political aspirations with the right to use their own bodies as they wished whether it be to ride bicycles or play tennis. However, there was more to women's sport than the struggle of privileged girls to break the mould of supine femininity. In certain respects female sport subtly reinforced the orthodox view of a woman's place. Women's sport outside school came to be rooted in a new kind of suburban culture centred around the family garden and the private club, which drew the public and the domestic domain more closely together than all-male sports. Female sport served as much to enhance woman in her domestic role as to liberate her from it. Women's sport struck a delicate balance between physical emancipation and social respectability. The recreational purpose of the female body was redefined in the late-Victorian period by permitting women a more active physical life whilst maintaining a rigid distinction between the capacities and character of men and women.

Sport was very much the preoccupation of privately educated middle-class girls. Working-class boys had little enough physical education in school, working-class girls usually had none at all. 'They might find a little wholesome physical exercise in cleaning out the school' was the only suggestion for female exercise from the Revd. James Fraser in a report of 1861 on popular education. Therapeutic gymnastics were introduced into girls' elementary education by the London School Board in 1878 and by 1885 700 teachers had been trained to supervise simple remedial exercise. Gym was quite actively promoted in Liverpool schools and was significantly encouraged by the drive for national efficiency in the years before the First World War. Sport, however, was rarely included. As with boys 'games for the classes, gym for the masses', seems to have been the rule within the school walls. When attempts were made to provide sport for munitions girls during the Great War it was found that 'they had never been accustomed to take part in team games, or indeed any form of exercise for pleasure'. The major changes in women's sport took place at the new and most expensive girls' schools like Roedean, Wycombe Abbey, and St Leonards in Scotland, which began to take the place of the 'academies for young ladies' where walking 'in crocodile' had been the only concession to exercise. The new schools were supplied with games mistresses from the private college of physical education at Dartford owned and run by the redoubtable Madame Bergman-Osterberg, whose influence in women's physical education before the First World War was enormous. Her pupils founded three further colleges of physical education—

Anstey, Bedford, and Dunfermline—long before Carnegie was established for men in 1933. Madame Osterberg was at the centre of a separate female tradition in sport, which combined team-sports with the practice of the Swedish gymnastics devised by Ling for female physical development. 'Women need health as well as men', Ling had stated and 'Madame' was committed to clarifying his meaning. Fitness and femininity were not opposed qualities. Both were needed to create healthy, moral, middle-class families.[42]

The blending of boys' games with a carefully graded set of exercises to promote suppleness, balance, and agility ingeniously undermined the reservations of the medical establishment. Instead of denying that women were different and demanding equal treatment, as feminists might do today, Madame Osterberg and her followers emphasized the need for separate development. Women's physiology required special strengthening exercises alongside sport as part of a broader programme of physical recreation. So they used the idea of female vulnerability for their own ends, stressing that only women could train women, bluntly rejecting male interference and creating a special place for themselves in the educational system. 'Let us once and for all discard man as a physical trainer of women. Let us send the drill sergeant right-about-face to his awkward squad,' exorted the zealous Swede. 'This work we women do better as our very success in training depends upon our having felt like women, able to calculate the possibilities of our sex, knowing our weakness and our strength.' Though initially unfamiliar with sports, Madame Osterberg soon saw the potential 'to combine these games with Swedish gymnastics and thus create a perfect training system for the English girl'. A new female occupation was created: the games mistress; those vigorous ladies drawn for the most part from affluent homes were schooled not only in the art of movement but in polite behaviour and good manners by their matriarch. Madame Osterberg was very strict in this respect even requiring the 'young ladies' to dine together in evening dress. She was in the business of training bourgeois girls, who in turn would go out to improve the racial quality of the élite. Her

---

[42] McIntosh, *Physical Education in England since 1800*, pp. 92, 193-4; S. Fletcher, *Women First* (1984), pp. 19-20.

'graduates' came in for more than their fair share of derision not only from men, for whom sexism was completely 'natural', but also from women, who did not wish conventional femininity to be challenged. Their ebullience and social confidence carried them through. Public attitudes were changing as they set out to preach the gospel of games, shrugging off the sly jibes of better-paid academic colleagues, whose library pallor was accentuated by the rude good health of these new additions to the staff room. Cheerfully brandishing their tennis-rackets and hockey-sticks, bustling about indoors and out, full of uncomplicated energy and optimism, such was the image of the games mistress.[43]

If Osterberg won cautious medical and educational consent to female physical education by turning it into a kind of science, Miss Lawrence of Roedean and Miss Dove of Wycombe Abbey guaranteed the respectability of team-sports for girls. Roedean was founded in 1885 and from the outset modelled itself on the athletic and moral style of the Victorian boys' public school with two hours' exercise a day in winter and three in summer. Alongside running, swimming, and gymnastics the girls were encouraged to play hockey, tennis, and even cricket. 'Considered as a means of training character games stand alone and they provide precisely that element in girls' education which hitherto has been lacking.' The missing element was 'the power of working with others'; this was the great virtue of sport, considered Miss Lawrence, for whom games were 'obligatory on all, as otherwise those very individuals whose characters most need the discipline they afford, will evade them'. Quite so; one can almost hear Miss Dove giving her crisp assent while appending a list of sporting qualities that would have done credit to the creator of Tom Brown: 'powers of organization, of good temper under trying circumstance, courage and determination to play up and do your best, even in a losing game, rapidity of thought and action, judgement and self-reliance, and, above all things, unselfishness.'[44]

---

[43] Fletcher, *Women First*, p. 31; J. A. Hargreaves, 'Playing like Gentlemen while Behaving like Ladies', *BJSH*, May 1985, p. 48. Hargreaves's excellent analysis may be supplemented on the medical side by P. Atkinson, 'Strong Minds and Weak Bodies', in the same issue of *BJSH*; see also K. E. McCrone, 'Play Up! Play Up! and Play the Game!', *Journal of British Studies*, 23 (1984), pp. 106–34.

[44] Fletcher, *Women First*, pp. 32–3.

These schools made hockey the game for middle-class schoolgirls and by the end of the century the *Girl's Own Paper* was singing the praises of hard-won house-matches. 'How different from us, Miss Beale and Miss Buss' ran the ditty, but even two such uncompromising upholders of academic standards were gradually won over to physical education. Admittedly under Miss Buss it was slow going and the North London Collegiate School did not get beyond callisthenics four times a week and a see-saw in the garden until the end of the century, though Miss Beale introduced games at Cheltenham Ladies' College in 1891. Soon the quiet spa was enlivened by the clash of sticks and the cries of girls urging on their school. So too were the ancient universities. Girton formed a hockey team in 1890 which sang 'Beat Newnham' to the tune of 'Knocked 'em in the Old Kent Road'. Tennis, croquet, and badminton were played at Oxford after Somerville and Lady Margaret Hall were opened in 1870. In addition to hockey rowing was introduced, though only on the Cherwell and in a recreational form so as not to incommode undergraduate oarsmen. Oxbridge women, therefore, set out to imitate the men without compromising their status as ladies. Doctors who had confidently predicted that either sport or study would use up the finite 'vital force' of the female were effectively put in their place. Writing in 1898, Miss Lawrence of Roedean could reflect with some satisfaction on the progress of games. 'We had to explain our position to hostile critics, and to encounter much opposition from the parents of our girls, and we felt we were carrying on a crusade,' she recalled. But the battle had largely been won. 'A wave of change' had come over public opinion. Games for public schoolgirls were coming to be seen as so desirable that the ingenuity of non-sporting pupils was sorely tested to escape the muddy pitch or the chilly pool. A good memory for menstrual cycles was required by a successful games mistress.[45]

Headmistresses had a good deal of autonomy within their own institutions and their girls could enjoy games in relative peace and privacy. But in the outside world women who took up sport were likely to have their appearance endlessly discussed and criticized. The legitimacy of sport for women and the kind of

[45] Ibid., p. 34; K. E. McCrone, 'The "Lady Blue" ', *BJSH*, Sept. 1986, p. 197.

clothes that could decently be worn led to a protracted and vituperative debate between those who saw sport as the enemy of femininity and the proponents of 'rational dress'. There was far more at stake here than the cut of this or the length of that. Clothes had a symbolic significance, which accounts for the remarkable amount of space devoted to the dress issue, especially in women's magazines. Cycling was singled out for particular criticism. Public reaction over whether or not women should be allowed to wear tailored culottes or 'bloomers' was often angry and derisive. Mrs Eliza Linton had for long been the self-appointed scourge of such conduct. As mass production of the modern safety-bicycle and the invention of the inflatable tyre made cycling a relatively cheap and safe activity, the anger of Mrs Linton grew. In 1896 she could contain herself no longer, denouncing the female cyclist in the pages of the *Lady's Realm* as lacking 'the faintest remnant of that sweet spirit of allurement which, conscious or unconscious, is woman's supreme attraction'. What Mrs Linton most feared was not so much the clothes themselves as what they symbolized. 'Chief of all dangers attending this new development of feminine freedom', she went on, 'is the intoxication which comes with unfettered liberty.' The undergraduates of Cambridge made the same point when they hanged a female student in effigy in 1897 complete with her bicycle in protest at the decision to put women's names on the class lists.[46]

Female cyclists were turning night into day, or so their elders thought. Personal transport meant private mobility and the prospect of freedom from surveillance, the right to go out and explore the world, to be in charge of one's own destiny. Advertisers played on this longing to flee the stuffy bourgeois household, depicting young men and women escaping from the dirty, overcrowded cities to rediscover an unspoiled and romantic rural world. 'There is a new dawn, a dawn of emancipation, and it is brought about by the cycle,' enthused Louise Jeye in 1895, 'free to wheel, free to spin out into the glorious countryside, unhampered by chaperon or, even more dispiriting, male admirer, the young girl of today can feel the real independence of herself,

---

[46] D. Rubinstein, 'Cycling in the 1890s', *Victorian Studies*, Autumn 1977, pp. 66–8.

and while she is building up her better constitution she is developing her better mind.' This sturdy independence of mind and body was all very well but from the parental point of view a girl's reputation, if not her virtue, might be at risk. Even Lady Haberton, a veteran cyclist and supporter of rational dress, was concerned lest her efforts be confused with 'free love'. 'Daisy, Daisy' sung by Katie Lawrence did not hold out the prospect of riches and comfort. 'It won't be a stylish marriage, we can't afford a carriage', admits the suitor. Whether or not their daughter would 'look sweet upon the seat of a bicycle made for two' was beside the point as far as the family of a 'nice' girl was concerned.

Apart from the problems of learning to balance and bruising encounters with hedges and pot-holes, there were other dangers to consider. 'Given a lonely road, and a tramp desperate with hunger or naturally vicious, it stands to reason that girls, or indeed any woman, riding alone must be in some considerable peril', thought Mrs Harcourt Williamson in 1897. In fact, the mundane hostility of the general public, especially the poor, was a more serious problem for the lady cyclist than the 'sturdy beggar'. 'Few would believe how insulting and coarse the British public could be unless they had ridden through a populated district with a lady dressed in Rationals', remarked a correspondent of the *Clarion*— the progressive organ of the cycling and socialist Clarion Clubs. Occasionally public resentment at privileged ladies careering through working-class streets could turn to violence. In the summer of 1899, for example, the editor of *Rational Dress Gazette* was struck with a meat-hook while cycling in Kilburn. Such incidents were rare, but the kind of angry reaction recorded by Flora Thompson was more common.

The wife of a doctor in Candleford town was the first woman cyclist in that district. 'I should like to tear her off that thing and smack her pretty little backside', said one old man grinding his teeth in fury [or was it something else?] One more gentle character sighed and said: 'T'ood break my heart if I saw my wife on one of they', which those acquainted with the figure of his middle-aged wife thought reasonable.[47]

[47] Rubinstein, 'Cycling in the 1890s'; J. Mackenzie (ed.), *Cycling* (1981), p. 24; R. Watson and M. Gray, *The Penguin Book of the Bicycle* (1978), p. 128.

In fact, the symbolic impact of cycling for women was more important than the reality of female participation. The right to be strong, swift, and independent certainly challenged received wisdom about women. 'Lifted off the earth, sitting at rest in the moving air, the London air turning into fresh moving air around your head,' wrote a breathless Dorothy Richardson, '. . . country roads flowing by in sun and in shadow . . . leaving you careless and strong.' Feminist enthusiasm for the bicycle competed with dire predictions of gynaecological damage and racial decline from the medical establishment. Though such fears were foolish and groundless, they none the less were widely accepted. The *Northern Wheeler* in 1892 confidently asserted that 'in young girls the bones of the pelvis are not able to resist the tension required to ride a bicycle, and so may become more or less distorted in shape, with perhaps in after life, resulting distress'. At all events the boom of the mid-1890s was short-lived with poverty and domestic controls keeping most women out of the saddle until the 'outdoor movement' of the inter-war years, which will be examined later. The Lord's Day Observance Society recorded the number and sex of cyclists passing the Red Deer in Croydon on a Sunday morning in 1904: 1,797 men and only 125 women. Higher church attendance rates for women does not seem by itself an adequate reason for this disparity. A more obvious explanation is that cycling—part feminist, part fad—had lost its immediate appeal. The avant-garde were moving on to the automobile leaving most young women still under the control of father or husband. Exploring the countryside, which appealed so strongly both to the lower middle-class heroes of H. G. Wells like the draper's assistant Mr Hoopdriver in *Wheels of Chance* and to intellectuals and literary men like Shaw, Jerome K. Jerome, and Arnold Bennett was still mainly the preserve of Edwardian man.[48]

If cycling remained a slightly dubious activity for the bourgeois girl, tennis was seen as a more positive force. A new kind of middle-class suburban culture sprang up as the railway-lines stretched out into the rural hinterland of the big cities. There was Wilmslow and Didsbury in Manchester, Gosforth in Newcastle

---

[48] Mackenzie (ed.), *Cycling*, pp. 24, 34–5. J. Lowerson, 'Sport and the Victorian Sunday', *BJSH*, Sept. 1984, p. 211.

and Edgbaston, the 'Birmingham Belgravia', which rose in population from 2,599 in 1881 to 16,368 in 1911. Here, amidst substantial family houses in quiet tree-lined 'avenues' and 'groves', tennis could be played in back gardens that might occupy the best part of an acre. The 'lawn' became a favoured site of informal upper middle-class amusement. Croquet, adapted from the French game *maille* or 'mallet', was introduced in the 1850s by a manufacturer with an eye for social trends and 'hardly a house with a lawn was without its croquet set'. The old children's game of battledore-and-shuttlecock was transformed on the Duke of Beaufort's estate at Badminton around 1870—hence the new name. Badminton required little space and was easy to play as a casual garden game as well as at club level. There were around 250 clubs in the Badminton Association by 1914. Lawn tennis was adapted from 'royal' or 'real' tennis by Major Gem, clerk to the magistrates of Birmingham, with the help of a Spanish friend named Perera who may have been familiar with 'pelota'. These two began playing with a couple of local doctors at the Manor House Hotel at Leamington Spa in 1872, which provided an appropriately genteel setting for the first tennis club. Meanwhile a Major Wingfield had interested Lord Landsdowne in a game, which he unhappily called 'Sphairistike' and was renamed 'lawn tennis' according to a certain Arthur Balfour, whose later elevation to the position of prime minister did not diminish his early enthusiasm for the game. Whether Gem or Wingfield deserves the credit as the founder of modern tennis is less important than the fact that Wingfield quickly saw its potential, publishing a set of rules and marketing the basic equipment in 1874. Happily the sales-book of Wingfield's early venture into sports manufacturing has survived and records the sale of 1,050 sets of tennis equipment, mainly to the aristocracy, between July 1874 and June 1875. By 1877 a tennis tournament was established at the All-England Croquet Club in the lush suburb of Wimbledon. Tennis at Wimbledon was a cuckoo in the nest, soon relegating croquet to a minor role and drawing over 3,500 spectators for the men's final by 1885.[49]

[49] J. Stevenson, *British Society 1914–45* (1984), p. 25; Hargreaves, 'Playing like Gentlemen', p. 32; K. G. Ponting, 'Lawn Tennis', in W. Vamplew (ed.), *The Economic History of Leisure: papers Presented at the Eighth International Economic History Congress, Budapest, August 1982* (1983), p. 74.

Tennis bridged the upper and middle classes. It is significant that both the country sports journal *The Field* and the MCC played a prominent part at its inception. Like cricket and rugby, tennis fitted neatly into the more open élite created by the expansion of the Victorian professions and commerce. Unlike other sports, however, tennis could be played by either sex or by both together. Therein lay its true social importance. From a gender viewpoint, tennis was the first truly national game—and so it has remained. Learning to play tennis well enough to make a pair for mixed doubles became an *art d'agrément*. Gentle athleticism went hand in hand with feminine adornment with the wayward shots of the daughters coming to rest in the flower beds from which mothers and aunts would cut blooms for the house. The privacy of the garden provided an opportunity to invite suitable members of the opposite sex for supervised sports. In a new world where the upper and middle classes had become too large and diversified for the kind of organized contact between neighbours that had governed more traditional forms of introduction and courtship, tennis filled a useful gap. Young ladies raised in the city could hardly get a husband at a hunt ball as earlier generations of marriageable 'gels' had done.[50]

New institutions were required. The purchase and management of lawns and buildings presented no difficulty for the well-to-do parent of nubile daughters, especially when the game itself was also well-suited to the middle-aged man past playing the vigorous team-games of his schooldays. As time passed and public school girls became mothers in their turn, the Edwardian tennis club came into its own. The Select Lawn Tennis Club formed in Hove in 1881 made its purpose clear enough by its name and layout with 'eight courts adequately sheltered by the foliage of trees'. The shelter afforded was not so much from the sun as from the intrusive gaze of the common herd. There were about 300 clubs attached to the Lawn Tennis Association by 1900 with a threefold increase over Edwardian years. By 1914 there were around 1,000 clubs and many smart hotels and country clubs were well equipped with courts. The popularity of tennis, especially for women, grew enormously with press coverage of Suzanne Lenglen and Little Mo, though Mrs Godfrey, still attending

50   Hobsbawm, 'Mass-Producing Traditions', pp. 298–300.

Wimbledon sixty years on, was perhaps more typical of the respectable British lady player of the 1920s, who tended to avoid sensational publicity. Nearly three million private suburban houses were built between the wars and what had formerly been a snobbish game spread down to the lower ranks of the middle classes. By the late 1930s there were nearly 3,000 clubs affiliated to the Lawn Tennis Federation each with its niche in the social history of suburbia. A reader of Richmal Crompton's 'William' books, set somewhere within commuting distance of the City— perhaps around Bromley Common where the former classics mistress built her home—will probably recall the moments when Ethel, the elder sister of the hero, was just about to fall headlong for a nice chap at the tennis club when her dishevelled brother would suddenly crash through a window or peer out from behind a potted palm. Bridge parties and dances, picnics and smoking-concerts, even elocution lessons, were part of the social life of the tennis club and its suburban constituency. Within the club there was room for more competitive play, especially for men at league and county level, but this rarely overshadowed the larger social purpose. Those who ponder the relative failure of Britain to produce outstanding players would do well to remember this.[51]

While it was nice for a girl to be able to play tennis, she was not supposed to become good at it. The suburban garden or club was for polite courtship and friendly relations between social equals. Vigorous play was permitted to men but hard, sweaty rallies and a fierce will to win were 'not the thing', even for energetic young ladies like John Betjeman's Joan Hunter Dunn. Great importance was attached to fashion. In 1879 a ladies' magazine recommended the following outfit for tennis: 'a cream merino bodice with long sleeves edged with embroidery; skirt with deep kilting, over it an old-gold silk blouse-tunic with short wide sleeves and square neck'. To complete the ensemble a 'large straw hat of the coal-scuttle type' was to be worn. Additional hair-pieces were also common. When one of the beautiful Langrishe sisters from Ireland was struggling with the elements on No. 1

[51] J. Lowerson and J. Myerscough, *Time to Spare in Victorian England* (1977), p. 126; LTA statistics kindly provided by H. Walker, Research Officer, SSRC Leisure Project, Centre for Continuing Education, University of Sussex.

court, her hair-piece blew off during a rally. 'Not the least disconcerted', she finished the point and picked up the offending item, 'as one would a mouse by the tail, deposited it with the umpire for safe keeping, merely remarking, "Sure, and it's a wonder it doesn't blow yer real hair off," and went on with the game as if nothing had happened.' Such wonderful sang-froid was unusual. Most girls put appearance before performance, though the more competitive ladies gradually liberated themselves from the athletic idiocy of their garments. Lottie Dod, 'the little wonder' of tennis, who won Wimbledon in 1887 when she was only fifteen, was permitted to wear a simple calf-length school-dress where mature women were not expected to show their ankles. Lottie Dod seemed to lose interest in tennis after winning easily for several years. She was a brilliant all-round sportswoman— a hockey international, a champion golfer, and archer amongst other accomplishments—who complained about the restrictiveness of tennis wear for women without risking her reputation with truly 'rational dress', although she did insist on a cricket cap rather than the usual straw boater.[52]

Men gradually came to accept female sport, provided its frontiers were carefully marked out. Herbert Chipp, the first secretary of the Lawn Tennis Association, put it like this:

Among the manifold changes and consequent uprootings or prejudices which the latter half of this century has witnessed, nothing has been more characteristic of the new order of things than the active participation of women in its sports and pastimes . . . Lawn tennis must claim a large share of the responsibility for the introduction of this new regime. But whether for better or worse, whether we disapprove with our grandmothers or approve with our daughters, times have changed, and we have to accept facts as we find them. And although the present movement may be (and undoubtedly is) carried to excess, and the athleticism of the *fin de siècle* woman appears too pronounced, still it cannot be denied that on the whole the changes which have been brought about must ultimately prove beneficial to the race at large—at all events physically. Whether the benefit will be as great morally . . . only time can settle.

No such masculine equivocation surrounded women's cricket or football teams. They were laughed at, scoffed out of existence.

---

[52] P. Cunnington and A. Marsfield, *English Costumes for Sports and Outdoor Recreation* (1969), p. 92; Ponting, 'Lawn Tennis', pp. 76–9.

Ladies had played cricket in Victorian country-house games and there had been an 'Original English Lady Cricketers' touring team in 1890, which drew large crowds to see well-bred ladies play under assumed names. But the side disbanded at the end of the season. Lady cricketers were regarded as engaging oddities. It was not until 1926 that some old school friends, who gathered at Malvern for a game between Cheltenham Ladies' College and Malvern School for boys, formed the nucleus of the Women's Cricket Association; a magazine was set up, a cricket festival begun, and some county grounds made their facilities available on occasion. But the sport was restricted to former pupils of public schools and there were probably no more than fifty active women's clubs. Only hockey was able to establish itself as a credible team-sport for women. The All-England Women's Hockey Association was formed in 1895 after hockey had been introduced as an exclusive winter game for men at Blackheath and refined in 1874 by the Teddington Cricket Club. The Hockey Association, formed in 1886, was initially confined to wealthy suburban London clubs along with Trinity College, Cambridge. This meant that ladies could take up a game that had achieved social respectability but was not yet widely known as a specifically male sport. Ladies' hockey was bedevilled with problems about proper clothing, the desirability of competitive play, and public admission. Yet solid progress was made.[53]

Athletics had a firm following amongst the social élite, especially at Oxford or Cambridge, but its failure amongst public schoolgirls was significant and predictable. Appearing scantily clad in public in a sport which was cheap and therefore open to lower-class participation was regarded as quite unsuitable for girls from 'good homes'. Nor did the working man take a more enlightened view of his daughter becoming an athlete. Female participation in the Olympics was largely restricted to figure-skating and equestrian events before 1914. In 1902 de Coubertin declared that athletics for women was 'against the laws of nature' and maintained this position throughout his life. As late as 1935 he wrote, 'I personally am against the participation of women in public competition . . . At the Olympics their primary role

[53] Ponting, 'Lawn Tennis', pp. 76–7; J. Bale, *Sport and Place* (1982), p. 89; J. A. Cuddon, *The Macmillan Dictionary of Sport and Games* (1980), pp. 411–12.

should be like the ancient tournaments—the crowning of victors with the laurels.' In 1936 one of de Coubertin's successors as president of the International Olympic Committee, the American Avery Brundage, bluntly confessed that he was 'fed up to the ears with women as track and field competitors'. While the percentage of women competitors in the Olympics rose from 4.4 per cent in 1924 to 8.1 per cent in 1936, the range of athletic events remained severely restricted. Before 1948 there were only three track competitions for women, all under 100 metres (the 200 metres came in 1948, the 800 in 1960, the 400 in 1964, and the 1500 in 1972). A Women's Amateur Athletic Association was founded in 1922 composed mainly of lower middle-class and working-class girls, elementary schoolteachers, typists, and shop assistants. The slowness of progress in women's athletics in Britain at a time when ten Oxbridge men won track medals between 1920 and 1928 reveals the absence of a 'leisure class' of female athletes. Swimming was in a similar position. The well-to-do held themselves aloof. National events for women were held in Scotland from 1892 and in England from 1901 but they were very much the poor relation, consisting of only a minimal programme in comparison to men. The great advances in women's swimming came from abroad, especially from the west coast of the United States, where class taboos on female sporting activity were less stringent.[54]

In terms of day-to-day post-school participation, women's sport flourished only in the more affluent suburbs of the larger cities. In addition to tennis there was golf, which required even larger amounts of time and money to enjoy. A ladies' section was formed at St Andrews in 1867 and others followed in the next twenty years. The Ladies' Golf Union was founded in 1893 with Lady Margaret Scott its first champion followed later by Joyce Wethered, Lady Heathcoat-Amory, who was English champion five times between the wars. Gentry ladies were attracted to a game which was rather like taking a walk with friends around a country estate. P. G. Wodehouse had a good eye for this sort of thing with lovesick young chaps, clad in plus-fours, trailing in the wake of adorably tweedy examples of the 'New Woman'. Its pleasant parkland setting and moderate physical demands

[54] K. F. Dyer, *Catching up the Men* (1982), pp. 221, 127–9.

made golf the perfect sport for the middle-aged and middle class of both sexes. From a handful of courses outside Scotland there were around a thousand in Britain by 1914. Even in quiet rural areas golf began to spread. Five new clubs were formed in Somerset in the 1890s and there were twelve by 1910. The collapse of agricultural prices had made it possible to acquire the hundred or more acres of farmland required for a course without too much difficulty in the late nineteenth century but competition from inter-war housing estates changed the picture. Initially the cost had been easily within the reach of the committees of middle-class men, who had normally financed the purchase through the issue of debenture stock, i.e. capital loaned to a company (the club) upon which only interest was paid for a fixed period. Club subscriptions would cover interest payments while a larger sum was accumulated to pay off the long-term loans. Debentures provided an excellent financial means for those with small capital surpluses to acquire a share in a large piece of real estate, access to which would have been beyond their means as individuals. Builders began to see the potential for combining superior residential property with recreation. The golf club became the preferred embellishment of the high-class housing estate, where the 'nine-to-five' commuters could meet at the weekend. St George's Hill, Chipstead, and Edgware were among those founded in this way. Stanmore on the wealthy fringe of north London was originally part of the Gordon estate and the golf-course was designed for the enjoyment of friends of the family. But the restrictive aristocratic ethic quickly gave way to the self-governing and incorporated private club based upon the principle of shareholding and providing collective access to a landed style of life. What more appropriate structure and setting for 'the open élite' of modern England could there have been?[55]

Hence the importance of the club-house. In Scotland the course itself took priority over social facilities whereas in England almost the reverse seems to have been true. Leeds Golf Club spent £3,500 on new facilities in 1909 and this was modest in comparison to the £8,000 spent by Royal Liverpool in the 1890s; golf and

---

[55] J. Lowerson, 'Joint-stock Companies, Capital Formation and Suburban Leisure in England, 1880–1914', in Vamplew (ed.), *Economic History of Leisure*, p. 63; on Stanmore GC, personal communication from G. P. Glass, who is writing a history of the club.

country clubs around London began to spend very substantial amounts. Walton Heath was opened in 1904 at a cost of £30,000 and the Royal Automobile Club at Epsom, which included a golf-course, ran to £70,000. Lord Eldon's mansion at Shirley Park near Croydon was similarly transformed into an exclusive country club including a golf-course. John Lowerson has traced the occupations of over 400 directors of registered companies running golf clubs before 1914 and found 62 from a landed, church, or army background, 135 from the liberal professions, and 153 from commerce and industry with a further 50 white-collar or skilled tradesmen. This was a world governed by the broad swathe of the male 'middle-middle' and 'upper-middle' class with a fair sprinkling of blue blood and a nod in the direction of the petty bourgeoisie.[56]

Women were admitted to the world of golf in significant numbers with the proviso that a degree of internal segregation was accepted. Areas of the club were reserved for each sex and woe betide the woman who wandered accidentally into the men's bar—that a woman might *intentionally* cross the threshold was too preposterous to contemplate. The ladies had their own 'section' and most clubs would not permit the few women with shares to vote or hold office. However, unlike the members of the artisans' sections, which were formed to raise income and give manual workers restricted access to the sport without diluting the social tone, women were separate but equal in status to the men. There was no shortage of middle-class women with time to spare. There were 1.3 million domestic servants in 1931. During weekdays ladies might outnumber the men at the club with bridge, whist, and afternoon tea as alternatives to trudging around the course. Suburban woman, armed with a 'daily' and new labour-saving machines, was a lady of some leisure who might reasonably aspire to break a 100. Golf offered a kind of half-shared, half-segregated suburban activity rather like the bourgeois family in which a strict division of labour coexisted with an emphasis on the companionship of the couple. More importantly, golf fostered a new kind of community life in the suburbs. As Walter Besant wrote in 1909, the suburbs 'have developed a social life of their own; they have their theatres, they have their lawn tennis clubs, they have their bicycle clubs'.

[56] Lowerson, 'Joint-stock Companies', p. 69.

In the Home Counties, in particular, the golf club helped consolidate the new routines of suburban life. Its trees, fairways, and greens epitomized *rus in urbe*. Calling in at 'the club' for tea or a drink after the shopping or a drive in the car was part of a new middle-class style of life. These were the sort of people who patronized Mr Edwards's sports shop in inter-war Tunbridge Wells, beautifully evoked by Richard Cobb, where the owner, always in a blazer, attended to the sporting purchases of the wealthy inhabitants and gave golf and tennis lessons too.

He seemed incongruous standing behind the counter of his own shop; indeed, he was not *quite* a shopkeeper, certainly not *just* a shopkeeper . . . Mr Edwards looked like, and spoke like, a gentleman; but he wasn't one. However, he was very much in demand as a tennis coach even with mothers of young girls . . . Mr Edwards gave the appearance of being a free man, *l'homme disponible*, ever ready to step into the breach, and make up a fourth in mixed doubles. There were rumours, he was generally *disponible* for other games as well.[57]

So much attention has been paid to the structure and dissolution of working-class communities that the careful building of networks of neighbours, friends, and acquaintances within the supposedly private and individualistic world of the middle class has been overlooked. Tennis and golf clubs were worlds within worlds, business contacts and mutual reassurance for the reasonably well-off, islands of sociability within the unfathomable seas of domestic privacy. Comfortably ensconced behind a gin and tonic at the 'nineteenth hole' or lining up a vital putt in the monthly medal, the golfer could forget the troublesome outside world and settle down to enjoy his or her modest affluence. The Depression, the poor, wars and rumours of wars, the dispiriting progress of socialism were temporarily forgotten. And if one felt the urge to set the world to rights, there was never a shortage of orthodox political economists whose opinions on trade unionism or rising taxation were happily similar to one's own 'common-sense' view of things. In London, anti-Semitism, veiled but unmistakable, made up the nastiest of these topics of conversation. The ladies might add dinner-party recipes or the names of new hairdressers to the list. In golf, family membership and male sociability were not incompatible. The oft-derided lady

[57] R. Cobb, *Still Life* (1984), p. 141.

golfer, who played off 36 but rarely to it, may have been an embarrassment on the course, but she quietly built and maintained the links between middle-class families that lay at the heart of the commuting life. Such was the dense social network of the suburb in which sportswomen were so thoroughly and happily entangled.[58]

[58] M. Stacey, *Tradition and Change* (1970), ch. 5; see also M. Young and P. Willmott, *The Symmetrical Family* (1973), pp. 232–3.

3
Living in the City:
Working-class Communities

BY 1900 the scale of working-class involvement in organized sport was astounding. During the Edwardian period upwards of six million people a year paid to watch First Division professional football alone, and half a million or more played in leagues affiliated to the Football Association in England and Wales. Scotland was even keener with two professional divisions of its own and a thriving semi-professional 'junior league' for a population under five million. In Lancashire and Yorkshire it was not only Association football that caught on but rugby too. The founding clubs of the Northern Union (later to become the Rugby League), read like a roll-call of the strongholds of the Industrial revolution—towns like Oldham and Rochdale, Halifax and Huddersfield, Leeds and Wakefield. Rugby was established in the mining valleys of South Wales, becoming a popular symbol of a new sort of Welshness. County cricket was also followed with great interest by the inhabitants of the newly urbanized industrial centres, especially in the great conurbations of the West Midlands, South-east Lancashire, and West Yorkshire—all of which contained between one and two million inhabitants by 1881. Greater London with its huge population of nearly five million was already the home of cricket. Lord's and the Oval were the shrines of what was seen as the national game.

The unifying thread which runs through this vast and diverse world of popular sports is the idea that workers make their own culture rather than having their play organized for them or sold to them. For popular sports have often been seen as the product of initiatives from above that were imposed upon, or passively adopted by, those below. This 'diffusionist' view of popular culture needs close and critical scrutiny. Hence section 1 of this chapter deals with the intention of moral reformers to divert popular recreation into approved channels and the relative failure of their efforts to promote truly 'rational recreation'. This leads us into the culture of working-class sport itself and the kinds of sociability and identity which working men created through playing and watching sports. How did the male industrial working class come to terms with urban life and what role did sport have in this process? This is the central concern of sections 2 and 3 which deal with participation and spectating respectively. Here football as the most popular sport has a specially prominent place, particularly as the working-class forms of cricket and rugby have been singularly neglected by writers steeped in the traditions of southern amateur sport. As Chapter 1 revealed, there were important continuities between traditional and modern sports. Bowls, darts, billiards, fishing, pigeons, and dogs lie within this submerged world of sporting entertainment which is the subject of section 4. Finally, the urban–rural dimension must not be ignored. The city was growing and changing so fast that casual or frequent contact with rural life became increasingly difficult. The desire of workers, male and female, to reverse the process by combining physical recreation with a brief flight from the city provides the theme of the fifth and concluding section of this chapter.

1. RATIONAL RECREATION

Concern over the way the lower classes amused themselves became increasingly acute during the third quarter of the nineteenth century. While there were real efforts to stamp out deliberate cruelty to animals for the purposes of sport, there was little or no idea before the middle years of the nineteenth century of the positive benefits that might accrue from teaching the poor how to play. The very idea of a 'play discipline' would have seemed absurd, utopian in scope, and excessively intrusive, smacking too much of puritan 'enthusiasm' for the Hanoverian gentry. Yet this is what a growing band of bourgeois idealists advocated during the second half of the century. Sports were to play a major part alongside the provision of parks, museums, libraries, and baths in the creation of a healthy, moral, and orderly work-force. Reformers soon learned that homilies were not enough. In fact, the rational recreation movement—as these broadly linked initiatives came to be known—would hardly have been necessary if either the Established Church or the Nonconformist sects had been able to carry out effectively their former role of moral education. But they were not. The Anglican Church in particular increasingly lost touch with the millions who were born in the new industrial cities. The old controls no longer worked in the sprawling anonymity of the city where squire and parson could never exert the personal influence over church attendance they had done in the countryside. Even before the religious census of 1851 revealed that a large proportion of the new urban working class did not attend any sort of church, there had been something akin to a moral panic. The indifference of the town labourer to the Church (explicit atheism was still uncommon) became of pressing concern because of middle- and upper-class fears for political stability and the sanctity of property. As the textile towns of the industrial north grew at what seemed a crazy pace with the coal, steel, locomotive, shipbuilding, and machine-tool industries also expanding very fast, the world of the small workshop went into decline. Chartism, the movement for radical democracy, was born out of the sufferings of the old handicraft workers and the violent swings in the trade cycle that affected the new industrial economy in the 1830s and 1840s. Fear of urban radicalism, above all, was what galvanized the rich into thinking about the poor and gave weight to the wider programme of moral reform and education that was proposed by a vigorous minority of evangelicals and idealistic political economists. Attention was first concentrated on the cities of the north which were thought to house the most concentrated and potentially disruptive social forces. However, as these areas gradually settled down and built up a distinctive cultural life of their own, reformers came to be more concerned with the capital itself in an effort to separate the potentially respectable and stable workforce from the 'dangerous' classes of unskilled, casual labour so heavily concentrated in the East End.[1]

It is against this background that the diffusion of modern sports, especially football, needs to be understood. Although most sports

[1] J. M. Golby and A. W. Purdue, *The Civilisation of the Crowd* (1984), ch. 4, provides an up-to-date introduction to rational recreation, but Bailey's *Leisure and Class* remains the best case study. For London see G. Stedman-Jones, *Outcast London*, esp. the preface to the 1984 edn.

clubs rapidly developed along independent working-class lines, the intention of their founders was usually to promote rational recreation under middle-class control. Sport in this context is best understood alongside the wider movement to shape the values and behaviour of the next generation of men through youth clubs. 'Youth', by which commentators usually meant inner-city working-class boys, was defined as a 'social problem' towards the end of the nineteenth century and efforts were made to direct the energies of what came to be called 'adolescence' into acceptable channels. The traditional institutions of youth with their licensed revels had gone, and new forms of control were required. Although the primary aim of the Boys' Brigade, founded in Glasgow in 1883, was to bolster up the appeal of organized religion through offering uniforms and military-style training, sport soon came to play an important part in the strategy of counter-attraction. Boys were to be lured off the streets by the prospect of banging drums, blowing whistles, and kicking balls. As time passed the Boys' Brigade and the Church Lad's Brigade, along with the older paramilitary groups like the Volunteer Force or non-military initiatives such as the Young Men's Christian Association, all were drawn into the use of sport as an instrument of social discipline and a source of recruits. In Birmingham, about a quarter of football clubs and a fifth of cricket clubs were explicitly connected to religious organizations between 1870 and 1885. Aston Villa, founded by young men in a Wesleyan chapel in 1874, is perhaps the best known such club but Birmingham, Everton, Fulham, Bolton, and Barnsley were also originally church-based. However, careful recent research on religion and leisure in Birmingham has revealed that most of these sporting initiatives came from the ordinary church members rather than from the clergy. Anglican congregations, in particular, were enthusiastic, founding approximately two sports clubs for every one set up by the Nonconformists. Most games, after all, had long enjoyed the patronage of the Established Church, though the evangelical revival meant that a change of minister could easily lead to a new stand against frivolity. H. R. Peel, the Rector of Handsworth from 1860–73, was 'an ardent and skilful cricketer' who promoted sport in the Handsworth Working Men's Club but his successor, the Revd. W. Randall, appeared to have no interest whatsoever in sport. 'Muscular Christians' amongst the clergy were less common than many suppose.[2]

Although some working-class children shunned the discipline and pious rhetoric of these socio-religious groups, the prospect of playing games was attractive, especially as sports were not organized officially as part of elementary education until after 1906. An observer of the industrial north around the turn of the century noted that 'when play is organized for youths of a particular age it is common for those of a higher age to lie and cheat in order to join', not only to get a game but to make sure of winning as well. The state permitted elementary schoolchildren to be instructed in drill through the 1870 Education Act, although it did not require this. It was not until the 1902 Education Act that a wider programme of physical education was recommended and instruction in this for trainee teachers was made compulsory only in 1908. The result was that the working classes did not learn to play in school in the way that fee-paying pupils did. Military drill fleshed out with some general exercise was considered to be all that the ranks required. Outside of school hours, however, dedicated improvers of the young, whether sporting parsons or schoolmasters, often made efforts to organize games of football or cricket. 'Some among the many who take an interest in the young would be glad to give a few hours on a Saturday afternoon, for the purpose of organizing a game of football,' claimed the author of an 'open letter' to the Brighton School Board in 1882. 'As things now are a section of our disbanded army of youngsters prowls around the streets, especially about the market-place, eating rotten fruit and doing themselves no good in any way.' Eventually regular teachers became involved and this led to the formation of the Brighton Schools' Football Association in 1892.[3]

Efforts to encourage sport amongst working-class boys did not extend to allowing them to play casual games in the streets. Such

[2] J. R. Gillis, *Youth and History* (1981), ch. 3, esp. pp. 128-31; D. D. Molyneux, 'The Development of Physical Recreation in the Birmingham District, 1871-1892', MA thesis (Birmingham Univ., 1957), Appendices A and B; D. Reid, 'Labour, Leisure and Politics in Birmingham, c.1800-1875', Ph.D. thesis (Birmingham Univ., 1985), pp. 137-8.

[3] S. Meacham, *A Life Apart* (1977), p. 167; J. Lowerson and J. Myerscough, *Time to Spare in Victorian England* (1977), p. 122.

was the enthusiasm for football in the northern cities of
Edwardian England that 'in courts and alleys, on vacant plots of
land, on brick-fields, indeed on any open space at all that may
be found, attempts are made to play the game, even though the
football be but a bundle of tightly rolled up string-bound papers'.
What these boys were playing was too close to the older traditions
of casual street football for the liking of rational recreationalists.
Street football was generally forbidden and these regulations were
supposed to be enforced by the policeman on the beat. The battle
between the bobby and the local boys entered into the lore of
the street and was the source of lingering resentment against
authority. 'We used to have a policeman who used to stop us
playing football round the back wall,' recalled David Smith, who
had grown up in Edwardian Stepney. He and his mates liked to
kick around a ball of sawdust and rags until some dockers gave
them a proper ball. But 'when old Bloodnut come on . . . he
pinched our ball, and he knifed it, pierced it.' To which the boys
replied by stealing the heavy cape with which policemen would
inflict a painful clip on a youngster's ear ('He done our football,
we done his cape'). A Bristol boy had similar recriminations
against the police. 'I remember one Bank Holiday Monday I was
kicking a ball about in the street' when a little later 'a copper come
up to me and said "What's your name? . . . You've been round
here footballing." Anyway something was said and he hit me over
the head with the bloody truncheon . . . I was done for breach
of the peace, footballing in the street.' The police, however, were
fighting a losing battle. This, at least, seems to have been the case
in Leicester around the turn of the century. Writing to sympathize
with the author of an earlier letter protesting about street football,
a correspondent to the *Leicester Mercury*, who signed his or her
letter 'Orderly', complained that

in every street of the town nearly, we find these brainless youths
annoying peaceable citizens by indulging in this horse-play. I have
repeatedly seen people rushed against and nearly thrown down by this
latest form of street nuisance. Remonstrance is out of the question . . .
the streets seem to be handed over for anything in the evening . . . street
government seems to be in a very primitive form yet.

Offenders, according to this source, were simply cautioned
and went on playing football in the street. Street culture

was stronger than the ability of respectable opinion to control it.[4]

Inner-city boys, living out on the street for a good part of the time, naturally thought of it as their playground. The high birth-rate meant that Victorian Britain was a very young society with around a third of the population under fourteen, spilling out of their crowded homes and colonizing the roads and pavements with their noisy amusements. From their earliest years children played round the lamp-posts and back alleys carrying on the ancient chasing, catching, and racing games that were passed on over generations. Such games, as the Opies have shown, are still played today despite the traffic and the existence of so many alternative attractions. 'No one used to say anything to my knowledge,' recalled a Newcastle man, '[but] we would find ourselves playing marbles, then marbles would vanish and we would be playing with various-shaped tops and whips, or tops and string.' Boys graduated from leap-frog, blind-man's buff, and British bulldog (where one or more children try to stop others from crossing the street) to the games also played by adults like 'tipcat', a kind of primitive cross between rounders and cricket, where a piece of tapered wood about six inches long (the 'cat') was struck with a stick. This game was so popular in the streets of mid-nineteenth century London that *Punch* remarked 'this mania for playing at cat is no less absurd than it is dangerous, for it is a game at which nobody seems to win, and which, apparently has no other aim than the windows of the houses and the heads of the passers-by'. The writer clearly did not understand the game, but he did reflect the increasing middle-class intolerance of such activities. There was little that could be done to stop the poor turning their children out of doors, but street games obstructed traffic and damaged property.[5]

---

[4] D. Rubinstein, 'Sport and the Sociologist 1890–1914', *BJSH*, May 1984, p. 21 citing Charles E. B. Russell's *Social Problems of the North* (1913), p. 100; S. Humphries, *Hooligans or Rebels?* (1981), pp. 203–4; J. Maguire, 'Images of Manliness and Competing Way of Living in Late Victorian and Edwardian Britain', *BJSH*, Dec. 1986, p. 281.

[5] I. and P. Opie, *Children's Games in Street and Playground* (1984), esp. pp. 10–11; J. Walvin, 'Children's Pleasures', in J. K. Walton and J. Walvin (eds.), *Leisure in Britain 1780–1939* (1983), p. 236.

Compulsory schooling was, of course, the single most important means of taming the young and clearing the streets. Looking back fifty years, Helen Bosanquet was impressed by the new respectability of street life in 1891, concluding that 'perhaps the most striking difference with the London of today is the mass of neglected childhood'. The armies of Dickensian waifs and strays were much depleted by 1900. Yet school was often still perceived as an unwelcome and autocratic interference in the lives of the poor both by parents and by children themselves. Instead of the noisy variety of street play, children were forced to sit still without talking and given only a couple of hours a week of physical training. If they were lucky they might have a playground, but a report of 1895 showed that 25,000 children within a mile of Charing Cross had no facilities for play at all. Exercising was often done in the classroom and school-hall. Children were lined up and forced to bend or stretch at the command of drill sergeants, who toured the schools at sixpence a day and a penny-a-mile marching money. Small wonder that children would risk corporal punishment to vary the tedious routine. E. G. Holland recalled his drill class of 1877 in Highgate where the male pupils would enliven the proceedings 'by firing pieces of orange-peel at a line of military drums with a finger catapult. The "ping" or "pong" according to the size of the drum that was hit fully compensated for the dreariness of the lesson.' Children in Liverpool were drilled at elementary school from the 1860s. Drill was easy for teachers to master and the endless 'slow march, quick march, left turn, right turn' was thought both to inculcate discipline and to give basic military training. From the mid-1880s, however, there were efforts to provide sports for children, or, to be more accurate, for boys. The example of Brighton has already been cited. In 1886 the Liverpool and District Teachers' Committee began a football competition which was very successful and in the 1890s the finals were played at the Liverpool FC ground at Anfield. School sports were encouraged in the 1890s. In 1898 there were four gala school-sports days organized for Queen Victoria's jubilee with a total of 10,000 competitors.[6]

---

[6] Bosanquet cited in J. Walvin, *A Child's World* (1982), p. 149; P. C. McIntosh, *Physical Education in England* (1968), pp. 110, 119; R. Rees, 'The Development of Physical Recreation in Liverpool during the Nineteenth Century', MA thesis (Liverpool Univ., 1968), ch. 10.

Despite these efforts to provide organized games after school or at weekends, the impact of sport on the elementary educational system was fairly restricted. Children did not enjoy most of the exercises foisted on them at school and resented interference with their traditional play in the streets. Adult workers were similarly cautious about attempts from above to provide them with sports, especially when those efforts came from employers. Industrial recreation programmes were not very widespread, although several individual projects were quite ambitious and extensive in themselves. What was later to become West Ham Football Club grew out of the philanthropic industrial policy of A. F. Hills, an old Harrovian just down from Oxford and full of plans for class collaboration through sport. He inherited the huge Thames Ironworks and installed himself democratically in the East End from where he felt he could preach more effectively to his workers. A whole range of improving activities were introduced along with savings and profit-sharing schemes. A magnificent sports stadium was the centre-piece of his vision. The various sports clubs that were set up would 'crown the labours of the Works with the laurels of the road, the racing-track, the field and the public hall'. Similarly the management of the huge railway-works, which turned Crewe from a village of a few hundred to a company town of 40,000 by the end of the century, hoped that 'by encouraging young people in athletic pursuits they assisted to make them healthy and in that way tended to make them better workmen'. At Cadbury's model industrial community at Bournville, the benevolent despotism of George Cadbury required women workers to learn to swim (for cleanliness) and men in heavy jobs to do weight-lifting to protect them from industrial injury. Good sports facilities were provided as part of a company policy which 'rested on the importance of quick, well-executed work. Athletics and swimming, medical and dental care, proper breaks for meals and rest—all that helps to develop manual dexterity and visual awareness which are the commercial object.'[7]

[7] C. Korr, 'West Ham United and the Beginning of Professional Football in East London, 1895-1914', *Journal of Contemporary History*, April 1978; A. Redfern, 'Crewe', in Walton and Walvin (eds.), *Leisure in Britain*, p. 122; C. Crossley, 'Travail, loisir et vie communautaire en Angleterre au xixe siècle', in A. Daumard (ed.), *Oisiveté et loisirs dans les sociétés occidentales au xixe siècle* (1983), p. 27.

As a whole the socio-religious impulse declined at the end of the nineteenth century. Meller's study of Bristol, where there had been a powerful concentration of improving activity amongst high-minded Quaker employers, reveals the growth of commercial, morally neutral forms of amusement. A similar pattern of 'religion and voluntary association in crisis' is evident in Reading. In Crewe the London and North Western Railway Company refused to extend the swimming-baths it had provided in its philanthropic heyday and withdrew support for an eminently 'rational' plan to expand technical education. Part of the explanation for this new hesitancy to promote corporate leisure may in specific cases have stemmed from the collapse of economic optimism and the squeeze on profits that accompanied the Great Depression from the mid-1870s to the mid-1890s. But a change in attitude amongst second- and third-generation employers was probably more important. Firms were increasingly run by managers. Capitalists could still rail against the fecklessness of the poor but they now did so from the golf club bar and the suburban lawn. Comfort and leisure removed from the dirt and danger of the industrial classes was what large shareholders were looking for, and this is what they found in the plush resorts of the south coast or on the Côte d'Azur.[8]

Even for those who retained the desire to foster older middle-class values of thrift, sobriety, and respectability among the poor, the task usually turned out to be too much for them. They retreated in despair and disgust. This was particularly evident in sport, and came to a head over the question of professionalism. The object of encouraging sport amongst the working class was not, as A. F. Hills put it, to 'hire a team of gladiators, and bid them fight our football battles for us'. Similar conflicts arose with the formation of Crewe Alexandra FC as a professional team, and at Reading too. The *Guardian* considered the decision to legalize professionalism and the setting up of a professional Football League in 1888 as 'the beginning of the end of an important social movement'. 'Spectatorism', as it was contemptuously called by many gentlemen-amateurs, was the antithesis of 'sport'. It was perfectly acceptable for keen players to watch others playing for

---

[8] H. Meller, *Leisure and the Changing City, 1870–1914* (1976), pp. 237–41; also S. Yeo, *Religion and Voluntary Association in Crisis* (1976), ch. 7.

the love of it, but it was quite another matter for thousands of working-class youths and men to shout and swear, roaring their team on to victory by fair means or foul. Far from being 'rational' this was no more than mindless fanaticism, obstinate and arbitrary partisanship devoid of sense, morality, or self-restraint; little different in fact from the mobs that had baited bulls or carried the bladder of a pig from one end of the town to another. Was it for this that the old games had been revised and refined in the best schools in the land?[9]

Nor could those who had seen sport as a means of social improvement come to terms with it as a source of profit. The concentration of population into large units created a market for mass entertainment on a new and hitherto unprecedented commercial basis. Just as taverns with a tradition of singing were turned into music-halls with paid entertainers, so successful football teams were tempted to fence off their pitches and charge admission to the crowds that collected to watch them. This new market for commercialized leisure shocked men like the Revd. Henry Solly, who had set up the working-men's Club and Institute Union (CIU). First drink and then commercial entertainment were brought into the clubs. Paid singers and comedians were hired to entertain men who wanted to drink and laugh after work rather than listen to lectures on bridge-building, religion, or economics. The size of working-men's clubs grew, just as bigger music-halls and stadia were being built for sports. The values of the market-place undermined moral education in sport as in other forms of leisure.[10]

It was not only the diminishing numbers of idealistic employers or evangelicals who were disturbed by this. There was also a good deal of anxiety from the ranks of the educated, radical minority of the working class and in particular from middle-class socialists who had their own dreams of creating a more elevated 'high' culture for the masses. The rise of commercial amusement was met with dismay. For socialists it seemed as if a kind of trivial hedonism, an apathetic consumerism was gripping the people. Hence the common ground between high-Victorian advocates of

---

[9] C. Korr, 'West Ham United', p. 219; E. Dunning and K. Sheard, *Barbarians, Gentlemen and Players* (1979), p. 195.

[10] T. G. Ashplant, 'London Working Men's Clubs, 1875–1914', in S. and E. Yeo (eds.), *Popular Culture and Class Conflict*, pp. 248–62.

capitalist paradise and the seekers after a socialist utopia. Socialists feared the weakening of the 'membership mode' of popular leisure; that is to say, the idea that working people should run their own lives, devise their own amusements, and build a strong and autonomous culture that would be morally superior to commercialized entertainment. Just as the middle-class wave of moral reform was breaking up, the socialists took over the old vocabulary of decency and self-improvement for a new purpose. John Burns complained that 'the poor were rearing up a race of people who could and did applaud sport in which they could not indulge, as did the Greeks and Romans in their days of degeneration', whilst a contributor to *Justice* complained that 'sport like every other thing is demoralized and damned by capitalism'. It was the mixture of commercialism and passivity that most concerned such critics. Blatchford complained that on seaside holidays the people 'sit for hours huddled like sheep in a pen and gaze blankly at the sea', and there were no doubt plenty of socialists who thought the same about professional football matches. The radical ideal of good recreation was the simple outdoor life, walking the hills, thrashing out the problems of society whilst taking in the beauty of the natural world. Activists in the trade unions or in labour politics tended to adopt either a Fabian seriousness or to cultivate a nostalgia for the earlier intimacy and the radical culture of the workshop. Men like Alfred Williams, the Swindon railway-worker and collector of old ballads, felt that the new generation of workers would even abandon the solemn institution of the Sunday dinner to buy a ticket for a match on Saturday afternoon. Carving the joint, singing old songs, and fighting the good fight for social justice were being sacrificed for tawdry shows or fanatical contests stirring up workers of one town into an irrational resentment of another group of workers like themselves who just happened to live elsewhere and support another team. Socialists refused to accept commercial sport as an authentic element in working-class culture. It smacked too much of bread and circuses, of an evil design to distract the workers from the historic mission of the proletariat. Karl Kautsky, the pre-eminent German Marxist of the late nineteenth century, complained that as far as British workers were concerned 'the emancipation of their class appears to them as a foolish dream . . . it is football, boxing, horse-racing which move them the deepest and to which their entire leisure time, their individual powers, and their material means are devoted'. Unlike the Social Democratic Party, which had provided German workers with an uplifting and self-sufficient socialist world of music, festivals, and sports, the British Labour Movement was relatively detached from the culture of British labour.[11]

Trade unionists, moderate and revolutionary socialists all made some effort to move into the world of popular leisure between the wars, though these initiatives largely took the form of a kind of radicalized rational recreation—socialist hikes, Co-op rambles, and the like. For the most part left-wing intellectuals like George Orwell detested the crude nationalism and mindless partisanship of sport; they preferred the critique of 'bourgeois' literature to the celebration of football, boxing, or bowls. Rank-and-file union activists remained too deeply embedded within the culture of independence, self-improvement, and respectable domesticity to take much notice of organized sport. In Scotland the strong temperance element in the Labour Movement particularly disliked the association between spectator sport and drink. John Clarke, the Labour MP for Maryhill, opposed the socialist corporation's decision to allow the Kelvin Hall to be used for boxing because it drew together 'an army of bookies, touts, pimps, card-sharks, pickpockets, prostitutes and . . . usually winds up in an orgy of drunkenness, assault and battery'. Dog-racing, which became a major spectator sport between the wars, was similarly regarded by many socialists, who often had only slightly less contempt for professional football. Like the good Victorians who had brought them up, they preferred the playing of football to the watching of it and Scottish Labour leaders endorsed the setting up of a Socialist and Labour Football League in Glasgow in 1922. Whilst moderate socialists maintained the rational recreation tradition in a modest kind of way, the new British Communist Party in the 1920s attempted to politicize leisure explicitly. Yet the British

[11] C. Waters, 'Social Reformers, Socialists and the Opposition to the Commercialisation of Leisure in Late Victorian Britain', in W. Vamplew (ed.), *The Economic History of Leisure: Papers Presented to the Eighth International Economic History Congress, Budapest, August 1982* (1983); Dr J. D. Young kindly provided the reference from Karl Kautsky, *The Social Revolution* (Chicago, 1902), p. 102; on the leisure provisions of German socialism see V. L. Lidke, *The Alternative Culture* (1985).

Workers' Sports Federation, which successfully agitated for improved rights of way for walkers and against the banning of Sunday sport, according to an internal minute of 1931 had no more than ninety member-clubs, of which only nineteen bothered to pay their subscription. Sport was certainly never a priority for the Labour Movement between the wars. Those who thought about it at all distrusted the growth of commercialized leisure provision but they were powerless to do anything about it.[12]

2. THE LIFE OF THE STREET

Organized sport came to have a central place in the new world of urban industrial culture but the spirit of 'fair play' as advocated in the public schools had little influence on the way the working class played or watched their sport, and the strictures of socialists none at all. The pub and the street were the focal points for those who learned to play in the shadow of the factory or the mine. Reformers had hoped sport would drive men away from drink and several social studies suggested this might be so. Alcohol consumption statistics certainly reveal that really hard drinking was on the decline from the late nineteenth century. Yet the relationship is not straightforward. Social drinking associated with sport may have increased. Most sportsmen had their 'local', and the new generation of publicans seemed to have taken over the role of sporting enthusiasts with as much gusto as the alehouse and tavern-keepers of the past. This was a powerful source of continuity in popular culture. Boxers and professional footballers notoriously looked to the drink trade to give them a living when their fighting or playing days were over. Bowling-greens and boxing-rings were built on to pubs. Football clubs were sometimes organized from pubs. Football, rugby, and cricket were usually accompanied by a few pints afterwards.

Sport provided the main topic of conversation in what was the chief social institution of the male working class. N. L. Jackson observed that spectators would frequently 'adjourn to the

[12] I am grateful to William Knox for drawing my attention to pp. 38-41 of his *Scottish Labour Leaders, 1918-39* (1984); S. G. Jones, *Workers at Play* (1986), esp. chs. 6 and 7, provides the first authoritative survey of both the topic and the period.

"football pubs" to discuss the results of the latest match, or the prospect of the next'. Tom Causer, an English lightweight champion of the 1890s, was the hero of Bermondsey, taking over the management of the Eight Bells in 1898 and staying a publican for the rest of his life. His son recalled how boxing and drinking went naturally together with his father 'over the bar talking to his friends for hours about boxing. When the pub was shut, say, Sunday dinner-time . . . he used to have customers in there telling 'em all about his life story.' Prize-fighting had normally been organized by publicans and with the increased popularity of boxing with gloves in the last quarter of the century certain pubs became well known for putting on contests. Boxing came to take the place of the old animal baiting, the ratting, and the cock-fighting that had gone on in the upper rooms and the courtyards of innumerable alehouses until the middle years of the nineteenth century. The line between being an amateur and a professional was hazy when it came to pub contests. Fighting, after all, was part of pub culture and some of the matches were little more than regulated brawls, extensions of the street-fighting tradition that was so much a part of the world of the poorer working class. In Bermondsey, which produced six British champions between 1897 and 1914, it was common for boys to fix up fights in the street. The famous referee Harry Gibbs recalled 'one lad Wally Dorney coming round and knocking on our front door. He announced he had come to fight Siddie Gibbs. Now my elder brother was always the diplomat. "Sorry", he said, "I've not got the time just now but our Harry'll fight you." So I went out to do battle.' Life in the Glasgow Gorbals was even tougher. The roughness of the street-corner world was sharpened by the fierce sectarianism of the city. Benny Lynch, who became world flyweight champion in 1935, had his face slashed by a Protestant razor-gang when he was still a boy. He came from an infant school that nurtured three future champions apart from Lynch all within a few years of each other. Fighting was part of the lore of the street in slum areas and spilled over into more organized pub fights. This tradition of hardness will be more fully examined in the discussion of hooliganism in a later chapter. What is important for the moment is to note how strongly working-class society was rooted in the street and the pub. Even residential streets often had several pubs; one in the Gorbals had fourteen, but for the most part a single pub served a couple or more smallish streets and provided the basic unit of male social life.[13]

Pubs were a significant force in the rapid growth of football teams. As we have seen, charitable and religious bodies certainly made a contribution to the introduction of team-games, but the efforts of local people to run their own sides was much more important. Unfortunately, very little is known about the hundreds and thousands of teams that were formed by groups of lads on the street-corners or by neighbours and workmates. Mason points out that as early as 1879 there was a string of clubs in Blackburn which had grown up apparently through the formalizing of street-corner teams with names like Red Row Star, Gibraltar Street Rovers, Cleaver Street Rovers; sometimes localities were even more precisely and parochially defined as in the case of George Street West Rovers. Neil Tranter's research on sport in late nineteenth-century Stirling has revealed that 37 out of 68 football teams founded between 1876 and 1895 had neighbourhood names with five sides taking street names though closer examination revealed that 'Our Boys' and 'Stirling Hawthorn' were described in the press as 'Cowane Street' teams. In Birmingham the association game took off dramatically in the late 1870s and early 1880s. There were only around twelve organized clubs in 1875 but within five years this figure had risen to 155, 22 of which ran two or more teams. Of 218 football teams mentioned in the local press between 1876 and 1884, 84 had connections with organized religion, 13 were named after pubs, and 20 were works' teams. What is all too often overlooked because it presumably seems too obvious to mention is that the remainder were usually given the name of a particular place. Place-names, however, are more significant than they seem. They underline the sustaining role of the neighbourhood in sport; despite vast changes in the city itself, loyalty to a street or parish was deeply held. In this respect, the success of church clubs is significant. Church sports clubs have tended to be understood in terms of the improving motives of the muscular Christians. But the clergy's support for rational recreation may have been less

---

[13] J. Hutchinson, *The Football Industry* (1982), p. 27; S. Shipley, 'Tom Causer of Bermondsey', *History Workshop Journal*, Spring 1983, pp. 30, 35; J. Burrowes, *Benny* (1982), pp. 81–2.

important to club-members than the fact that sports had traditionally been run on a parish basis. Historically, the parish and the locality had been virtually synonymous. Residential solidarities of various sorts were no less important in cricket which had grown in Birmingham from the rather broader base of 69 clubs in 1871 to 214 in 1880; here 64 were church-based, 16 were pub teams, and 25 came from firms. Again most of the teams that were formed seemed to have been around the street or suburb, and the same was true of Liverpool where Rees counted a total of 148 cricket clubs in 1890, 61 of which had street- or place-names, while 30 were of church, 20 of works, and 18 of school origin. Of course, it is impossible to work out the precise basis of a club's composition from its name, as Jeremy Crump points out in his table of football-club origins in Leicester in 1893, which lists 16 church names, 2 works' clubs, 10 street or neighbourhood clubs along with 7 'others'. Historical imagination has to fill in the significance of scrappy data.[14]

What is more certain is that football lost its public school aura very rapidly. There was a marked increase in competitive league play in the early 1890s. There were 203 football clubs in Liverpool by 1890 and no less than thirteen local amateur leagues by the end of the century. This enormous increase in the number of working-class youths and men playing team-games led to severe pressure on a very scarce resource: the land itself. The National Playing Fields' Association was not created until the 1920s and during the nineteenth century clubs had either to buy or rent their pitches unless the municipality came to the rescue. Studies of Birmingham, Liverpool, and Glasgow have revealed a varying degree of enthusiasm for sport among local authorities. Parks had been laid out in the middle years of the century primarily as places to walk rather than places to play. Gradually by-laws forbidding organized games in public parks were amended and space was made available for the laying out of pitches, though demand always far exceeded supply. In Glasgow initial resistance on the part of the municipality gave way to fairly extensive provision

[14] T. Mason, *Association Football and English Society* (1980), p. 31; Tranter cited in R. Holt, 'Working Class Football and the City', *BJSH*, May 1986, p. 8; Molyneux, 'Development of Physical Recreation in the Birmingham District', appendices A and B; Rees, 'Development of Physical Recreation in Liverpool', p. 69; J. Crump, 'The Amusements of the People', Ph.D. thesis (Warwick Univ., 1985), p. 378.

for swimming, golf, and ball games in the public parks after 1890. In Liverpool cricket teams had been known to play before breakfast in order to get a pitch. By 1930 there were 172 football pitches and eighty-nine cricket fields provided by the municipality in Liverpool but, as the foundation of the National Playing Fields' Association in 1926 emphasized, there was still a serious shortage of space. Some of the thousands of youngsters who watched Liverpool or Everton might well have preferred to play themselves but lacked the opportunity. 'The youths who sit on office stools, or on the tail-boards of goods vans . . . yet feel an appetite for active recreation', remarked the Revd. Harry Jones in 1891, 'yet are deplorably ill-provided with opportunities for its satisfaction.' Publicans sometimes came to the rescue if there was open land adjoining their establishment. Newton Heath, which later became Manchester United, started in this way and Tottenham Hotspur were nurtured in their early years by the brewery which ran the White Hart and provided a ground in the lane running behind the pub. Church clubs had an advantage here. The Church of England, in particular, was a large landowner and was in a good position to ask for concessions from prominent local citizens in the form of the odd field for a game of football. Employers, as we saw, occasionally sponsored sport by providing facilities. Works' teams, for example, were very popular in the Crewe locomotive works, which provided twenty-seven out of thirty-nine clubs in the Crewe and District league in the 1912–13 season. But these clubs were run by the employees themselves with little or no support from the management. They found their own grounds and helped pay for them by holding dances and organizing outings. Such ventures are best seen as a development of artisan traditions of good-fellowship and community rather than part of a capitalist welfare system.[15]

The same can be said of rugby in South Wales. Mine-owners and iron-and-steel firms played only a small part in the spread of the sport amongst their workers. Individual instances of patronage apart, the phenomenal pace at which rugby spread

---

[15] P. Bilsborough, 'The Development of Sport in Glasgow 1850–1914', M.Litt. thesis (1983), ch. 5; see also Rees, 'Development of Physical Education in Liverpool', ch. 8; Redfern, 'Crewe', p. 129; J. Hutchinson, 'The Development of Professional Football, 1870–1914, with special emphasis on Scotland', important doctoral research kindly provided by the author.

through the valleys is the most eloquent testimony to the self-generating power of popular culture. For rugby largely lacked the support that the chapels gave to choral societies and had to rely on the natural enthusiasm of the waves of English and Irish immigrants as well as the native Welsh who were sucked in by dramatic economic expansion in the last quarter of the century. Rugby became a way of affirming a new kind of Welshness both distinct from the popular sporting tradition of England and from the old world of bardic culture and Welsh-speaking. A single valley might contain dozens of different teams. In the 1890s in Pontypool and district there were the Ironsides, the United Friends, Tranch Rovers, Garn and Varteg Pride, Cwmffrwdoer Rovers, Panteg Harlequins, Cwmbran Black Watch, Ponymoil Wanderers, Pontynewynydd Lilies of the Valley, Talywain Red Stars, Trosnant White Stars, Varteg Dark Blues, Panteg Artillery, Cwmbran Harriers, Cwmffrwdoer United, Abersychan Albion—and these were only some of the many local rugby teams. In the bigger centres there was the same mixture of work and street sides found in football. Swansea had clubs with names like Goat Street and East Side Rovers, while Llanelli had Gower Road and Prospect Place Rovers alongside explicitly works-centred teams like Wern Foundry and Copper Mills Rangers. Neighbourhood was all important in popular team-sports and altogether more important than in middle-class teams which might be composed of men who lived a fair distance from each other but shared ties of education, occupation, and status.[16]

Whether we look at rugby in the South Wales valleys or Association football in the northern textile towns, the sheer density of the network of local leagues and the speed with which they were set up are remarkable. This was not the achievement of well-intentioned middle-class reformers; it was the work of the members, of the people themselves. Playing team-sports was a way in which men created and sustained close-knit groups in the context of unprecedented urban upheaval. Joining a local team was never just a question of taking exercise. Exercise in itself was not something that young men who worked physically all day strictly required. But team-sports offered more than exercise; to be part of a team was to have friends, to share a sense of loyalty

[16] D. Smith and G. Williams, *Fields of Praise* (1980), pp. 11–12.

and struggle together, and to represent *your* street or workshop, *your* patch of territory. Representing the village or the guild had always been an important part of achieving full adult status for male youths and were deeply rooted in traditional forms of play. But what was to be done with a population which had been uprooted? How did a man make a new kind of life in a new environment? Communities are not just collections of individuals; the urban whole had to be more than the sum of its parts. A sense of meaning was not something that rational recreationalists could create for working-class youth, it was something they had to make for themselves. By taking up revised forms of the old games men and boys built a new life for themselves—re-creating something of the face-to-face intimacy and scale of village society. Teams gave a sense of belonging and a sense of pride; older rites of passage, which were increasingly lost as the apprenticeship system declined, were replaced by new kinds of male association.

Unfortunately, we know very little about the composition of these teams. They kept no records and did not attract the attention of journalists. All we can do is speculate that the young men, who joined a local team, may well have played alongside brothers or cousins; footballers were probably childhood playmates who graduated from street games to street teams, formalizing friendships through clubs, which would organize dances and outings, rather like the ancient 'bands of youth' with their 'captains' and licensed revels had once done. This, at least, was the way sports were played by my father and uncles in the respectable working-class world of Edwardian Tyneside. Neil Tranter has ingeniously checked the names of 1,800 sportsmen appearing in the press in the Stirling area against the census data for 1881 which gives the occupations of 982 of them. Football was by far the most popular game with about one-sixth of all males aged 15–44 belonging to a club (the next most popular game was cricket with one club per 215 males aged 15–44). Of 315 footballers whose occupation could be traced almost three-quarters came from skilled working-class occupations with only one in ten from unskilled labouring work. Cricket had a more even social distribution with a third coming from small business, clerical groups, the liberal professions, and the landed, though again the unskilled were under-represented, comprising only 6.8 per cent of the 177 cricketers traced. The extent to which it is possible to generalize from these findings about club composition in large industrial cities is uncertain, although research by the Sports Council since the 1960s confirms that participation in sport runs roughly in inverse proportion to occupational status.[17]

Team-sports provided emotional as well as physical rewards. Being in a team was to be 'one of the lads'; it gave warmth, simple shared values and objectives, and an endless source of banter. Tearing around, hurling yourself into tackles, sliding through the mud, and just pushing yourself through a hard and exhausting match was supremely worthwhile because it bound you to your side; even very fine individual players can rarely win a game by themselves. Pitches are too rough and confined, the tackling too hard, and the referees too lenient to encourage rank individualism. Football and rugby are collective experiences, and even cricket is essentially a team game, although it gives greater scope to individual bowling or batting talent than the winter ball games. Football as a game to play was successful not only because it was convenient and simple, and therefore well suited to the physical constraints of industrial cities and the timetable of factory life. The appeal of football was more than a matter of its adaptability. There were all sorts of other games that could be fitted into factory routine but none that could give the intense sense of belonging, of tired and thirsty solidarity, of shared triumph or consolation that the rugby and Association forms of football extended to those who wore the same colours on a Saturday afternoon. The size of the team—a dozen or so along with a few friends and supporters—provides the ideal blend of intimacy and variety. After a match a club could have a drink as a group, big enough to split up into a few adjoining tables yet small enough to share a joke together. As men grew older they eventually drifted away from the game. With the exception of the cheerful fanatics who wished for nothing more than to be allowed to run the line or race on to the pitch with a wet sponge once in a while, married men in their thirties presumably stopped playing; they moved on to less taxing sports like bowls, leaving behind the odd enthusiast to shout on the old side or pick the team, devising tactics in his own managerial fantasy world, or

[17] N. L. Tranter, 'The Social and Occupational Structure of Sport in Central Scotland during the Nineteenth Century', *IJHS*, Dec. 1987, pp. 302–3.

fixing up travelling arrangements and doing the paper work required by the local league. Such men, familiar figures to all who have watched amateur matches at the park, were the life-blood of football, the unsung comic heroes of so many cold Saturday afternoons; the 'boy-men' not of the public schools but of the people.

The working-men's club became the central focus of the social life of adult workmen. But as these clubs grew in size with an average membership of between 500 and 700 at the end of the century and some with several thousand members, loss of intimacy and friendliness came to be a problem. The clubs had started on a small scale but were increasingly becoming the major providers of commercial entertainment. 'I am among hundreds of men and yet I know no one' was how one man put it. One solution to this was the informal creation of 'sub-clubs' within the wider organization, and sport played an important part in this process. Differing sporting interests helped to break down the unwieldy numbers in big clubs into smaller, more sociable units. The St Pancras Club had rowing, cricket, and billiards and in 1884 organized boxing as a winter evening amusement. However, older sports like quoits and skittles continued to be popular and were better suited to team-play. Quoits had been a favourite pastime of the north-eastern miners and was also enjoyed in East Anglia, where there were numerous village leagues. In the south and west skittles was more popular and in 1900 an Amateur Skittles Association was formed in London. Both quoits and skittles, which had been so much a part of traditional village sports, were easily adapted to new forms of communal amusement in pubs and clubs. However, it was the ancient sport of bowling that was probably most important in the creation of friendly little clubs. The old sport of road or moor bowling, so beloved of Northumbrian miners, where men would see who could cover an agreed distance in the fewest throws, was suppressed as traffic increased at the end of the century and access to open spaces became more tightly regulated. Lawn or green bowling, however, was extremely popular both on the flat greens of the south and over the deliberately 'crowned', uneven surfaces of the north.[18]

[18] Ashplant, 'London Working Mens' Clubs', p. 248; on bowling and bowls generally see J. Arlott (ed.), *Oxford Companion to Sports and Games* (1976), pp. 77–92 and J. A. Cuddon, *The Macmillan Dictionary of Sport and Games* (1980), pp. 123–30.

Crown green bowling was a 'flat cap and false teeth' kind of sport, ignored by the rest of Britain but keenly followed in the mining and textile towns south of the Ribble and north of the Trent. Most pubs and clubs had their greens which were lovingly tended and whose individual variations were often the subject of years of studious observation and debate. Bowling was close-knit and convivial. At Cradley Heath near Birmingham the landlord of the Hand of Providence would send his son round to collect the sixpenny green-fee and take orders for drinks at the same time from those who would congregate on summer evenings for games in the local league. Bowling offered both an urban and a rural, an individual and collective aspect. It was played for the most part one against one but competitions were normally between different clubs whose rivalry could be as sharp, if more subdued, than rugby or football. Bowling remains at the heart of a half-forgotten world of popular sport nicely evoked in Brian Jackson's account of the working-class culture in Huddersfield in the 1950s and 1960s. Here the running of bowls had largely become a club activity as the pubs expanded to become more comfortable, less fiercely masculine places, and had built over their greens in the process. Municipal councils had done something to make good the loss, and in Huddersfield the council provided greens in the public parks that could be hired out. Interestingly this caused friction with the clubs who wanted 'to build around the green the familiar, interlocking cells of community. The official who turned out the lights at the presentation ceremony was implying, brusquely, that he didn't like the unfamiliar and inconvenient activities that grew around a plain municipal bowling-green.' Councils naturally saw their parks and greens as public places rather than as kinds of cultural property where habitual users had special rights.[19]

Just as northerners tended to prefer their own 'league' version of rugby to what they saw as the more effete and pretentious game of Rugby Union, so the crown green brigade tended to regard southern bowlers as snobs who lacked the skill to negotiate anything but a flat surface. Bowling in the south was certainly less uniformly proletarian. The Southampton Bowls Club claimed to date from the twelfth century and no less a middle-class hero

[19] B. Jackson, *Working Class Community* (1972), pp. 108–10.

than W. G. Grace was the first president of the English Bowling
Association in 1903. Bowlers made particularly careful
concessions to modern forms of organization, preserving their
old traditions in new county associations set up in the 1880s and
1890s. Lawn bowls was even adapted for indoor competition on
the urging of the ever enthusiastic Dr Grace. In Scotland, where
the rules of flat green bowling had first been formalized by a
Glasgow solicitor in 1849, the Edinburgh Winter Bowling
Association was set up in 1905. North of the border bowling, like
the more culturally distinctive curling and golf, may have
attracted a broader social mix including a substantial number of
skilled manual workers. Tranter has traced 111 bowlers in Stirling
of whom 60.5 per cent were clerical, farming, or small business
people and 27.9 per cent were skilled workers. In the south of
England bowling remained popular but still segregated by social
class as Stacey's well-known study of Banbury in the 1950s
reveals. The middle class had their Chestnuts club and the clerks,
shopkeepers, and manual workers their Borough Bowls and
British Legion club. Although both shared broadly Conservative
and Anglican affiliations and permitted limited mobility amongst
long-term residents, the broad social distance between their
members was maintained.[20]

In a survey of Sheffield in 1889 the Medical Officer of Health
remarked that the city 'more closely resembles a village than a
town, for over wide areas each person appears to be acquainted
with every other, and to be interested with that other's concerns'.
Within the city a complex network of informal friendship and
of club membership helped humanize the industrial landscape. The
working class preferred to take part in sport at this level rather
than joining a club beyond the familiar frontiers of the street, the
pub, and the local church. The immediate locality, along with
the working-men's club which was part of it, was the setting for
the thousands of teams which turned the thriving life of the street
corner with its gangs and games into more permanent competitive
channels. Playmates became team-mates, playing in clubs which
more or less formalized the gangs or youth groups of the street.
Even when working people got away from home, they did so

---

[20] Tranter, 'Social and Occupational Structure of Organised Sport in Central
Scotland', p. 302; M. Stacey, *Tradition and Change* (1970), p. 86.

collectively and often took their sports with them. Trips to the seaside were an escape from the physical environment rather than the human one, from neighbourhood rather than neighbours. During the Oldham Wakes Blackpool became 'Oldham by the sea' as whole streets moved into boarding-houses close to each other, playing and drinking together much as they did at home. Sports both reflected and reinforced this building up of intimate communities within the city. The new professional football clubs with their thousands of spectators, however, created a different and more extensive kind of community. What was the nature and appeal of this second level of popular involvement in sport?[21]

3. SPECTATING AND CIVIC PRIDE

Popular as the playing of sport became, the watching of it was probably even more popular. Every large city had its football, cricket, or rugby ground; many had several huge stadia, and even small industrial towns often had a permanent semi-professional team in their midst. The towering brick walls, the clanking turnstiles, the peeling match posters, and the cries of street-corner programme-sellers are ingrained in working-class life. But what do we know more precisely about the men—for it was overwhelmingly a masculine event—who filled the row upon row of terraces which were so oddly empty for all but a few hours on a Saturday?

Watching professional football appears to have been rather more popular amongst skilled workers than with the unskilled, especially if we classify as skilled the million or more miners, who were probably keener on sport than any other group of workers and for the most part earned higher wages than the unskilled. Tony Mason has weighed the scanty evidence carefully but unfortunately there is only one hard statistic available and this comes from a peculiar and macabre source: the Ibrox disaster of 1902 when twenty-five were killed and over 500 injured after a stand collapsed. Of the 249 casualties whose occupations were

---

[21] P. J. Waller, *Town, City and Nation* (1983), p. 76; J. K. Walton and R. Poole, 'The Lancashire Wakes', in R. Storch (ed.), *Popular Culture and Custom* (1982), p. 113.

identified there were 166 skilled workers and fifty-three unskilled, but the relatively high cost of admission (a shilling), the nature of the fixture itself (an international match), and the difficulty in categorizing some of the occupations all urge caution when it comes to drawing firm conclusions about the nature of the crowd from this evidence. What is not in doubt is that the broad swathe of more or less skilled workers could certainly afford to watch football. Sixpence a week was manageable for those in regular employment but it was more than the casual worker or the unemployed man could easily afford. References to cyclical unemployment causing a fall in attendances crop up from time to time. The Pilgrim Trust, which carried out a careful investigation of the effects of long-term unemployment in Liverpool in the 1930s, noted the wretched spectacle of men on the dole silently lining the streets and watching those in work make their way to the game. The precise nature of working-class representation remains unclear, and the same is true of the age structure of the crowd. Contemporaries could not agree on whether watching football was more popular with the old or with the young. Again the only definite evidence comes from the Ibrox disaster when most of the victims were found to be in their twenties and thirties with a fair sprinkling of those in their forties, but local games may well have attracted a wider age-span. As the game became more popular and the Wanderers and Old Etonians yielded to the might of the Lancashire mill-towns, football came to be seen as vulgar and not quite respectable for the bulk of the middle classes. And yet football was never an entirely working-class sport. All clubs had reserved seating accommodation and this kind of price segregation guaranteed the continued presence of small business men and retailers. The educated professions and bigger business men, however, were normally restricted to the directors' box. If the coverage given to professional football by *The Times* before 1914 is anything to go by, the best people had scant regard for the game except as a relic of happier days when it was the preserve of Old Etonians and a few other ancient public schools.[22]

By the mid-1890s the newly formed Football League had firmly established itself, expanding from the initial twelve to sixteen

---

[22] Mason, *Association Football*, pp. 154–7, 148; C. Andrew, 'Football Crazy', *Listener*, 10 June 1982, p. 7.

clubs and attracting around two million spectators through the turnstiles; this figure shot up to six million by the season 1905–6. Professional football had become the major form of male entertainment in Britain. What made so many men pay to stand for a couple of hours on cold grey afternoons, unprotected from the rain and the wind, without proper toilets or refreshments, and herded together like cattle? What was it about football which exerted so strong a pull on all those faces in crowd photographs, the odd bowler amidst the rows of flat caps, heads wreathed in the smoke of Woodbines and wrapped in mufflers? Explanations fall into two kinds: those which focus on the special qualities of the game itself and those which emphasize the changing character of the working class. Was there something unique about football, or was its success no more than a product of the evident need for entertainment in the new urban world? These different approaches need not be mutually incompatible. Looking for a single cause of the success of football is unwise and unnecessary. A synthesis of the structure of the game and the context in which it developed show how the two elements acted together to sustain and reinforce its massive appeal.

Many of those who watched professional football must have played the game themselves, although how many is hard to say. This was one of the most remarkable aspects of the spectacle. Persons attending theatres or concerts for the most part do not act or play instruments, but it seems reasonable to suggest that from about 1900 onwards many football supporters had either kicked a ball around with their friends or perhaps even played in one of the thousands of local teams. The weekly number of spectators, which probably varied between 300,000 and 400,000 in Edwardian England, was not so far removed from the number of registered amateur players. Presumably, those in amateur leagues, who played on Saturday afternoons, graduated to the terraces as they got older. The chance to watch others do what you had tried to do yourself was very tempting. Football crowds loved to denigrate the talents of professionals in favour of their own. 'I could've wafted it wi' my cap', moaned many a portly spectator when a forward missed a difficult chance. Listening to the catcalls, of course, was all part of the fun and particularly noisy supporters would get to be known by players and by other spectators. After the noisy rebukes and the collective head-shaking that would go on when the home side missed a goal, quieter and wiser counsels of 'old hands' might be heard above the din muttering that the ball was greasy, the marking tight, or the goalkeeper well-positioned. Watching football involved a kind of unspoken dialogue between the rational assessment of the strengths and tactics of each side and a fierce loyalty to one of the two teams. Spectating was certainly a more intelligent activity than middle-class observers were willing to concede. However, to say that men watched football because they had played the game and understood it still begs the question. What was there about football that proved so irresistible whether as a game to play or as a popular spectacle?

There was definitely a marked and rapid transformation in the style of play. The best teams of the 1870s and early 1880s adopted a cavalier approach concentrating on individual flair and all-out attack, which suited the public school style and spirit. But this kind of play was quickly replaced by the careful balance between defence and attack, and the smooth movement between the two that can only be produced by long and short passing between players. Soon these methods, which were first introduced by the Lancashire teams, were widely accepted. A clear division of labour emerged between the defence whose job was to mark the dangerous attacking players of the opposing team, the half-backs who had to fetch and carry the ball between defence and attack, and the forwards themselves. Forward play involved a subtle blending of skill and strength with wingers to provide pace pulling the defence wide and crossing the ball accurately in the path of the central goal-scoring players. Football very quickly assumed what is broadly speaking its present form. Watching football required the spectator to see how the team was playing as a unit as well as how individuals fulfilled their particular role within it.[23]

Marxist theorists like Rigauer have seen the emergence of this modern form of play and its subsequent elaboration as an analogue of industrial capitalism itself. The division of labour within a team was rather like the specialization of skills that went into the production of iron and steel or, perhaps more appropriately,

---

[23] J. Walvin, *The People's Game* (1975), pp. 70–4; for a fuller discussion of styles of play see Mason, *Association Football*, ch. 7.

the manufacturing of machinery. Teams had to have their hard men, the centre-halves who could give and take 'a bit of stick' and the lumbering full-back who could clear his lines. 'Give it some shoe, lad', the crowds would shout at a defender under pressure. The defence had to work together while the mid-field was where sheer energy, the ability to work, to get through prodigious amounts of running were most important. Forwards, however, had to have skill; they had to be able to do the unexpected, to pop up unmarked or turn suddenly and shoot from an acute angle; they needed the vision to run into open spaces, to make themselves available for a pass, and most importantly to hold the ball at their feet twisting, feinting, and then accelerating past a defender. The crowds loved a forward to take on a back and leave him lunging in the mud—a Steve Bloomer or a Billy Meredith—but it was the overall team performance that mattered most at the end of the day. Football reporters often used industrial analogies in their match reports; teams were like 'well-oiled machines', men had legs like 'pistons', or were 'dynamos' with 'sledge-hammer' shots. The capacity to work hard, to take punishment, and to play your required role in the team performance were the qualities the crowds looked for and, it is argued, an appreciation of such high levels of team performance and specialization was particularly well-developed in those whose working lives were dominated by similar considerations.[24]

As skilled workers were probably the largest group of spectators, the question arises as to the nature of the connection between the kind of talents required at work and those which were displayed in sport. Can we make a link between the de-skilling of industrial work, which from the late nineteenth century onwards was tending to turn craftsmen into machine-minders, and appreciation of skill in sport? Despite trades like shipbuilding, which remained very much the preserve of the time-served tradesman, the twentieth century has seen the rise of new industries and the technological rationalization of old ones. Wage differentials based on skill have had to be enforced by union militancy rather than by the logic of the market itself. The degree

[24] B. Rigauer, *Sport and Work* (1981), offers a theory but no historical evidence.

to which sport fostered judgement and admiration for physical dexterity that no longer found a privileged place at work is a notoriously tricky issue. Historical evidence is unavailable, and to assert in the face of this that leisure was either a 'compensation' for the mechanizing of work or an 'extension' of work skills poses the problem too simply and arbitrarily. The great variety of sports themselves and the different forms in which each could be practised whether as a keen or casual competitor, a regular or occasional spectator, defy easy analysis.

Clearly some of the more traditional sports, especially those involving the breeding of animals, had firm roots in artisan custom. Watching football, however, may have been more attractive as a competitive than as a craft-based display of skill. Skilful players were certainly appreciated but at heart, as a West Bromwich and England winger of the 1890s later remarked in his capacity as sporting publican and club director, the crowd go 'to see a stern fight between keen rivals, and if their chosen side happens to win I don't know if they care much beyond that'. If football was primarily about winning matches rather than admiring individual skill, can it then be argued that the capitalist work-ethic was reinforced by competition at play? It is easy to show that a crudely manipulative 'bread and circuses' approach does not make sense, but to suggest that in their recreation workers insidiously learned to accept 'the rules of the game' in sport and in life, is a more complex proposition. Did workers 'internalize the conditions of their own subordination' in the cumbersome language of neo-Marxism by learning from sport that competition, nationalism, and aggression were just part of human nature? Such notions, subtle or otherwise, run into serious difficulties. At bottom, this kind of approach involves what are no more than assertions about the 'inner meaning' of sport, which it is assumed the working class will absorb in whole or in part. But can football as a spectacle or sport as a whole be reduced to such crude terms? And even if it were plausible to simplify its meaning in this way, how do we know the message was understood? Social control may have existed as a motive in the minds of some employers, but they were few and their influence on their workers seems to have been restricted to say the least.[25]

[25] S. Wagg, *The Football World* (1984), p. 10. J. Hargreaves, *Sport, Power and Culture* (1986), provides the most thorough case for a 'hegemonic' understanding of sport.

Far more convincing is the view that sports were very much an area of free expression and cultural independence. Working men made their own culture, as Edward Thompson and others have insisted, even if they did not do so 'in conditions of their own making'—to borrow Marx's celebrated formulation. They shaped so-called élite sports in their own image and according to their own values and traditions. Football crowds were no blank sheet upon which 'the ruling class' could write. Nor were football matches purely commercial events foisted upon a passive proletariat. Culturally, spectators were just as much 'members' as 'customers' of League football clubs. Workers were not dumb, credulous creatures, easily manipulated by politicians and profiteers. Rather than imposing the competitive principle through play, it may well be that the workers *sought* outlets for competition which were not available at work. As McKibbin has intriguingly suggested, the very high level of informal shop-floor control by workers in British industry meant that in their day-to-day lives men did not learn to compete so much as to co-operate. Competitive productivity within and between firms was something managers naturally hankered after but rarely achieved. In reality, men in the large firms which became the norm in British industry set their own quirky, humane rules on how the job was to be done, obstinately imposing arbitrary lines of demarcation and refusing to compete with one another in a way that would make work less bearable and drive out the older man who still needed to make a living. There is perhaps a stronger case for saying professional football provided a competitive edge to a co-operative life than in seeing the League championship as the apotheosis of capitalist values. The plain truth is that we do not know how football was culturally related to work. The game has no agreed 'essence', no single or uncontested meaning which can be explained in terms of work. The best we can do is suggest a range of insights which may have had an influence on different groups of workers at different times.[26]

Whatever its inner meanings, spectator sport must still be set within the changing material conditions of the working classes.

---

[26] The most sophisticated theoretical use of Marxism to analyse the meanings of sport is R. Gruneau, *Class, Sports and Social Development* (1983). On informal control of workplace see R. McKibbin, 'Work and Hobbies in Britain, 1850–1950', in J. Winter (ed.), *The Working Class in Modern Britain* (1983).

All too often this amounts to no more than a nod in the direction of shorter hours and rising incomes. Economic historians of sport perhaps inevitably tend to over-simplify the issue, which they see in terms of the creation of a new market for leisure industries amongst urban workers who had lost touch with the culture of their forebears and not yet created one of their own. It is not so much that this view is wrong—although football was a poor investment in financial terms for most directors of clubs—it is more a question of failing to get to the heart of the matter. The crucial question is less 'Why was there a rapid growth of commercial entertainment in the later nineteenth century?' than 'Why did this specific form of sporting activity have so great an appeal to this social group?' It is certainly true that the provision of the Saturday half-day for skilled workers in the 1860s and 1870s and for large numbers of the unskilled from the later 1880s explains the *timing* of matches, but it does not explain why it was football rather than some other game or even a completely different leisure activity that was so popular. Similarly, there is no doubt that the general improvement in real wages for urban manual workers, ranging from around a quarter to over a third in more skilled trades during the formative decades of Association football, speeded up the process of commercial specialization that created the professional Football League. But why were so many prepared to pay their sixpence to watch in the first place? The mere possession of small weekly surpluses cannot explain the manner in which that money was spent any more than the spread of an urban rail-network can in itself account for the use which was made of it on Saturday afternoons. Time, money, and mobility may have been necessary conditions for the rise of professional football but they are hardly sufficient ones. It is not enough to say that football just happened to be easily adapted to new circumstances and leave it at that.

Possibly more central to explaining the success of football in terms of the wider transformation of society was the process of urbanization itself. Of the twelve teams that formed the Football League in 1888 all came from towns of over 80,000 except Accrington and Burnley. Whatever its 'rational' attraction or its suitability in terms of time and space required, the supreme appeal of football lay almost certainly in its expression of a sense of civic pride and identity. The massive expansion in the scale and size of urban communities in the second half of the nineteenth century created new problems of identity for their inhabitants. Despite the success of professional football in a few smaller industrial towns like Darwen, which was probably the first team to hire professional players (Love and Suter, the 'Scotch Professors' from Partick), professional football was essentially a big-city phenomenon. There were thirty-six towns of over 100,000 in 1911 in Great Britain and almost all of them had professional teams. In essence, football clubs provided a new focus for collective urban leisure in industrial towns or cities that were no longer integrated communities gathered around a handful of mines or mills. The urban population was dispersed over a wider area and further segregated into working-class and middle-class suburbs. Cities were made up of dozens of sub-communities. As far as *playing* football or cricket was concerned, the neighbourhood was all important. But the inhabitants of streets were also the citizens of new cities, which were on an altogether different scale from the towns of the early Industrial Revolution. They were members of larger administrative, political, and economic units; and these in turn were integral parts of a nation of forty million and of a great Empire, as the popular press constantly emphasized. These inhabitants of big cities needed a cultural expression of their urbanism which went beyond the immediate ties of kin and locality. A need for rootedness as well as excitement is what seems most evident in the behaviour of football crowds.

The problem was how a new urban identity could be made real. When Blackburn was a town of a mere 30,000 or so in the first half of the century 'to belong' to Blackburn was a rather more straightforward proposition than at the end of the century when it had nearly 130,000 inhabitants. This was even more evident in the case of giants of the industrial revolution like Liverpool, Manchester, Glasgow, and, of course, London itself. The shift from living close to work to commuting on the bus or train was becoming commonplace. In 1905 the LCC estimated that 820,000 working men made extensive journeys to work in London and this same pattern was repeated on a smaller scale elsewhere. At the same historical moment as this upsurge of urbanization was leading to the knitting together of hitherto separate towns into huge conurbations in South-east Lancashire, West Yorkshire,

Clydeside, and Tyneside, important changes in working-class attitudes were taking place. While most men remained entrenched in their immediate localities, they also became more aware than ever before of the national dimension to their lives. The press, the railway, and the ballot all contributed to widening working-class horizons, while changes in the structure and strategy of business led trade unions to expand rapidly from the 1880s onwards often on the basis of nation-wide agreements. Literacy and the rise of Labour helped to bring about a shift away from the more purely localized and restricted preoccupations of earlier generations. When picking the British trade unionist most representative of his members, Eric Hobsbawm chose Herbert Smith, the flat-capped miners' leader who combined being a national figure with an unshakeable attachment to Barnsley FC.[27]

Professional football helped flesh out a distinctive sense of place within the wider framework of national competition. By following the progress of your team within the national league you could assert your membership of the city; it gave you something to belong to and something in common with thousands of other men. When you went to the pub in the evening you might have travelled a few miles from work. You might not know other men from your work-place, so you could not always exchange gossip about the shop-floor. But football, and to a lesser extent other sports like cricket and boxing, were an endless source of argument and banter. 'The best you can say for football', wrote a Glaswegian critic, 'is that it has given the working man a subject for conversation.' The novelist is better placed to capture the feeling of a football crowd than the social scientist, though few creative writers have concerned themselves with the game. J. B. Priestley is the honourable exception, and in *The Good Companions* he pinned down the spirit of northern football better than most:

It turned you into a member of a new community, all brothers together for an hour and a half, for not only had you escaped from the clanking machinery of this lesser life, from work, wages, rent, doles, sick-pay, insurance-cards, nagging wives, ailing children, bad bosses, idle workmen, but you had escaped with most of your mates and your neighbours, with half the town, and there you were, cheering together, thumping one

[27]   E. Hobsbawm, *Worlds of Labour* (1984), ch. 11, esp. pp. 202, 212.

another on the shoulders, swopping judgements like lords of the earth, having pushed your way through a turnstile into another and altogether more splendid kind of life . . . It offered you more than a shilling's worth of material for talk during the rest of the week. A man who had missed the last home match of 't United', had to enter social life on tiptoe in Bruddersford.

As two of Priestley's characters chew over a poor match on the way home, Jim says to Jess,

'Yon new centre forward they've getton—MacDermott or whatever he calls hissen—he'll nivver be owt, nivver. He was like a great lass on t'job. And what did they pay for him? Wer it two thahsand pahnd? . . . Watson were worth twenty on 'im—ah like the lad if they'd let him alone. An then they go and get this MacDermott and pay two thahsand pahnd for him to kick t' ball ower top.' Jim lit his yellow monster of a pipe and puffed away with an air of great satisfaction. He had obviously found a topic that would carry him comfortably through that evening, in the tap room of the Hare and Hounds, the next morning in the East Bruddersford Working Men's Club and possibly Sunday, Monday and Tuesday nights.[28]

Of course, in the largest cities it was normally not realistic to confine support to a single team. Both the market and the motive for the running of two or more clubs were there. In Liverpool, Manchester, Edinburgh, Birmingham, Dundee, and Nottingham there were two teams and usually several more near by. In Glasgow there were half a dozen clubs as there were in Edwardian London. Clubs were spread around the big cities drawing on geographically well-demarcated areas for their support such as West Ham United enjoyed in the East End of London. As the population grew and the conurbations spread, the need to define that part of the city to which you belonged became more acute. To a certain extent this had always gone on as the role of football in the inter-parish conflicts of the pre-industrial city revealed. The conflicts of rival clubs in the same city in a sense took those deep-seated traditions and regulated them in accordance with the new conditions of urban life and a wider national consciousness. Hence the enormous crowds for local derby matches as teams and their rival communities of supporters battled for who was

---

[28] J. H. Muir, *Glasgow in 1901* (1901), p. 193; I am grateful to Dr J. D. Young for this reference. J. B. Priestley, *The Good Companions* (1929), pp. 4–7.

to rule the locality both in a sporting and in a wider symbolic sense.

The largest football crowds were often found in Glasgow, where a huge influx of Catholic Irish into the mines of Lanarkshire and the factories of Glasgow was balanced by Protestant migration from within Scotland itself, topped up around the turn of the century by the movement of militantly anti-Catholic Orangemen from Ulster into the shipyards of the Clyde. Glasgow can claim to have been the first and most fanatical footballing city in Britain. There were half a dozen professional teams in the city itself and even more in the surrounding industrial and mining communities. But these strictly local loyalties were dwarfed by the enormous support for Celtic with its openly Irish nationalist sympathies and Rangers with their fierce anti-catholicism and support for the cause of Ulster. Rangers and Celtic were two tribes in which territorial loyalties were widened into religious and political ones, so that there were plenty of Scots who in effect supported two teams: their local team and either one or the other of 'The Old Firm', who, as the term suggests, profited considerably from their mutual antagonism. Late Saturday afternoons in Glasgow were ruled by 'fitba supporters new back frae their gem', often travelling in horse-drawn brakes organized by small groups of fans and roaring 'obloquy and ridicule at any rival club whose brake may pass theirs'. Of course, the fanaticism of this new social type—the supporter—was observed south of the border too. Sport had become too serious. The modern working man had lost touch with the old self-improving traditions; 'politics, religion, the fates of empires and governments, the interest of life and death itself must all yield to the supreme fascination and excitement of football.'[29]

The role of sport in promoting and expressing these urban loyalties is most apparent in the reception given to teams winning a major trophy. When Preston won the FA Cup in 1889, the town took to the streets in an intense and spontaneous celebration of welcome with a crowd of 30,000 surrounding the station and a band playing 'See the Conquering Hero Comes'. 'Around the

---

[29] Muir, *Glasgow in 1901*, p. 184. Bill Murray's *The Old Firm* (1984) provides an extensive analysis of Rangers and Celtic. Rubinstein, 'Sport and the Sociologist', p. 20 for a survey of Edwardian social observation of sport.

team swarmed hundreds of fanatics, each of whom struggled to get a handshake with some member of the team.' When the trophy itself was revealed ('the bit of silver plate') 'the wildest enthusiasm prevailed. Hats were thrown up, handkerchiefs waved, and sticks flourished' and thus the huge and excited entourage made its way to the town hall where the team would be formally thanked for the distinction and celebrity they had brought the town. Similar scenes greeted Tottenham Hotspur in 1901 after they had won the Cup in a replay against a Sheffield United side containing a couple of the best players in the country—'Fatty' Foulke, the twenty-two-stone England goal-keeper who could punch a ball almost to the half-way line and the outstanding mid-field player of the age, 'Nudger' Needham. It mattered little to the huge crowd that gathered after midnight at Tottenham station that their side was composed of five Scots, two Welshmen, an Irishman, and three northerners. It was the territory of the crowd not the players that counted. No southern team had won the Cup since the Old Etonians. The birthplace of the players was of little significance to the crowds that blew horns, threw confetti, and chanted snatches of popular songs changing the words to celebrate the team. 'There were so many people, so tight together, you could have walked on their heads', was how one report put it. Many of them returned to White Hart Lane the following night to watch an animated picture show in honour of the victory. Similar instances of communal revelry could be multiplied dozens of times up and down the country. On a smaller scale those early bastions of industrialization in south Lancashire and in north and west Yorkshire, which clung to Rugby League, were the scene of more intimate celebrations. Richard Hoggart recalled the Hunslet club bringing home the national trophy in the 1930s 'into the heart of the district on top of a charabanc. They went from pub to pub in all the neigh-bourhood's main streets, with free drinks at every point, followed by crowds of lads prepared to risk staying out hours after their bedtime for the excitement of seeing their local champions.'[30]

Professional football embodied the ambiguities of modern urban life perhaps better than any other single social

---

[30] D. Morris, *The Soccer Tribe* (1981), p. 111; B. Butler, *The Giant Killers* (1982), ch. 2; R. Hoggart, *The Uses of Literary* (1958), pp. 108–10.

phenomenon. On the one hand it sustained a sense of belonging; on the other those who represented the legions of supporters were often not local at all. They were 'mercenaries'—as the indignant élite of amateurs were inclined to label the new breed of professionals. Frequently players came from far afield and a thriving transfer market was soon established. Yet lack of local players did not stop Spurs' supporters celebrating the winning of the Cup, and most Geordies or Scousers were happy enough to have outsiders playing for them provided the team was successful. So players who often had no organic ties with their club were given the collective task of bringing glory to the birthplace of their supporters. In the search for new kinds of solidarity and new forms of social life to give shape and meaning to an industrial civilization, football proved to be a potent source of masculine cohesion. In a world where industrial production and urban life had cut loose from the more intimate and human scale of the past—where factories employed thousands of men and cities housed hundreds of thousands—supporting a football club offered a reassuring feeling of being a part of something even if the crowd itself were for the great part strangers to one another. Supporters achieved symbolic citizenship. Through regular encounters with other clubs, the members of a crowd in a sense found out who they were. By supporting one side against teams representing different towns, men were constantly affirming and defining their own pride of place. Hence the cultural as well as the commercial importance of the league system.

So far, so good; but this kind of blind territorial affiliation must not be pushed too far. Crowds were not unconditionally loyal and support for a side could vary according to its playing success. This seems to have happened in Edwardian Leicester where Leicester Fosse had a core of committed fans running into several thousand and a further body of less loyal supporters who would come when the side was winning but fell away when the team was losing and star players were sold. Football cannot be explained in terms of territory *alone*. That is not the purpose of my argument. Bound together with the sense of urban community there was the sheer excitement and beauty of the thing—the perfect pass that suddenly switches the play from end to end, the shuffle and swerve that turns a defence and sends a winger away with the time to cross to a centre-forward tearing past his marker, the sudden reflex movement of a goalkeeper twisting and diving full-length to save a fierce shot. In the end these moments are instinctive and aesthetic, beyond social and historical analysis.[31]

Sport was a kind of subtle and ubiquitous male language, a bond between husbands whose wives had their own world of neighbours and relatives. Women ran the family; men had their place within the household, but the house was not *their* space. Interfused with the ideas of territory, grace, and drama was an ideal masculinity. Professional football was about 'maleness' rather than 'manliness'. The working class imbued sport with a masculine value-system of their own which differed markedly from the manly Christian ideal. Football enshrined older forms of toughness and rudeness, which stoutly resisted the 'civilizing process' of fair play and sportsmanship. Although the conduct of the crowd was quite orderly by earlier standards, they happily transgressed the 'limits of decent partisanship' in terms of middle-class standards of language, gesture, and style.[32]

The team symbolized the men who supported it. Its characteristics were their characteristics, its virtues their virtues. What the anthropologist Clifford Geertz has said about Indonesian cock-fighting could cautiously be applied to football: if a cock-fight is a kind of 'deep play' in which a people see their individual and collective values expressed—'a story people tell themselves about themselves'—so regular matches played at the same time, in the same place, by the same rules, in a sense set out infinite variations of the same story. Football was like a mirror that reflected back the image the crowd wanted to see. It was a celebration of intensely male values: 'grit' was the great virtue, in the north especially, but there was also sticking at the task, persisting, and never letting your mates down even if you were injured or dropping with tiredness. In a way football was like a saga where skill and cunning were valued but hardness, stamina, courage, and loyalty were even more important. Fairness and good manners were not held in high regard. The crowd, of

[31] Crump, 'Amusements of the People', Ph.D. thesis (Warwick Univ., 1985), p. 392.
[32] Maguire, 'Images of Manliness', contains some useful evidence of rowdiness; see also Holt, 'Working Class Football', for festive traditions.

course, often displayed these attitudes in their own behaviour. Supporters never accepted the notion that the contest should be confined to the pitch. As early as 1876 a game between Queen's Park and Vale of Leven involved 'yelling, hooting and calling out to the players' as well as 'coarse and vulgar pleasantries'. Football was 'a man's game'.[33]

The middle-class amateur told himself a different story. He had greater pretensions to being 'civilized'. He claimed to put less of a price on victory than the working classes for whom winning was all important. The middle-class sportsman saw himself as someone who could hold his passions in check and for whom the enjoyment of the game was more important than the result. Just as the middle class used spectator sports as one kind of flattering mirror, working-class men used them as another. Pursuing this 'reading' of football a bit further, both groups regarded the referee as a regrettable necessity, but for diametrically opposed reasons. The public school ideal was 'self-government' and respect for the rules in themselves; in an ideal world enforcement of rules should not be needed, but the next best thing was absolute and unquestioning acceptance of the referee's decision even if it was wrong. To refuse 'to walk' when given out or to appeal against a decision in rugby was the height of bad form; and even if you silently loathed the opposition you were expected to clap out the batsmen of the opposing team. For the working-class spectator, however, the referee was the enemy, the representative of authority, of 'Them' against 'Us'. If he gave a decision against a home side then woe betide his eyesight and his parentage. Hence the contempt of middle-class idealists for professional football. 'The game has become the British bull-fight and has made those that look at it as callous and brutal as any Spaniard', wrote a student of Glasgow life, adding that 'behind the referee's back everything is permitted'. The crowd was shamefully partisan. 'If an offence is committed by his own side the working man will not protest.' Indeed 'he will greet with a roar of delight some ungoverned brutality or clever, underhand trick, which, if practised on himself by a fellow-workman, he would resent until his dying day.' Claiming throw-ins or corners

---

[33] C. Geertz, 'Deep Play', *Daedalus*, Winter 1972; Bob Crampsey, *The Scottish Footballer* (1978), p. 19.

as a matter of course, regardless of what the player or spectator knew to have actually taken place was part of the game. Two linesmen as well as a referee were required for professional matches by 1898-9.[34]

Professional football in England was largely a northern game before 1914, and when their teams played clubs from the south their perception of the northerner as tough in comparison to the 'soft' southerner was at stake. Bitter local rivalries might be temporarily suspended in order to see that the hated Arsenal were sent back to London with their tail between their legs or that the North won the periodic representative match against the South. Southerners had to be shown what northern men were made of. When Swindon played Barnsley in the semi-final of the Cup in 1912 the star Swindon player, a theological student from Warminster College, H. J. Fleming, was mercilessly kicked from the moment the game began and was carried off injured. He did not play again for nearly a year. All this was done with the evident approval of the Barnsley crowd who jeered the young man who had compounded the crime of coming from the south by being middle class as well. 'To stop an opponent by maiming him is not football as understood in the south', complained the *Daily Express*, 'and it is certainly not "cricket".' With this, at least, the Barnsley miners with their cry of 'Gi' it some clog' would have been in full agreement.[35]

Even county cricket in the north was not quite 'cricket' in the south. Cricket was the English national sport in the sense that it was followed by the middle and the working classes, both in the north and the south. Although playing cricket was often more difficult for working-class boys, who could not afford proper equipment and did not have access to a pitch, it was still keenly followed as a spectator sport. An Edwardian observer of working-class Birmingham thought it strange that despite 'the comparatively small extent to which boys play the game, they nearly all take a great interest in County Cricket'. London youths similarly displayed a 'breathless and extravagant interest' in Surrey and 'the most amazing knowledge . . . of the personal appearance, character and moral weakness of each individual player'. County cricket, however, never made any concessions to the requirements

[34] Muir, *Glasgow in 1901*, p. 191.   [35] Butler, *Giant Killers*, pp. 51-60.

of the working class. County games were normally played during the week to allow amateur players to get away for the weekend. Hence the popularity of local professional leagues like the famous Lancashire League, which came into existence alongside professional football to suit the needs of the factory workers. These games could attract large crowds and produced some very fine players despite the contempt in which they were held by the grandees of the county game. As in professional football, local animosities were fierce and the crowds, which often ran to five or six thousand, could be as unruly as at a football match. The *Bacup Times* complained about the 'deplorable ill-spirit and ungovernable excitement' of the spectators in the Bacup–Haslingden matches in the 1870s. Yet the League game was more than a matter of parochial feuds. S. F. Barnes, the outstanding bowler of the Edwardian period with twenty-nine Test matches to his credit, played the bulk of his cricket in the Leagues. Nelson signed the great Australian fast bowler E. A. Macdonald in 1922 and paid him £700 a year; they later acquired the services of Learie Constantine from the West Indies, who stayed with them from 1929 to 1938, reputedly earning up to £1,000 a year. Learie Constantine came to love Lancashire and to be loved by the people of Nelson, who flocked to see him and the rest of their team. This was cricket as a community game. 'On any fine afternoon in the week there are three nets going . . . it is not surprising to have thirty to forty people practising and hundreds of people looking on estimating the form of the coming matches,' recalled Constantine. There were at least twenty-six matches a season timed to suit the mill-hands who finished on Saturdays before eleven and could 'get home, do a little shopping, have lunch and get down to cricket in good time for the start of the game' at two. There were even mid-week matches so that shop assistants, who worked on Saturdays, could watch the town's team from time to time. Here cricket was as neatly dovetailed into the needs of the people as football. The 'first-class' game sneered at the League form with its poor pitches and quick results. Batsmen had a hard time on this kind of wicket and county amateurs were not anxious to try their luck. The history of cricket, which has been very much in the hands of privileged MCC men, has ignored the importance of the League game. League cricket was 'second class'. Like the black baseball leagues in the

USA, League cricket ran a 'parallel system' of popular sport which is only now beginning to receive its due.[36]

County cricket never quite made the conquest of the north that it did of the south, although two of the greatest teams were northern. Lancashire and Yorkshire from their strongholds of Manchester and Leeds drew on the northern working class for the bulk of their support as did the new football teams and Rugby League sides. Yorkshire and Lancashire were formed within a year of each other in 1863 and 1864 respectively and the Roses match was the highlight of the summer months played at Bank Holiday before 20,000 or more. A deep sense of Lancastrian pride first inspired the young Neville Cardus as he grew up in one of the poorer parts of Manchester around the turn of the century. He always relished Roses matches 'spikey with antagonism . . . the old familiar occasion as it always was and always will be'. Yorkshire, in particular, who won the County Championship more often than any other side before 1914, were not given to rash gestures or dangerous declarations. Yorkshire cricket was based upon a particularly fierce sense of territory which still forbids the recruitment of players born outside the county. Wilfred Rhodes and George Herbert Hirst, both born in the Pennine industrial village of Kirkheaton in the 1870s, were the two greatest all-rounders of the age and both played for Yorkshire in its heyday. Hirst managed the double of a thousand runs and a hundred wickets fourteen times whilst Rhodes took over 4,000 wickets and made nearly 40,000 runs, moving up the England batting order from number eleven to number one in the process. Both were utterly devoted to Yorkshire. Regional chauvinism is a neglected aspect of Labour history. 'George Herbert', as Hirst was known locally, first played on the windy, stone-walled Kirkheaton pitch after leaving school at ten and Rhodes, born in a farm-cottage, lost his job on the railway for clocking off early to get to a Saturday afternoon match. Playing in the vigorous local leagues paved the way for a Yorkshire trial and for fame from the Dales to Scarborough, where the season would end with a

---

[36] McKibbin, 'Work and Hobbies in Britain', p. 133; K. A. Sandiford, 'English Cricket Crowds in the Victorian Age', *JSH*, Winter 1982, pp. 13–14; J. Hill, ' "First Class" Cricket and the Leagues', *IJHS*, May 1987 (see p. 72 for Constantine) and a further paper to be published in R. Holt (ed.), *Sport and the Working Class in Modern Britain* (MUP forthcoming).

'festival' of cricket. Lord Hawke, the captain, shored up the strong Yorkshire loyalty of his players with good wages and they rewarded him with a period of sustained success unmatched to this day. Yorkshire played to win, and if that meant a dour, stonewalling stand until the bowling of the opposition was blunted, then so be it. 'Teams of the North of England are not wholly to blame for playing the game in the rather inglorious way they frequently do play it', Cardus explained. 'So long as the public in this part of the world continues to hold the view that championship laurels are "worth while" at any price, the price will occasionally be stiff indeed.' The Boycott tradition goes back a long way; even in the early years of the County Championship there were complaints that cricket was 'becoming a matter of hard work'.[37]

By inverting the amateur maxim that the game itself was more important than the result, northern cricketers incurred the wrath of the southern establishment. 'Average mania is as fatal to cricket as trade unions are to commerce' as one indignant gentleman put it. Cricket reached a peculiarly English accommodation between the upper classes that ruled it and the mixture of middle- and working-class people who watched it. In principle cricket was based on the old institution of the county, though in practice this increasingly meant siting grounds in the most populous areas. Surrey played at the Kennington Oval rather than in the lush heartlands of Dorking or Guildford and Middlesex was to be found in St John's Wood. County teams might maintain a limited number of fixtures in smaller places, but the older idea of cricket as a movable feast was giving way to the commercial logic of the big ground. This was mainly for the benefit of the suburban middle classes, who increasingly took county memberships in the late nineteenth century. So it was in the leafy suburbs of the big cities that the counties made their new grounds. When Warwickshire moved to Birmingham in 1885 despite the protests of small county towns, they set up shop in Edgbaston and were rewarded with a rise in membership from a mere fifty-one county stalwarts in 1885 to 1,225 members in 1893. Working-class people could neither afford to become members of county clubs nor would

---

[37] N. Cardus, *The Roses Matches, 1919–39* (1982); A. A. Thomson, *Hirst and Rhodes* (1986), esp. pp. 28–9.

1 The last days of street football: Shrove Tuesday 1846 at Kingston upon Thames

2 Suppressing cruel sports: the police arresting cock-fighters in Great Windmill Street in April 1865

3 The persistence of old sports: Essex farm-hands playing quoits, c. 1900

4 Traditions of paternalism: the Master of the Hunt serving out presents at the Chertsey Workhouse, January 1914

5 Amateurism, the
Establishment, and
'the Doctor': the
Pavilion at Lord's
during the
Gentlemen vs.
Players match, 1891

6 The national game: a keen game of street cricket in London's East
End, probably 1920s

7 Sport and the Raj: maharajas mixing with Indian army officers in the Hyderabad Contingent polo team

8 Tennis as courtship: bright young things at the Queen's Club, 1918

9 'A good walk spoiled?': the pleasures of golfing at Ganton, 1913

10 'The good life': women joining in the hiking craze of the 1930s

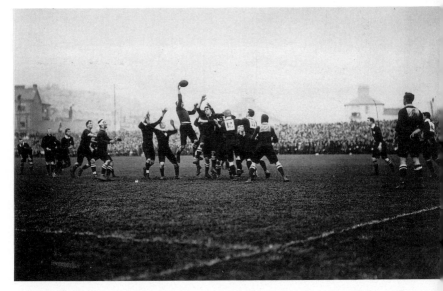

11 Sport and national identity: a passion for rugby shared by Wales and the Springboks, December 1906 at Swansea

12 The heyday of spectator sport: possibly the first Wembley Cup Final, 1923

13 The invention of sporting traditions: the England vs. Scotland game, Crystal Palace, 1905

14 Athletics in a mining village: risking a jump in the streets of Fryston, Yorkshire, *c.*1950

15 Miners and their greyhounds: Fryston, Yorkshire, *c.*1950

16 Darts as an outdoor sport: a competition on Tyneside, 1938

they have been socially acceptable. That the working classes maintained such an interest when little or no attempt was made to make cricket more attractive to them is remarkable. Yet by 1900 most of the sixteen first-class counties could expect to play to crowds that rarely fell much below 10,000 and sometimes rose to 25,000. Lord's could hold 30,000 spectators by the end of the century and was quite often full to capacity. In 1892 around 100,000 people, spread over three days, watched the popular Nottingham vs. Surrey game and the arrival of the Australians on the scene generated great interest, especially when they played the northern counties. The best part of 40,000 turned up to watch Yorkshire play the Australians in 1902. If county cricket made few concessions to the working class, it did peg its prices. It cost the same to go to a football match lasting an hour and a half as to attend a cricket match for the entire day. The only trouble was that you might have to lose a day's pay in the process. No wonder cricket for the working classes was partly a holiday entertainment whereas football provided the staple diet of popular sports for most of the year.[38]

4. GAMBLING, ANIMALS, AND PUB SPORTS

There was a particular cluster of popular sporting activities that middle-class society either ignored or attacked. These were sports which in one way or another involved gambling. The fact that most forms of betting were illegal make such activities even harder to explore. Yet no survey of popular sport would be complete without taking account of a time-honoured interest in animals and making wagers. Horse-racing is the best place to start as it attracted more interest and adverse criticism than any other form of working-class gambling. Off-course betting had been outlawed in an act of 1853 and remained illegal until 1960. Once the battle against animal-baiting and cock-fighting had been won, social reformers and evangelicals turned their attention to the rooting out of the ancient custom of staking money on a contest

---

[38] C. Brookes, *English Cricket* (1978), p. 117; Molyneux, 'Development of Physical Recreation in Birmingham', pp. 90–1; Sandiford, 'English Cricket Crowds', p. 6.

of uncertain outcome. Risking small incomes was dangerous and gaining money without effort was wrong. Those imbued with the ethic of work and thrift certainly disapproved of the sums wagered by the aristocracy. But the power of the House of Lords and the fact that those with large amounts of surplus income could hardly be prevented by law from wasting it meant that all gambling could not be stopped. Instead there was a selective ban which applied to those who could neither afford to attend horse-races in person nor were accepted as credit customers by turf accountants. What frightened Victorian reformers was not so much the ruin of the aristocracy as the fact that the railway, the telegraph, and the popular press would combine to cause an enormous increase in betting. Instead of going to the races once or twice a year, or gambling on the occasional prize-fight or athletic contest, improved communications would permit a whole new industry to arise which would encourage and profit from habitual gambling.[39]

This caused alarm not only to evangelicals but also to those with a vision of modest material progress for the common man. Artisan radicals and socialists were as outspoken in their criticism of gambling as they were of drink. The two were often linked in the minds of reformers as twin evils feeding off each other in a culture of misery and sloth that dragged decent men into crime and vice. These lurid visions usually had little to do with the reality of betting and were fed by the very illegality that was forced upon bookmakers and ordinary gamblers. With the prohibition of pub betting and the publican's fear of the Licensing Committee, gambling moved out on to the streets. What ensued became part of the lore of working-class life, a ritual game of cat-and-mouse. Bobbies chased bookies as respectable opinion demanded a periodic crack-down on the fecklessness of the poor. Bookmakers employed look-outs to warn of the arrival of the police and runners to take the money and give out betting-slips. Every street would have someone touting for trade or a man who made a few bob taking bets from his mates at work. The sale of sporting papers rose enormously. Before the later nineteenth century there had been no newspapers catering for popular gambling on horse-racing but from the 1880s the *Sportsman*, the

---

[39] W. Vamplew, *The Turf* (1976), provides a sound general history.

Sporting Life, and the *Sporting Chronicle* were all selling over 300,000 copies a day. The mass press permitted the publication of starting prices and the provision of much more detailed information about the runners. The amount spent on illegal off-course betting is by its very nature extremely difficult to assess but estimates rose as high as £400 million per year by the inter-war years. In an 'average working-class area' of Glasgow, a bookmaker told the Select Committee on Betting Duty in 1923, around £300 a day was taken by six bookmakers working twelve tenement closes. A survey of 1951 found that no less than 44 per cent of the adult population bet on horses, though many of these gamblers would confine their interest to a flutter on the Derby or the Grand National.[40]

Horse-racing is possibly the best example of a sport that remained very exclusive in social terms but also had a huge popular following. The railway and the newspaper meant the lower classes could keep up their well-established enthusiasm for holiday racing, and the building of a substantial number of enclosed courses, starting in 1875 with Sandown Park, much extended the calendar of events. Many of those present probably came from among the poorer urban groups as the bulk of middle class opinion and some skilled urban workers tended to frown upon the sport with its connotations of crime and dissipation. As Wray Vamplew neatly puts it, 'we do not know how many spectators at race-meetings nutritionally could not afford to be there'. Despite the success of the enclosed courses, it was the Whitsun saturnalia of Derby Day that epitomized popular fascination with racing and the strong sense of continuity that it imparted to popular sport. As many as a quarter of a million Londoners and others were drawn to the Epsom Downs with its card-sharps and fortune-tellers, prostitutes and tipsters by the hundred. The Derby was the great day out for the capital and not a tenth of those who came can have had much chance of actually seeing the race. But this hardly mattered. There was the prospect of a drink, a 'flutter', and a glimpse of the rich and the high-born. Some old habits lingered on into the brave new world of regular racing. Glasgow prostitutes would make a special trip

[40] R. McKibbin, 'Working Class Gambling in Britain 1880–1939', *Past and Present*, Feb. 1979, pp. 152–5.

to the Musselburgh races and their sisters from the east would
go west when there was racing at Ayr. But cock-fights and the
bare-knuckle fighting that had formerly accompanied the races
were decisively suppressed by enclosure. The racing calendar
linked to hiring fairs and country festivals was in decline. Racing
was now the sport of punters who rarely saw a race.[41]

For those who found it difficult to accumulate capital, who
were a prey to lay-offs, accidents, and illness it is hardly surprising
that gambling was popular. The chance of a small windfall was
a source of hope as well as amusement. Viewed from this
perspective, as McKibbin points out, the popular passion for
gambling which the middle classes found so perplexing and
distasteful makes much more sense. Most working people did not
believe it was possible to save enough to really improve their lives.
The effort required would just make a hard life worse. Popular
culture was more concerned with the present than the future—
the main thing was getting by, staying cheerful, and joining in.
Working people who refused to 'have a go' on a sweepstake might
be considered mean. There was a strong belief in luck as well as
in calculation, and this was the kind of thing that encouraged
street-corner games of pitch-and-toss. Pitch-and-toss 'schools'
were extremely common, often run by local bookmakers who
would employ a 'hard man', perhaps a small-time boxer, to keep
an eye on proceedings. This was how Benny Lynch's manager,
Sammy Wilson, got a start as a bookmaker in the streets of
Glasgow. Dwarfing these little ventures, of course, was the
growth of the football pools. Betting on the results of individual
matches had gone on from the beginning, and like the wagers
made on runners or boxers there was a good deal of careful
calculation involved. But once a system of betting on the results
of a whole series of games was introduced the element of skill
was lost. The football pools were often won by someone picking
out the draws with a pin or by writing down birthdays or bus
numbers. The simplicity of the idea created a huge potential
market which in turn offered the prospect of enormous prizes
for a very small stake. It was the provincial newspapers that first
promoted this form of betting, though specialized companies
soon moved in. A survey carried out in Liverpool in 1907 showed

[41] Vamplew, *The Turf*, pp. 41–2, 137; M. Wynn Jones, *The Derby* (1979).

that nearly 80,000 coupons were collected in a single week. Filling in a football coupon was part of the ordinary working-class way of life between the wars when it was estimated that around ten million took part. Not to do the pools was thought a bit odd, especially amongst men who were forever moaning about their luck or mulling over next week's forecast. This reached almost obsessional proportions during the Depression. The *Investor's Chronicle* estimated that pools expenditure rose from £10 million to £40 million between 1934 and 1938.[42]

The anti-gambling lobby naturally tended to lump together all forms of gambling as foolish and dangerous. A Select Committee of the House of Lords looked into the matter in 1903 and recommended the stiffening of fines for loitering for the purpose of betting and these were enacted in the Street Betting Act of 1906. What most critics failed to understand, however, was that most was done for small stakes on a controlled weekly basis. The availability of 'sporting intelligence' allowed the punter to think carefully about the horses he was going to back and make a calculation based on the horse's past form, the jockey, the course, the going, and maybe even the trainer or the owner. Such complex calculations were the subject of endless private cogitation and group discussion at work. Very few were shrewd enough to win regularly, and for the most part all the bookmaker had to do was to wait for the punter to make a mistake. But this is not really the point. Picking winners for small weekly stakes gave working men a rare opportunity to exercise their judgement. Families were rarely ruined in this way, although middle-class critics persisted in asserting without proper evidence that they were. No doubt there was needless distress, but there was also the occasional windfall. Nevertheless public libraries still persisted in pasting out the racing news before allowing the public, especially the unemployed, to read the papers. Lady Bell, in her famous survey of the life of the workers in her husband's iron-and-steel works in Middlesborough, was much exercised with the problem of gambling. Despite the exaggerated fears that run through her account, her description of men awaiting the results

[42] Burrowes, *Benny*, pp. 82-3; Mason, *Association Football*, pp. 181-5; *Investor's Chronicle and Money Market Review*, 8 Jan. 1938, cited in S. Jones, 'The Economic Aspects of Association Football in England, 1918-39', *BJSH*, Dec. 1984, p. 295.

of a race evokes the popular passion for betting as vividly as any
punter could wish:

> I have the picture in my mind of a winter's day, when the huge, cumbrous
> ferry boat, which plies across the Tees, taking the men backwards and
> forwards from their work, was going slowly back in the late afternoon
> with the toilers who had finished their day's work. As it reached the
> shore some other men going across to the works from the town were
> waiting to board it, among them a man of about sixty carrying his bag
> of tools in one hand and the evening paper in the other. He stood facing
> the crowd, as, with one question on their eager faces, they jostled across
> the gangway. And in one word he gave them their answer, the word
> they were waiting for—the name of a horse. It ran through the crowd
> like the flash of a torch, lighting up all the faces with a nervous
> excitement; and it seemed to the onlooker that there was not a man there
> whom that name did not vitally concern.[43]

Of course, there had always been other sorts of gambling,
particularly on the outcome of athletic events. When the Amateur
Athletic Association became more firmly established as the
dominant body in athletics, it adopted a high moral tone and a
tough line on betting. Several athletes entering events under false
names were prosecuted and subsequently imprisoned in the
1880s, although it was not until the stiffening of the law in 1906
that the AAA could exclude bookmakers from their events. Arthur
Wharton, the black son of a Wesleyan minister from the Gold
Coast, became the first man to run an AAA's hundred yards in
ten seconds in 1883. But how could a poor immigrant resist the
chance to earn substantial amounts by subsequently taking on
professional challengers? Amateurism in its pure form was
impossible for a man like Wharton, who also played for several
professional football teams and tried his hand as a racing cyclist
as well. A lively, if largely forgotten, tradition of professional
athletics survived in the twentieth century, although magistrates
were often unfriendly. In Northumberland the commercial
'sporting-grounds' of the common people—the Victoria Grounds,
the Fenham Park Grounds, the Gateshead Borough Gardens, and
the Bedlington and Killingworth grounds patronized by miners—
were closed down after prosecutions for illegal gambling in
1875-6. In 1887 the Lillie Bridge stadium in Fulham, which was

[43] Lady (Florence) Bell, *At the Works* (1969), pp. 263-4.

used for professional events, was burned down. Angry punters had gone on the rampage after a race between two top sprinters was abandoned 'because, it was said, the competitors and their managers were unable to agree which of them should win'. Powderhall in Edinburgh has maintained an unbroken tradition of running professional handicaps since it was built in 1869. Large crowds of up to 10,000 were common for the weekly races. The famous New Year sprint over 130 yards, where the top runners frequently carried thousands of pounds of backers' money, was a major sports event, attracting a record crowd of 17,000 in 1909. The speed of professional sprinters was cultivated in secret training sessions and subject to all manner of spying and speculation. Professional times were faster than the best amateur performances. The vitality of athletics as a popular gambling sport has been overlooked because of the subsequent national and international success of the AAA and the Olympics. The Olympic Games, especially the London Games of 1908, glorified the amateur athlete as a symbol of British prowess in the world. British manhood had to be seen to triumph both physically and morally on the world stage, and thus the old professional tradition was pushed to the sidelines. Like professional League cricket or the Rugby League, professional athletics were never accepted amongst the middle and upper classes, who set the rules concerning what was morally acceptable for the nation in sporting matters.[44]

The most significant development of professional sport for gambling purposes in the twentieth century was greyhound-racing. The matching of greyhounds for speed and killing ability was an ancient sport and much in favour with nineteenth-century gentlemen who formed the National Coursing Club in 1858 to regulate competition between the largely aristocratic clubs like the Swaffam Club, the Altcar Club, and several others. Huge crowds came to see the Waterloo Cup held each February on the Sefton Estates at Altcar near Liverpool, which was in essence an open national championship for greyhounds. The success of such events provides an important reminder of the adaptability and

[44] A. Metcalfe, 'Organised Sport in the Mining Communities', *Victorian Studies*, Summer 1982, p. 14; P. Lovesey, *The Official Centenary History of the Amateur Athletic Association* (1979), p. 43; *Oxford Companion*, p. 24. On Arthur Wharton see *West Africa*, 3 June 1985. I owe this reference to Dr R. C. C. Law.

appeal of country sports to industrial workers as well as farm-labourers and landowners. An attempt to adapt coursing to urban needs by racing greyhounds on a track was made at the Welsh Harp at Hendon near London in 1876. Various meetings were held but without great success because running races in a straight line made it fairly easy to pick the best dog and hence results were too predictable. It was not until the 1920s that an American variant involving the dogs running round a circuit was introduced, which combined just the right mixture of speed and skill to make the outcome uncertain. Twenty-five thousand pounds was spent on a track at Belle Vue in Manchester in 1926 and the following year the White City in London started greyhound-racing. These tracks sprang up in most of the major cities of Great Britain in the late 1920s, offering cheap gambling and a night out for ordinary working people who found it difficult to go to horse-racing. Sixty-two companies with a total capital of £7 million were registered for greyhound-racing in 1927 alone. Britain was 'going to the dogs' and by 1932 the annual attendance at licensed tracks in London had risen to 6.5 million. Several of the leading tracks drew 200 to 300 bookmakers. In 1928 a National Greyhound Racing Society was set up to regulate the sport and prevent corruption, but this poor relation of the Jockey Club was never fully accepted by the greyhound-racing public and there were a large number of 'flapper' tracks, makeshift circuits sometimes no more than a field where working men would race their dogs. In Scotland greyhound-racing was the second most popular spectator sport after football by the late 1930s with big tracks in all the major cities, but 'gaff' or makeshift tracks also flourished in 'old unlovely mining communities like Armadale in West Lothian, Auchinleck in Ayrshire, Thornton in Fife, Wishaw in Lanarkshire or Wallyford near Musselburgh'.

Whippets were a popular pet in pit villages and only slowly gave way to the larger greyhound as the favourite racing dog in the 1930s. They were small enough to keep in the house and might even pay their own way by catching live rabbits in the fields as well as chasing them from a trap. As dog-fighting declined in the second half of the nineteenth century, informal dog-racing developed as a more humane animal sport. Dog-racing was a world of its own with all sorts of ways of 'stopping' a dog or speeding it up, a rich tradition of potions and tricks passed on from father to son or picked up around the tracks. Handlers would squeeze the poor creature's testicles, jerk its tail, or even feed it a meat pie to slow it down and improve the odds for the next race. When the aim was to win the owners would 'stand behind the winning-line beckoning their "bairns" with their favourite object—a feeding-bowl, a bit of blanket, a tin can, a bonnet, a rag or a rabbit skin'. 'Slipping' whippets, as it was called, was quite an art. So was the training of them. A man would set up an old bicycle-frame on a piece of waste ground with a cloth rabbit attached to the rear hub by a long string. The father would slip the dog while the son furiously turned the pedals and the creature would race after the 'hare'. Sometimes the tunnel-visioned dogs would crash into the bike itself and require impromptu surgery. A friend of mine recalled seeing her father stitch together his greyhound after an accident in Edinburgh in the early 1960s. This kind of thing together with carrying home bloody paper-bags of sheep's-head and offal were the less attractive aspects of a sport that gave a manual worker the chance of raising a good dog and making money. Champion dogs were greatly prized, even given the best chair beside the fire and, in some accounts, their trophies displayed alongside family heirlooms on the mantelpiece of 'the room' at the front of the house.[45]

Breeding, feeding, and training dogs whether for the big tracks or the small ones was not quite as popular an activity as keeping pigeons. Miners were the most enthusiastic pigeon-fanciers whether in Britain, northern France, or in Belgium, where the sport was enormously popular. Often living in industrial villages close to the countryside and older sporting traditions, cooped up for long periods in dark, cramped coal-seams, miners seem to have had a particular feeling for the natural warmth and graceful speed of dogs and birds. The breeding of these birds as message-carriers together with the spread of the rail network meant that pigeons could be raced either by individuals or clubs over long distances. Before the introduction of rings and time-clocks in the Edwardian period, owners had to gather their bird as it returned to the coop and then run to the registration point

[45] S. Jones, *Workers at Play* (1986), pp. 38–45; on training greyhounds I defer to the oral history carried out by Billy Kay for the Odyssey programmes for BBC Scotland (see the *Scotsman*, 19 Jan. 1985) and to the personal recollections of Janis Stirton, whose father trained greyhounds in Edinburgh in the 1950s.

where the tag placed on the bird before release would be checked. Shorter races were informally organized and often involved angry accusations of cheating by losing owners, although during the twentieth century these contests have been largely replaced by the more highly organized long-distance club events. Pigeon-racing offered a mixture of attractions; the skill of the individual fancier is both rewarded by winning club trophies and by winning prizes and bets. But the trip down to the club, usually a back room of a local pub, for the synchronizing of clocks, the ringing, and the filling in of forms was a social event. Getting birds to fly well, the kind of hard corn to feed the young, and a hundred and one other tricks of the trade were passed on from one generation to another as closely guarded family secrets. In the Cumbrian country town of Wigton, Jeff Bell recalled joining his first pigeon club with his brother towards the end of the First World War. Jeff and his brother 'used to fly in what was called the South End Club and they had a lot of adult members—Pattison lads and a lad called Storey. There were Hill's boys . . . and there were Blair's lads, West Street. All round that area everybody had a small loft, not a lot of pigeons but small lofts and we used to race from about a hundred and fifty mile. A shilling a bird.' A bit of sponsorship from the brewery and a few improvements in timing methods were the main changes in sixty years. For Jeff Bell the routine of cleaning out the lofts every morning never changed. It was a cosy addiction. 'Pigeon flying's a disease,' as an old Wigton fancier used to say, 'it's the poor man's racehorse.' In Bolton in the 1930s Mass Observation came to much the same conclusion. One interviewee fed his bird according to a strict street pre-race formula. 'On Wednesday night I give the cock two cod liver oil capsules' to clear the bowels. From Thursday onwards a cake of 'Rape, White Mullet, Dandelion, Sesame, Lettuce, Hemp, Linseed, Golden Pleasure, Mauve, White Spanish and Thistle seeds' bound with demerara sugar and sherry was administered. Then 'the motions of the birds are carefully watched and should be jet black with a smear of white on top.' Men went to their grave refusing to divulge how they fed and bred their pigeons or which bait they used to fish a particular stretch of river.[46]

[46] J. Mott, 'Miners, Weavers and Pigeon Racing', in M. Smith, S. Parker, and C. Smith (eds.), *Leisure and Society in Britain* (1973), and Hoggart, *Uses of Literacy*, p. 328; M. Bragg, *Speak for England* (1976), pp. 381–5; *The Pub and the People*, by 'Mass Observation' (1987), p. 288.

Fishing too was often linked to betting by working men. The great popularity of angling testified to more than nostalgia for the countryside. The number of registered anglers in Sheffield, for example, grew from around 7,000 in the 1860s to over 20,000 by the end of the century. These fishermen did not normally set out for a solitary, contemplative day by the river as a harassed business man or weary lawyer might do. Instead they organized themselves into over 200 clubs, often based on the local pub, and ran club competitions which might involve hiring excursion trains and 'pegging down' extensive stretches of river-bank. Prizes were offered by local tradesmen, brewers, and newspapers and there was a highly developed though informal system of betting on the results. There were 464 individual entries for an angling competition in Bolton just before the Second World War on the Lancaster Canal. The event was predictably run by a brewery and one pub alone entered twelve teams. The prize-giving, which took place in the upper room of a pub a few days later, was a sociable affair. A pianist performed 'The Bells of St Mary's', 'Swanee', 'On the Mississippi' and accompanied a local man who got up to sing. 'He's a good singer, yon man, but yon pianist'll knock bottom right out o' two pianos if 'e plays like that all neet', remarked one of the anglers. The evening went off noisily with more singing and talk of prize catches, good bait and big bets. One landlord won a side-bet of a hundred black puddings, which his grateful regulars consumed at a single sitting. 'Sacks of potatoes, a sack of corn, flour, a case of oranges, joints of beef, legs of pork' were placed as bets along with bottles of spirits and even 'a box of kippers' and 'a dozen pounds of tripe'.[47]

Betting was even important in bowls, especially of the northern crown green variety. Significantly, the two classic events of northern bowls took place at Blackpool. Workers wanted some special sporting entertainment on seaside holidays when whole towns would descend on Blackpool at the same time. The 'Talbot Handicap' became the great event of the northern bowler's year. The 'Talbot', begun in 1873 by the enterprising proprietor of the Talbot Hotel, attracted over 1,000 entries and became to bowling

---

[47] J. Lowerson, 'Brothers of the Angle', paper delivered to the Society for the Study of Labour History's conference on Sport and the Working Class, 24 Nov. 1984 (abstract in *Bulletin of the Society for the Study of Labour History*, Spring 1985); *The Pub and the People*, pp. 291–4.

what Belle Vue was to brass bands: *the* prestige event that was talked about in pubs and clubs throughout the North. A second bowling tournament established 'national' status in the North in 1907 when the Waterloo Hotel set up a similar open handicap tournament, which quickly attracted the maximum of 1,024 competitors that permitted a winner over ten rounds of individual competition. Whether staking a few pence on an 'end' between friends or picking the winner of the Waterloo or the Talbot, the idea of winning money was never considered 'unsporting' in the North. A visitor to a casual competition on a pub green observed knots of men standing near a drinks-hatch watching play and calling out 'Ah'll tak two dollars', 'I'll take 14 bob to 8', with bookies' runners sitting near by, who presumably would also tout for business on the horses.

Billiards, which normally involved the placing of side-bets of a modest sort, became the most popular indoor game. It offered older men the blend of skill, drinking, banter, and gambling they found so congenial. Billiards had been enjoyed from at least the sixteenth century as a tavern and as a country-house pastime, but it was not until the nineteenth century that advances in manufacturing and technology provided smoother tables, sprung cushions, and perfect balls. John Roberts became well known as the unofficial British champion in the mid-Victorian era and this mantle was then assumed by his son, who became the first official champion in 1870. The son brought back the more complex game of snooker from a tour of India in 1880, but for a long time snooker, which has become so popular in this century, was the poor relation to billiards. Thurston's Club off Leicester Square was the mecca for billiards. 'When the world is wrong, hardly to be endured, I shall return to Thurston's and there smoke a pipe among the connoisseurs of top and side. It is as near to the Isle of Innisfree as we get within a hundred leagues of Leicester Square', sighed J. B. Priestley.

The *Daily Mail* did not shift its sponsorship from billiards to snooker until 1936 by which time Joe Davis, surely one of the best-known names in the entire world of popular sport, had established complete dominance of the game, playing exhibition matches in all major cities of Great Britain. Not surprisingly Blackpool was a popular venue in the summer where those who struggled manfully to make a break that ran into double figures could watch the master make a hundred. Davis was a unique phenomenon, unbeaten and unbeatable, drawing large crowds wherever he played. During the Second World War he raised £125,000 for charity and the public paid £12,000 in 1946 to see the championship final against his brother Fred. Davis then retired from active competition but ruled snooker administratively for twenty years more. Yet for most of the 'high period' of industrialization it was those who tirelessly manœuvred the three balls round the table in combinations of pots, in-offs, and cannons who were the heroes of the public bar: men like Inman, six times champion, Willie Smith, Walter Lindrum, and Tom Reece, who made a record unfinished break of 499,135 points in 85 hours 49 minutes over three days in 1907 before the rules were changed to prevent perfectibility. Inman and Reece were great rivals, shrewdly playing up their dislike and contempt for each other to stimulate public interest. Reece once demanded that Inman should pay to be present because he was 'just a spectator'. Banter was all part of the act, which could even extend to gymnastics. Clark McConachy used to 'warm up' the audience by walking round the table on his hands. All this, of course, was long before anyone dreamed that snooker would become a stable winter entertainment for millions of television viewers. Televised snooker is another story, which will be told later.[48]

Both billiards and snooker were very 'clubbable' activities and often linked to other forms of voluntary association. Tens of thousands of men spent much of their spare time doing a bit of drinking at the British Legion with their friends and playing a couple of frames. Kingsley Kennerley, the amateur billiards champion in 1937, started by joining Congleton Brass Band Club. Ray Reardon recalled how he began to play snooker in the 1930s at the Miners' Institute in Tredegar in the Rhondda. Unemployment had left many men from the valleys with nothing to do but hang around the miners' welfare listening to the clinking of the balls, eking out their beer and tobacco between spells at the table. Billiards and snooker were patronized by the top and bottom echelons of society, from the royal table at Sandringham to the scruffy back room of a workman's bar. But the rich and

---

[48] C. Everton, *The Story of Billiards and Snooker* (1979), provides a simple outline, which is enlivened by D. Trelford, *Snookered* (1986), esp. p. 47.

the poor rarely, if ever, met at the table. The rich played casually as individuals not as part of a club competing with others. Despite a brief schism in 1908, when the amateurs went their own way for a few years, the Billiards Association held together a sport that was played in the gentlemen's clubs of Pall Mall and the seedy halls of the inner cities where 'sharp' players could always make a pound or two from the optimism or naïvety of the newcomer. 'The sign of a mis-spent youth' was a jibe that stuck to both billiards and snooker, which certainly had their share of shady characters hovering on the margins of crime. Sadly there was no Damon Runyon to bring them to life.[49]

Rounding off these individual games, which mixed chance and chat—'to have a bit crack' as northerners would say—with a test of dexterity or judgement, there was the game of darts, which now claims six million or more casual players. As a kind of domesticated archery, darts in various guises had been around for centuries. But in its modern form with the clock-board and flighted cylindrical darts it dates from the turn of this century. A curious legal case in 1908 established it as a game of 'skill' rather than of 'chance'. 'Foot' Anakin, a northern publican with huge feet, threw three double-twenties twice in succession at a Leeds Magistrates' Court after a junior clerk, who had never played the game, was instructed by the bench to have a go and missed the board entirely with two of his first three throws. The magistrate swiftly pronounced darts to be a 'skilful' and therefore a legal pub activity. This, in practice, allowed men to back themselves or others for a pint or a few bob during an evening at the pub dartboard. Darts is a good example of the power of popular culture to create private languages for players. Shouts of 'fish-shop', 'swans in a lake', or 'three in a bed' must have perplexed casual visitors to dart-playing pubs. Darts, relatively cheap and so deceptively simple, was taken up by the mass-circulation Sunday papers, a sure sign of its popularity. In 1937 the King and Queen were photographed throwing darts while opening a social club in Slough and inadvertently gave the game a further boost. First the *People*, always anxious to outflank its populist Sunday rivals, started the Lord Lonsdale Trophy in 1938 and the *News of the World*, which was read by around one in two British people, soon jumped on the bandwagon. Darts, pigeons, and bowls took their place alongside dog- and horse-racing, football and cricket in its columns.

This odd miscellany reflects the way games were experienced in practice: the newly regulated amateur or team-sports rubbing shoulders with older games that mixed gambling, drinking, and conversation with knowledge of animals or co-ordination of hand and eye. Working-class sport has been seen too exclusively in terms of football, boxing, or cricket. The fact that around eighteen million entry tickets were sold for licensed dog-tracks alone in 1931 or that there were half a million pigeon-fanciers and a thousand homing-clubs tends to be forgotten. This is partly a matter of class bias in reporting—golf, for example, which had fewer adherents got much more coverage—but it was also a question of age. Despite books like *The Boy Fancier* (which happily turned out to be nothing more than a juvenile handbook of pigeon-racing) raising birds or casting a fly required maturity and knowledge. So did rolling woods across a green, calculating the bias, and waiting for a gentle satisfying knock as your bowl edged out another and settled beside the jack. This was no country for young men. It was a world of cap-shifting, head-scratching, and the odd involuntary click of false teeth. When older men could no longer play vigorous team-games like football, they could fall back on activities that called for experience, guile, and patience. As time passed women took up bowling—the only area of desegregated contemporary working-class sport.

This assortment of different sports constituted a kind of submerged tradition, sustaining skills and providing satisfactions which the hurly-burly of the playing-fields did not. Although the equation between the declining demand for skill at work and its displacement into the world of play is a risky business, those who used their tools—the prized symbol of the skilled man—to build kennels and coops in their backyards or near the allotments where they grew their prize leeks and 'chrysanths' were surely cultivating a kind of craftsmanship. Just as sport could never be cut off from its wider social context at the collective and public level, so in the private course of an individual life the pleasures of competitive exercise mingled with the enjoyment of making and digging, of working a piece of wood, or raising a plant from seed. We tend to think of sport as being one of a number of popular leisure alternatives, an option in a range of consumer choices, though 'choice' is not quite the right word for activities that were largely determined by age and by sex, and most importantly by the habits and customs of the immediate community. There was no point in flying pigeons if no one else flew them. Most people did what their neighbours did. A limited but absorbing and convivial range of entertainment was available and arbitrary divisions between one activity and another are misleading. Men did not raise pigeons *or* watch football, play bowls *or* plant marrows. They frequently did some or all of these things as well as singing in choirs and playing in brass bands. Television has recently rescued darts, snooker, and even bowls from the condescension of the public school tradition, recognizing and reinforcing their importance in the living culture of urban Britain. Horses and dogs, fish and birds were important too, drawing upon a deep-rooted fascination for animals as well as providing an outlet for the urge to gamble that ran through so much of popular sport. Here was another link between modern Britain and the world before the fields and woods were turned into cities and suburbs.

5. FLIGHT FROM THE CITY?

Until the inter-war years getting out of the city often amounted to no more than a quick trip to the seaside once a year. Unlike France, where shooting-permits were relatively cheap and there was plenty of unenclosed land, field sports in Britain were very much the preserve of the gentry or the rich. Coarse-fishing was competitive but there was also the casual side to the sport where a man and his son or a friend might just go off for a day in the peace and quiet, sitting by a canal waiting all day for a bite perhaps, or using the train to go further afield. The numbers who amused themselves this way are by definition extremely difficult to assess. One informed estimate suggests that by 1914 there were between 150,000 and 200,000 working-class anglers. Even harder to calculate are the numbers of those who simply went off for long walks. The Victorians were prodigious walkers. The habit of casually tramping long distances in the manner of Thomas Hardy's country characters was also a feature of urban artisans, like Job Legh in Elizabeth Gaskell's *Mary Barton*, who knew 'the name and habitat of every plant within a day's walk of their dwellings'. This was part of an older tradition which was mostly lost on a new generation of urban workers, who were getting used to taking cheap trains or trams to get to work.[50]

Although the bicycle brought the possibility of cheap personal mobility by the Edwardian period, clubs organizing cycling trips or country rambles were suburban and predominantly middle class. In 1880 the Young Men's Christian Association took up rambling (the Manchester YMCA were truly 'muscular Christian', organizing weekend rambles of up to seventy miles) and a London Federation of Rambling Clubs was formed in 1891 to take advantage of the secondary rail network to escape the noise and dirt of the city. The Rucksack Club, begun in Manchester in 1902 by former members of the exclusive Alpine Club, set up several branches and seemed to exert a particular appeal to lawyers. Even the Clarion cycling clubs with their explicit commitment to socialism tended to recruit mainly from the aristocracy of labour along with the teaching profession and a sprinkling of Fabian intellectuals. Cycling was a craze in the 1890s. Membership of the Cyclists' Touring Club shot up to nearly 60,000, from which it declined to around 15,000 by the outbreak of the First World War as well-off Edwardians deserted the bicycle for the car. It was all very well for D. H. Lawrence's Paul Morel to ride out of a Nottinghamshire mining village and discover nature, but most workers preferred the security and familiarity of 'the match' on a Saturday afternoon. Sunday morning was spent sleeping off the excesses of Saturday night. Moreover where open country was close at hand there was no need to buy a bike. Traditionally there had been community tramps to the moors on holidays, and it would be interesting to know whether this custom was still in force in the more isolated mill-towns of the north of England. Taking the train or the tram to the end of the line was one way out of the big conurbations. The question is how many of them bothered to get off and explore the countryside when they got to the terminus?[51]

[50] Lowerson, 'Brothers of the Angle'. E. Gaskell cited in A. Holt, 'Hikers and Ramblers', *IJHS*, May 1987, p. 57.

[51] H. Walker, 'The Popularisation of the Outdoor Movement', *BJSH*, Sept. 1985, pp. 142–3; the author kindly supplied additional statistics of membership of the Cyclists' Touring Club.

It is hard to know how far shortage of money prevented workers from 'discovering the countryside' or whether they were simply disinclined to do so. For those whose families had migrated to the towns within one or two generations, the poverty of country life, which affluent urban tourists overlooked in their search for natural beauty, may have lingered in the memory. At any rate workers were less inclined to indulge in the bouts of utopian ruralism than middle-class artists and intellectuals. Admittedly, a good bicycle was still rather expensive for a working man, but there were plenty of second-hand machines and easy hire-purchase arrangements. Staying overnight even in a very cheap room could strain the budget, but given what a skilled man was prepared to spend on a holiday at Blackpool, cost alone does not seem to have been the main obstacle. More important was community loyalty and the familiarity of the neighbourhood. For girls there was the added issue of parental control to consider. Most young workers before the First World War were unable or unwilling to use the trains or the bicycle to 'get away from it all' as middle-class youth did, although shorter cycling excursions did become more common. Apprentices preferred a few days beside the seaside in the company of their mates, drinking and chasing the girls, to invigorating walks over mountains. It was to remedy this state of affairs that a Congregationalist minister from Colne, T. A. Leonard, pioneered walking-holidays in the Lake District for his parishioners around the turn of the century, and later established the Holiday Fellowship in 1913, which expanded considerably, guiding new generations of enthusiastic northerners from the gentler climbs like Cat Bells at Derwent Water to the full rigours of Great Gable, Red Pike, Striding Edge, Scafell, and the Langdales. The Lakes entered the folk memory of the North—youthful achievements recalled in old age without a Wainwright to guide and prod the memory—bringing back the sense of enchantment that popular 'mountaineering' brought to city people.[52]

The real change seems to have come after the First World War, which approximately doubled money wages, with unskilled

[52] Here private and public histories merge. I was brought up on tales of trips to the Lakes made by my father from the 1920s onwards. My parents went to Newlands with the Holiday Fellowship about nine months before I was born.

workers benefiting the most (their hourly rate rose from about half to three-quarters that of skilled men). Women workers not only earned more but they acquired a new freedom to do 'male' jobs, a greater sense of independence and dignity, which culminated in female suffrage. The material advantages of the war were short-lived, especially for women, who were quickly forced back into the home or traditional areas of poorly paid female employment, but the awareness of wider possibilities and horizons had an impact on female behaviour. Despite the spectre of long-term unemployment in the staple industries, which emerged after the brief restocking boom of 1919–20 and continued to plague the economy for most of the inter-war years, falling prices pushed up the value of the earnings for those in work. There was a gradual move towards paid holidays with one and a half million manual workers benefiting from them in 1925 and four million by 1937. Hours of work fell, though not very significantly, dropping from an average of fifty-four in 1900 to forty-six and a half in 1938. Men still worked on Saturday mornings throughout the inter-war period. Yet the idea of the 'weekend', formerly the prerogative of the country house and affluent suburb, assumed a new importance, especially amongst the young of both sexes.[53]

By the 1920s cycling trips, either casually arranged by small groups of friends or more formally organized through the clubs run by the Cyclists' Touring Club, the National Cyclists' Union, and other bodies, were commonplace. Groups of touring cyclists became a familiar addition to the landscape. J. B. Priestley noticed them on his *English Journey* in 1934 near Bradford. 'I remember wondering exactly what pleasure they were getting from the surrounding country, as they never seemed to lift their heads from the handle-bars, but went grimly on like racing cyclists . . . but perhaps they call an occasional halt, and then take in all the beauty in a deep breath.' The mixture of competitive sport and the countryside may have seemed strange to Priestley but it was a perfect combination for urban youth. There was the speed of the machine to give you a thrill, a long hard pull, and then a fast downhill stretch, clocking up the miles before stopping for a look

---

[53] A. Howkins and J. Lowerson, *Trends in Leisure, 1919–39*, a review for the Sports Council and the SSRC (1979), p. 9.

around or a drink in a café or pub. Exertion and endurance, skill in riding and 'tuning' the machine, periods of rest and conversation, the swift and communal rather than the slow and solitary contemplation of nature: these were the new joys of the road.[54]

The bicycle has a special place in the history of private life. Getting a 'big' bike came to be a kind of rite of passage for the working-class boy (parental expectations of female behaviour continued to put girls at a disadvantage, though persistence might eventually purchase the freedom of a gleaming ladies' roadster). 'A sign of arrival at real adolescence is the agreement from one's parents to the buying of a bike on the hire-purchase system,' as Richard Hoggart recalled of the 1930s, 'then one goes out on it at weekends, with a friend who has bought a bike at the same time, or with one of those mixed clubs which sweep every Sunday through town and out past the quiet tram terminus.' Alan Sillitoe summed up this love affair with the bicycle amongst young working-class men and women, which continued into the post-war years. 'I rode a dozen miles out into the country, where fresh air smelt like cow-dung and the land was coloured different, was wide open and windier than in the streets: marvellous. It was like a new life starting up, as if till then I'd been tied by a mile long rope by the ankle at home.'[55]

So much has been written about the hardships of the Depression that the excitement and liberation of youth, which was as important in its own way as the better-known 'youth culture' of the 1960s, is sometimes overlooked. Sports-club dances, trips to the country, hiking, swimming, popular music on the radio, weekly visits to the new dance-halls and cinemas were open to the unmarried, whilst plentiful housing and small families meant that young married couples could still enjoy some leisure. No sooner had the bicycle been democratized than there was the even more exhilarating prospect of powered private transport. Not the motor car, which remained a middle-class possession until the 1950s, but the motor cycle; motor bikes were far cheaper and simpler to run than cars. Skilled workers could afford to buy a BSA or an AJS, which they would lovingly strip down and

[54] Priestley cited in J. Mackenzie (ed.), *Cycling* (1981), pp. 85–6.
[55] Hoggart, *Uses of Literacy*, p. 329; Sillitoe cited in Mackenzie, *Cycling*.

reassemble in garden sheds or at kerb-sides before taking off for a spin with a girl-friend clinging on. This is just what Dixie Dean, the footballing hero of the late 1920s liked to do, until he came crashing off and was almost killed. Road deaths shot up to over 7,000 in the mid-1930s—a figure that would have amazed and alarmed previous generations. But middle-class consumers and their working-class counterparts, motorists and bikers, were agreed that 'progress' could not be stopped. Caravans and the new excursion buses jostled with cars, lorries, motor bikes, and cycles on the road. Mobility began to be seen as inherently desirable by working people. Male conversation increasingly turned on 'decarbonizing', 'adjusting tappets', 'feeler gauges' and gaps for plugs and points along with the ritual moans about punctures. People who spent their working lives using technology to manufacture goods for others now had their own machines to maintain. Technology became a hobby, old artisan skills found new outlets as men did their own servicing, even sometimes making their own spare parts, paving the way for mass car ownership in post-war boom. Taking photographs of the trips that the internal combustion engine had made possible completed this 'brave new world' of domestic technology, bringing family and countryside together in innumerable 'snaps' of smiling faces and celebrated 'beauty spots'. The social history of the motor cycle between the wars, to which a side-car could be added to transport a small family, has been obscured by the more sensational antics of the next generation of motor-cyclists, whose leather jackets and long hair spread moral panic in the 1950s.[56]

Walking too seemed to take off as a healthy outdoor recreation. New excursion tickets on the intricate rail network combined with the development of the rural bus service meant that it was now much easier to get into the countryside. LMS line offered 'ramblers' tickets' with 'a choice of over 300 tours from the Manchester district' mostly to the Peak District. 'The Sunday morning queues of ramblers on London Road [Piccadilly] station stretched down the station approaches,' recalled an enthusiast, and 'the platforms rang to the sound of . . . ex-army boots which they nailed themselves.' Suddenly educated working-men were

---

[56] J. Stevenson, *British Society 1914–45* (1984), ch. 14, gives a useful general outline but there is no social study of motor-cycling between the wars.

espousing the kind of romantic anti-urbanism that had first captured the hearts of the middle classes at the end of the nineteenth century. Some of the new walkers, of course, had time on their hands as a result of long-term unemployment. John Nimlin from Glasgow told how in 1930 he and other friends on the dole 'explored Loch Lomond and the Campsie Hills', starting their own climbing club. 'I believe that during the slump there were many despairing and disillusioned men who found a new meaning to life in the countryside', he claimed. How true this was at the national level is hard to say. The Pilgrim Trust's study of unemployment in Liverpool noted the passive and hopeless state of those who had been out of work for more than a year. Betting rather than hiking was their hobby. Walking in the country, as a recent student of the phenomenon puts it, 'was a pursuit of the lower-middle and upper-working classes, people frequently characterized by a certain earnestness and the taste for self-improvement'.[57]

There was an important social distinction here between 'ramblers' and 'hikers'. Ramblers saw themselves as an élite with an interest in topography and natural history and tended to be drawn from the liberal professions with university dons prominent. They wore knee-breeches, long woollen socks, and tailored jackets. Hikers, on the other hand, were fair-weather walkers, clad in a unisex outfit of ex-army shorts, aertex shirts, and boots that scandalized the old guard, who wrote indignantly to *The Times* on the subject of 'youth and maidens in hideous uniforms'. Hiking and biking were very important for women in providing the first opportunities for shared physical recreation with men in a working-class world where the sexes still occupied separate spheres. Eileen Gooding, an office-worker from Croydon, found walking had become a fashion amongst her contemporaries, who just took off into the countryside independent of organized clubs. Chatting at lunch-time to others 'I quickly found there was quite a bit of competition in this— they called it hiking—you know, "we went hiking and we did so many miles on Saturday and so many miles on Sunday". The great thing seemed to be to get out and pick up this challenge,

[57] B. Rothman, *The 1932 Kinder Trespass* (1982), p. 12; Stevenson, *British Society*, p. 392; A. Holt, 'Hikers and Ramblers', p. 61.

to get into the open air.' Closely tied in with this was the development of the Youth Hostel Association, copied from the German model and supplying overnight accommodation at a shilling a night. From its inception in 1930 the movement grew dramatically with almost 300 hostels by the end of the decade providing over half a million overnight stops. Although the facilities were spartan, supervised, and segregated, hiking did offer new prospects for courtship in a more wholesome and romantic setting than the front parlour or the back row of the 'pictures'. The YHA found its initials were popularly translated by young women as 'Your Husband Assured'. The enjoyment of nature had to compete with the pursuit of more conventional goals.[58]

It is interesting to speculate here about the influence of the horrors of the Great War on popular recreation. For an articulate and active minority the 'flight from the city' was associated with a wider rejection of capitalist civilization and militarism in favour of rural peace, beauty, and quietness. There was a strongly pacifist and internationalist element in the 'outdoor movement' of the inter-war period. This is particularly evident in the most famous confrontation between walkers and landowners at Kinder Scout in the Peak District in 1932. Large estates in the Peak District had been fairly tolerant of small groups of walkers, but the craze for hiking led them to restrict access to protect their paths and grouse moors. The fact that so large an area of wilderness between Sheffield and Manchester was closed to the public played into the hands of the 'access to mountains' activists led by the Clarion clubs, the ILP, the Woodcraft Folk, and the communist-backed British Workers' Sports Federation, who played the major role. On 24 April 1932 some 400 hikers turned out to confront the Duke of Devonshire's gamekeepers, singing 'The Manchester Rambler' and fanning out to claim common rights to the heights of Kinder Scout with its 'boxing-glove' stones, rocky, moorland desolation, and beautiful reservoir invitingly near to the eastern limits of Greater Manchester. Five were arrested for riotous assembly and later convicted by a packed jury of landowners and army officers. They were sentenced to between two and six

---

[58] Walker, 'Popularisation of the Outdoor Movement', pp. 150–1; A. Holt, 'Hikers and Ramblers', p. 57.

202 *Living in the City*

months each. The cause had its martyrs, notably Benny Rothman, a young Mancunian who led the Trespass, and large protest meetings followed, addressed by Arthur Henderson and the popular radio philosopher C. E. M. Joad amongst others. The right to ramble was a good cause for the Left. Despite the continuing obduracy of the landed interest, the Kinder Trespass was a moral victory for the rights of ordinary city people to enjoy the open countryside, dramatizing the importance of democratic access to open spaces and helping to pave the way politically for the National Parks and Access to Countryside Act of 1949. Since then there has not been the kind of active enjoyment of the nature which radical ramblers had hoped for. Taking a 'run' into the country by car or a bus trip through the Lakes or Dales has become the favoured means of seeing the countryside. Hill-walking and rambling are certainly popular but the aura of 'alternative' middle-class culture still clings to them. For most urban workers, especially the younger ones, a short afternoon on the terraces is infinitely preferable to a long day on the hills. From the 'outdoor pursuits' perspective what is even worse is that watching sport or enjoying a guided tour of beautiful countryside can now be done without getting out of an armchair.[59]

[59] S. G. Jones, 'Sports, Politics and the Labour Movement', *BJSH*, Sept. 1985, p. 168; Rothman, *Kinder Trespass*, gives a first-hand account with superb photographs.

4

Empire and Nation

SPORT played a major role in the transmission of imperial and national ideas from the late nineteenth century onwards. Cricket, in particular, came to have a special meaning for the Empire. The first Imperial Cricket Conference was held at the height of the Boer War in an atmosphere of colonial fervour. The regular Test matches between England and Australia that began in the 1880s were tremendously popular in both countries by the end of the century. When Victor Trumper brought his famous Australian side to England in 1902 the England team included in its ranks an Indian prince. In India itself cricket spread down through the noble and merchant élites and won a popular urban following between the wars. Likewise in the West Indies the exercise and entertainment of the white colonist came to be the ruling passion of the common people. What began as manly exercise for a master race slowly came to be a kind of common language superficially obscuring divisions of ethnicity, religion, and economic interest. How did this happen? What role was initially envisaged for imperial sports and how did their significance change as the Empire itself evolved into a self-governing 'Commonwealth of Nations'? These are the questions which are examined in turn in the opening discussion of the colonial rulers and the following section on the spread of athleticism to the indigenous élites. What reaction did the cult of specifically Anglo-Saxon sports provoke amongst those who wished to be free of imperial domination? The study of sport and imperialism leads naturally to nationalism; for it was through the channel of imperial ideology that 'British nationalism'—or more accurately the attachment to a certain idea of Englishness—was most fervently expressed and this was met by the rise of Dominion nationalism, which is the subject of section 3. Against this was ranged not only the kind of cultural separatism expressed in Ireland through the spread of Gaelic games, but also a more complex blend of dependency and assertiveness found in the relationship of Wales and Scotland with England. 'Domestic' sporting nationalism is examined in section 4 and the chapter concludes with an attempt in section 5 to disentangle ideas of 'Englishness' from the complementary and over-lapping sense of 'Britishness'. Sport, as it turns out, provides an excellent tool for looking at loyalties that social historians have tended to play down in comparison with class-based forms of solidarity.[1]

1. COLONIAL ÉLITES

The extent and importance of sport in the public school curriculum has already been established. There was a close relationship between the creation of this muscular élite and the extension of formal control over large areas of Asia and Africa by the British government in the later nineteenth century. Though public school sport was in the first instance not specifically intended to train the lieutenants of Empire, it came rapidly to be seen in this light. While Frenchmen could not quite bring themselves to accept that the battle of Waterloo had been won 'on the playing-fields of Eton', aristocratic reformers like Baron de Coubertin certainly thought the encouragement of physical vigour and group co-operation in games had played an important part in the acquisition of the British Empire. The Germans were also struck by the 'imperial sportsman' as a distinctively British type. As a German observer of British sports later remarked, 'the great tasks offered by the Empire, with its varied problems for the pioneer, often demand the strong energetic character rather than the bookworm'. The British were perceived as active and resourceful, if academically limited. Foreigners often envied their sheer ability to get things done, especially in relation to the running of an empire, which was ascribed in part to energy and common sense derived from games.[2]

---

[1] D. Cannadine, 'The Context, Performance and Meaning of Ritual', in E. Hobsbawm and T. Ranger, *The Invention of Tradition* (1983). J. M. Mackenzie, *Imperialism and Popular Culture* (1986), ch. 1, challenges the view that British imperialism was an élite phenomenon and stresses the pervasiveness of imperial propaganda and the responsiveness of the public to it.

[2] R. Kirchner, *Fair Play* (1928), p. 13; R. Holt, *Sport and Society in Modern France* (1981), p. 63.

It was in this imperial light that public schoolmasters tended to see their task. J. E. C. Welldon, the headmaster of Harrow from 1881 to 1895 and a fervent imperialist, conceded that 'Englishmen are not superior to Frenchmen or Germans in brains or industry, or the science or apparatus of war.' In what, then, did their superiority reside? It was 'the health and temper which games impart' that set the British apart. 'The pluck, the energy, the perseverance, the good temper, the self-control, the discipline, the co-operation, the *esprit de corps*, which merit success in cricket or football, are the very qualities which win the day in peace or war.' 'In the history of the British Empire,' he concluded, 'it is written that England has owed her sovereignty to her sports.' Despite the occasional 'flannelled fool' or 'muddied oaf', it was Newbolt rather than Kipling who set the tone of reverence for games as the source of physical and spiritual strength. The resolute schoolboy, who plays out a difficult innings in fading light with the same resolve that he later takes command of a desperate situation with 'the Gatling jammed and the Colonel dead', sums up the heroic ideals of generations of schoolboys brought up on tales of imperial adventure and the thriving new genre of schoolboy fiction.[3]

The importance of sport from the point of view of the educationalist and the soldier lay not simply in acquiring fitness or in being competitive, but in the sense of solidarity, duty, and service it inculcated. Hence the strong preference for team-sports over individual ones. Baden-Powell put it like this when writing to the boys of his old prep school after the Boer War: 'While you are yet boys is the time to learn to do your duty . . . At football you do your duty not by playing to show yourself off to the onlookers but to obey the orders of the Captain of the team and to back up so that your side will win the game.' 'What is the justification of the games we play so much here', wrote Cyril Norwood, the Master of Marlborough and future headmaster of Harrow, 'save the ideal of service?' Leading headmistresses joined in as well. Girls had to be prepared physically to stand shoulder to shoulder alongside their husbands in the outposts of Empire. 'Most of the qualities, if not all, that conduce to the supremacy of our country in so many quarters of the globe', wrote Miss Dove

---

[3] J. A. Mangan, *The Games Ethic and Imperialism* (1986), pp. 35–6.

of Wycombe Abbey, 'are fostered if not solely developed, by means of games.' Examples of this kind of homily are legion and spread quickly through the grammar school network. They were endorsed in the press, in Parliament, and within the imperial administration itself. A contributor to the *National Review* of 1906 was moved to remark that Kent had won the County Championship 'because they were imbued with that co-operative and sporting enthusiasm, that superb playing for the side and not for the self, that sacrifice of the individual for the team's sake'. Was there not, he concluded, 'something Imperial both in the form of the Kent team and the popular recognition thereof'?[4]

What headmasters and other ideologues of Empire were inclined to say would have been of relatively little consequence if those with practical experience of colonial administration had not been in agreement. As the Empire expanded in the late nineteenth century both the need for recruits and the increasing cultural importance of athleticism combined to promote the cause of the sportsman. Recruitment to the Indian Civil Service remained academic but athletes moved in elsewhere. The Sudan Political Service provides the best example of this process at work. Set up in 1899 to supervise the administration of Sudan, it recruited entrants through an interview system mainly based upon recommendations from trusted dons in Oxford and Cambridge. The ideal recruit was a sportsman with a good second, but if the candidate was deficient in any respect then it was better to be a poor scholar than a poor sportsman. G. R. F. Bredin, who served from 1921 to 1948, wrote that selection boards 'attached considerable importance to the athletic records of candidates. Such activity was regarded as an indication not only of physical fitness (important in a climate which was often unhealthy) but of personality, initiative and capacity for judgement and control of subordinates.' No wonder an aspiring entrant declared that he would 'row himself into the Sudan', a country which came to be known as 'the land of Blacks ruled by Blues'. In fact, of 393 entrants to the administrative grade seventy-one had full representative sporting honours from Oxford or Cambridge, and many more were highly proficient sportsmen drawn for the most

---

[4] Mangan, *Games Ethic*, pp. 48, 97; P. C. McIntosh, *Physical Education in England since 1800* (1968), p. 132; C. Brookes, *English Cricket* (1978), p. 141.

part from the older established public schools. Eton, Rugby, Winchester, and Marlborough alone supplied nearly a quarter of the entrants. Sport played a more significant role in colonial recruitment in the Sudan than elsewhere in the Empire, but this was a difference of degree rather than of kind. In East Africa, for example, 'it helped the applicant's cause if, in addition to a good degree, he had some kind of athletic record'. The value attached to sport in the colonial service is nowhere better summed up than in the obituary for A. F. Mummery, the daring climber killed on Nanga Parbat in the Himalayas in 1895, the kind of man who 'made our race the pioneers of the world, which in naval warfare won for us the command of the sea, which by exploration and colonization has given the waste lands of the earth to Anglo-Saxon enterprise . . . whilst Englishmen possess this quality they will manifest it in their sports'.[5]

So much for 'character training', what of the real life of the Empire? Sport was not just a matter of education for Empire, it was a major source of recreation and entertainment for the colonialists. This élite was not only a ruling class, it was often a leisure class as well. When the United States were still the Thirteen Colonies southern landowners had begun emulating an English-gentry style of life devoted to horse-racing, which explicitly excluded poorer white settlers and slaves. Horse-racing remained important in the old south, especially in loyalist circles. In colonial South Australia important government officials and big landowners set up the Adelaide Hunt Club in 1846 and sponsored horse-racing. Later tennis, golf, and yachting were brought into the charmed circle of 'superior' amusements. 'Where a score or so of our sons are found there is found cricket', observed Trollope in 1868. Sport helped both to relieve the tedium of a distant posting and to integrate new arrivals into the small world of colonial society. This could be useful as well as pleasurable. 'The fact that most members played games and participated in sports together gave them a similarity of outlook which was clearly reflected in their handling of administrative matters', remarked an authority on the sporting Sudan. Such

---

[5] A. H. M. Kirk-Greene, 'Imperial Sidelight or Spotlight?', in *Proc. XI HISPA International Congress*, ed. J. A. Mangan (1987), pp. 1–11; see also Mangan, *Games Ethic*, ch. 3, esp. p. 74; G. J. Stewart, 'The British Reaction to the Conquest of Everest', *JSH*, Spring 1980, p. 37.

gatherings were especially important in maintaining contacts between settlers and officials in dispersed rural communities. 'Our countrymen are not to be scared by the sun from the pursuit of the national game [cricket]. They are as much Englishmen in Africa as in England', remarked Lord Bryce in the 1890s. Sport could even be used by angry settlers to make a point to colonial officials. In 1907 a fancy-dress football match in Kenya for charity was 'disrupted by leading settlers dressed as colonial officials with rows of medals made out of tin lids and red tape who pegged out quarantine, forest, native and game reserves until the entire pitch was out of bounds'.[6]

'Joking' political incursions aside, British sports served overwhelmingly to express and enhance the solidarity of colonial society. Providing amusement for those far from home isolated amidst an alien and sometimes hostile population, sport was not so much a luxury as a necessity, a means of maintaining morale and a sense of shared roots, of Britishness, of lawns and tea and things familiar. For the more humble middle-class emigrant sports also underlined that transition from a suburban to an essentially landed style, which added to the appeal of the Empire. Where else could the son of a shopkeeper mix with a gentleman? How else could a man acquire 'broad acres' and prestige so quickly? For the price of a private education, the settler could become a kind of squire copying or adapting the pastimes of his 'betters' back home. The rows of dusty tusks and mangy heads that adorned the walls of club and bungalow bore witness to this. Taxidermy was the true art of empire. Hunting, of course, had never been only a form of amusement. It was often vital for a man to ride in order to be able to fulfil official functions and the ability to shoot was a useful reminder to subject races of the underlying reality of imperial rule. In the early phases of colonization explorers and soldiers often paid their porters in meat—neatly combining sport and conquest. Once the land was mapped and the native subordinated, 'big-game' hunting ceased to be a source of the simple heroism fostered by Rider Haggard and G. A. Henty. It became a matter of slaughter by expensive

---

[6] J. A. Daly, 'Sport, Class and Community in Colonial South Australia', in *Proc. XI HISPA International Congress*, ed. Mangan, pp. 346-9; Kirk-Greene, 'Imperial Sidelight'; T. Ranger, 'The Invention of Tradition in Colonial Africa', in Hobsbawm and Ranger, *Invention of Tradition*, pp. 216-17.

high-velocity weapons and of conspicuous consumption, especially by rich Americans.

This military dimension of imperial sport was most evident in India. The Viceroy hunted on the grand scale, affirming his precedence with the gun and the size of his kill. Fear of Russia to the north and of internal subversion meant that a third or more of the entire British army was stationed in the subcontinent. In the early days of the East India Company most whites went hunting, but under the Raj the Indian Forest Service increasingly regulated access. This was done not only on a racial basis with the Indian hunters classified as 'poachers' but on social lines too. Game was for officers and administrators as it was at home. In order to maintain the fitness and morale of officers—what the ranks were expected to do is not so clear—a wide range of sports were developed, the most original and distinctive of which was 'pigsticking'. This became the passion of cavalry officers deprived of fox-hunting and involved the running down and spearing of a boar from horseback. Only mature animals, which were often strong and dangerous, could be hunted. The sport was organized by 'tent-clubs', the first of which was founded in Poona in the early nineteenth century. Pigsticking reached its prime in the later part of the century with the establishment of the Kadir Cup by the Meerut Tent Club in 1874. This was awarded to the outstanding individual rider whilst the Muttra Cup was a team-event in which three representatives of a tent-club or regiment competed in a series of heats to see who could kill the most 'pig'. The sight of a British officer at full gallop, spear in hand, alarmed not only the pig but also perhaps chastened the local population, who were required in their hundreds to act as beaters.[7]

Popular as it was amongst the officer corps, pigsticking not surprisingly failed to win acceptance elsewhere unlike polo— the other equestrian team-sport begun by the British in India. Polo in various forms had been played in Asia for thousands of years— the Mongols were said to have used skulls instead of balls—but was in decline in India when Captain Sherer came across it in Assam in the 1850s. The first modern club was set up in Calcutta

---

[7] J. A. Cuddon, *The Macmillan Dictionary of Sport and Games* (1980), pp. 602–3; J. M. Mackenzie, 'Hunting and the Imperial Élite', in Proceedings of the Fourth Annual Conference of the BSSH, 1986, pp. 58–69.

in 1862 and from there the game spread rapidly amongst cavalry officers and Indian princes, who spent vast fortunes on it to demonstrate their importance within the Raj. 'The polo cult was so strong in India around the turn of the century it occasioned little surprise when one military commander replaced all non-playing officers with playing ones, underlining the essential lessons thought inherent in the game.' The first polo match in Britain was played between the Tenth Hussars and the Ninth Lancers on Hounslow Heath in 1870 in a game that 'was more remarkable for the strength of the language used by the players than for anything else'. Polo was played by army officers in parts of West Africa where traditions of horsemanship dating back to Islamic conquest by mounted warriors were strong amongst the local rulers. It was also found in South Africa, but reached its peak in South America where the sport became a passion amongst the great ranchers of Argentina, who were often of British descent and tied closely to Britain by the economic bonds of 'informal' Empire.[8]

Not all the sporting innovations of the imperial army were so clearly linked to the need to maintain the cavalry in a state of readiness. Games were essential to fill in long evenings where there was little other source of entertainment. The clink of ivory billiard balls was a familiar sound in the clubs of the Raj. Odd varieties of billiards using coloured balls such as 'slosh' and 'pyramids' were well known in the mid-Victorian period. One of the rules of a game with coloured balls played at the Garrick Club in the 1860s stated that 'in the event of the yellow ball being involved in a foul stroke, it is the custom for the watchers to cry out the word "Bollocks" '. The honour of devising and naming the game of snooker, however, goes to the officers of the 11th Devonshire regiment stationed in India. Alternate potting of red and coloured balls livened up the game and when a player missed an easy pot a fellow officer called him a 'snooker', which was army slang for a novice. It is one of the minor ironies of history that what is now the most popular televised indoor sport had its origins amongst pigsticking and polo-playing army officers,

[8] H. A. Harris, *Sport in Britain* (1975), p. 168; also J. Arlott (ed.), *Oxford Companion to Sports and Games* (1976), p. 696; B. Stoddart, 'Sport, Cultural Imperialism and Colonial Response in the British Empire', in *Proceedings of the Fourth Annual Conference of the BSSH*, 1986, p. 8.

and was introduced to Britain by a professional billiards champion employed by the Maharaja of Jaipur.[9]

This was all very well for officers and gentlemen but there was still a need for a more inclusive kind of entertainment that would offer something to other residents, to the ranks, and to the wives. As far as participant activities were concerned the 'lawn' sports made good progress; the laws of badminton were first codified in Poona in 1870 and lawn tennis was also popular within the British community and later amongst Anglo-Indians. Colonial spectator sports naturally varied according to climate and local conditions. Attempts to play rugby in India came to so little that players in Calcutta decided to melt down their assets to make the Calcutta Cup, which they presented for competition between the Rugby Unions of England and Scotland, complete with snake-handles and surmounted by an elephant. Cricket was more leisurely and better suited to colonial life in warm climates. From 1892 there began the series of Presidency matches between the British and the Parsees at Bombay, which was expanded to include representative sides of Hindus and Muslims and drew large numbers of spectators. Alongside cricket, and perhaps more important as a pure spectacle and focal point for colonial society, there was horse-racing. Racecourses were built from Hong Kong to Nairobi. Racing had the aura of aristocracy about it; it was 'the sport of kings' where graceful beasts were paraded on fine turf. It appealed both to the smart and fashionable and to the ordinary man, the punter with a few pence to put on. Hence the great success of racing amongst the poorer immigrants of what became the white Dominions as well as in northern India, the Far East, and Africa. 'When I arrived in Cairo, less than a year after the battle of Tel-el-Kebir had been fought,' remarked Lord Cromer, 'every department of the Administration was in a state of the utmost confusion. Nevertheless a racecourse had already been laid out and a grandstand erected.' If there was an element of 'bread and circuses' about this, it was not so much the people as their rulers who sought entertainment.[10]

[9] D. Trelford, *Snookered* (1986), pp. 17, 25.
[10] R. Hyam, *Britain's Imperial Century, 1815–1914* (1976), p. 151.

2. THE IMPERIAL IDEA AND 'NATIVE' SPORT

Sports may have been seen initially as training and amusement for a colonial élite, but as the Empire expanded the value of building cultural bridges through games became more important. There were two quite distinct aspects to this. First there was the obvious advantage of keeping on good terms with local rulers by assimilating them to some degree into 'the British way of life'. The number of those who had to be brought into the cultural fold grew ever larger as the difficulty in holding down 'the natives' and the need for assistance with routine government tasks became more acute. In addition to this there was the strategic problem of a vast and sprawling Empire surrounded by colonial rivals. 'Over-commitment', which was exacerbated by the successful outcome of the First World War and the transfer of German colonies, gave the maintenance of good relations with 'native' élites a higher priority. Playing together was one way of helping this process along. Second, there was the related but separate issue of promoting loyalty to the Crown amongst white emigrants to Canada, South Africa, and Australasia. This was particularly important where linguistically distinct and politically hostile groups like the Boers or the French Canadians were concerned. A loyalist culture had to be fostered and sustained. Sports were thought to help create a climate of relations that would bind the Empire together. Representative events of various kinds would permit the expression of a legitimate sense of Dominion pride and independence within the wider imperial framework.

These ideas were not precisely stated or set out as colonial policy, except to a limited degree in the case of India. On the whole the British state preferred to give general encouragement and latitude to a wide variety of officials, missionaries, and educationalists. By refusing to impose their culture formally, the British weakened indigenous opposition to it. The cultural imperialism of the British tended to be more insidious than French or German efforts to stamp their territories with their customs and values. This was particularly true of India. Sports in the subcontinent came to be seen as an integral part of a wider process of incorporating the indigenous rulers into the Raj. After the Indian Mutiny of 1857–8 a new relationship between the princes and the British was established, which guaranteed them certain privileges in return for loyalty to the Crown. A viceroy was established; 'durbars' were held where honours and great titles were bestowed upon princes; an order of knighthood was even established in 1861. The aim was to incorporate the indigenous rulers partially into the Raj and thwart insurrection in the future. The princes not just to be imbued with Western values but with a distinctively British sense of priorities. British hegemony in India was to be underpinned by the princes themselves, who were not merely to be 'bought off' but rather were to become honorary English gentlemen. In this way they would come to see the superiority of British culture at first hand and uphold the status quo out of conviction rather than from greed or from fear.[11]

Lord Curzon, that most superior of superior persons, outlined the proper education of an Indian prince as follows: he had 'to learn the English language, and become sufficiently familiar with English customs, literature, science, modes of thought, standards of truth and honour, and . . . with manly English sports and games'. It was this kind of thinking which lay behind the setting up of the 'Chiefs' Colleges' in the 1870s and 1880s. These schools were reserved for the nobility and offered a very similar curriculum to an English public school. Games were no less highly regarded at Mayo or Rajkumar College than at Harrow or Eton. Chester Macnaughten, the head of Rajkumar and pioneer of this kind of teaching, delighted in reading from *Tom Brown's Schooldays* to his charges. He was especially fond of the passage where the captain of the eleven discussed the need to keep the team steady; but perhaps this was to be expected in a school where young princes sometimes came accompanied by numerous retainers ready to launch a sudden attack on a rival student prince, who might have slighted the honour of their lord. It obviously took time for such institutions to settle down, but by the Edwardian era the battle seemed more or less won. Mayo College had 'three cricket and football elevens, each with a capital ground' and five English games masters, noted an admiring journalist on a visit from Britain. Of course, many great Indian families spurned such innovations, preferring their ancient Hindu and Muslim curricula taught by private tutors or through a well-established

---

[11] B. S. Cohn, 'Representing Authority in Victorian India', in Hobsbawm and Ranger, *Invention of Tradition*, ch. 5, esp. pp. 181–2.

educational system. On the other hand, it did become fashionable amongst the high-born to send at least one son to be educated in England. Frank Richards gave Greyfriars an obligatory Indian, who despite his comically long-winded English was a 'good fellow' and could be counted upon to rag the 'fat owl' Bunter with Bob Cherry and the other chaps. Moreover, whether they were educated in the 'Chiefs' Colleges' or in England, the most illustrious often went on to Oxford or Cambridge to finish their academic and athletic education.[12]

Most famous of these 'oriental gentlemen' was Prince Ranjitsinhji, Maharaja Jam Sahib of Nawangar, known universally as 'Ranji'. He learned to play cricket at Rajkumar College before going to Cambridge and subsequently scoring a record 3,000 runs in 1899, captaining Sussex, and playing for England. If ever there was an honorary Englishman, it was Ranji. He served as ADC to Sir John French in 1915, went grouse-shooting and had an estate in Ireland. He was watched as appreciatively by the ranks of the comfortably retired at Hove as he was back in India, elegantly glancing the fastest of bowling away to the boundary; the late cut was virtually his invention. Ranji eventually returned to India, where he became Chancellor of the Chamber of Princes, distributing his patrimony lavishly on cricket and diplomatic entertaining with hospitals and schools benefiting from what little was left over. Cricket, in fact, came to be a major source of expenditure. Subsidizing tours seems to have been among the favourite extravagances of the Indian aristocracy. The Maharaj Kumar of Vizianagram ('Vizzy') brought over Hobbs and Sutcliffe to play in a series of private matches. Like their English counterparts, the Indian aristocracy tended to leave the hard work of bowling to the lower classes and naturally expected their station gave them the right to the captaincy. There was an unseemly struggle for the position among the Indian side to tour England in 1932. The team was originally to be captained by the Maharaja of Patiala, one of the richest and most flamboyant of the princes. 'He strode out to the crease, jewels flashing in the sun. The people adored him and if, plumb in front to the first ball he received, he was given not out, who cared?' When Patiala had to withdraw the vice-captain, the Prince of Limbdi, prepared

---

[12] J. A. Mangan, *Games Ethic* (1986), ch. 5, pp. 125, 133, 137.

to take over but this met with stiff resistance from 'Vizzy', the deputy vice-captain. Another ruler, whose formal precedence could not be questioned, had to be brought in. The only trouble was that the new captain had nothing like the knowledge needed for a test captain. Status was more important that virtuosity. When Vizzy got his turn in 1936 he was a splendid social success, but a disaster on the field, constantly altering the batting order and indulging in wildly eccentric field-placing. Ironically the best of the princely cricketers, who came after Ranji also played for England. The Nawab of Pataudi not only made a record 238 not out for Oxford against Cambridge, he even produced a useful century for England in their notorious tour of Australia in 1932. Unlike the members of the Yorkshire side, those who played for England did not really have to be born on their native heath—a title and a couple of years at Oxford or Cambridge were all that was required.[13]

Cricket was not the only means of anglicizing the indigenous rulers. Polo was never the sole preserve of the Indian army. Keeping strings of polo ponies was a satisfying form of conspicuous consumption for maharajas, who supplied some of the best players and were in close and competitive contact with the élite of the Indian army as a result. The Maharajas of Alwar, of Kishengarh, and Jaipur along with the Nawab of Bhopal were among some of the best players in the Raj. Billiards and snooker were another source of common interest between the Indian palace and the officers' mess. It was the Maharaja of Cooch Behar at the Calcutta Club in 1885, who passed on the rules of snooker to John Roberts, the world billiards champion, and this is how the game got back to Britain. Roberts himself had formerly been retained at a huge fee by the Maharaja of Jaipur, who installed him in the palace and gave him a hundred servants. Six full-size billiard-tables were brought to Jaipur by elephant and the Maharaja spent £5,000 organizing a single tournament. Going by the maxim of the diplomat Sir Hercules Robinson that 'a similarity of taste in amusements is a guarantee for common sympathy in more important matters', the British had little to fear from the sporting princes.[14]

---

[13] A. Ross, *Ranji* (1983); R. Cashman, 'The Phenomenon of Indian Cricket', in R. Cashman and M. McKernan, *Sport in History* (1979), pp. 196–8.
[14] Trelford, *Snookered*, pp. 24–5; Hyam, *Britain's Imperial Century*, p. 151.

The cultivation of British sports amongst the Indians was not confined to a handful of great families. Other élite elements were also drawn into games, especially cricket. The Parsees, an important group of merchants and members of the liberal professions originating in Persia and based around Bombay, took up cricket and organized regular fixtures with the British as part of their role as brokers between the British and the bulk of the Indian population. The Parsee side beat the British in 1886 and a few years later an Islamic and then a Hindu 'gymkhana' or 'playing-space' for cricket was formed. Cricket matches between the Presidency and these Indian teams were held at Bombay and Poona and drew large crowds. Sectarian differences were too deeply rooted to permit caste or religious mixing on a large scale. British hopes that shared sports would diminish inter-community feuding soon gave way to the acceptance of bitter divisions—a tolerable state of affairs for those who ruled a land 'too divided to rule itself'.[15]

High-caste Indians were taught 'to play the game' at fee-paying secondary schools often run by athletically inclined muscular Christians like Cecil Tyndale-Briscoe, younger son of an Oxfordshire gentry family and Cambridge oarsman. He dedicated himself for fifty years to *Character Building in Kashmir* (as he entitled a pamphlet on his activities for the Church Missionary Society) after the Bishop of London, shocked by his theological ignorance, had told him 'you are only fit to teach the blacks, there now!' Football, rowing, and boxing were the major weapons in his campaign to bring enlightenment and stamp out sodomy amongst the pupils. Gymnastic exercises were also tried, though this did not please the sporting missionary, for whom 'a holy Brahmin . . . hanging by his hocks—his only apparel being a very filthy night-gown telescoped over his head . . . was not a pretty sight'. The Hindu prohibition against touching leather would have discouraged lesser men from choosing football as a means of 'grinding grit into Kashmir', but not the robustly ethnocentric Briscoe. Bringing up the rear with his riding-crop, the 'dirty, smelling, cowardly crew' were 'shooed down the streets like sheep on their way to the butchers' by teachers armed

---

[15] Cashman, 'The Phenomenon of Indian Cricket', in Cashman and McKernan, *Sport in History*, pp. 191–3.

with sticks, who then drove them on to the field of play. Pupils tried to kick the ball but generally missed it, 'their clogs flew in the air . . . while their night-gowns flapped in one another's faces'; those struck in the face with the ball screamed they were polluted by the leather ball and had to be washed and reassured. All was not in vain. In 1922, after thirty years of struggle, he was able to watch a good game of Indian schoolboy football carried on in the spirit of fair play. He had persisted and football had at last won some limited acceptance. As he sowed the seed of sport in the stony ground of Kashmir, he took comfort in this little verse:

> . . . it isn't discussion, or staring or fussing
> will coax us a crop from the clay;
> Its draining, manuring, persisting, enduring,
> Its patiently pegging away.[16]

The introduction of Anglo-Saxon sport to the people of India met with some resistance, mostly of a passive kind. Many just ignored these strange, exhausting activities or abandoned the practice as soon as they left school. Tyndale-Briscoe called his autobiography *Fifty Years against the Stream*, and for the zealous missionary of exercise India must often have seemed a weird and dispiriting place. Active resistance to British sports seems to have been fairly uncommon, but there is evidence of limited but determined intellectual opposition to modern games in Bengal. The British did not particularly like the climate, the topography, or the inhabitants of Bengal. 'A low, lying people in a low-lying land' ran the colonial sneer. A Bengali had 'the grit of a rabbit'—an image with which the Bengali élite itself appeared to concur. It was against the 'self-image of effeteness' that a small number of Bengali cultural nationalists took issue. They rejected any involvement in Anglo-Saxon sports and demanded the restoration of the ancient physical culture of the Bengali people, in which circus strong-men and acrobats featured prominently. As a national hero they chose the unlikely figure of a former circus performer who became a colonel in the Brazilian army. The indigenous Bengali rulers naturally resented their leadership being usurped by a 'social bandit', whose largest engagement was said to have involved only fifty men. So they donned their flannels

---

[16] Mangan, *Games Ethic*, ch. 7, esp. pp. 184–5, 190.

and went out to bat with the British. The native élite mostly rejected their own culture and tried to win the respect of the Raj through sport. Nationalist opposition to Anglo-Saxon sports, therefore, was limited and ineffective. Members of the liberal professions in the Congress Party were far more likely to have absorbed the values of fair play at school than to have cultivated ancient Indian sports. In fact, much of the strength of the Congress case against the Raj was that the British were not playing 'fair'. Once an educated élite had proved beyond reasonable doubt that they were fit for self-government, it was simply 'not cricket' to deny them their chance. The British were refusing to play by their own rules, and this line of argument had more impact on the liberal middle-ground of British politics than more ideologically inflammatory forms of nationalism.[17]

By the 1930s cricket had become a major urban spectator sport, especially in the south of India, with capacity crowds for the first test series between England and India in 1933–4. Support for the Ranji Trophy, an inter-state competition introduced in 1934 in honour of India's foremost player, was strong. At the top level, however, cricket remained something of a princely enclave. If India had a national sport it was hockey. Field hockey had been introduced by army officers in the 1880s in Calcutta and spread quickly. This is perhaps because it resembled a kind of stick-and-ball game that had been played in different forms in different parts of the subcontinent into the nineteenth century. Indians certainly showed themselves to have a remarkable flair for the game, even changing the shape of the stick so that the ball could be dribbled more easily. A federation was formed in 1925 and India entered the Olympic Games in 1928 and won the gold medal. They repeated the feat in 1932 and again in 1936 at Berlin where they satisfyingly annihilated the Aryan opposition 8–1 in the final. Major Dhyan Chand, who scored six of these goals, was a national sporting hero.

Promoting sport for the improvement of subject colonial peoples came to be quite widely canvassed around the turn of the century, though it was never systematically carried out. 'The moral teaching force of cricket in malarial jungle, sandy desolation, or the uttermost islands of the sea' was just one

---

[17] J. Rosselli, 'The Self-Image of Effeteness', *Past and Present*, Feb. 1980.

example of the kind of thinking to be found throughout the Empire. In Ceylon, the headmaster of Trinity College 'used to conduct a post-mortem on the previous day's match . . . and would describe with pitiless accuracy every moment when a player held on to the ball when he should have passed, or committed a slovenly piece of fielding at cricket.' In Africa Sir Frederick Lugard proposed to educate the sons of the Nigerian chiefs through 'a strong British staff of the right type, who in the daily social intercourse of the play fields will impress on the boys what the school expects of its members'. This was also one of the aims behind the setting up in East Africa of Budo College in Uganda. 'The discipline of work and games in a boarding-schol' was the means chosen by Bishop Tucker and the other founders 'to build character'. A former pupil of the school remembered its hearty imperial flavour where the boys allegedly petitioned the head to adopt as the motto of Budo the dying words of Cecil Rhodes: 'So little done, so much to do.' 'When we come out at four, we go and play football', remembered one boy, 'on one side eleven and on the other side eleven, and we arrange every man in his place.'[18]

In the West Indies there were similar efforts to use secondary education to create a separate and culturally pro-British stratum. In Barbados, which as a small Caribbean island can claim to have become in proportional terms the most passionate and successful cricketing force in the world, three élite schools—Harrison College, The Lodge, and Cobermere—systematically promoted the game and the ideals of imperial sportsmanship it enshrined. Such was the success of the enterprise that decolonization had little impact on the system of athletic education. The new black rulers had been brought up in the school of fair play and saw no reason to change significantly the syllabus or spirit of élite education in what came to be known as 'Little England'. A classic account of this process of 'cultural reproduction' has been provided by the black historian, novelist, and socialist C. L. R. James. James came from a modest, respectable, and religious family in Trinidad with educational ambitions. He won a scholarship to

[18] Hyam, *Britain's Imperial Century*, p. 151; Mangan, *Games Ethic*, pp. 176–7; J. A. Mangan, 'Gentlemen Galore', *Immigrants and Minorities*, July 1982, p. 155; T. Ranger, 'The Invention of Tradition in Colonial Africa', in Hobsbawm and Ranger, *The Invention of Tradition*, p. 222.

Queen's Royal College, a racially mixed secondary school staffed by masters steeped in the traditions of the minor public schools and Oxbridge. The 'college boys' were set apart from the street boys; the street boys 'shouted and stamped and yelled and expressed themselves fully in anger as in joy', but the college boys with their education in the art of 'fair play' were required to keep a 'stiff upper lip'. James steeped himself in the middle-class culture of the British boy, reading the *Boy's Own Paper* and *The Captain*, worshipping at the shrine of Dr Grace and memorizing the averages of C. B. Fry with the awe of a young Harrovian reciting *Wisden*. James grew up in the public school tradition, fostered alike by cricket and by art, under the stern gaze of Mr W. Burslem MA—the appropriately 'Arnoldian' headmaster. The impact of this education on James was not a matter of crude propaganda, but rather a subtle blending of 'high' culture with physical culture. 'How not to look up to the England of Shakespeare and Milton, of Thackeray and Dickens, of Hobbs and Rhodes?' That was the question. Despite sharing a socialist philosophy, James could never stomach Nye Bevan's mocking of the 'Tory' morality of 'playing with a straight bat'. Nor did he later sympathize with the popular fanaticism of those who saw West Indies representative cricket mainly as a chance to inflict humiliation on the former colonial power. This 'wasn't playing the game'. He maintained an attachment to the principles of 'fair play' despite their imperial provenance. Similarly in Barbados 'the colonial radicals were products of an educational system which stressed the virtues of classical learning and cricket practice. Chris Braithwaite, Mitchie Hewitt, Hugh Springer, Frank Walcott, and others did not see any contradiction in supporting British forms of recreation while denouncing British forms of exploitation.'[19]

So the celebrated case of C. L. R. James is instructive and not unusual. The extent to which a black revolutionary retained an underlying belief in the games ethic underlines the insidious influence of British culture on the educated few. Its deeper significance in the West Indies lay in the way cricket reflected

---

[19] C. L. R. James, *Beyond a Boundary* (1963), ch. 2, esp. p. 38. K. A. Sandiford and B. Stoddart, 'The Élite Schools and Cricket in Barbados', *IJHS*, Dec. 1987, pp. 333–50; K. A. Sandiford, 'Cricket and the Barbadian Society', *Canadian Journal of History*, Dec. 1986, p. 367. I am grateful to Keith Sandiford for drawing this article to my attention.

the colonial racial hierarchy and the aspirations of the Afro-Caribbean majority. For racial segregation was built into colonial sport. Many whites simply refused to play in or against teams with black players. 'The stubborn refusal . . . to take part in any game in which poor coloured men are engaged is a persistent exhibition of artificial greatness that finds no place where intelligence or decency encamps', observed the *Barbados Globe* in 1895. Nor was racism just a matter of 'white' or 'black' clubs; there was a series of intermediate distinctions based on lightness of skin colour and on occupation in Trinidad club cricket, which determined its structure. The Queen's Park club took white officials and a handful of the most distinguished 'coloured' families but no blacks. Shamrock catered for the Irish Catholics and other whites plus some middle-class coloureds. Again there were no blacks. James thought it would have been easier for him to have joined the MCC than either of these clubs. Then came Maple, a brown-skinned team which ranked itself above Shannon, who were made up of the better-educated blacks. Finally there was Stingo, the leading black working-class team. Despite the fact that all these teams with the predictable exception of Queen's Park played on the same large area of grassland, they all had their separate club-houses and played each other 'with deadly seriousness'. In Barbados the first clubs, Pickwick and Wanderers, founded in 1877 and 1882 respectively, were for the white élite with Leeward and Windward following in the 1890s for poorer whites. Spartan, set up in 1893 for middle-class non-whites, split in 1915 because of its policy of excluding lower-middle-class blacks and they formed the Empire Club in 1915. Empire in its turn would not take poor rural blacks, who did not get a chance to play in their own clubs until the 1930s.[20]

Cricket was a far more complex social force than imperial propagandists realized. Playing Anglo-Saxon games did not make all sportsmen reassuringly pro-British. A game like cricket was capable of carrying several 'political' meanings depending upon whether the player was a white official, a brown-skinned sales clerk, or a black dock-worker—as two of the outstanding non-white players of the 1920s were. Representative cricket did,

---

[20] James, *Beyond a Boundary*, ch. 4; Sandiford, 'Cricket and the Barbadian Society', pp. 362–3.

however, help to provide an opportunity for the expression of a new national confidence in which black and brown differences were partially submerged by a rejection of colonialism. Learie Constantine and George Headley showed that West Indian cricket was capable of producing world-class cricketers. Yet recognition was slow to come. The captaincy was denied to a series of black players culminating in a snub to Frank Worrell in 1960 that sparked off rioting during the visit of the England team. Behind this lay the pressing question of national independence. Brown and black could unite around national cricket as a symbol of dignity and freedom, though racial discrimination remained with the better seats occupied by those with lighter skins. The Test match became so important because it both dramatized these tensions while offering a satisfying refutation of white superiority. The batting of Worrell, Weekes, and Walcott and the bowling of Valentine and Ramadhin helped promote cricket as a source of national pride in the crucial pre-independence decade after the Second World War. As other countries began to see the West Indians as great cricketers, so they grew in confidence and began to see themselves in the same light. Cricket helped to create a wider Caribbean culture bridging the differences between islands which, combined with a favourable climate, has produced a seemingly endless supply of brilliant cricketers like Gary Sobers, Viv Richards, and a host of superb fast bowlers. The top Caribbean cricketers have become Carnival heroes, celebrated in popular song and expected to play not just well but with 'style, panache, flamboyance, an ostentatiously contemptuous defiance of the opposition'. Cricket in the West Indies is half British and half rooted in the street culture of 'expansiveness, camaraderies, unruliness, jesting, joking, verbal and bodily bravado, clowning—in a word *playing*'. The crowd antics at big matches became part of the spectacle itself, spilling over occasionally into rioting when the pace of national independence and the progress towards the eventual appointment of a black captain was too slow. And yet all this has taken place within a wider international context of Commonwealth co-operation. Cricket is a living expression of post-colonial solidarity. Such is the paradox of sport and decolonization. Cricket has helped both to sharpen a sense of nationalism and to soften its impact on Britain through the maintenance of close sporting contacts between former colonies and the 'mother country'.[21]

3. DOMINION CULTURE AND THE 'MOTHER COUNTRY'

It was in Canada, South Africa, Australia, and New Zealand—the white Dominions which achieved statutory self-determination between the wars—that the role of sports as a means of reconciling nationalism with membership of the Empire was most important. Canada was the odd man out in the sense that it did not play Test cricket and had a large French-speaking minority, who were not exactly receptive to British culture. Moreover the proximity of so powerful a neighbour led to the introduction of American spectator sports alongside more distinctively Canadian ones like ice hockey. Whilst shared sports were less important in Canada than elsewhere in the Dominions, they remained influential amongst the loyalist élite educated at exclusive private boarding-schools such as Upper Canada College, founded in 1836 by Sir John Colbourne, who requested a 'cargo' of Oxford sportsmen to staff it. 'British feelings cannot flow into the breasts of our Canadian boys through a more delightful channel than that of British sports', remarked the *Toronto Patriot* of the time. Britishness in this context meant conservatism, for the correspondent went on to add that 'a cricketer, as a matter of opinion detests democracy and is staunch in his allegiance to his king'. Cricket was also played in the United States, and North America was important enough to be visited by the first England touring team in 1859. The Canadians sent a side to Britain in 1880 and contacts have been maintained since at a minor level.[22]

Why did cricket 'fail' in Canada and succeed elsewhere in the Dominions? Part of the answer lies in the way the game became trapped in its own exclusivity. Cricket was played by too few

[21] R. D. E. Burton, 'Cricket, Carnival and Street Culture in the Caribbean', *BJSH*, Sept. 1985, pp. 187–8; H. Tiffin, 'Cricket, Literature and the Politics of Decolonisation', in R. Cashman and M. McKernan, *Sport: Money, Morality and the Media* (1982), pp. 177–94.

[22] R. Gruneau, *Class, Sports and Social Development* (1983), pp. 103, 117–28; J. A. Mangan, 'Imperial Reproduction', in Proceedings of the Third Annual Conference of the BSSH, 1985; also Mangan, *Games Ethic*, ch. 6; G. Redmond, *The Sporting Scots of Nineteenth Century Canada* (1982), pp. 117–28.

to permit serious competition except with the United States, where the sport came largely to be confined to Philadelphia and 'old money'. French Canadians were never likely to have much time for a game that was so quintessentially English. Moreover, climatic factors and the pattern of British emigration itself further weakened its appeal. The presence of so many Scots and the coldness of the weather favoured curling rather than cricket. Canada, in fact, has become the leading curling nation in the world with half a million players. Though curling helped to maintain links with Scotland, the sport was too peripheral to have much significance in imperial terms. The creation of a distinctive form of football, however, was a different matter. Here the role of the United States was crucial. The Ivy League universities influenced their Canadian counterparts like McGill to develop along broadly American lines. The Canadian Football Union was set up in 1891 to regulate a game, which is different from American football only in technical detail. American commercial interests and players moved into Canadian football and ice hockey so that sporting links with the United States became stronger than those with Britain.

Athletics, however, have provided some common ground between Britain, Canada, and the rest of the Empire. The first British Empire Games, later to be renamed the Commonwealth Games, were held in Hamilton in 1930. The idea had first been floated by J. Astley Cooper as part of a Pan-Britannic Festival as early as 1891, but the establishment of the Olympic Games shortly afterwards cut the ground from under the proposal and, despite early enthusiasm, it eventually lapsed. Athletics were organized as part of the Festival of Empire for George V's coronation in 1911, but they formed a fairly minor part of the celebration and involved only Canada and Australasia. Canada eventually won the Empire Trophy presented by Lord Desborough, but an Australian journalist complained that 'all the enthusiasm was shown by the colonials . . . the British public did not take the meeting seriously'. The successful revival of the idea in the later 1920s is historically interesting and requires to be placed in a wider imperial context. The implementation of the Statute of Westminster was about to establish the full constitutional autonomy of the Dominions. This loosening of the formal bonds of Empire came at the same time as new economic pressures were being placed upon the relationship between the Dominions and Britain. The prices of primary produce were falling and the capacity of the Dominions to purchase industrial goods from the 'mother country' was reduced accordingly. Despite the ending of free trade and the Ottawa agreements of 1931 on preferential imperial tariffs, there was increasing economic strains on the maintenance of good imperial relations. This is *not* to say the British Empire Games were simply devised to hold together through the bonds of sport an institution which was under constitutional and economic strain. The political economy of the Empire was not the 'cause' and the Empire Games the 'effect'. The relations between imperial governments and between the departments of the British state itself were much too complex for that. Nor was the Amateur Athletic Association, or the other sporting bodies involved, subject to direct state control. On the other hand, to view the Empire Games *purely* as the culmination of a long-term trend within athletics for greater international competition is surely naïve. The pervasiveness of imperial propaganda between the wars created a climate where the members of the relevant sporting bodies—many of whom were active in other areas of public life—were increasingly inclined to consider organizing a specifically imperial event. Growing criticism of the stridency and chauvinism of the Olympic Games also played a part. Imperial athletes sought an affirmation of the 'fair-play' spirit, and significantly it was the Dominions which most fervently advocated this ideal. Canada agreed to host the first British Empire Games in 1930 with the venue, the city of Hamilton, agreeing to bear any overall loss there might be. 'Boosterism' blended with a celebration of cultural ties which were now free from formal imperial control. Constitutional liberty released the floodgates of Dominion sentiment. Sport came to be seen as an integral aspect of the 'Commonwealth'. The Games took their place alongside other displays of imperial achievement, custom, and industry at the periodic inter-war Empire exhibitions.[23]

Of the many contacts between the sportsmen of the Empire, most took place outside the framework of the Empire Games.

[23] K. Moore, 'Sport, Politics and Imperialism', in Proceedings of the Fourth Annual Conference of the BSSH, 1986, pp. 46–57.

Cricket and rugby were the games which Britain and the white Dominions of the southern hemisphere shared with most enthusiasm. Football was not an 'imperial' game. Soccer tours were organized and football was widely played, especially in South Africa, which provided Liverpool with a string of outstanding players between the wars, but Dominion football internationals never took hold. This preference for rugby was partly a result of the public school education of important officials and settlers, and partly a response to the sudden professionalization of football in Britain. The dispersed and relatively small populations of the Dominions could not hope to sustain highly paid professional soccer teams to compete with the English or the Scots. However, the amateurism of Rugby Union, and its weakening as a result of the schism with the northern clubs in 1894, permitted countries like New Zealand and South Africa to play the British on equal terms—some would say more than equal terms. The South Africans won their first Test series in 1903, and then beat Wales and Ireland on their 1906 tour and drew their match with England. Only the year before this the All Blacks had won thirty-two out of the thirty-three matches on their British tour, and the controversial try which lost them the game against Wales is disputed to this day by their fervent supporters. South Africa and New Zealand had firmly placed themselves at the heart of international rugby despite being on the other side of the world.[24]

Rugby and cricket Test matches were the real stuff of Dominion sport. Lively interest in Britain was nothing to the absolute passion with which All Black or Springbok matches were followed at home. The seeds of a triangular exchange between Britain, South Africa, and the Antipodes were sown around the turn of the century, but it was not until after the Great War that the pattern of regular touring was firmly established. Between the wars there was a busy and cheerful traffic of sportsmen on the luxury liners to and from South Africa, Australia, and New Zealand. Sporting memoirs abound with tales of pleasant voyages to the Cape on the *Windsor Castle*, or the long haul to Australia through Suez, which was a kind of imperial itinerary in its own right with stops in Aden, Ceylon, and Singapore. Bilateral

[24] J. Reason and C. James, *The World of Rugby* (1970), p. 35.

dominion contacts, notably the ferocious rivalry between the All Blacks and the Springboks, were as important in emphasizing the shared culture of the British Empire as visits from British teams themselves. Within Britain the regular presence of visiting cricket and rugby teams of very high quality both provided a focus for national effort and a break from the familiar round of domestic competition. The visit of an Australian touring team as early as 1880 prompted Lord Harris to claim 'the game of cricket has done more to draw the Mother Country and the Colonies together than years of beneficial legislation could have done'. This remained the received wisdom. For the British the enjoyment of 'our' games by 'our' people, wherever they were, was a wholesome expression of the naturalness of Empire.[25]

The reception of sport within the Dominions, however, was more complex than the British public imagined. These countries were not a blank sheet upon which the British could write what they wished. The meanings attached to games varied from place to place according to racial and political divisions and aspirations. In South Africa, for example, British sports were drawn into the conflict between the Dutch-speaking and English-speaking groups. British settlers made little effort to conceal their contempt for the Boers. 'It is worth considering the Boer at sport,' wrote John Buchan, 'for there he is at his worst. Without tradition of fair play, soured and harassed by want and disaster, his sport became a matter of commerce' (shooting game for profit). Buchan thought that the Afrikaners simply 'were not a sporting race'. They were resented as interlopers or patronized as bumpkins. Just at the moment when the rebellious Boers were inflicting embarrassing damage on the British army, South Africa took its place at the first Imperial Cricket Conference. Subsequently the Boers did not feel either welcome or inclined to participate in the game, which remained very much an expression of Anglo-Saxon separateness and superiority in the eyes of Afrikaner farming people. Test cricket between South Africa and England was an Anglophile 'family' affair. No significant writing on the game appeared in Afrikaans for fifty years. The victory over the visiting England side in 1907 by a South Africa armed with a

[25] K. S. Inglis, 'Imperial Cricket', in Cashman and McKernan, *Sport in History*, p. 155.

unique trio of googly bowlers was not a matter for Boer rejoicing. The brilliance with which the young Jack Hobbs spotted the spin on the following tour, nipping down the wicket to smother the turn, may have moved *Wisden* to superlatives but the tricky business of off-breaks bowled with a leg-break action was a closed book to the Dutch speakers.[26]

Perhaps surprisingly the Boers did not reject all British sports. They developed a keen interest in Rugby, which became a kind of ruling passion in the rural areas between the wars and a vehicle for a Afrikaner self-expression and identity. Jaapie Krige, a centre with mesmerizing footwork, had been the hero of the Springbok touring side of 1906 and the Boer element came to predominate in the great Springbok sides who dominated world rugby in the 1930s. The Springbok prop-forwards 'Boy' and Fanie Louw and the hooker Jan Lotz had a five-stone advantage over any other side in the world. 'Skrum, skrum, skrum' was the guiding principle despite the brilliance of their backs, who were fed by Danie Craven, inventor of the spectacular 'dive pass' and later to preside over the turbulent politics of the game as president of the South African Rugby Board from 1956. The way the Springboks perceived the game is of the utmost importance. The controlled power of their forwards, their speed, and the fierceness of their tackling offered an image of the Afrikaner people, which stood in stark contrast to the apparent 'softness' of Anglo-Saxon cricket. 'Borselling', where team-mates would lift up a player and ceremonially beat his backside, symbolized their tight male bonding and toughness. The Springboks may have been playing an 'imperial' game but they were playing it to assert themselves as a proud and independent people, whose attitude to the British Crown was ambiguous to say the least. Loyalty to the Empire was not uncontested or straightforwardly assimilated through sport.[27]

The point here is not to suggest that the world of rugby was necessarily more aggressive or weighed down with masculine ritual in South Africa than elsewhere. Rugby seems to have promoted a strong male group conformity and a certain social conservatism wherever it was played. What varied from one context to another was the degree to which the supporters of

---

[26] R. Archer and A. Bouillon, *The South African Game* (1982), pp. 18, 87.
[27] Ibid., ch. 2; Reason and James, *World of Rugby*, ch. 5.

representative teams stressed national self-assertion over the wider loyalty to the Empire. The collective identity of New Zealand males was certainly bound up in the performance of the All Blacks but in their case sporting success reinforced the dominant political culture of loyalty to Commonwealth and monarchist traditions. Colin Meads, the most-capped All Black, was a loyal subject of the Crown *and* a patriotic Kiwi. All Dominion sport mediated the desire for national self-determination and identity with a sense of imperial purpose. Even South African rugby fostered a kind of fondness for old enemies and was also popular with English-speaking loyalists. The relationship between the elements of nationalism and imperialism varied according to the historical experience of the individual state. Nowhere was the sense of shared culture and of Dominion independence more finely balanced than in Australia.

When Frederick Robert Spofforth took the wicket of W. G. Grace with his second ball in a match against the MCC during the first Australian tour of England in 1878, he gave notice of a new power in the world of cricket. When 'the demon bowler' took 14 for 90 four years later in an official Test match at the Oval, even *The Times* acknowledged the beginning of 'a new epoch in the history of the game' and offered an obituary for English cricket, whose 'body will be cremated and the Ashes taken to Australia'. A group of Melbourne ladies subsequently provided the England captain with an urn containing the incinerated remains of a bail and the legend of the Ashes was established. From that moment the struggle for the Ashes became the focal point of sporting contact between England and Australia. This quaint trophy was a symbol both of the rivalry and of the friendship between the two peoples. Cricket had spread quickly in Australia where leisure time and earning power tended to be significantly higher for working men than in Britain. The biannual tours to win the Ashes were certainly popular in Britain, especially with poorer county sides coming to depend on their share of the tour to prop up the balance sheet. But in Australia, where there was less top-class spectator sport available, an England touring team was *the* major entertainment and attracted massive public support. In the 1880s private tours organized by English professionals like Arthur Shaw and Arthur Shrewsbury of Nottingham or James Lillywhite of Sussex were highly profitable.

By the Edwardian period an England tour was expected to gross around £25,000 with crowds of up to 35,000 turning up to watch Saturday play.[28]

The Australian cricket team became a major focus for cultural nationalism. As early as the 1890s it was starting to be said that the best service England could do for imperial unity was to take home a losing team. F. R. Spofforth by rights should have been their first sporting hero but he inconveniently cherished his old landed Yorkshire roots, settling back in Britain in 1888 where his 'father rode as straight as the best with the York and Ainsty hounds'. 'Anglo-Australians', middle-class settlers who never considered themselves anything but British at heart, were common enough at the time but they were not the stuff of national myth. The problem was compounded by being a bowler. Takers of wickets have fared worse than scorers of runs in the heroism stakes. In Victor Trumper Australia found a national hero, a batsman of the class and power of Fry or even Grace himself who was truly an ordinary 'Aussie'. His maiden Test century at Lord's in 1899 was effortlessly executed and followed by 300 not out against Sussex. The Test series of 1902, still considered by many to be the finest of all time, brought together a magnificent England side which included C. B. Fry, Ranjitsinghi, and the great Yorkshire all-rounders George Hirst and Wilfred Rhodes. When Gilbert Jessop, 'the Croucher', and one of the most aggressive run-makers in the history of the game, and batsmen of the class of Francis Stanley Jackson and John Tyldesley are added, this undoubtedly was one of the strongest England sides of all time. Their captain, Archie MacLaren, was also a fine batsman holding the record for a county score of 424, though modestly comparing himself to Trumper as 'an honest selling-plater in the company of a Derby thoroughbred'. Against them were ranged an Australian team, which included several players who had made centuries against England; alongside 'the immortal Victor' there was Monty Noble, a brilliant tactician and one of the finest Australian all-rounders in the history of the game.[29]

[28] D. Ibbotson and R. Dellor, *A Hundred Years of the Ashes* (1982), ch. 2; Inglis, 'Imperial Cricket', pp. 151-2.

[29] R. Cashman, 'F. R. Spofforth', Proceedings of the Fourth Annual Conference of the BSSH, 1986, pp. 29-45; M. Down, *Archie* (1981) and L. H. Brown, *Victor Trumper and the 1902 Australians* (1981), reviewed in the *Times Literary Supplement*, 26 June 1981, p. 720.

The series began sensationally when Australia, in reply to England's 376 for 9, was dismissed for 26—the lowest ever score in an Ashes match—after an overnight downpour made the slow left-arm spin of Rhodes virtually unplayable. The rain then came to the rescue of Australia and rain again stopped play in the second Test at Lord's. The Australians performed soundly at Sheffield in the next encounter with Noble taking 11 for 103 to win the match. England now had to win the fourth Test. Despite a superb century before lunch in the first innings by Victor Trumper on a sodden wicket, England dominated, bowling out Australia for 86 in the second innings and needing only 124 to win. They lost quick wickets but Rhodes kept his end up and England had reached 120 for 9 when the tail-ender Fred Tate swung wildly at a simple ball and was bowled. England lost by three runs in what came to be known as 'Tate's match'—the poor man had also dropped a crucial catch. English honour was redeemed in the final Test at Lord's when Gilbert Jessop came to the wicket at 48 for 5 with England needing 263 to win. In what a contemporary called 'an innings that will be remembered as long as cricket is played' Jessop made 104 in 77 minutes off 80 balls. Hirst and Rhodes saw England home with a famous last-wicket partnership to win the Test by a single wicket. But Australia retained the Ashes. Everyone had something to cheer about, Trumper's and Jessop's centuries, marvellous bowling, and desperately close finishes. There were sudden and devastating collapses by both sides redeemed by exceptional individual efforts. The true beneficiary of such a series, every twist and turn of which was followed by large crowds and in the papers, was the institution of the Test match itself, and with it the sense of being culturally so close to people who lived so far away. Cricket was the only game which could draw strong support from all sections of English society and, despite fierce competitiveness on the field, imperial sentiment was strengthened by this 'invented tradition' of Empire.[30]

In Australia things were not quite this simple. It was all very well for the English to make much of the 'imperial' quality of the game. The problem was that imperialism was often perceived as no more than a kind of English nationalism of the middle and

---

[30] Ibbotson and Dellor, *A Hundred Years of the Ashes*, pp. 48–52.

upper classes. The gentlemen who ran the Empire from Whitehall were also quite likely to be members of the private club at Marylebone to whom cricketers all over the world were expected to defer. This understandably grated on the poor emigrant, who had travelled so far to escape the class structure of the old country. If we add the descendants of those who came on convict-ships as well as a large Irish element, enjoyment of the imperial game was shot through with feelings of collective resentment and self-assertion. Australian cricket was an odd mixture. Affection for the 'Old Country' was tinged with a sharply democratic 'Jack's as good as his master' attitude. Certain elements in the crowd were overtly hostile from early on. The 'Poms', especially those amateurs who were gentlemen both in the sporting and social sense, were fair game and were expected to maintain their famous stiff upper lip in the face of crude provocation from the crowd. It was during the 1890s, when the Test match emerged as a national institution in Australia, that barracking by sections of the crowd became a problem and a source of complaint. 'We have been insulted, hooted at and hissed', wrote A. E. Stoddart, who captained the England touring team in 1897–8, 'in every match and on every ground without exception.' 'Pommie bastards' they became—possibly derived from the English gentleman's taste for Pommery champagne in preference to Australian beer—and 'Pommie bastards' they remained.[31]

Australian cricket tended to divide between the 'British' style of amateur official and the more down-to-earth 'Aussie' professional. There was a real struggle for control of the game which the 'gentlemen' officials only won with difficulty in 1911–12. Enlistment, which the Australian Cricket authorities had urged upon its players, and the consequent loss of life in the trenches, affirmed the depth of shared sentiments whilst suffering sharpened the popular consciousness of Australia's separate interests and needs. Cricket dramatized the ambivalence of the Australian public to Britain. The touring team of 1921, which included Gregory and Macdonald in the pace attack and

---

[31] Scyld Berry, 'Mike Brearley—Pommie Bastard', *Observer*, 10 Feb. 1980; see also W. F. Mandle, 'Cricket and Australian Nationalism in the Nineteenth Century', *Journal of the Royal Australian Historical Society*, Dec. 1973.

Macartney and Bardsley with the bat, is probably the greatest Australian side to have visited Britain with the exception of Bradman's 1948 team with the devastating bowling of Lindwall and Miller. Cricket was able to satisfy the desire of the lower-class immigrant to beat England whilst appealing to the 'British' establishment in Australia as an imperial sport. This kind of division became open and explicit in the history of football where the southern and western states favoured an Irish form akin to Gaelic football ('Aussie Rules') whilst the northern ones split along predictably class lines to create a Union and League game which closely mirrored the divisions in 'the Mother Country'. This says a good deal about the problem of 'Britishness' in Australia.

All this brings us to 1932 and the 'bodyline' tour. The bones of the business can be set out quite simply. After being soundly beaten by Australia in England in 1930 mainly as a result of the remarkable batting of Bradman, whose 334 at Headingley broke the existing Test record, England had to find a way to contain the 'Don' and win back the Ashes. The England captain, Douglas Jardine, for all his Oxford amateurism, was a grim competitor. Like some of his Australian critics, he did not believe simply in 'playing the game for its own sake' and being a 'good loser'. Jardine had only one advantage in comparison to Bradman's Australia. He had a formidable pace attack at his disposal in the form of Larwood, Voce, Bowes, and Allen. To be able to draw upon four fast bowlers was extremely rare in the days when spin was still regarded as essential for a balanced side. The fact that Harold Larwood was possibly the fastest bowler of all time gave Jardine a potentially strong hand to play. It was the way he played that hand which caused the trouble.[32]

Bradman had proved a magnificent player of spin bowling. If he had any weakness at all it was perhaps a tendency to play too much off the back foot and to hook the high fast ball on the line of the body. Whether the 'bodyline' assault was coldly premeditated by Jardine or it was Larwood himself who hit upon it while bowling to a momentarily nervous Bradman during the 1930 series may never be fully resolved. What is more important

---

[32] The bodyline series is probably the best-researched controversy in the history of the sport; L. Le Quesne, *The Bodyline Controversy* (1983), is sound; see also R. Mason, *Ashes in the Mouth* (1984); R. Sissons and B. Stoddart, *Cricket and Empire* (1984), is particularly valuable for the broad historical context.

is that both captain and bowler were determined to use intimidatory bowling to unsettle Bradman. Larwood always claimed it was a fair tactic but it was precisely the legitimacy of playing this way which was at the heart of the controversy. Though he was slightly built, mentally Larwood was a tough professional, an ex-miner, who believed the batsmen who got the glory had to be able to take punishment and show courage when it was needed. Jardine also felt intimidatory bowling was legitimate. He set a leg-side field and waited for a simple catch as the batsman tried to protect himself from a sharply bouncing ball aimed at the upper body and an unprotected head. In brief, the tactic seemed to work. Bradman's test average slumped from over a hundred to a mere fifty—still well ahead of the rest—but England regained the Ashes.

The real trouble came in the third Test at Adelaide when the Australian captain was felled by a short-pitched but straight ball from Larwood. What really incensed the crowd was Jardine's switch to a full leg-field immediately after the accident. Later the Australian wicket-keeper Oldfield was struck on the head, again from a straight delivery from Larwood, and the crowd roared angry abuse at the England team. Jardine, who was believed to loathe Australians and to enjoy baiting them by his supercilious attitude, silk handkerchief, and Harlequin cap, was the main target. When drinks were brought out, a voice from the crowd was heard to shout, 'Don't give *him* a drink, let the bastard die of thirst.' Jardine had been barracked in the earlier 1928–9 tour of Australia and was said to have deeply resented it. He had even requested that spectators be forbidden to attend net sessions. At the end of the day's play the England manager, 'Plum' Warner, who had been born in Australia and captained several successful pre-war tours, went to enquire about the injuries after the game and received what has since become the best-known rebuke in the history of the game. 'Of two teams out there,' said Woodfull, 'one is playing cricket, the other is making no effort to play cricket.' There are several versions of the precise form of words he used, but the message was unmistakable and Warner left deeply hurt. Privately he urged Jardine to desist from the tactic but without success. The England captain was master in his own house. Laconic to the end, his only comment afterwards was that 'those of you who had seats got your money's worth—and then some'. The commercial cynicism of the gentleman-amateur made an odd contrast with the impeccable sentiments of the Australian captain to the effect that 'this great Empire game of ours teaches us to hope in defeat and congratulate winners if they manage to pull off victory . . . it is not the individual but the team that wins the match'.[33]

A bad situation was made worse by the reporting of Woodfull's words to the press. Both Bradman and Fingleton had been in the dressing-room and worked for newspapers, though they strenuously denied the leak. It was the newspapers which dramatized the whole event. 'Not cricket' roared the Australian popular press, and matters became much worse when the Australian Cricket Board surprisingly made public a telegram they sent to the MCC which read, ' "Bodyline" bowling has assumed such proportions to menace the best interests of the game . . . in our opinion it is unsportsmanlike.' To have been a fly on the wall of the Long Room at Lord's when this arrived would have been a rare treat. The MCC have diplomatically 'lost' the records of their discussions but their icy reply insisting the word 'unsportsmanlike' be withdrawn and offering to cancel the tour is well known. By implication the Australian cricketing authorities and public were questioning the good faith of the British in the common morality that bound them together. This was a very serious matter. Politicians in Whitehall and the Australian prime minister applied pressure behind the scenes for an honourable compromise. Relations between the two countries were at a particularly sensitive point with plummeting agricultural prices threatening a debt crisis between British banks and the primary producers in Australia. Enflaming Australian nationalism was the last thing the British government wanted after it had just carefully constructed a Commonwealth constitution, which preserved loyalty to the Crown whilst recognizing the autonomy of the Dominion governments, and a system of trade based on 'imperial preference'. Close links between the Conservative Party, which dominated the National Government, and the MCC committee ensured that wider imperial considerations would have been well understood. On the one hand the MCC could not contemplate

[33] B. Stoddart, 'Cricket's Imperial Crisis', in Cashman and McKernan, *Sport in History*, p. 134; Le Quesne, *Bodyline Controversy*, p. 43.

the public humiliation of accepting that their side was 'not playing the game'. So the MCC had to stick by its man for the duration of the series and the Australians withdrew the word 'unsportsmanlike'. But in the time-honoured traditions of the British establishment Jardine was quietly ditched despite his success and Larwood was never selected for England again. Interestingly Larwood felt he was a victim of the British class system and eventually migrated to Australia where he was very popular. The Aussies always blamed Jardine. There was only one thing worse that a gentleman who did 'play the game', and that was one who didn't. Hearing of Jardine's appointment to the captaincy, one of his former masters at Winchester had remarked presciently, 'Well, we shall win the Ashes—but we may lose a Dominion.' The Empire was more important than the Ashes. Leg theory was not revived and national competitiveness was duly reined in.[34]

4. CELTIC NATIONALISM: IRELAND, WALES, AND SCOTLAND

Sport as an imperial activity was very much the preoccupation of the English, especially the propertied classes of England. There were plenty of athletically inclined Scottish missionaries, of whom Eric Liddell, the gold medallist in the 1924 Olympics, who went off to China at the height of his career, is the most famous. But in the 'spiritual' rather than the strictly factual sense the proposition holds good. English public schoolmen certainly saw themselves, and were in turn seen by others, in this light. 'Playing the game' was a combined physical and moral activity, an exercise in the art of being 'British', which most of those who ran the Empire unconsciously translated as 'English'. Nor did 'English' refer to the customs and values of England as a whole. Class differences were immensely important. Association football, for instance, never became an imperial sport along the lines of cricket, rugby or athletics because the public schools soon shunned a game that had become so popular with the working class. Football was played in Canada, South Africa, Australia, and there were always individual enthusiasts for it among the imperial

[34] Stoddart, 'Cricket's Imperial Crisis', p. 132.

élite; but in the same way that the most popular of British games never captured the readership of *The Times*, so football also failed to become officially established as an institution of Empire. To this way of thinking, football, though indisputably of British origin was not really 'English'. Visiting salesmen and artisans, often coming from north of the border, were the great disciples of football; South America and Europe, where the governing hand of the 'Blue' was absent, took up football but neglected rugby and cricket. French rugby was the exception to the rule, and here the influence of English wine-merchants and retired Indian Civil Service people was evident. But even they could do little for the cause of cricket, which remained an inscrutably Anglo-Saxon mystery to the French.

'Englishness' itself was rarely understood by foreigners for whom 'England', 'Britain', and the 'United Kingdom' were obstinately synonymous. Yet within Great Britain and the island of Ireland national difference was the very stuff of sport. Although 'Celtic nationalism' provides a convenient general term for the sense of possessing a distinct territory, culture, and history, there were two quite separate elements within it. The first and most dramatic was the root-and-branch rejection of British sports by Irish cultural nationalists. This involved the setting up of an alternative tradition of Gaelic games with its own administration, funding, and regulations. The playing of any 'foreign' games were declared to be formally incompatible with participation in Gaelic sports. The other dimension to 'Celtic nationalism' took less extreme forms; sports were shared with the English and used as a means of asserting claims for the recognition of special ethnic and national qualities. The cultural identity of modern Scotland and Wales was not so much a question of kilts or Eisteddfods as of 'fitba' at Hampden and rugby at the Arms Park. 'Scottishness' and 'Welshness' were constantly fed by a sense of antagonism towards the English as the politically and economically dominant force. Sport acted as a vitally important channel for this sense of collective resentment, which was the nearest either people came to a popular national consciousness. Football gave the Scots a way of fighting the 'old enemy', whilst addiction to rugby came to be one of the major ways by which the English defined the Welsh and the Welsh came to see themselves. Cultural identity was a two-way process.

(i)   *Ireland*

'If any two purposes should go together they ought to be politics and athletics,' wrote the *Irishman* in 1884, 'our politics being essentially national, so should our athletics.' Gaelic games took their place in the forefront of a new Irish resistance to British culture in the late nineteenth century. This sprang from an increasingly strident rural populism lead by an educated urban élite, which took advantage of the introduction of the secret ballot to organize a powerful nationalist grouping at Westminster for the first time. The struggle to establish peasant proprietorship over the landlordism of the Anglo-Irish ascendancy, which had politicized the countryside and helped turn Parnell into a national leader, coincided with the spread of new forms of British sport. This would not in itself have been so significant had it not been for the wider 'modernization' of Ireland that was taking place. The nub of the matter is this: the railways and the rise of literacy together with the telegraph, the rotary printing-press, and improved road transport, all of which underpinned the rise of nationalism and the creation of the modern political party, also permitted the rapid distribution of British goods and customs. The rural isolation that had kept much of Ireland out of the grip of British culture was being eroded. In 1852 Sir William Wilde had complained that 'the faction fights, the hurlings and the mains of cocks that used to be fought at Shrovetide and Easter . . . are past and gone these twenty years'. The habit of 'coat-trailing' as a ritual challenge to fight seems to have declined in the first half of the nineteenth century and, as in Britain, the fairs of Ireland, which had played so great a part in popular recreation, seem to have become steadily more business-centred and better policed. Archbishop Croke, a pillar of the Catholic Irish establishment, sounded the alarm with a ringing denunciation of the 'the ugly and irritating fact that we are daily importing from England, not only her manufactured goods . . . but her fashions, her accents, her vicious literature, her music, her dances and her manifold mannerisms, her games also and her pastimes, to the utter discredit of our own grand national sports, and to the sore humiliation, as I believe, of every genuine son and daughter of the old land.'[35]

[35] W. F. Mandle, 'Sport as Politics', in Cashman and McKernan, *Sport in History*, pp. 100–1; E. Malcolm, 'Popular Recreation in Nineteenth Century

So the whole spectrum of Irish nationalist politics—Croke from the Church, Michael Davitt from the Fenians, and Charles Stewart Parnell for the Home-Rulers—came together in 1884 to lend their patronage to the newly formed Gaelic Athletic Association. The ostensible aim of the GAA was to resurrect and reorganize the ancient games of Ireland, the most famous of which was 'hurling', a stick-and-ball game from the same family of sports as Highland shinty and field hockey. Croke bemoaned the fact that this and other Irish sports 'amongst men and boys may now be said not only to be dead and buried, but in several localities to be entirely forgotten and unknown'. Croke was probably exaggerating, but in the areas of strong British settlement or influence, especially Dublin, football had long been established and in its modern forms seemed set fair to carry all before it. Hence the urgency of finding an alternative. It was the son of an Irish-speaking farmer from Clare, Michael Cusack—mocked by Joyce as a 'broadshouldered deepchested stronglimbed frankeyed redhaired freelyfreckled shaggybearded' self-appointed epitome of the Irish race—who found a solution to the threat from English sports. Cusack had ironically been making a good living cramming students for the British Civil Service examinations when he devised a means of playing both hurling and Gaelic football on the same pitch. He stressed Irish ethnic distinctiveness through sport. This crude populism had the effect of turning the Anglo-Irish gentlemen of Trinity College, who had formed a hurling team in the 1860s, quickly into hockey players. 'Gaelic' football permitted the handling, kicking, and bouncing of the ball. This innovation both restricted the spread of soccer and, by being coupled with hurling, a game that involved great skill and practice from childhood, helped to sustain the general cause of Gaelic games. A prospective Gaelic games player, who had not spent his youth slashing at weeds on the long country walks to school with his ash-stick or 'hurley', could hardly hope to master the art of lifting the ball on to the stick without the hand and balancing it there whilst running.[36]

Ireland', in O. MacDonagh, W. F. Mandle, and P. Travers, *Irish Culture and Irish Nationalism* (1983), pp. 40–5.

[36] D. Greene, 'Michael Cusack and the rise of the GAA', in C. C. O'Brien, *The Shaping of Modern Ireland* (1960), p. 77; T. Garvin, *The Evolution of Irish Nationalist Politics* (1981), p. 64; T. McGurk, 'The Last of the Craftsmen', *Hibernia*, 11 Sept. 1980, p. 27; I am grateful to Mike Hopkinson for this reference.

That the British have never given Gaelic games the credit they deserve is hardly surprising. From the beginning the GAA was fiercely anti-British not just in cultural terms but in a quite specific political sense. The formation and early history of the GAA is arguably the most striking instance of politics shaping sport in modern history; it is certainly the outstanding example of the appropriation of sport by nationalism in the history of the British Isles and Empire. Not content with promoting their own games, they proceeded to ban the playing of others. The 'Ban' meant that anyone who had played 'foreign', that is 'British', sports was prohibited from GAA-organized events. Members of the Royal Irish Constabulary or the Dublin Police were banned whatever their sporting inclinations. This 'steadfast rule' was maintained for over eighty years. The Ban was the most audacious and successful challenge to British sports mounted anywhere in the world. It had been passed at the GAA conference of 1887 where the Irish Republican Brotherhood had staged a take-over. In the next few years the GAA was little more than a front organization for Fenianism and was infiltrated by paid informers for the authorities posing as new players. One such spy, with the code name 'Emerald', was asked by the secretary of the Kerry GAA in the early 1890s 'if he would wish to become a man'. When 'Emerald' replied that he was a man, the GAA chief merely said that 'he was only a boy, but that he could make a man of him'.[37]

Male pride, athletic prowess, and political commitment went hand in hand in the early years of the GAA. The objections of the Church eventually forced the Fenians to share control with a broader spectrum of Irish opinion in the 1890s and there existed a range of nationalist positions within the movement. One of the leading hurling sides in Cork were called the Redmonds in honour of Parnell's successor, whose nickname of the 'Sporting Reds' ironically came from a rather English scorn for the win-at-all-costs mentality. Other hurling teams backed different factions in the confusion following Parnell's death. Despite these internal divisions, the GAA prospered mightily in the 1890s with 41 clubs and over 10,000 members by 1901 (and these

---

[37] Garvin, *Evolution of Irish Nationalist Politics*, p. 67; for the early politics of the GAA see W. F. Mandle, 'The IRB and the Beginnings of the Gaelic Athletic Association', *Irish Historical Studies*, Sept. 1977.

figures come from cautious police estimates, which excluded the Dublin area). National championships were set up and followed by crowds of up to 80,000 watching the hurling or football finals at the 'national' stadium named Croke Park in Dublin amid much kissing of rings and patriotic ritual.[38]

In Cork, where Gaelic games had avid support, a crowd of 20,000 turned up for the opening of the new Gaelic athletic grounds in 1904. Parish rivalries remained powerful. The city was divided between Glen Rovers north of the river and Barrs to the south, while nearby Blackrock had its famous 'Rockies'. Their mortal rivalry was suspended when their best players combined to play for Cork against other county teams. Jack Lynch is perhaps the most famous such son of County Cork, though whether becoming the Taoiseach was accounted a greater honour than being the first man to win six successive All-Ireland senior championship medals is no easy question to answer. The GAA neatly harnessed the old parish and provincial loyalties of rural Ireland to create a liberated area of national life where the Gael was free of the garrison. The hurley stick became a symbol of Irish freedom, a 'weapon' to drive out the British. Two thousand hurleys draped in the national colours were borne aloft at Parnell's funeral. Gaelic games were also a part of the expatriate nationalism of the Irish, especially in the United States; there St Patrick's Day became an annual festival of Irishness, in which Gaelic sports played a part along with shooting competitions with 'a life-size Indian as a target'.[39]

Within Ireland the GAA managed to prosper through the turbulent years of Home Rule agitation and civil war by maintaining its 'broad church' position. Although the GAA in public played down its paramilitary role to please the clerical element and avoid British surveillance, amongst many of the rank-and-file there was a continuing tradition of nationalist militancy. When the Monaghan Gaelic Football team were on their way to play the final of the Ulster championship in January 1922, the team included several IRA men with papers linking them to an attempt to release Republican prisoners under sentence of death

[38] Garvin, *Evolution of Irish Nationalist Politics*, p. 91.
[39] T. Horgan, *Cork's Hurling Story* (1977), pp. 13–17, 29; R. B. Park, 'British Sports and Pastimes in San Francisco 1848–1900', *BJSH*, Dec. 1984, p. 311.

in Londonderry gaol. However, it was only in Clare that the GAA actually split between the pro- and anti-Treaty sides in the Civil War. A National Games was held in 1924 attracting a total of 140,000 spectators, which was partly designed to heal wounds and to assert the role of sport in the development of a new national culture. Under the Free State and Republic the GAA became a bastion of rural, Catholic Ireland—Fianna Fail at play— celebrated in the columns of the *Cork Examiner* by Ireland's most famous sporting journalist, P. O. Mehigan, or 'Carbery' as he signed himself. Born in 1884, the same year as the foundation of the GAA, he became a minor civil servant in Dublin and London before returning to his native County Cork to work as a customs officer and to play Gaelic games. Carbery was a simple, unshakeable, sentimental Irish nationalist. He loved nothing better than 'humming along' the country roads on his 'little motor cycle' from one match to another, singing the praises of everything Irish from the songbirds in the hedgerows to the men of the hurley. He wrote prolifically not only on sports—*Carbery's Annual* was the Gaelic sportsman's favourite Christmas present—but about anything 'Irish' into which category he lumped together among other topics 'Busy Blackbirds', 'Spring', 'West Cork Jewels', 'Killarney—Heaven's Reflex' and other touristical pieces. 'Glamorous Galway' with its Race Week and breakfasts of 'trout, salmon, home-cured streaky bacon, fresh eggs, crisp toast, marmalade and bastible cake' came in for special praise. In 'December Storm' he broke off from a description of 'mounting waves breaking snow white over rocks and cliffs' to reassure his readers that 'the danger of "wheat midge" has been grossly exaggerated'. From fertilizers to football, nothing that might entertain the small farmer escaped him. For their part his audience seemed to relish the peculiar blend of lyricism and practical sense he brought to his work.[40]

To Carbery Gaelic sports were bound up with 'the lovely tapestry' of Irish life, its characters, and religion. His talent as an arch-propagandist of popular nationalism was at its best in his biographical sketches of great Gaelic sportsmen. In 'Dan Fraher's

[40] M. A. Hopkinson, *The Irish Civil War* (1988); I am grateful to him for showing me his manuscript. W. F. Mandle, 'The GAA and Popular Culture', in MacDonagh, Mandle, and Travers, *Irish Culture*; P. D. Mehigan, *Vintage Carbery* (1984), pp. 67, 81.

Famous Field' Carbery sang the praises of a draper from Dungarven, a GAA champion, who 'lived his own distinctive Irish life from cradle to grave'. Old Dan was 'like some ancient Irish chief talking rapid Gaelic and dishing out hospitality with a liberal hand'. At long last his patriotism caught up with him and 'his locks were silvery when the grand old warrior suffered his last term of imprisonment in the Black and Tan days'. Another favourite of Carbery was Father Tom Jones, a handball champion from Tralee before he entered Maynooth College to study for the priesthood. In addition to his sporting prowess, he was a scholar, Gaelic translator, and musician. Better still the good Father had suffered for Ireland with 'Black and Tan revolvers to his head and a rifle muzzle in his back'. Sporting nationalism has survived best amongst the nationalist population of the north. Gaelic games flourished amongst Catholics after partition as a link with the Republic. The GAA in Ulster named their Belfast stadium 'Casement Park' and individual clubs have been very active in support for Republican prisoners with the revival of the armed struggle to impose unity since the late 1960s.[41]

Amid such fierce politicising of sport, one might have thought British sports would have withered away in Ireland. Yet this was not so; they not only survived, but even managed to prosper in a modest fashion. The hostility of the nationalists in no way deterred the landed classes and may even have acted as an incentive to participate. Irish gentry ladies were prominent in both golf and tennis from the outset. These sports were well suited to a country-house environment and provided a welcome alternative to hunting, through which the solidarity of country society and the Anglo-Irish ascendancy has been reinforced. There was nothing like riding over a peasant's fields for letting him know who was in charge, and the sport was strongly opposed by the Land League. Despite the hostility of small farmers and financial difficulties, hunting carried on. The Westmeath, for example, had nineteen different masters between 1854 and 1913 and the Kilkenny was saved from extinction by the intervention of Sir Hercules Langrishe of Knocktopher, a gentleman so skilled in hunt calls that 'he could play "gone away" on a gun barrel'.

[41] Mehigan, *Vintage Carbery*, pp. 22–3, 56–7; J. Sugden and A. Bairner, 'Northern Ireland', in L. Allison (ed.), *The Politics of Sport* (1986), pp. 91–9.

The female side of the family were not only famous for their beauty but distinguished at tennis and in the saddle. Most famous of hunting ladies was Mrs Somerville, who not only became Ireland's first female Master of Foxhounds, but with her second cousin ('Ross') described the hilarious fox-hunting exploits of Major Sinclair Yeates, the famous 'resident magistrate' of *Experiences of an Irish R.M.* Such was the leisured society of rural Ireland, which survived in a modest kind of way the upheaval of independence and civil war. In the world of Molly Keane with the old landed interest isolated by popular nationalism, hunting helped to fill in the time and keep county friendships alive.

In athletics, Irish competitors were very successful winning a total of eighty-five gold medals in the AAA annual championship between 1885 and 1912. Dennis Horgan, a huge shot-putter who warmed up by drinking a dozen eggs in a pint of sherry, was the star performer. He even continued his winning streak when a metal plate had been inserted in his head after he was knocked out in New York while acting as an auxiliary policeman. The anglicizing element is easily overlooked when analysing the GAA but it reflected the importance of an alternative view of Britain within Ireland, especially amongst elements of the middle class who distrusted Catholic or radical nationalism. Association football gained a fair following, partly among the northern Protestant working-class but also amongst Catholics in Belfast, Londonderry, and in Dublin. An Irish league of semi-professional teams was formed based in Belfast in 1890. Belfast Celtic were set up in emulation of the new Glasgow club in 1891 whilst Linfield and Glentoran upheld the Unionist cause. There were several sectarian incidents between rival fans before 1914. During the Anglo-Irish War in Belfast shots were fired into a chanting 'Fenian' football crowd in 1920. There was also the 'Bloody Sunday' shooting of Michael Hogan, a Tipperary player, and twelve others at Croke Park in Dublin on 21 November 1920. With Partition a separate Football Association of the Irish Free State was formed and, to complicate matters further, several prominent Catholic clubs in the north applied to join. There followed a long, bitter, and often ludicrous wrangle over which of the two associations could call itself 'Ireland'; this was not finally resolved until the name 'Northern Ireland' was imposed on the Six Counties by FIFA in 1954. The tortured organizational history of football neatly encapsulates the conflict between nationalism and Unionism in the 'states of Ireland', and underlines the significance of political conflict in 'British' sports beyond the GAA. For all this the standard of play was surprisingly good. The Republic managed to beat England 2–0 at Goodison Park in 1948 to inflict England's first defeat at home by a foreign country. The fact that eight of this team were playing in the English League is an indication not only of interest in the game despite the Ban but also of the lack of a strong commercial base. Ireland 'North' and 'South' lacked the resources for successful professional football despite their relative success in international competition, producing players like Blanchflower, Best, and Pat Jennings in the North and Liam Brady or Frank Stapleton in the South, all of whom have had to cross the water to earn a living at the game.[42]

Significantly the only team sport to escape the divisive effects of political and sectarian conflict has been the game of rugby. The Ireland rugby team ignores the frontier drawing players from north and south alike, although in the north very few Catholics are involved and the leading clubs tend to be part of a wider Unionist social network. Social class provides the clue to the allegedly apolitical status of Irish rugby. Rugby began in Ireland as an élite game. Trinity College formed a club in 1856 (the second oldest in existence) and the North of Ireland club set up in 1868 was made up of old boys from Marlborough and Cheltenham. The Irish Rugby Union was formed in 1879 with strong representation from higher education and old-boys' clubs in the major cities. The hostility of the GAA may, ironically, have helped to maintain the unity of Irish rugby. Middle-class outcasts clung together after the partition of Ireland in 1922 with internationals played alternately in Belfast and Dublin. De Valera could perhaps have denied southern rugby the facilities for cross-border co-operation, but staunch nationalist though he was he did not interfere. 'Dev' apparently had a soft spot for this heretically integrated activity.

Irish players sometimes found themselves lining up in the same Oxford or Cambridge team and a few played together for the British Lions (a unique experiment in 'inter-national' integration);

[42] P. Lovesey, *Official Centenary History of the Amateur Athletic Association* (1979), p. 48; *Oxford Companion*, pp. 314–17.

players might be members of the liberal professions, sharing a common interest in the law or medicine, or have business contacts spanning both parts of the country. The gospel of fair play provided a bond for the privileged, which is perhaps best exemplified in the career of Cameron Michael Henderson Gibson, MBE; Mike Gibson, the great stand-off half and centre for North of Ireland, Ireland, and the British Lions in the 1960s and early 1970s, came from a Protestant middle-class family in Belfast and was educated at Cambridge. 'There was nothing he could not do, except perhaps believe he was as good as he really was' was the verdict of the famous Welsh coach Carwyn James, who marvelled at his modesty and selflessness. The Irish, more than any other of the Home Unions, have retained something of the old morality of the game—the dash, the daring, and the idea of enjoying the game 'for its own sake'. The spirit of the public school game was safe in Ireland, though their insouciance and small pool of players has meant that they have won the Triple Crown less often than the other unions. Yet the support of affluent urban Ireland has not wavered. When Ireland were chasing the title in 1952 everything rested on the outcome of the final game against Wales at Lansdowne Road. With tickets at a premium an advertisement offered a Rolls-Royce for four first-class stand tickets. 'What year is the Rolls?' was apparently the only response to the offer. In Ireland nationalism has further complicated the class divisions between games which were so evident in Britain. Instead of football as the popular game Ireland has Gaelic football and hurling but like England and Scotland it has kept rugby as a well-bred alternative. Class and nationalism interact through sport in powerful and complex ways.[43]

(ii) *Rugby and Welshness*

In Wales rugby developed quite differently. Instead of being a middle-class game cut off until recently from popular sentiment, rugby in Wales has been thoroughly democratized and is patriotic to the point of chauvinism. Instead of inventing or reviving their own games in the face of the invasion of English sports, the Welsh took the winter team-game of the English public schools and

[43] D. Smith and G. Williams, *Fields of Praise* (1980), p. 337.

turned it into a vehicle for their own brand of 'Celtic nationalism'. Why rugby, why Wales? This is the question that always crops up in relation to Welsh sport. In particular, why was it that football failed to gain a large popular following among the miners and metalworkers of South Wales when these occupational groups were such ardent soccer players and spectators elsewhere. Football, to be fair, did quite well in North Wales. The village of Chirk produced Billy Meredith, who battled away hopelessly against the English for the Welsh international team for most of his long and otherwise successful playing career for Manchester City and Manchester United. Despite being born only a hundred yards across the border, Meredith was a staunch Welsh patriot. But as an Association rather than a rugby footballer, he never achieved the heroic national status Wales accords to her greatest players.

There were two stages in rugby's conquest of Wales. The first concerns the implantation of the game in the southern valleys; the second relates to its place in the new industrial and democratic culture of Wales around the turn of the century. The relative remoteness and inaccessibility of the valleys running north from the coast of south Wales meant that the local form of folk-football ('cnappen') probably survived longer than elsewhere. Old forms coexisted alongside the playing of the modern game of rugby by the pupils of Llandovery College, a new public school for the Welsh gentry staffed from Oxford and Cambridge in the 1860s. Indeed the early forms of modern rugby before the rule requiring the ball to be released when grounded must have been rather like 'cnappen' with 'a quarter of a hundred heavyweights leaning up against each other' and 'the ball lost in the ruck'. Initially the liberal professions took the leading part in the founding of clubs along the coast at Neath, Cardiff, and Newport in the 1870s. This preceded the main wave of immigration into the area with the huge expansion of coal production in the 1880s. Moreover the bulk of immigrants came either from the west of England or from Ireland rather than from areas like west-central Scotland or Lancashire, where the Association form of football was already established. A soccer-playing tradition was not imported into Wales.[44]

---

[44] Ibid., ch. 2; *Fields of Praise*, provides a unique combination of a social and a centenary history of the Welsh Rugby Union,; see also K. O. Morgan, *Rebirth of a Nation* (1981); for Meredith, see J. Harding, *Football Wizard* (1985).

The new immigrants took up the revised form of the indigenous game in the densely packed industrial villages clinging to the hillsides around the pits. The nature of this settlement did not favour the large-scale commercialization of sport in the manner, for example, of textile production. Tight-knit communities of a few thousand unable to move easily on an east–west axis made for fierce local rivalries, but restricted the potential for gathering the very large crowds needed to sustain professional football, which predictably did best in the larger coastal towns. Merthyr was large enough to support professional soccer but this collapsed with the depression in the mining industry in the 1920s. Aberdare, twenty miles north of Cardiff, had a population of 40,000 by 1890 supporting not only professional football but professional athletics, boxing, and producing several of the world's top professional cyclists. While it is a myth to believe professional sport had no following in Wales rugby certainly dominated both as a participant and a spectator sport.[45]

The continued success of an 'amateur' sport in an overwhelmingly working-class area seems at odds with historical logic until two further factors are taken into account: one financial, the other cultural and political. Welsh rugby was not 'amateur' in quite the same sense as English or Scottish rugby. Despite periodic investigations by the Welsh Rugby Union, which under Walter Rees's autocratic fifty-year stewardship remained amateur in principle, a good deal of broken-time payment in the form of 'reasonable expenses' was connived at by the clubs. The Welsh Rugby Union itself was not above honouring its greatest player by launching a testimonial fund for Arthur Gould. When Scottish and English representatives on the International Board indignantly refused not only to contribute but warned of the impropriety of the gift, the Welsh withdrew from the Board and bought Gould a house with the funds. Relations were patched up after a season without international fixtures, but the message was clear. Wales would not submit to external scrutiny of its affairs. The amateur code was officially enforced through the good offices of the WRU but an official inquiry admitted in 1907 that some clubs 'were in the habit of paying and receiving hotel or travelling expenses in excess of the sum actually disbursed'.

[45] G. Williams, 'How Amateur Was My Valley?', *BJSH*, Dec. 1985, pp. 259–60.

This is probably the reason for the failure of the Rugby League game after efforts to introduce it in Aberdare and Merthyr. Some of the very best players were lured to the Northern Union by large signing-on fees and the offer of good jobs, but good club players in South Wales had little incentive to turn to the semi-professional form when in practice they could make as much by remaining 'amateur'. So Wales was able to square the circle. A game hemmed in by middle-class social restrictions was able to attract and retain good working-class recruits because the governing body did not inquire too closely into limited contraventions of the code.[46]

So much for the 'financial' factor; it has to be mentioned but its importance should not be overstated. More important in the success of Welsh Rugby Union was its new cultural role as Wales moved rapidly away from a rural and bardic past and into the industrial world. 'Welshness' had to be created amongst the migrants who flocked to the coalfields from Ireland and the west of England in the forty years before the First World War, giving Wales the highest immigration rate outside the United States. The one and a half million or so workers clustered around the southern industrial region knew little or no Welsh; the legends and literary traditions of the ancient Britons passed them by. Yet they came to a land that was undeniably different, that had maintained its separate identity. This provided the context for the second stage in the history of Welsh rugby: namely the process by which a game that had become popular was turned into a defining characteristic of Welshness both by those outside Wales, who needed labels to pin on the new society, and by the new inhabitants of the valleys who sought an identity for themselves. Rugby took its place alongside chapel choirs, self-education, and socialist unionism in the new canon of Welshness. A rugby-playing, chapel-going, musical man, educated by 'the Fed' (the mining union) was the ideal type, the new Welshman. The different elements in this composite caricature were sometimes incompatible. Winning scholarships to Oxford was hardly a popular or a sporting accomplishment (working-class boys unlike their public school counterparts were expected to be clever rather than athletic). For every minister who propped up the front row there was another like the Revd. John Rees of the Rhondda who

---

[46] Smith and Williams, *Fields of Praise*, pp. 94–5.

thought that 'even an ape would not disgrace itself by seeking its pleasures in kicking a football'. If men wished 'to frequent pubs, theatres or football fields', he thundered, 'then let them, in the name of the living God, remain outside the Christian pale'.[47]

Despite the forces of revivalism, rugby in Wales became 'the one great pastime of the people'. As a unifying, inclusive cultural force it outstripped politics and religion, drawing together coal-heavers and coal-owners in a common passion for the national side. The Crawshays, iron-masters from Merthyr, even formed and financed their own touring team in 1922 'to enable men from all walks of life to take part in a rugby tour'. For Geoffrey Crawshay, a nostalgic squire sporting a green cloak, his 'Welsh XV' was the natural culmination of a long-standing family tradition of bardic culture and paternalism. Edwardian Wales witnessed the invention of rugby as a distinctly 'Celtic' phenomenon. Rugby was held to embody the unique ethnic virtues of the Celt as Wales took the Triple Crown in six of the twelve seasons after 1900. This success was no accident, enthused the press,

we all know the racial qualities that made Wales supreme on Saturday . . . the great quality of defence and attack in the Welsh race is to be traced to the training of the early period when powerful enemies drove them to their mountain fortresses. There was developed, then, those traits of character that find fruition today. 'Gallant little Wales' has produced sons of strong determination, invincible stamina, resolute, mentally keen, physically sound.

Wales claimed the soul of rugby, others could have the body. Thomas Jones, secretary to Lloyd George, put his finger on it— 'a game democratic and amateur is a rare thing—a unique thing to be cherished'; Scottish and English rugby was 'aristocratic', but in Wales rugby 'has made a democracy not only familiar with an amateur sport of distinguished rank but is in reality a discovery of democracy'. Rugby became a new Welsh myth, a unifying belief; a strand in the national character that gained strength from being so tightly entwined with the idea of ancient liberties reborn, of a rich and independent culture. Rugby gave Wales a special

[47] Smith and Williams, *Fields of Praise*, p. 101.

place in the wider framework of the Empire. The great struggle with the All Blacks in 1905 confirmed the Welsh and the New Zealanders as the leading rugby nations. Rugby helped reinforce imperial attachments as well as more narrowly national ones. 'Proud as he was of being a Welshman,' remarked the MP Tom Ellis in 1910, 'he confessed to a still greater pride that Wales was part of the British Empire.'[48]

Wales needed new heroes and Rugby supplied them in plenty. Arthur Gould, born in Newport in 1864 of an English father, was the first of these. He was a tree-climbing child prodigy (hence his nickname 'Monkey') and a superb athlete as well as being the greatest centre three-quarter of the age. When Wales beat England 12–11 for the first time on Welsh soil Gould was carried off shoulder high by the huge crowd. His try-scoring exploits were celebrated in countless conversations in pit and bar. Gould himself does not seem to have taken his role as standard-bearer of the people too seriously. After a game with Scotland in 1896 he duly greeted all and sundry with the words 'Cymru am byth' ('Wales for ever'), confessing 'I don't know what it means but I've been told to say it.' Gould's confusion was shared by his supporters whose knowledge of their native language was usually no better than his. The first singing of Welsh hymns seems to have taken place in 1910 at Cardiff against Scotland, but 'long before its conclusion a popular music-hall song replaced it'. The chant of 'Teddy Morgan' to the tune of 'Clementine' was another favourite. The Cardiff factory-girls, who turned out to cheer Wales in 1905 with their ribbons and feathers, amused themselves by humming 'Dolly Gray', 'The 'Orse the Missus Dries the Clothes on', and 'Bill Bailey'.[49]

The mixture of Welsh patriotism with the new popular culture of the music-hall is evident in the success of the James brothers of Swansea. These 'curly-headed marmosets', the 'performing fleas' of Welsh rugby, would jinx round a defence one minute and walk on their hands the next to amuse the crowd. This proletarian side of Welsh rugby with its 'characters', colour, and entertainment sometimes clashed with what the authorities

[48] Ibid., pp. 173–4; G. Williams, 'From Popular Culture to Public Cliché', in J. A. Mangan (ed.), *Pleasure, Profit and Proselytism* (1988), p. 16. I am grateful to Gareth Williams for supplying me with this article ahead of publication.
[49] Smith and Williams, *Fields of Praise*, pp. 93, 140.

deemed to be the proprieties of the game. Before the 1911 Triple Crown match with England a well-known acrobat came on to the field with a bicycle and a couple of chairs to perform an act that had apparently gone down well at other rugby matches. The secretary of the Union, Walter Rees, was outraged at this affront to what he saw as the dignity of the fixture. The police were ordered to remove the man instantly. This turned out to be easier said than done. He was eventually overpowered by seven constables, who 'were pelted with oranges and subjected to all manner of derision' by the crowd. The egregious James brothers were eventually signed up by scouts from the Northern Union, who had to circulate cautiously round the valleys for fear of communal wrath at the luring away of local and national talent. One who resisted was Willie Trew, a slightly built Swansea boilermaker of the Edwardian era, who 'drifted through Welsh rugby like the ghost in the machine'. A pack of pitmen or policemen (as was more often the case between the wars) was all very well but the pace and artistry of a single back, turning a game with a swerve of the body—that was the stuff of which Welsh heroes were made.[50]

Welsh rugby was badly hit by the decline in the coal industry between the wars. The crowds were as large as ever and their 'Cymric' character more polished than before—the great tradition of communal singing took root in the 1930s—but the best players were more easily tempted by offers from the Rugby League. Wales did not win a Triple Crown in the forty years from 1910 to 1950. The post-war years, however, saw the renaissance of Welsh rugby in the international arena. Coal was king again, for a brief moment, and new industry poured into the area. This was the age of Gwilliam, the huge history teacher who was like a 'blank page between the Old Testament and the New' and treated all men as his pupils, of Ken Jones who ran gloriously alongside Bleddyn Williams, the son of a coal-trimmer, whose eight sons all played for Cardiff. The mixture of powerful miners and grammar school boys patiently coached by a dedicated handful of teachers was the secret of Welsh rugby; men like Ned Gribble at Tonyrefail GS, who was a leading figure in the Welsh Secondary Schools' Rugby Union. Alongside the power of WSSRU was the

[50] Smith and Williams, *Fields of Praise*, pp. 76–7, 187.

more flamboyant influence of the Urdd, the Welsh League of Youth, which not only imbued Cliff Morgan with an unshakeable pride in Welsh culture but also nurtured Barry John and Carwyn James, respectively the most gifted player and the greatest coach of modern times. The old Welsh culture was catching up with the new as rugby was given a bardic gloss. The great Welsh side of the late 1960s and early 1970s drew on men like Barry John, Gareth Edwards, and Gerald Davies among others, who all came from mining families but forsook the pits for an education and the chance of a middle-class career. Perhaps the sense of Welshness was especially sharp for those who made the break from manual labour with its fierce solidarities and sense of place. Welsh as they were and proud of it, the demands made by the public on their national heroes was enormous. Barry John, 'the King' as he came to be known, retired prematurely from the game when he found he could not go into a shop or pub without the worship of his countrymen stifling his freedom. He was continually pestered, his privacy invaded, and his family bothered; although in principle still an amateur playing for fun, he was a 'star', the conqueror of the All Blacks, a great Welshman. It was all too much for him. He escaped his public and the clutch of the press with the same mazy step and calm elusiveness with which he had drifted through a packed field of players to drop a goal or score a try.[51]

(iii) *Scottishness and 'Fitba'*

Sport in Scotland was no less a vehicle for nationalism than in Wales. Unlike the Irish, the Scots did not try to build up their indigenous sports at the expense of the modern team-games from England. Although the game of shinty remained popular in the Highlands, it made no impact in the central belt where over two-thirds of Scotland's population was concentrated by the end of the nineteenth century. Ironically, it was the English aristocracy who fell in love with the Highlands, especially with the stalking and fishing to be found in what was one of the last wildernesses in western Europe. It was the annual visit of the 'English' monarch

[51] Ibid., pp. 341–2, 419–21; G. Williams, 'From Grand Slam to Great Slump', *Welsh History Review*, June 1983.

to Balmoral, which revived the declining traditional sports and in 1866 turned the summer athletics at Braemar into the Braemar Royal Highland Gathering. This was done mostly for the benefit of the Anglicized Scottish aristocracy, who could parade their 'traditional' costume invented by an eighteenth-century Quaker industrialist from Lancashire. Dressed in their kilts with the special clan tartans (ingeniously devised by the manufacturers to improve sales), the laird could meet the lord and enjoy a brief glimpse into the inner circle of the court. 'Tossing the caber' was the image of Scottish sport that appealed to the English, who liked to think Scotsmen spent their lives eating porridge in kilts and hurling tree trunks around deserted glens. The Highland games were certainly a modest success, providing employment for a band of semi-professional athletes, who toured the rudimentary circuit that developed in the north and in the Borders, but they made little or no impact on the great industrial conurbation of the Clyde and Lanarkshire or the cities of Edinburgh, Leith, and Dundee in the east.[52]

Industrial Scotland did not wear the kilt. Like South Wales it had its own identity to forge, its own kind of Scottishness to create that was far removed from the 'Benn and Glen' variety so beloved of the romantic expatriate. Those for whom popular artists and the publishers of calendars laboured so tirelessly had a sentimental attachment to rural Scottishness, but their response to the massive urbanization that had made Glasgow the second city in Great Britain was ambiguous. There was a civic pride that radiated from the new university and municipal buildings which coexisted with a bourgeois and Presbyterian anxiety at the tough, hard-drinking world of the shipyards and railway-shops, of razor-gangs and the Gorbals. Concern at the direction of popular culture in Scotland hardened into distaste among the liberal professions and governing élite of the capital. Scotland was too sharply divided to permit the common pursuit of Scottishness in sport. The concentration of population in Glasgow enabled the city to sustain no less than six senior teams in the Scottish League. 'Fitba' was the working-man's game. Devotion to it was more complete

---

[52] H. Trevor-Roper, 'The Invention of Tradition', in Hobsbawm and Ranger, *Invention of Tradition*, pp. 20–32; G. Jarvie, 'Class, Social Development and the Highland Games', paper delivered to BSSH, Glasgow, July 1985.

and more passionate than anywhere else in the English-speaking world. Rugby was the game of the Edinburgh public schools with an exclusive foothold in Glasgow via the Academicals and West of Scotland. Later Alan Glen's School and Hutcheson's Academy abandoned the kicking game for the handling one and completed the process by which the social and academic élite cut themselves off from the people's game.

So the Scots carried on a dual rivalry with the English. There was the competitive but gentlemanly struggle for the Calcutta Cup. Rugby was steeped in the traditions of imperial service via schools like Loretto, Merchiston, and Fettes and it was natural that Edinburgh should host the first game against England in 1871 at Raeburn Place on the exclusive fringe of the Georgian New Town. In 1873 six public school clubs formed the Scottish Football Union (declining to name their sport after an English school until 1924). An annual fixture against Ireland in 1877 and against Wales from 1883 was added to the game against England. While a similar pattern of domestic 'internationals' emerged in the Association game in the same period, rivalry in rugby was less sharply focused on England than in football. The passionate, obsessive need to beat the English, which has been the driving-force of Scottish international football, was muted by the public school code and the fact that an influential minority of Scotland players had polished their rugby at Oxford and Cambridge. Between 1884 and 1891 four Lorettonians held the captaincy of Oxford and in 1900 both Oxford and Cambridge were captained by boys from Loretto.[53]

National rivalry in rugby was friendly but in football it was fanatical; that, at least, was the way things turned out. To begin with, the Association game was also an élite pastime. The first soccer international was held on the grounds of the West of Scotland Cricket Club in 1872 in Glasgow. Football at that date was dominated by the Queen's Park club, formed in 1867, and the foundation of the Scottish Football Association in 1873 and the Glasgow Rangers club in the same year heralded the rapid expansion of the game in Scotland. By the time the Celtic Football and Athletic Club was set up to raise money for the relief of the

[53] A. M. C. Thorburn, *The Scottish Rugby Union* (1985), pp. 1–2; J. A. Mangan, *Athleticism in the Victorian and Edwardian Public School* (1981), p. 58.

Catholic poor in 1887 football was already quite popular with industrial workers. By 1894 there were two divisions of the professional league. Considering its population size and resources, no other country has sustained the scale and quality of professional football attained in Scotland. By the early 1890s ministers of religion were complaining about the new popular passion. 'The Saturday evening sporting paper is the young man's Bible and sermon', remarked the Presbytery of Dumbarton whilst in Hamilton 'on Saturday afternoons men do nothing but attend or discuss sports'. This tradition of fanaticism is nicely caught in Robin Jenkins's novel about Drumsgart, a 'junior' team of 'young hopefuls and old has-beens' who win the Scottish Junior Cup. 'Junior' football with its fervent semi-professional clubs run on a shoe-string became a testament to the depth of feeling for the game in Scotland. *The Thistle and the Grail* captures a little of this Gallic intensity. For the Scots 'fitba' was emotionally *their* property; they did not acknowledge or respect English precedence in the matter; they resented the constant haemorrhage of the most-gifted Scottish players to England which began when the first 'Scotch professors' were hired by Darwen even before professionalism was legalized. Only Celtic and Rangers could hang on to quality Scottish players. Teams like Newcastle and Sunderland always had plenty of Scots in the team alongside local talent. The highly successful Scottish international side of the late 1920s was full of 'Anglos' like the Newcastle centre-forward Hughie Gallacher, who started with Airdrie, or Alex James, he of the 'shorts' flapping below the knee and hair slicked down with a centre parting. He passed from Kirkcaldy's impoverished Raith Rovers to Preston North End, and from there he was transferred for £9,000 to become the mainstay of Herbert Chapman's great Arsenal side, which won the English League four times in six seasons after his transfer in 1929. Not one of the winners of the English League Championship between 1920 and 1939 played without a Scot in the team. The Newcastle side of 1926–7 had seven and the victorious Sunderland team of 1935–6 had eight. This drain of the best players from Scotland to England remains a constant reminder of economic inferiority. Profits from transfers to England has helped to keep many smaller clubs afloat. Mournful speculation over 'who'll be next to go' is a staple topic of conversation north of the border mingled with a fierce pride in the capacity of the country to keep replenishing the stock.[54]

The economic domination of English football aggravated a broad, if politically unfocused, resentment against the English. Scotland, after all, was a nation in its own right; it had its own education and legal system; it was distinctive in religion and had been constitutionally separate from England until 1707. But Scotland had no nationalist party worth the name and no political assembly of its own. Rather it was incorporated into the Westminster system and governed through the office of Secretary of State for Scotland (a late nineteenth-century afterthought and a political graveyard for the ambitious minster). When democratic politics came to Scotland it was popular liberalism with its antagonism towards the landed Anglicanism of rural England and its sympathy for religious dissent which first took hold to be followed by the rise of socialism in mining and shipbuilding communities. The class consciousness of 'Red Clydeside' was an odd amalgam of nationalism and internationalism; Scottish anger was expressed in the language of Marx, yet beneath the intellectual sophistication of the leadership lay a good deal of uncomplicated resentment of the power of Tory majorities from the English shires to determine the fate of urban Scotland.

This explains the extraordinary importance attached to the annual confrontation with England at football. It was not just a question of beating the 'auld enemy'. Part of the obsession with the game may have come from a sense of past wrongs and ancient triumphs, of Culloden, Bannockburn, and the rest. But history was not the heart of the matter; the crowds might wave the Stuart flag but this was no Jacobite legacy. The desperate need to win 'the England game'—no other international fixture was played with the same passionate seriousness—sprang from more than just the desire of a small, poor country to cut its larger and richer neighbour down to size. Public attachment to the battle also grew out of the very disunity of Scottish football itself. The conflict between Celtic and Rangers was no ordinary club rivalry; nor was it confined to Glasgow. Celtic and Rangers drew support from a

[54] Bill Murray, *The Old Firm* (1984), pp. 5–9; T. C. Smout, *A Century of the Scottish People* (1986), p. 154; Bob Crampsey, *The Scottish Footballer* (1978), pp. 32–40; J. Walvin, *The People's Game* (1975), p. 124.

wide area of central and southern Scotland. Sectarianism of a more muted kind also lay beneath the Hearts and Hibs split in Edinburgh and the Dundee and Dundee Hibs division (renamed Dundee United in 1923 in an effort to avoid controversy). Rangers' supporters, bolstered by Orange immigration from Ulster around the turn of the century, saw themselves as bastions of true Scottishness in contrast to the Catholic Irish immigrants, whose numbers were undermining the native Protestant traditions of Scotland and who even wore the colours of a separate national movement. Significantly, neither Celtic nor Rangers, despite their wealth, were inclined to buy players from England. By 1980 112 international players had played for Rangers but not one of them was English. The Protestantism of Rangers is so well known that the militant Scottishness of their supporters and management has been overlooked. This idea of Scottishness clashed strongly with the hybrid nationalism of Celtic supporters, who disliked the English for very different historical reasons. It was only through their joint hostility to England that the two opposing traditions could recognize fleetingly their common loyalty to Scotland.[55]

The prestige of the fixture steadily increased. Scotland was the first country to have a national stadium—named ironically after an English parliamentarian. Hampden Park with its unique capacity of 150,000 was begun by Queen's Park in 1893 and gradually established itself as an international venue in preference to the huge rival stadia of Celtic and Rangers at Parkhead and Ibrox. The facilities for professional football in Edwardian Glasgow were unique in the world. When England herself acquired a national stadium after the First World War, the biannual trek to Wembley began in earnest with up to 30,000 Scots descending on the capital in a wave, a kind of ritual of reversal where the Scots took possession of London for the day. By the 1930s the Wembley trek was *the* great cultural event for the working-class Scottish male. 'Wembley Clubs' were formed in the work-place, in pubs, and working-men's clubs to collect weekly contributions for the patriotic bonanza. The *Glasgow Herald* of 1936 estimated that 30,000 Scots subscribed a shilling a week to the Wembley Clubs and the *Daily Record* claimed a total of 60,000 Scots would travel to London in 1938. There was

[55] Murray, *The Old Firm*, gives a good account of the sectarian issue.

a serious shortage of tickets for the battalions of fans with their 'tammies', bagpipes, and banners of Wallace and Bruce with the device 'Forget Flodden and remember Stirling Bridge and Bannockburn'. Some took drums with them, others came armed with rattles, accordions, and tin frying-pans. The 'send off' at big stations like Glasgow Central was an event itself with reports that 'women danced "war dances" to send their trippers on their way'. Beating the English on their own territory was always sweet, and never sweeter than the 5–1 thrashing of England by the 'Wembley Wizards' in 1928. This game has gone down in Scottish folk-memory and the match ball is still kept in a place of honour by the SFA. England had Dixie Dean at centre-forward, fresh from scoring sixty goals in a season, but the dipping crosses of Alan Morton (a mining engineer whose qualifications, stature, and smart appearance earned him the name of 'the Wee Society Man') and the heading of Alex Jackson, who, like Alex James, was playing in England at the time, destroyed England and made for a historic victory. Honours have been even in the England–Scotland game and the relative success of the 'junior' partner created a truly massive popular interest in Scotland. The world record attendance for a sporting fixture was set at Hampden in 1931 with a crowd of over 130,000, and soon after a staggering 149,415 watched the first all-ticket England–Scotland match in 1937. No other match in Britain could command such an attendance. One in three or four of the working-class male population of the west of Scotland were physically present and thousands more were locked out.[56]

A national tradition was born, established, and still flourishes—'part of a sturdy subculture of symbols, slogans, heroes and myths which sustains an apolitical, inverted, but palpable sub-nationalism which combines a strong identity of being Scottish with a very weak national project'. The Hampden 'roar' was unique, striking fear into the most determined of English players. 'It shook me and my colleagues in the England team . . . You could sense the enthusiasm of the crowd being transfused into the veins of the Scottish players,' remarked Stanley Matthews. 'I thought to myself "what a noise" . . . that is when I could think', said

---

[56] K. McCarra, *Scottish Football* (1984), p. 52; H. F. Moorhouse, 'Scotland against England', *IJHS*, Sept. 1987, pp. 195–9.

Tommy Lawton. The fact that the flame still burns as strongly in the cosmopolitan age of television and air travel might seem surprising, but no one who saw Scotsmen swinging from the goal-posts and digging up the Wembley turf in 1977 could doubt that it does. Draping themselves in the lion rampant of red and gold, singing the battle-lament 'Flower of Scotland', and clenching their fists and their cans in triumph or defeat, the battle with England goes on. Being totally or partially 'guttered', 'steaming', 'blitzed', 'stocious'—contemporary Scots seems to have as many words for the moods and stages of drunkenness as the Eskimos have for snow—has always been all part of the experience. Many of the visitors to Wembley in the 1920s had attracted 'undue notice by the attention which they had obviously paid to the bottle', remarked a contemporary witness. Hard drinking, after all, is part of the self-image of working-class Scotland. *No Mean City* bred no ordinary, fair-weather supporter. A Scotland fan could not let the side down by staying sober for the England game; a fact which makes the success of recent efforts by the SFA to ban alcohol at domestic fixtures all the more remarkable.

In a land of 'No Gods and precious few heroes' football has come nearest to filling a cultural void. Style has been important in Scotland. Jim Baxter, for instance, controlling an England game from midfield with an unhurried artistry that contrasted with the dull efficiency of a well-marshalled 'engine-room' that England could always be expected to produce. Jim Baxter became a legend because he would not adjust to the physicality and tireless running that was the hallmark of the Rangers team; nor did he respect the sectarian traditions of not mixing with Catholics off the field. In the 1967 Wembley game 'Baxter strolled across—can you see the slightly hen-toed saunter, the socks crumpled, the florid, gallus expression?—and, as he prompted his team-mates into more advantageous position, he played "keepie up" . . . I could feel myself gasp at him, at his sense of theatre, his exact awareness of how we Scots felt about winning and the English.' 'Slim Jim' was his own man and that was what Scotland wanted for itself. Jimmy Johnston, the little winger from a huge housing estate, who became Celtic's 'flying flea', the tearaway who scuttled past a full-back like a thief pursued by 'the polis', was another popular hero, whose fame came not just from his playing skill but from the way he lived like a 'Glasgae kid', stealing a rowing-boat and drifting drunkenly out to sea while training with the national team. Managers, however, were expected to be different from players; managers had to be 'gods', players were only 'heroes'. Managers had the collective responsibility of the nation on their shoulders and woe betide them if they were not equal to the task. When Ally Macleod returned with a humiliated Scottish squad from Argentina in 1978 he was cast out by those who only weeks before had idolized him. The Scotland manager had to be serious and successful; the press unfairly weighed in and word got round that the unfortunate Ally was a bit of a 'balloon' in the parlance of the time (i.e. a foolish person, brightly coloured, and full of air). In stark contrast was Jock Stein, son of a Lanarkshire miner and a miner himself for several years before becoming a professional with Albion Rovers at Coatbridge. In 1951 at twenty-nine he joined Celtic, later becoming manager of the Celtic side that won the European Cup in 1967, a man of gravity and determination, who died in harness watching the side qualify for the 1986 World Cup. Jock Stein, Matt Busby, and Bill Shankly—perhaps the most outstanding managers in modern British football—all came from around Bellshill near Glasgow.[57]

While it is absurd to call football a 'religion' in the sense of a spiritual system of belief, it does come close to the more restricted definition offered by Durkheim, namely a set of beliefs and practices through which a society collectively worships an idealized form of itself. The increasing division of labour in the work-place and the impact of large-scale urbanization was undermining shared beliefs. Collective life itself was under threat in huge industrial communities where citizens could no longer assemble together to carry out the ceremonies through which they found a sense of purpose and identity. Durkheim put it like this: 'The old Gods are growing old or are dying, and others are not yet born . . . it is not a dead past, but life itself which can give rise to a living cult'; more specifically 'the only way of renewing the collective representations which relate to sacred things is to retemper them at the very source of religious life, that is to say in assembled groups . . . Men are more confident because they

---

[57] R. Jenkins, *The Thistle and the Rose* (1983), p. 3; Moorhouse, 'Scotland against England', p. 197; Stanley Matthews, *Feet First* (1948), p. 43; Tommy Lawton, *Football is My Business* (1946), pp. 74–5; Bob Crampsey, *Mr. Stein* (1986).

feel themselves stronger; and they really are stronger because forces which are languishing are now reawakened into consciousness.' Literacy and rationalism, class conflict, and the decline of compulsory church attendance have all combined to promote the indifference or antagonism of the majority of urban workers towards organized religion. There is a lack of collective and public ceremony in contemporary society. In this restricted sense employed by Durkheim football could be said to be a 'religion'. Support and symbolic trappings varied according to the unit represented with the nation commanding the largest numbers and the most elaborate ritual. The singing of 'Abide with me' at Wembley Cup Finals after the First World War even attempted to bring organized religion into the game directly but without success. Good tunes and tangible, immediate, national objects of devotion were what was required. The blanket labelling of sport as a 'religion' is too vague to be meaningful but when applied to specific national forms, to rugby in Wales or football in Scotland for example, the intense identification of certain individuals with the national collectivity seems sufficiently powerful to qualify as 'an elementary form of religious life'.[58]

5. ENGLISHNESS AND BRITISHNESS

What became of the English amidst so much Celtic passion? Englishness and English nationalism are unjustly neglected subjects, especially where sports are concerned. Part of the blame attaches to the English themselves, who chose to obscure the matter, often preferring to call themselves 'British' when they meant 'English' and vice versa. Foreigners picked up the habit too, either from sheer ignorance or by copying the usage of the English themselves. Behind the confusion there was a simple logic. England dominated the British Isles. It was greatly superior in population and resources and until 1922 governed the whole island of Ireland as well as Scotland and Wales. Hence the use of 'English' to mean 'British' reflected the distribution of power

[58] A. Giddens, *Capitalism and Modern Social Theory* (1971), p. 122; see also E. Durkheim, *The Division of Labour*, with its appeal in the Preface of 1902 for a new collective life for industrial workers.

within the state. British imperial values were largely the product of the *English* public schools. But the nature of the English was not a matter the English felt inclined to explain. The formation of a distinctive English national culture in the late Victorian and Edwardian era is undeniable but still not widely understood. The new consciousness of English culture that arose at this time ranged from an interest in the purity of the English language and its literature to music, folklore, landscape, and the idea of games as an embodiment of the English spirit.

Beneath the stuffy, benign image of public service cultivated by British imperialism lay a more strident belief in the mission of the English people. The English, after all, had been the first to personify the nation in the robust shape of John Bull; they were also the first to have a national anthem. Sports were not just the source of high-minded ideals, they were inseparably associated with the more down-to-earth, assertive, and patriotic Englishness. Pugilism was considered peculiarly English in the early nineteenth century; Tom Brown thought fighting 'the natural and English way' to settle quarrels. The impact of the Victorian conscience and the drive for respectability undermined the status of physical combat as a mark of Englishness and raised up cricket in its place. It is not just the famous cricketing morality that matters here; it is the identification of the English with the style of the game and its heroes. W. G. Grace was not an English national hero because he 'played the game' (which he most emphatically did not); it was his boundless energy, his competitiveness, his huge stature, and simplicity that made him the quintessence of Englishness. 'He played in the Grand Manner,' wrote that other embodiment of the sporting English hero, C. B. Fry. 'He stood bolt upright and swept into every stroke, even a defensive back-stroke, with deliberate and dominating completeness. He never hedged on his stroke; he never pulled his punches.' Here was a new John Bull whose only concession to self-doubt was whether or not to take a quick single.[59]

In cricket the Established Church found an institution as English as itself. 'Is it wrong to pray to beat the Australians?' wondered

---

[59] G. Redmond, 'Moral Tales for Manly Boys', in Proceedings of the First Annual Conference of the BSSH, 1983, p. 68; W. F. Mandle, 'W. G. Grace as a Victorian Hero', *Historical Studies*, Apr. 1981, p. 359.

an anxious public schoolboy. 'My dear boy, anything which tends to increase the prestige of England is worth praying for', came the smooth reply. 'Put your whole soul into the game and make it your very life,' went one sermon, 'hit clean and hard at every loose ball for the least bit of work that helps anyone nearer God is blessed work and gladdens the Captain's heart.' J. H. Parsons of Warwickshire was ordained 'after the Archdeacon of Coventry had talked him into it between innings' and his team-mates supported his new vocation by excusing him from the slips on Saturdays 'so that he could prepare his sermons while fielding in the deep'. Free-scoring vicars were the stuff of English legend. The clergy of Somerset made 453 for 9 in 215 minutes; as true gentlemen their batting was stronger that their bowling and the opposition replied with 454 for 1 in 122 minutes. English cricket came to have a special place in the Anglican heart beside the King James Bible and the Book of Common Prayer. It was a clergyman, the Revd. James Pycroft, who, in 1851, published the first serious work on the early history of the game in the shires of southern England. Another vicar, Revd. J. R. Napier drifted in and out of Lancashire cricket picking two choice fixtures against Yorkshire and the Australians before rejoining his flock.[60]

Beside the village church there was the village green. Cricket more than any other game was bound up with the ruralism of an England overburdened with great cities. Village cricket was a uniquely English version of the pastoral. Dickens was an early devotee with Mr Pickwick's game between Dingley Dell and All Muggleton. When A. G. Macdonell's hero set out on a Scotsman's voyage of discovery into the mysteries of Englishness, he went to a fairy-tale village in deepest Kent. Here he was enchanted at his first sight of rural England:

White butterflies flapped their aimless way among the gardens. Delphiniums, larkspur, tiger lilies, evening primrose, monk's hood, sweet peas, swaggered brilliantly above the box-hedges, the wooden palings and the rickety gates. The cricket field itself was a mass of daisies and buttercups and dandelions, tall grasses and purple vetches and thistledown, and great clumps of dark red sorrel, except of course for the oblong patch in the centre—mown, rolled and watered—a smooth, shining emerald of grass, the pride of Fordenden, the Wicket . . . the parson shook hands with the squire. Doves cooed. The haze flickered. The world stood still.

---

[60] C. Brookes, *English Cricket*, p. 141; Harris, *Sport in Britain*, p. 86.

Village cricket, the English and the English countryside were at one.[61]

Close-fought village games with teams of odd characters in idyllic settings was a minor theme of English writing. Unique amongst English sports, cricket has not lacked serious literary attention. After the Great War there was a special need for reassurance, to know that the essence of England had survived, to forget the carnage, and enjoy English pleasures undisturbed. Hugh de Selincourt, a London-born literary critic and minor novelist, who had fled the metropolis for the peace of Pullborough and the Sussex Downs, wrote *The Cricket Match* in 1924 based on his experience as captain of the village side of Storrington. The book soon became a minor classic with the players in the team a kind of tapestry of the oddities and virtues of the English character: from the young Horace Cairie who prays 'Oh God, please bless mum and dad and keep me safe in the night, and oh God, please make me a sportsman' to the dashing Edgar Trine in the Big House, Teddy White with his racing-tips, and the brooding presence of Paul Gauvinier, the captain caught up in the seriousness of the enterprise and yet aware that life was a still more difficult business. Cricket was supposed to bring together the classes in a uniquely English way before they went back to their separate social worlds. This was the way *The Cricket Match* ended:

At length the band stopped playing and dispersed, the gossiping groups broke up and straggled away, some singing uproarious catches along the still lanes. Slowly the square emptied, the colours went out of the sky, the night descended peacefully on the village of Tillingfold. Rich and poor, young and old, were seeking sleep.[62]

The grip of cricket on the middle-class English imagination became very strong from the late nineteenth century, merging with the melodies of Elgar and the imagery of 'the thatched cottage awash with hollyhocks'. The nostalgic dream of peace and harmony that was country cricket can never have been quite the same for those who daily lived with the reality of agricultural

[61] A. G. Macdonell, 'England, Their England', in A. Ross (ed.), *Penguin Cricketer's Companion* (1981), p. 120.
[62] H. de Selincourt, *The Cricket Match* (1980); see esp. introduction by Benny Green.

decline and rural poverty. Nor did the northern working class invest the game with the same kind of Englishness that took hold of the south. It was the unforgiving duels of batsman and bowler, the strange mixture of guile and grit which particularly appealed up north. Northern cricket was less sentimental; 'village' cricket had been professionalized in the Lancashire League and denatured—a shameful act to judge by the deafening silence of an otherwise eloquent band of cricket-writers for whom Englishness was everything. It is as if the inhabitants of the mill-towns, who were the backbone of the League, had betrayed their birthright. 'The neglect of League cricket, particularly in the South,' wrote C. L. R. James, 'passes comprehension. The only reason that makes sense to me is that it is wilful. The South does not want to know.'[63]

Despite differences in the way the game was interpreted north and south of the Trent, it remained the true national sport of the English. Football was the property of industrial workers, rugby of the middle class. Only cricket was universal. Just as the era of Grace was over a new star rose in the firmament. Jack Hobbs was the authentic English hero of the inter-war years. The first of twelve children born to a Cambridge college servant in 1881, he was 'The Master'; the first working-class sportsman to receive a knighthood. To walk out of the pavilion to open the England innings with Jack Hobbs, whom Archie Maclaren called 'the perfect batsman', was the dream of an entire generation of Englishmen. He was the greatest run-maker in English cricket scoring 61,237 runs and 197 centuries from 1905 to 1934. His significance for England, however, was more than a matter of statistics. He was an artist; he had a kind of grace and power, an elegance in his play that moved the most knowledgeable of critics to marvel. When relatively early in his career he made 62 not out on an appalling wicket against the Australians, C. B. Fry recalled that 'as a spectator at the other crease I have to say that this was as great an innings as I ever saw played by any batsman in any Test match, or any other match'. But it was not this cricketing talent alone that made him an English hero; it was the reserve, the modesty, the shy humour, the very 'gentlemanliness'

---

[63] R. Colls and P. Dodd (eds.), *Englishness* (1986), marks out the field properly for the first time; James, *Beyond a Boundary*, p. 130.

of this professional that won the heart of the nation. Hobbs combined the effortless superiority of the amateur with the respectability and perseverance of the artisan. He was a true aristocrat of labour; he drank very little and was never known to swear or behave in an unseemly manner. He was immaculately turned out and a regular church-goer. He accepted the division between amateur and professional without complaint, retaining the habit of calling amateur players 'Mr' and never strove for the captaincy of either Surrey or England. Hobbs did not offer any challenge to the system. He was a contented, happily married family-man, who made a good living from his sports shop in Fleet Street and never lost his dignity. He was a comfortable sort of hero. Just the man to send out to open the innings for England. And this he did into his late forties, sharing no less than twenty-six stands of a hundred for England, eleven, including three consecutive ones in 1924–5 in Australia, with Herbert Sutcliffe in a partnership that became a popular legend.[64]

Just as the General Strike came to a head, the mature Hobbs was at the height of his fame, passing Dr Grace's tally and making a record sixteen hundreds in the single season of 1926. Class relations in England, despite the depth of bitterness over pay and conditions in the mines, did not degenerate into the class war which Marxist parties predicted and tried to organize. The working class retained a certain confidence in the system. They preferred to express their newly acquired sense of unity and purpose through the institution of the Labour Party with its firmly parliamentary and gradualist approach to socialism. They trusted the propertied classes to 'play the game', to respect the verdict of the electorate just as a sportsman accepted the decision of the umpire. The monarchy was now cast in the constitutional role of referee between the political contestants. The fact that the English nation at least shared certain simple ethics, embodied in their admiration for men like Hobbs, may in a loose but important sense have helped to maintain a climate of public trust. We are *not* talking here of bread and circuses. Sport, especially cricket, was never a vehicle for crude social control; rather it provided a shared vocabulary of 'fairness' and embodied a set of principles

[64] J. Arlott, *Jack Hobbs* (1981), *passim*; a model short biography of a sportsman.

for the decent organization of public life. It was the ruling classes who had most thoroughly absorbed these ideas. Hence Stanley Baldwin resigned in 1929 'because it would have been "unsporting" not to have done so'. Earlier the King was advised in relation to the first Labour Government that 'the general feeling of the country [was] that, true to British ideas, the Government, whoever they should be, should have a fair chance'. It was this all-pervading spirit of fairness which most impressed a German observer. Sport played an important part in the creation of a stable and democratic political culture. ' "Fair play" is a great conception', he wrote,

for in these two words are summed up all that English education and ethics hold most dear. The words are untranslatable, and it would be an injustice to cramp them into a rough and ready formula. The value of certain things lies in their very vagueness and lack of precision . . . Everyone, be he sportsman, soldier, politician, statesman, journalist, employer or employed, finds in these two words guidance and admonishment affecting the whole scope and meaning of his work . . . Fair play means regard for one's neighbour and seeing the man and fellow player in one's opponent.[65]

This is dangerous ground. It is easy and tempting to over-simplify as George Trevelyan did when he claimed that 'if the French *noblesse* had been capable of playing cricket with their peasants, their *chateaux* would never have been burnt'. The Trevelyans were well-intentioned Whiggish landowners in south Northumberland, who may have oiled the wheels of rural deference by maintaining some common sports. But that is not the point. These common sports were in decline from the early nineteenth century in an England rapidly taken over by urban sprawl. It was not so much that a new paternalism arose to replace the old but that new 'rules of the game' were forged and agreed by both sides. Hence the social and political importance of the games analogy. 'Rules' were binding on rich and poor, employer and employed, noble and commoner alike. This became part of a 'national tradition' of work and play, sport and politics, through which the British recognized themselves and were recognized by others. The scope for radically reactionary politics was

[65] R. McKibbin, 'Deference and Democracy', *Times Higher Education Supplement*, 15 Feb. 1982, p. 13; Kirchner, *Fair Play*, p. 18.

circumscribed by this sense of abiding by the rules. Even if trade unions caused disorder and left-wingers threatened sweeping reforms, one still had to play the constitutional game. To ignore the will of the people as French and German conservatives did would not have been 'English'. This lay behind Pierre de Coubertin's admiration of the English. As a Liberal nobleman he urged his class to accept the Republic and as a citizen of the world he tried to apply the principle of fair play more widely through the institution of the Olympic Games. If France was to break the cycle of revolution and counter-revolution, she needed a gradualist politics born out of a sense of give and take, a consensus that certain constitutional forms were 'above politics'. In France the monarchy was fatally compromised by reactionary catholicism whereas in Britain the working classes came to trust the monarchy and the state apparatus as being more or less neutral, like a referee ensuring 'a good game'.[66]

The king was expected to be a 'sport', both in theory and in practice. George V began the tradition of royal attendance at the FA Cup Final in 1914 and this came to be a new national ceremony with the opening of Wembley stadium in 1923. The 'White Horse' final of that year when a single mounted policeman managed to control the huge crowd that spilled out on to the pitch became a symbol of decency and orderliness. The President and Secretary of the FA were knighted in 1927 and 1931. Attendance at major sports events became an accepted part of the royal itinerary, and the current royal family have a genuinely distinguished record of sporting achievement—albeit of an equestrian sort, which avoids popular team-sports and physical contact with commoners. Leading public figures have been seen to be similarly keen on sport. Lloyd George was a golfer and so was Ramsay MacDonald (presumably reassuring the upper middle classes that he was not going to destroy civilized life entirely); Balfour loved tennis and so did Birkenhead; Baldwin watched football and even gave a lecture on the game; Lord Grey was a great fisherman; so is Lord Home, whose autobiography is so full of fishing and cricketing analogies that one reviewer could not decide whether it ought to be catalogued under sport or politics. Harold Wilson's enthusiasm for Huddersfield Town and for the

[66] Holt, *Sport and Society in Modern France*, pp. 63–4.

England World Cup squad of 1966 was all part of the bluff populism of a northern intellectual in politics. Ted Heath is a fine yachtsman. Even Mrs Thatcher has a golfing husband.[67]

The use of sport as an ideological tool was for the most part informal. Britain defined its political distinctiveness in part through the 'small state', which left its people free to get on with their own lives. The government was aware of the potential of sport as a source of social stability as discussions in the Home Office concerning the civil unrest after the First World War reveal. But a campaign to promote sport for 'social control' was not attempted. Some funds were provided for industrial recreation programmes, mainly for miners, but private corporate initiative was more important. A National Council on Sport in Industry was set up in the 1930s, which was quite strong in the newer industries of the South and the West Midlands. This body openly aimed at 'incorporating' the work-force by the lavish provision of sporting facilities. A few of the older industrial concerns like Pilkington's also provided their workers with sports facilities in the paternalist tradition, but the concept of leisure provision as an integral part of a 'salary and conditions' package was most fully developed by large stores, banks, public corporations, and multinationals such as the opulent Lensbury Club on the banks of the Thames near Richmond provided for the employees of Shell in the 1930s.[68]

For most people the local authorities were the main providers of recreational facilities. From the preoccupation with fresh air, flowers, and cleanliness the tradition of municipal socialism moved on to provide playing-fields as well as parks and swimming-baths. Supply, however, was far behind demand. The London County Council had 350 pitches with a thousand teams applying to use them in 1929. In 1925 the Duke of York launched the National Playing Fields Association to secure facilities for sports in urban areas where the building boom was putting even

[67] McKibbin, 'Deference and Democracy'; S. Wagg, *The Football World* (1984), ch. 3.

[68] S. Jones, 'The Political Control of Association Football', paper presented to the Society for the Study of Labour History, conference on Sport and the Working Class, Nov. 1984; there is a useful body of research on the history of industrial recreation in the United States but as yet little has been done on Britain, especially for the twentieth century.

greater pressure on the limited amounts of open space. This body
raised £1.5 million which went towards the purchase of 6,000
acres of land and provided over a thousand recreation grounds
between 1927–33. The National Playing Fields Association is
especially interesting in the way it combined private charity with
royal patronage in a typically British alternative to formal political
initiatives through government. This was 'rational recreation' by
another name and usefully supplemented the work of the
municipalities. Liverpool increased the number of municipal
cricket pitches from 50 to 79 and the number of tennis-courts
from 170 to 400 between 1921 and 1930 in addition to the 179
football-pitches they ran. Rates rather than national taxes were
the source of public subsidy for sport. Even when the fear of
German rearmament pushed the Conservative Government into
passing the Physical Training and Recreation Act in July 1937 only
part of the £2 million allocated over three years was to be spent
on sport. The traditions of Victorian liberalism were hard to shake
off. As Nye Bevan pointed out, 'there is no need to seek the
justification of national well-being for playing, because your own
well-being is a sufficient justification'. It was not until
'Butskellism' and the 'welfare capitalism of the Macmillan and
Wilson years that the state accepted a prime responsibility for
the provision of sports facilities culminating in the setting up of
the Sports Council with its slogan of 'Sport for All'.[69]

Despite Bevan's fine phrases, the Labour Movement between
the wars did not advance a great deal from its Edwardian neglect
of popular culture. Efforts were made but they did not come to
very much. With the Depression and the threat of war sport
seemed politically trivial on the Left. A British Workers' Sports
Federation (BWSF) was founded in 1923 but fell victim to the
bitter hostility between communists and democratic socialists in
the 1920s. It was gradually infiltrated and taken over by the
British Communist Party and mainstream Labour supporters set
up an alternative, the National Workers' Sports Association, in
1930 which brought together established progressive groups like

[69] Jones, 'Political Control'; McIntosh, *Physical Education*, pp. 224, 242; John
Hargreaves, 'From Social Democracy to Authoritarian Populism', *Leisure Studies*,
1985 (4), argues that the 'welfare consensus' is now being undermined and a return
to private provision and 'Victorian values' is under way; S. Jones, *Workers at
Play* (1986), p. 95 for interwar provision.

the Clarion cycling clubs. At its height the BWSF claimed 6,000 members in 1931 but even this small number may be an exaggeration. The organizers were too keen on attacking the 'bourgeois' sports establishment and the official political parties to organize proletarian sport effectively at the grass roots, although they were effective in popular protests against the ban on Sunday games and mass trespasses such as the famous tramp over Kinder Scout in the Peak District in 1932. The BWSF lacked funds because it lacked the support of organized labour. It also fell victim to the dominant values of 'depoliticized' sport. Socialist sport with its baggage of doctrine was inherently suspect to the 'common-sense' view that sport and politics were quite separate spheres of life. Communists were deeply suspicious of sport as entertainment and yet it was just this kind of commercialization which working men enjoyed so much on Saturday afternoons. Most of all 'communist' sport with its tours of the Soviet Union and constant propaganda for the Workers' State was 'un-British'. Foreign connections spelled death to any association trying to become an established part of British popular culture. The Left was much less successful than the Right in laying claim to the 'good things' of English life, including sport. Conservatives tended to take cultural possession of cricket in particular. Englishness was part of their credo. England, as Orwell remarked in 1940, 'was rather like a stuffy Victorian family', which despite its differences had 'a private language and common memories, and at the approach of an enemy it closes ranks'.[70]

This tradition of thought and feeling in English sport is distinct from the cruder forms of partisanship. Nationalism in English sport has become more pronounced in recent years as the imperial role through which it was formerly expressed has disappeared. At first English patriotism in sport was relatively weak, restrained both by the amateur code in Rugby and cricket and by the strong class-based and regional following of football. To the northern working-class football supporter 'North' against 'South' games were probably more engrossing than the home internationals. Beating a London club was something a Geordie could more readily appreciate than beating a Scotland side containing some

[70] S. Jones, 'Sport, Politics and the Labour Movement', *BJSH*, Sept. 1985, esp. p. 166; Orwell cited in J. Stevenson, *British Society, 1914–45* (1984), p. 472.

of his own club's players. As time passed a genuinely popular and national press slowly stoked up the flames of English nationalism. But the mentality that made the Scots so keen to beat England was much less apparent in English attitudes to the Scots. Between the wars the depressed and deprived northern cities waged a battle with the richer southern clubs, especially with Herbert Chapman's Arsenal, that was possibly more important than national rivalry with Scotland.

English football was too self-absorbed to give itself wholeheartedly to the national cause. Club loyalties were too strong and the League programme too exhausting. Moreover the rulers of the game did not encourage it. English football remained proud and insular; relations between the Fédération Internationale de Football Association (FIFA), which was set up without English support in 1904, were always difficult. At heart the English felt football was their property and were disinclined to co-operate with foreigners. Admiration for the originators of the game tempered Continental irritation with this variant of 'splendid isolation'. Disputes over the definition of amateurism further soured relations between the wars. Although England played twenty-three internationals on the continent of Europe between 1929 and 1939, England was not a member of FIFA and did not take part in the new World Cup. It was not until after the Second World War that Britain officially and fully opened itself up to the 'world game'. By the time England started to take the rest of the world seriously, the rest of the world no longer had anything to learn from us. When England finally entered the World Cup in Brazil in 1950, they were defeated 1–0 by parttimers from the United States. Admittedly this was a freak result, but there was nothing freakish about the lesson in short passing delivered in 1953 by the Hungarians at Wembley. It was no longer possible to look down on these faintly ludicrous foreigners trying to play our game. It was the chauvinistic condescension of the English themselves that now seemed foolish.[71]

International competition was taken more seriously in other sports, especially in athletics. The setting up of the Olympic Games, partly based upon the Baron de Coubertin's anglophilia, institutionalized 'the nation' in athletics from the outset. England,

[71] Walvin, *The People's Game*, pp. 121–2.

Scotland, Ireland, and Wales were required to compete together as a single nation-state rather than as four 'countries'. Coubertin did not wish to promote nationalism, which he defined as hostility to other countries. On the contrary, he sought to foster 'patriotism', which he felt combined the love of one's own country with an acceptance and appreciation of the love other peoples felt for theirs. Sport was to be the means of recognizing differences between peoples within the wider framework of a common humanity deriving from Greek culture—'the Esperanto of the races' as Jean Giraudoux was later to put it. The Olympic Games aimed to foster a religion of patriotism, directing the new power of national identity into constructive and peaceful channels. Hence the significance of the sacred plants, flights of birds, wreaths, and other religious symbols and ceremonies. Unfortunately, the real nature of the Games quickly changed. The first Olympic Games in Athens in 1896 was happily chaotic, with visiting tourists carrying off medals unexpectedly. 'Such was the informality of these Games that a British lawn-tennis player entered the Olympic tournament simply to secure a court to play on.' A little of this lingered on in Paris in 1900 but by 1904 in St Louis commercial influences—the Games were linked to the World's Fair Movement—and a nascent athletic nationalism were already undermining the Olympic ideal.[72]

By the time the Games came to London in 1908 individual eccentricity and utopianism had largely been crushed by the weight of national expectation. A total of around 300,000 spectators watched 1,500 competitors from nineteen nations. The British press and public came to feel their 'racial virility' was on trial. The spread of a crude social Darwinism was making nations increasingly sensitive about their sporting prowess. Sport would reveal 'the survival of the fittest'. These ideological undercurrents were aggravated in Britain by the revelations of the physical weakness of recruits during the Boer War (three out of every five had been rejected in Manchester). Unofficial pressure groups such as the National Birth Rate Commission and the Eugenic Education Society were formed. The government set up a committee to review the question of racial deterioration. 'National efficiency' was the new watchword. The British were especially anxious

---

[72] J. J. MacAloon, *The Great Symbol* (1981), ch. 8, esp. pp. 258–9.

about German economic penetration and naval rivalry. 'International sport came to be seen ambivalently both as an agent of international peace in a world moving inexorably towards war and as a means of reviving threatened national morale.' It seemed imperative to do well in front of one's own people as proof of the vitality of the race and the relatively poor British performances were seen by racial activists as a sign of decay. Set against this was the deep-seated belief in enjoying the game for its own sake, of being a good sport, and playing with style rather than training scientifically to win. The balance between nationalism, 'professionalism', and science on the one hand and individualism, the games ethic, and 'effortless superiority' on the other set the tone of inter-war representative athletics.[73]

This mood was cleverly captured in the film *Chariots of Fire*, which follows the preparations and Olympic fortunes of two British athletes in the Paris Games of 1924. Harold Abrahams is criticized by his Cambridge tutors for being too Semitic in his single-minded pursuit of victory in contrast to the young Lord Burghley's studied casualness. Abrahams is thrown together with another outcast from the English way, the Scot Eric Liddell, whose need to win comes from a Calvinist belief that 'God made me fast'. Apart from Douglas Lowe, who maintained the Oxbridge tradition with victory in the 800 metres in both 1924 and 1928, the best British athletes between the wars were generally of modest origins—athletics was a cheap sport to take up—but possessed of quiet tenacity and willing to submit themselves to tedious training schedules to win national honour. Albert Hill, a railway-guard who had done three years in the trenches, was just such a man. He won both the 800 and 1,500 at the first post-war Games at Antwerp in 1920 under the guidance of Sam Mussabini, who trained professional runners and later coached Abrahams. Then there was the frail, bespectacled figure of Sydney Wooderson, a corporal in the Pioneer Corps, who got rheumatic fever running the 'Stalin Mile' in Manchester in 1944, and became a kind of symbol of the dowdy, underfed, indomitable Englishman whose courage and endurance would defeat Hitler. Athletes increasingly

---

[73] J. Lowerson, 'Sport and National Decay: The British and the Olympics before 1914', abstract in N. Müller and J. K. Rühl, *Olympic Scientific Congress 1984 Official Report* (1985), p. 384; G. R. Searle, *The Quest for National Efficiency, 1900–14* (1971) for Darwinian influences on policy.

were seen as standard-bearers of the race—unpaid, unspoiled patriots.[74]

The kernel of nationalism at the heart of British sport revealed itself most clearly in war. Public schoolmen with their ideals of service seemed positively to relish the prospect of a 'good game' with Germany. Boys at Marlborough thought the Great War 'was like a glorified football match in which, if peace did not come, they might take their places in the English team'. Sport was called to the colours. The action of Captain Nevill of the East Surrey regiment became a symbol of this. 'As the gun-fire died away', he 'climbed on to the parapet and into no man's land, beckoning others to follow' and with a good kick 'the ball rose and travelled well towards the German line.' This act of bravado rather than the pity of the football match between British and German soldiers at Christmas 1914 set the tone for official wartime sports propaganda. Despite the fact that football grounds were used extensively for recruiting, there was strong moral pressure to stop the Football League for the duration of the war. 'Duty Before Sport' demanded the *Evening News* and reluctantly the clubs acceded. 'You have played with one another and against one another for the Cup,' declared Lord Derby in 1915, 'play with one another for England now.' A 'Footballers' Battalion' had been formed in December 1914, but middle-class opinion was determined that professional working-class sport be stopped altogether in the name of patriotism. This view prevailed against angry protests by sporting papers like the *Athletic News* that a 'clique of virulent snobs' was seeking to deprive the poor 'of the one distraction that they had had for over thirty years'. The Hunt, however, did not exercise a self-denying ordinance, although élite opinion was divided over the morality of maintaining a racing-programme. In the end a very limited number of meetings was accepted as a way of maintaining the bloodstock—the northern munitions areas were excluded. Local league cricket was especially popular in the north in the absence of the county game (suspended for the duration). Boxing and pedestrianism also flourished in a climate where escapism was at a premium and team-sports were curtailed. With the introduction of conscription the argument that sport was a disincentive to enlistment lapsed,

[74] Lovesey, *Centenary History of the AAA*, pp. 68–75.

though in official eyes wartime sport was still seen as faintly immoral and a potential hindrance to the war effort.[75]

During the Second World War, however, more care was taken to maintain morale at home between Dunkirk and D-Day by organizing not a full League programme but a host of representative matches—home internationals, inter-service games, as well as friendly professional fixtures. Football was enlisted for the Home Front. England was split into North and South with a challenge cup competition. 'Games followed one on top of each other in a seemingly endless stream', recalled Denis Compton. Eighty-five thousand watched Charlton and Chelsea play in the Southern Cup in 1943 and 440,000 attended various games on Boxing Day 1943. Touring teams of star players were set up to entertain the troops. Despite the odd cat-call of 'D-Day dodger', one soccer party was worth five ENSA shows in battle areas—this, at least, was the view of one Commanding Officer. Football was certainly more entertaining in wartime. The ban on Sunday games was lifted, and a system of guest players was permitted. Referees were even allowed to wear glasses. Occasionally a rank beginner bluffed his way into a professional team like a recruit to a Chelsea side who claimed he had played for Motherwell—anger on the Chelsea bench soon turned to hilarity as he failed even to make contact with the ball let alone kick it in the right direction. Removal of the fear of relegation led to much higher goal-scoring feats. The unsung hero of wartime entertainment has to be Albert Stubbins of Newcastle United, who scored no less than 230 goals during the war, surpassing the feats of more famous players like Tommy Lawton, Stan Cullis, and Joe Mercer, whose presence at the Aldershot army-camp was a wonderful bonus for the local supporters as well as the troops. Instead of snuffing out 'the people's game', the more imaginative officials and politicians of Churchill's Britain used football as a useful prop for national morale and as a source of army physical-education instructors.[76]

---

[75] C. Veitch, ' "Play Up! and Win the War!" ' *Journal of Contemporary History*, July 1985, pp. 363, 374–5; D. Birley, 'Sportsmen and the Deadly Game', *BJSH*, Dec. 1986, pp. 288–310, provides a useful and broad survey.

[76] J. Rollen, *Soccer at War, 1935–1945* (1985), pp. 16, 20, 54–7, 173; Rollen offers an extraordinarily detailed catalogue of events but the main developments are outlined in Walvin, *The People's Game*, pp. 137–45.

The growth of a more fanatical, even violent, English nationalism in football from the 1950s goes beyond the scope of this chapter. This subject is best understood in the context of the wider changes in crowd behaviour which will be examined in Chapter 5. Let us leave English football at its height before the impact of television and post-industrial affluence. The vast post-war crowds supported England with a cheerful, modest patriotism in keeping with the sense of solidarity, austerity, and respectable socialism of Attlee's Britain. Yet relief and jubilation at the successful conclusion of the war soon turned to apprehension, especially amongst the educated governing élite. The war had exhausted Britain economically. Foreign assets had virtually all been sold, the United States dominated the world economy, and British industry desperately required reconstruction and diversification. In foreign policy America, with the atomic bomb and the Truman doctrine determined the course of an emergent Cold War with the Soviet Union. Britain was relatively speaking on the sidelines. India was granted independence in 1947 and for the first time the future of the British Empire in Africa began to look uncertain. 'Britain was losing an Empire and searching for a role.' British morale, especially its élite English element, badly needed a lift.

This was the setting for the conquest of Everest by a British-led expedition in 1953. The fact that it was a New Zealander and a Nepalese who actually reached the summit did not prevent the ascent being hailed as a great British triumph by the press. On the contrary, it showed how a new post-imperial co-operation could overcome the greatest of obstacles. This theme was echoed in the Queen's Speech of 1953 which spoke of the Commonwealth bearing 'no resemblance to the empires of the past . . . it is an entirely new conception, built on the highest qualities of men . . . moving steadily towards greater harmony between its many creeds, colours and races'. The climbing of Everest coincided with the crowning of the new queen and there was much talk of a 'second Elizabethan Age'. *The Times* compared the conquest of Everest with Drake's circumnavigation of the globe. It was the manner of this triumph as much as anything else that pleased the British. There was a charming amateurism and eccentricity about the expedition. Umbrellas had been carried up to 13,000 feet. Sir John Hunt played the part of the cultured, competent, phlegmatic Englishman reading the *Oxford Book of Greek Verse* while organizing supplies and technical support with a minimum of fuss. There was still hope for Britain if the old qualities of stoicism and the knack of handling 'native' races could be combined with the scientific and management skills needed in the modern world.[77]

Another sporting triumph followed hard upon the conquest of Everest and gave added reassurance to the nation, especially those steeped in the amateur spirit for whom the demolition of English professional football by Puskas and the Hungarians was not a matter for much regret. On 6 May 1954 at the small Iffley Road stadium in Oxford, Roger Bannister, a medical student at the University, broke the four-minute mile with the help of a couple of friends, Chris Brasher and Christopher Chataway. Despite the apparent informality of the occasion, this was no glorious undergraduate fluke. The sub-four-minute mile was a superbly planned and executed achievement. The record was broken by scientific training and pacing in which two first-class athletes sacrificed themselves to permit Bannister to break the record. A blend of the old virtues and the new, which the public seemed to understand and appreciate, united these two very different achievements. Bannister and Hunt gave the English hope for the future within the British Isles and more importantly in the wider post-imperial world. Not since a bony young Yorkshireman, Len Hutton, batted into a third day in August 1938 against Bradman's Australia to pass the Don's record score for a test match had the British known such transcendent moments of self-belief through sport. Hutton, later to become the first professional captain of England and knighted in 1956, joined the ranks of those who had to embody the hopes and expectations of an England creaking under the weight of its industrial and imperial past, but whose sense of destiny was still quite strong.

[77] Stewart, 'British Reaction to the Conquest of Everest', pp. 22–9.

5

Commercialism and Violence

IT is becoming commonplace to think of sport as a 'leisure industry'. In recent years there have certainly been dramatic moves to open sport up to the forces of the market. The maximum wage and the retain-and-transfer system in football, and the distinction between gentlemen and players in cricket has been scrapped. Tennis also abandoned the amateur and professional labels and simply called all competitors 'players' from 1967. Most recently a change of heart on the part of the athletics authorities now enables top competitors to earn very large sums which are held in 'trust funds'. This technicality permits athletes to remain 'amateurs'. Only Rugby Union holds out against the commercial tide despite widespread speculation about covert payments to players. Cricket, the game of the British amateur *par excellence*, is now sponsored by tobacco firms and insurance companies whilst footballers advertise everything from double-glazing to Guinness on their shirts. The Football League was recently sponsored by a Japanese camera manufacturer whose name had to be repeated when publishing or broadcasting results. A newspaper and now a bank have since taken over. In return for media coverage and the 'clean' image of sport, sponsors are prepared to provide big injections of cash. This new rush to make profits from sport provides a contemporary context against which to measure the earlier degree of commercialization. To what extent were large profits made from spectator sports and what kind of earnings and working conditions could a professional sportsman expect? What role have newspapers, the radio, and television played in sport? This leads us to the composition and behaviour of sports crowds, especially at football matches and the current debate about the reasons for hooliganism. How far are money and the media responsible for the misbehaviour of football supporters? Or is aggression leading to violence endemic in sport and sports spectators?

1. SHAREHOLDERS AND PROFESSIONALS

Professionalism was the limited form through which amateurs permitted market forces to enter the world of sport. There was a long-standing tradition of professionalism, which centred around jockeys and pugilists for the most part. Sporting gentlemen of the pre-Victorian period saw no harm in making money through playing games so long as this was a matter of gambling; nor did they mind mixing with others of a lower class, who derived the bulk of their income in this way, provided distinctions of birth were recognized and preserved. Peers played cricket with the Hampshire farmers of Hambledon without needing to designate their status officially as 'gentlemen' or 'players'. Yet in Victorian Britain the alliance of wealth and birth formed in the public schools infused sport with a new idealism whilst simultaneously segregating the élite from members of the lower classes taking the same form of exercise. What were the implications of this for the process of commercialization? More striking than the provision of popular entertainment for profit was the remarkable degree to which the landed interest, the liberal professions, and even sections of the business community itself excluded commercial forces from sport.

The rule of sport by amateurs kept capitalism at bay in British sport. All sports came to make sharp distinctions between those who received payment and those who did not. Some amateur associations went as far as legal prosecution to prevent any payment or profit being derived from the activities they controlled. Of those sports where payment was permitted, there was little concession to the creation of a free market. Footballers were hedged around by restrictions on personal mobility and income whilst the residence qualifications for county cricketers prevented a cricketing equivalent of the football transfer system. Even the breakaway 'Northern Union' required rugby players to have a source of income outside of the game and paid them in principle for 'broken time'.[1]

The historical hostility to commercialism among the ruling bodies of sport is indisputable. Yet there were areas of commercial penetration. Sport certainly responded to the demand of the

---

[1] See above, pp. 103–9.

urban worker for entertainment. Professional football is the obvious case. With hundreds of thousands of paying spectators each week, with rising transfer fees, and the registration of clubs as limited liability companies surely it is reasonable to conclude that professional football was 'a business'? Plausible as this may sound, the proposition is flawed; the organization of football, for example, was quite unlike that of the music-hall or the cinema. Spectator sport may have been partially commercialized but it never became a capitalist leisure enterprise. Careful research by Tony Mason, Wray Vamplew, and others has uncovered the financial structure of football from company records. Professional clubs formed themselves into limited liability companies not to speculate in the entertainment business but to make legally secure the cost of providing facilities. It was not just a matter of handling gate-money and paying the players. More important was the status of loans raised to buy or rent land and erect a stadium. Even this was hardly big business. The initial sums were often quite modest as football clubs tend to grow gradually, first drawing crowds on a casual basis and then fencing in a field and charging admission; from this point a wooden stand might be built and earth piled up into which steps could be cut. Fulham even invited the public to dump their refuse in the ground in order to erect rudimentary terracing and so, I am told, did Stirling Albion. Purpose-built stadia generally followed from club success rather than being built speculatively in the hope of profit. There was no 'futures market' in football. Between 1889 and 1910 fifty-eight clubs moved into new grounds, though there was often continuity of land use in the sense that 'at least 35 out of the current league grounds were recreational or sporting grounds in some form before the clubs moved in'. Club directors were cautious and strictly functional in their building plans. Archibald Leitch, a mechanical engineer from Glasgow, provided the standard design for stadia with three open sides and a two-tier grandstand running the length of one of the longer sides of the rectangle. Much as their fans loved them for all their quirks, the aesthetics and comfort of a ground did not cross the mind of many football directors. They did not seek to attract new customers by the excellence of their pitches or facilities as music-hall proprietors did through the plushness and extravagance of their theatres.[2]

---

[2] S. Inglis, *The Football Grounds of England and Wales* (1985), p. 13.

Building and running a stadium that would hold tens of thousands of spectators was an expensive business and not usually a profitable one. Only six out of sixty-two leading clubs paid their shareholders any dividend in the season 1908–9 and they were restricted by the FA from paying a dividend of more than 5 per cent. 'No one who is out for a business return would look at football shares,' commented a leading sporting paper. 'Hundreds [of shareholders] have for years maintained guarantees at banks', continued the article, 'and thousands have helped to create clubs by taking shares without hope of seeing their money back or any return on it.' The same was broadly true of Scotland. Only Rangers and Celtic made much money—hence the original meaning of the term 'The Old Firm'—and Celtic was pledged to donate to Catholic charities. The small annual profits of the Edinburgh and Dundee clubs were interspersed with losses and no dividends were distributed to shareholders. There were odd cases of profiteering such as the rental and catering concession held by Mears at Chelsea, but these were the exceptions that proved the rule. When 'King John' Houlding, a self-made brewer and prominent local Tory, tried to use his position on the Everton board to jack up the rent paid to him by the club, there was a shareholders' revolt and Houlding eventually left the club to form Liverpool FC. Profiteering was morally unacceptable to most Everton shareholders; this was even true of business men like Hartley, the jam-maker, and Hudson, the soap-manufacturer. When there were contracts to be handed out directors may have tried to help one another, but that can hardly have been a sufficient reason for buying up large blocks of shares.[3]

Although there was no direct financial incentive for the purchase of shares, the bulk of those who took them up were involved in business. Of 740 directors of football clubs from 1888–1915 that have been traced there were only forty-two skilled manual workers and a mere four unskilled. Similarly there were only thirty-two 'gentlemen'. Manufacturers and managers, wholesale and retail, financial and commercial businesses, the

---

[3] T. Mason, *Association Football* (1980), p. 48; id., *The Blues and the Reds* (1985), p. 4; W. Vamplew, 'The Economics of a Sports Industry', *Economic History Review*, Nov. 1982, p. 556; S. Tischler, *Footballers and Businessmen* (1981), stresses the indirect benefits to directors but the evidence presented does not sustain the author's wider argument.

building trade and the food and drink trade made up approximately two-thirds of the group. Naturally directors tended to be drawn from the larger shareholders. The thirty-four English clubs examined by Tony Mason were mostly run by smallish groups of substantial shareholders, though shareholding was sometimes quite widely distributed as in the case of Woolwich Arsenal with 900 manual workers holding shares in 1893. In Sheffield a small, interconnected group of industrialists dominated football, passing down their directorships from father to son like family property. Many directors continued in office long after they could hope to participate effectively. Alderman Wardley of Sheffield Wednesday remained a director until he was over ninety. Attendance at AGMs was small and directors were returned unopposed. At West Ham the club was run by two families involved locally in business on a modest scale. As they controlled an absolute majority of shares, the club was effectively closed. No new members of the board were elected, though the odd family friend was co-opted from time to time.[4]

Vamplew suggests shareholding was rather more democratically distributed in Scotland with skilled manual workers making up 19.1 per cent of shareholders in twenty-three clubs up to 1916. Publicans were still the most important occupational group, holding between them almost a third (31.2 per cent) of all shares. Perhaps a stake in a popular club would give profitable returns indirectly through the sale of drink. The degree to which publicans 'invested' for this reason in football is unknown but the pecuniary advantage at first sight seems doubtful. There was all the difference in the world between meeting a retired sporting hero behind the bar and meeting a shareholder or even a director. Probably publicans were just carrying on an old tradition of involvement in popular sports. Being a major shareholder or a director was rather like holding some honorific office within the community; it brought its own private and social satisfactions which could not be measured financially. Publicans were frequently men of working-class origin, who sought prosperity without leaving their community.

[4] Mason, *Association Football*, p. 32; N. Fishwick, 'Association Football and English Social Life, 1910–1950', D.Phil. thesis (Oxford, 1984), p. 91; C. Korr, 'The Men at the Top', in W. Vamplew (ed.), *The Economic History of Leisure. Papers Presented at the Eighth International Economic History Congress, Budapest, August 1982* (1983), pp. 1–16.

They had a certain prestige within the neighbourhood and influence within the world of football was part of this process of 'making good'. Similar feelings influenced middle-class shareholders and directors too. Investment in soccer offered a sense of self-importance and pride at running an organization around which so much local interest was centred; the club made you 'someone' in the town, a big fish in a small pool. Arnold Bennett caught this splendidly in the story of Denry Machin, an ambitious and well-off young councillor, who brought back a local footballing hero to the town at his own expense. 'Two days later a letter appeared in the *Signal* (signed "Fiat Justitia") suggesting that Denry, as some reward for his public spirit, ought to be the next mayor of Bursley.' When he was duly elected, Machin merely remarked to his wife ' "You'll be mayoress to the youngest mayor . . . And it's cost me, including hotel and travelling expenses, eight hundred and eleven pounds six and sevenpence" ' (the cost of the transfer fee from York). Such was the 'psychic capital' to be earned from investing in football.[5]

If football was a business, it was a very peculiar one. Clubs did not compete with one another to attract larger crowds by reducing their prices. Nor did they make any serious efforts to derive income from a huge fixed asset, which was used for only a few hours a week. Even the payment of players was regulated in such a way as to prevent clubs competing in a free market for talent. As the game became more popular in the 1880s lack of regulation enabled the best footballers to play clubs off against one another and bid up their own wages. It was to stop this that amateurs within the FA, who disliked professionalism in principle, were willing to accept it in practice. Professionalism was legalized partly in order to place a limit on the bargaining power of players. 'Clubs who employ paid men will be only too glad to possess a strong authority over them' was how the *Athletic News* put it. Hence the acceptance of professionalism did not set up a free market in football but bound players legally to one club and determined the maximum wage that could be paid to them. The Football League was a kind of non-profit-making cartel in which the power of the largest clubs was limited by the smallest. This

[5] Vamplew, 'Economics of a Sports Industry', p. 557; 'New Blood' by Arnold Bennett, cited in V. Scannell (ed.), *Sporting Literature* (1987), p. 203.

was just as the amateurs of the FA thought it should be. Nor were there frustrated breakaway movements from a handful of top clubs. For they could still buy the best players through club transfers and were in a position to provide small additional incentives to players without increasing their wage-bill.[6]

Cricket was even less open to the winds of free competition. County cricket made little concession to spectators. Amateurs wanted to get off to the country for the weekend rather than performing for the benefit of playing spectators. 'The amateurs in the two teams went out grouse-shooting during the morning', disclosed one account of Surrey against Derbyshire at Glossop in 1902. The professionals sat around waiting for the gentlemen to return before the match was called off. The interests of the crowd were simply not considered. The English 'national' game was largely played at times when the English nation was otherwise engaged. 'Cricket', remarked Pelham Warner sternly, 'is not a circus, and it would be far better that it should be driven back to the village green . . . than yield a jot to the petulant demands of the spectator.' County matches frequently produced dull play and drawn games. But there was no question of any of the first-class counties being relegated for poor results. County clubs were financed partly through gate-money and partly from the subscriptions of members. The idea of being part of the 'county' was socially appealing. County membership was not quite the same as holding a season-ticket for a Football League club. Kent and Yorkshire even refused to recruit from outside of their territorial frontiers. Wearing the county tie was a mark of modest social distinction and with that went the responsibility of meeting debts and subsidizing the side. In 1937 county cricket was estimated to have lost £30,000. The losses of individual counties were relatively small and every four years the visit of the Australians helped to replenish the kitty. Titled county presidents were also of great value. Patronage did not die out with industrialization; it lived on through the honorific offices of county clubs and national bodies. In Derbyshire Will Taylor, the county secretary, would do his sums at the end of the season before phoning the Duke of Devonshire at Chatsworth. 'Now then, Taylor, what's the damage this time?' the Duke would ask

[6] Mason, *Association Football*, p. 73.

and on being told he would briskly reply 'Cheque in post tomorrow. Good day to ye.' Crowds had begun to fall from a first-day county average of almost 15,000 in the 1890s to under 10,000 between 1906 and 1914. The relative failure of cricket as a popular spectacle lay 'in the deliberate refusal of its administrators to modernize. Cricket, in essence, stifled itself by remaining too true to its pre-industrial origins.' Lack of an alternative summer team sport protected cricket between the wars and it benefited from a brief post-1945 resurgence in numbers, but then numbers fell so dramatically that by 1965 they stood at about a third of the post-1945 years. It was the imminent collapse of the county game which finally pushed the men of Lord's towards a more businesslike and consumer-conscious outlook.[7]

Until recently both football and cricket administrators simply took the loyalty of the crowds for granted. Average attendances in the First Division doubled between the Edwardian period and the 1930s. Approximately 30,000 was the average crowd in the season 1937–8 and cup games often attracted double this number. In Glasgow a Rangers–Celtic cup-tie in 1937 attracted a crowd of almost 150,000. The tragedy at Bolton in 1946, in which thirty-three were killed and 400 injured, was the result of admitting 85,000 fans with more clambering over walls or vaulting the turnstiles. The demand from the public for football was so great, the FA and the League had no need to 'sell' the game. Instead of profiting from the enormous interest in gambling on football results through the 'pools' system, the FA's puritanism led to a futile and absurd confrontation in 1936, which involved the withholding of fixture lists to frustrate the pools companies. The hostility of the FA arose not just from a lack of commercial sense but from a more profound belief that gambling was wrong. Elements of a morally uplifting 'rational recreation' tradition survived in football despite the payment of players. The gambling issue underlined the central fact that professionalism and commercialism were not synonymous.[8]

[7] D. Kynaston, *Bobby Abel* (1982), p. 125. Kynaston is, from a historical viewpoint, superior to the many other cricketing biographers of 'the golden age'; W. Vamplew, 'Profit or Utility Maximisation', in id. (ed.), *Economic History of Leisure*, p. 49; G. Moorhouse, *Lord's* (1983), p. 135; K. Sandiford, 'English Cricket Crowds', *JSH*, Winter 1982, p. 15.

[8] S. Jones, 'The Economic Aspects of Association Football in England, 1918–1939', *BJSH*, Dec. 1984, p. 289; on the FA's response to the football pools see S. Inglis, *Soccer in the Dock* (1985), ch. 7.

Of course, there were some economic changes during the century spanning the formation of the FA and the ending of the maximum wage. In the inter-war years, for example, transfer fees rose dramatically, the job of manager was defined, and revenue from advertising came to be more important. Herbert Chapman, the manager of Arsenal, proved to be the prototype. These changes, which were limited to the big club sides, will be examined later in relation to media interest in sport. For the moment let us take a look at the fortunes of the professionals, mostly unsung and unremembered, who played cricket or football for pay. 'Obedient servants' they have been called, and that for the most part is just what they were. Until very recently professional sportsmen have been regarded by directors as skilled workmen; footballers' incomes were not calculated in the same way as transfer fees according to market value but in relation to what other working-class men could expect to earn. By such standards both footballers and cricketers, provided they were among the minority who avoided injury and played in the first team, were quite well off for a few years. They were paid about double what a skilled man could expect for a fifty-hour week in return for working part-time at something that they enjoyed. Spectators were not surprisingly unsympathetic to the rare protests of professionals about the maximum wage and the retain-and-transfer system. Their employers were quick to stoke up popular envy through the press if players even temporarily forgot their good fortune.

Yet both professional footballers and cricketers were subjected to unreasonable restrictions and working practices. In most cases they gained very little financially from their employment. In cricket there were very few opportunities with only fifteen first-class counties and the Lancashire League sides, who had only one full professional per team. Professional batsmen were frequently in competition with 'gentlemen' who did not charge for their services in the conventional manner. County cricketers were paid for the summer and only the best were given a reduced wage to see them through the winter. Of twenty-four professionals retained by Lancashire in 1899, seventeen were paid £3 a week as a basic wage during the season with the remainder getting less. All received reduced winter wages with eleven given nothing at all. Match fees and bonuses for winning pushed up the wages of the best players, but travel and hotel expenses had to be met out of the £5 or £6 payment for away games. Most significant for a county player was the opportunity to have a benefit match. This was not done for players with less than ten years' service and a longer period was usually required. Benefits were notoriously unreliable. If a player was granted a good fixture, if the weather held fair, and if the player was popular with the supporters, a good sum might be raised. Mandle's calculation of an average benefit of £816 in the 1890s indicates a threefold increase since the 1860s, and would have been enough perhaps to start a man off in a small business. The 'benefit' was in fact a deferred payment, which both tied a player to a single club and was of no value to those who through loss of form or injury were not able to serve the county for a long enough period.[9]

Bobby Abel, the son of a cockney lamplighter from Rotherhithe, played for Surrey from 1881 to 1904. At the time only 'W.G.' had made more first-class runs than the 'Little Guv'nor' with his 32,669. 'He gathers runs like blackberries everywhere he goes', said C. B. Fry. With his cap pulled down over one eye and the crowds shouting 'Go to it little 'un', he was a stalwart of Surrey and England. Had he not been followed as a Surrey opener by Jack Hobbs, then perhaps he would be better known to posterity. He was a dedicated professional, who claimed 'I sacrifice everything for cricket, never stop out late and always take the greatest care of myself.' Whenever he was out he set himself the task 'to study how and why until I discovered how I should have played the ball that beat me'. Abel was granted a benefit in 1895 after fourteen years with the club and took the Surrey–Yorkshire game. The Bank Holiday fixture was habitually requested and refused for benefit matches and the stand receipts were also withheld. Abel managed to make £730, which helped to develop a sports shop beside the Oval, though this later failed and he was rescued from penury by a public appeal launched by the *Daily Mail* after the First World War.[10]

Players like Abel of international calibre were increasingly resentful of the special payments made to famous amateurs. Grace

[9] W. Vamplew, 'Playing for Pay', in R. Cashman and M. McKernan, *Sport: Money, Morality and the Media* (1982), p. 112; W. F. Mandle, 'The Professional Cricketer', *Labour History*, 1972, p. 3.

[10] Kynaston, *Bobby Abel*, esp. pp. 17, 136–9.

openly demanded payment of £20 a match from Gloucester and more for Test matches; *Wisden* could only comment that 'nice customs curtsey to great kings'. At Surrey the 'amateur' W. W. Read was employed as 'assistant secretary' to the club for £250 a year—a post he relinquished when he ceased to play. Entry fees to the Stock Exchange were put up by members of the Surrey committee in the late nineteenth century to help impecunious gentleman-cricketers. Harry Wood, a professional for twenty years with Surrey and along with Abel one of three who went 'on strike' in 1896 demanding a £20 match fee to play the Australians, left the game a bitter man. He believed that if 'I had played cricket as a "gentleman" I should have made sufficient out of my "expenses" to retire by now.' This was probably an exaggeration, though the resentment was understandable. Amateurs always claimed that (W.G. apart) only legitimate hotel and travelling expenses were met, though 'testimonials' were sometimes arranged to give the gentleman a decent send-off. Grace notoriously pocketed £9,000 from his second testimonial while more modestly W. W. Read managed a respectable £1,000 from a Surrey vs. England fixture specially resurrected for him.[11]

Then there were the sheer indignities of a professional cricketer's life—the separate entrances, changing facilities, menial jobs to do around the club, even the placing of the man's initials after his surname to signify servile status. When Kent played Surrey in 1890 a fine spread was laid on for the gentlemen but the professionals 'were left to shift for themselves, and thought themselves lucky to get a bit of bread and cheese'. Even the otherwise haughty Surrey committee was moved to complain about this lack of common courtesy, though naturally they did not go so far as to suggest meals should be taken in common. The Middlesex secretary of the Edwardian years, who was also secretary of the MCC, Sir Francis Lacey, mixed a curt politeness with public condescension in his treatment of the professional staff. At the start of each season he would stand with his chief clerk at the gate of Lord's with 'a pile of contracts on heavy blue legal paper, everyone tied with a piece of pink ribbon. As each cricketer stepped forward he would refer to the man by his surname and say, "Here's your contract and here's your first day's

---

[11] Kynaston, *Bobby Abel*, pp. 127–31, 142–5.

wages, and I hope you've wintered well." ' Not even the most
distinguished professionals were treated any differently, including
'Patsy' Hendren, who after Jack Hobbs made more first-class
centuries than any other player. Patsy's brother Dennis also
played for the club and did not appreciate the secretary's habitual
greeting: 'with me bleedin' ribs pokin' out of me skin, breakin'
me neck to get at that six and eight' (the initial sum dispensed
by the Secretary), Dennis Hendren had not 'wintered well' and
did not believe Middlesex looked after its players out of
season.[12]

Wally Hammond took over from Hobbs as the Great Man of
English cricket. He played his first match at the age of 17 for
Gloucester in 1920 and continued until after the Second World
War. He was the supreme all-rounder—the best since Grace—
but with a self-confessed 'allergy' to publicity which perhaps led
his reputation to suffer after his retirement. Hammond changed
his status from professional to amateur partly through taking a
directorship of a tyre company in 1938—he liked to drive fast
cars—and was then selected to captain England. He was the first
ex-professional to be so honoured. His career neatly illustrates
the expanding commercial possibilities for famous sportsmen
outside the field of play. Taking money for playing still
disqualified a man for the highest honours in amateur eyes, but
profiting from sporting fame indirectly through directorships did
not.

The subordinate status of professionals lasted a very long time
indeed. When the distinction was abandoned in 1963 some old
'players' steeped in traditions of the game even mourned its
passing. Most professionals were a deferential, biddable lot. The
ending of what amounted to class segregation was less a matter
of the democratic spirit of professionals finally asserting itself than
of the decline of the amateur. A combination of higher taxation
and more rigorous academic standards led to a dearth of first-
class amateurs. Gentlemen had to take their fortunes and their
education more seriously. Even Oxbridge men had less time and
money to spare. Things had changed since the 1920s when Lionel
Hedges, a Tonbridge and Kent cricketer and Oxford blue, had
dismissed 'a seedy looking middle-aged gentleman [who] called

[12] Ibid., p. 125; Moorhouse, *Lord's*, pp. 108–9.

on him on the morning of a match. Imagining him to be a reporter, Lionel said to him brusquely, "I have nothing to say to you." The man tried to expostulate but Lionel repeated, "I have nothing to say to you." It only afterwards transpired that the seedy man was not a reporter but his tutor, with whom he was not otherwise acquainted.' After the Second World War the comfortable, leisured life cushioned with a decent income from stocks and shares was hit both by inflation and the liquidation of Britain's foreign assets. When Keynes had talked of the 'euthanasia of the rentier' he had not been thinking of cricket, but the MCC had to face the reality of the decline of the leisured classes. From 175 out of 450 county cricketers in 1949 the number of amateurs fell to 72 out of 370 in 1961. It was becoming difficult to put together a Gentlemen's eleven worthy of the name. So Lord's decided that all men should henceforth be 'cricketers' and the Gentlemen and Players fixture was duly abandoned. By this time professional cricketers' earnings had fallen behind average manual wages. Cricketers were no longer even financially privileged workers and there was no representative body to fight for them until the Cricketers' Association was formed in 1968. Since then their incomes, though still relatively low, have improved somewhat. The benefit has remained crucial to the county cricketer, and with assiduous planning and work the sums raised from them have gone up dramatically. Cyril Washbrook's £14,000 in 1948 remained a record until the early 1970s. Nowadays the holding of dances, raffles, and pub talks along with the fixture has pushed up the sums enormously, although if inflation and house prices are taken into account even £50,000 or over is hardly a fortune for a man who has to find a job and keep a family.[13]

Professional footballers fared little better than cricketers and were less likely to be able to pursue their occupation for as long. On the other hand, there were many more openings for footballers than cricketers. There were 448 players registered with the Football League in 1891 but this figure rose to around 5,000 by the Edwardian period. During the 1890s the FA left

[13] K. Sandiford, 'The Professionalization of Modern Cricket', *BJSH*, Dec. 1985, esp. pp. 271-2, 280-1, provides an outline of the economics of cricket since 1945; for Hedges, see J. Morris (ed.), *The Oxford Book of Oxford* (1978), p. 379.

wages to the discretion of individual clubs, but there were complaints that top players were able to use this freedom to extract large sums from the directors despite their contractual bondage to a particular club. Moreover, poorer clubs were anxious not to find themselves in a wages-auction with richer ones and the FA finally set a £4 a week maximum in 1900, which was raised in 1909 to £5 for senior professionals with a club. Although well above the best wages of a skilled man, it was neither market-determined nor received by all registered professionals. Wage regulation applied only at the upper limit. There was no 'minimum wage' and clubs tended to take on large numbers of hopefuls at low rates. Vamplew has worked out that almost half of the players registered with First Division clubs in 1910 never played a League match. Many players retained part-time jobs or worked odd shifts at the pit. Of twenty-eight new signings for Aston Villa in 1893–4 half never played and only one continued with the club for more than three seasons. The same seems to have been true of other clubs. Most working men claimed to know someone who had once been given a trial or had been 'on the books' of a club for a spell. Wages rose with inflation after the war to £8 a week but only a minority of players on a club's books received this. Of full-time professionals playing for a major club like Sheffield United in 1934–5 only four out of twenty-one were on the maximum wage. Benefits for long-serving players were discretionary and unlike cricket were subject to tax.[14]

This, of course, is only the official, public side of the story. The extent to which the maximum wage was regularly breached is difficult to determine. Naturally, players and directors did not want to broadcast systematic evasion of FA rules. For most players in the lower divisions the issue simply did not arise. They would have been only too happy to accept the maximum. But in the commanding heights of the First Division with huge crowds and ambitious directors, there is no doubt that incentives were given to players. One way of evading restrictions was to find sinecure posts for good players; one man was given the job of checking the advertising posters for the club, though the most common trick was for club directors, who were often substantial

[14] Vamplew, 'Playing for Pay', p. 124; Fishwick, 'Association Football', p. 213.

employers, to find part-time or simply bogus jobs for which payment was made. Another ruse was to offer houses at low rent or for sale, or to offer signing-on fees far in excess of the £10 theoretically permitted by the FA. Old cars were sold to clubs at inflated prices and on one occasion a player sold his dog to a director. From time to time the authorities got wind of these breaches of regulations and punished clubs, but they did not regularly inspect the books and revelations of extra payments tended to emerge as a result of other inquiries. Such was the case at Manchester City in 1905–6. Billy Meredith, the 'Prince of Dribblers' and the club captain, was suspended for a season for attempting to offer a bribe to an Aston Villa player. Meredith at first proclaimed his innocence but friction between the player and the club led to further disclosures. Meredith claimed he had offered the bribe on behalf of the manager and that the players were to be offered a team bonus of £100 if they won the League. An FA investigation revealed that the club had regularly breached the maximum wage restrictions in the season 1904–5. As a result seventeen players were suspended for six months, fined a total of £900, and forbidden to play for the club again. Two directors were suspended for a year and the chairman and manager banned from football for good. The FA was determined to set an example, but here the difference between the largely amateur FA and the Football League was important. The League was controlled by the club chairmen, some of whom were undoubtedly also involved in making extra payments. The supreme irony of the Manchester City affair was that several rival clubs, notably Manchester United, signed the suspended players, offering substantial signing-on fees (contrary to FA rules) as well as a transfer fee to the club. Billy Meredith and Herbert Burgess, the 'Mighty Atom' as the fans called him went to Manchester United along with Jimmy Bannister, Meredith's partner in City's attack. Presumably they were offered inducements to sign and paid over the odds when they helped to win the League championship for City's rivals two years later.[15]

There seems little doubt that the richest clubs went on evading the maximum wage regulation. As the FA handed over control of this aspect of the game to the League, it was not likely that

[15] Inglis, *Soccer in the Dock*, pp. 12–22.

club chairmen would encourage investigations that might damage themselves. The memoirs of great inter-war players like Dixie Dean, Tommy Lawton, and Stanley Matthews politely skate over the issue, but a Manchester United player in the 1920s recalled a telling incident involving the club captain, Frank Barson. Barson's powers of tackling and leadership were so highly regarded that United had paid £5,000—a huge fee at the time, especially for a defender—for his transfer from Aston Villa in 1922. When the former blacksmith from Barnsley 'walked into the United dressing-room, he would put a hand on to a shelf in search of a package before he took his coat off. In the package was the few bob he got extra, because he was half the team. One day, there was no package and he said to the trainer, "Where's the doin's? I'm not taking my bloody coat off till I get it." ' That illegal payments to players in the top clubs was widespread and continued throughout the period of the maximum wage emerged from evidence of overpayment by Sunderland in the 1950s submitted anonymously to discredit the chairman, Bill Ditchburn, a wealthy local business man, who used to go out to buy fish and chips in his pink-and-mauve Rolls-Royce. Ditchburn covered up the extra payments through a hugely inflated figure for the purchase of straw to protect the turf from frost. He was barred for life from the game and angrily hired his own team of detectives to collect evidence to prove that all the other major clubs were also evading the regulations. This 'evidence' was never published but he persisted in his belief that his only crime was that he was found out. Trevor Ford, the aggressive Welsh centre-forward, who had been signed for Sunderland as part of Ditchburn's lavish spending programme (earning Sunderland the name of 'The Bank of England club'), confirmed that abuse of the system was widespread in the First Division.[16]

Most professionals, however, did not have the market value nor did their clubs have the resources to behave like this. Just how hard a school professional football was emerges from Ward and Alister's imaginative oral history of Barnsley between 1953 and 1959. The club had thirty in its youth squad in 1951 and there was competition even to get a game for the fourth team. Despite

[16] Jones, 'Economic Aspects of Association Football', p. 294; Inglis, *Soccer in the Dock*, pp. 116–40.

relegation to the Third Division the club kept a playing staff of thirty-eight, twenty-five of whom came from the Barnsley area and were almost all miners or the sons of miners. Even first-team players had odd jobs and reserves often worked shifts at the pit or elsewhere. Johnny Kelly, an established player, ingeniously devised his own brand of detergent, which he mixed up in his bath at home and delivered in an old van with the registration number AGE 100. Clubs such as this were rather like workshops with the old pros as time-served tradesmen who expected the young apprentices to clean their boots and learn their trade. These lads were often touchingly naïve. Away games gave working-class youths their first taste of comfortable living. Many had never stayed at a hotel or even had a cheap meal away from home. When one youngster was asked by a waitress what he wanted for 'a sweet', he replied 'a Nuttall's Minto'.[17]

What became of most professionals after their brief sojourn in the game? Their lack of other skills or a decent education often pushed them into routine manual labour, though jobs within football did increase between the wars. The most successful players certainly did well; Stanley Matthews had a hotel in Blackpool and Jackie Milburn, the folk-hero of Tyneside, ran a coach firm. But they were exceptional. Of the eleven who won the Cup for Manchester United in 1948, most of whom were internationals and all in the first rank of senior professionals, five went into football coaching and management, three ran newsagents' shops (customers presumably enjoyed discussing the sports headlines with men who had once made them), two worked in factories, and one became a night-telephonist. Only one of the five who stayed in football was able to keep his position within the game until retirement. Even Johnny Carey, the club captain and reckoned to be the most versatile player of all time (he had played in ten positions for United including goalkeeper), finished his working life modestly in the treasurer's office of Trafford Borough Council after having gone the way of all managers in the grip of impatient and often ignorant directors. Such were the small gains to be made from a playing career at

---

[17] A. Ward and I. Allister, *Barnsley* (1981), pp. 10–13, 52; a splendid tribute to an unglamorous club, which uses interviews to evoke its spirit and humour. Most club histories are sadly lacking in 'feel' for the people who watched and played.

the very top. Ordinary club professionals had far fewer opportunities. A few like Hughie Gallacher, the marvellous centre-forward
for Newcastle and Scotland in the 1920s, could never adjust to the
sudden loss of fame and took their own life. But there were probably
a great many more who simply took advantage of too many of the
free pints they were offered too often and slipped into alcoholism.
It was hard to be a hero one day and a 'has-been' the next.[18]

Arthur Hopcraft's *The Football Man* evokes perfectly the life of
the footballer at the fag-end of England's industrial heyday as men
like Nat Lofthouse, the son of a coal-man from Bolton and a 'Bevin
Boy' in the war, led the England attack in the tradition of big,
fearless centre-forwards. In the 1940s and early 1950s football
remained the ruling passion of working men without cars and
televisions, whose world still revolved around the communal life
of the works, the pub, and the match. Derek Dooley, the young
Sheffield Wednesday centre-forward who scored forty-six goals in
his team's Second Division championship victory in 1951–2, was
the kind of hero every northern boy dreamed of becoming. His
father was a steel-worker. He had often been out of work during the
boy's early years in the west of Sheffield 'where the city meanders
in a smokey, greasy straggle of workshops into Rotherham'. The son
learned his football in a shared backyard or on 'patches of grit and
oily grass, hemmed in by the crouched streets, with the rusty
swings and roundabouts, which creaked under a cafuffle of ragged
children. Jackets made goal-posts, and: "If you went down you
got up with a lump of a cinder in your knee." ' School football
matches were desperately hard-fought, especially when the
secondary modern had a chance to beat the grammar school. This
was no place for the frail ball player. Hardness was cultivated and
admired. Hopeful youngsters clashed with old timers playing out
their last few seasons in the reserve leagues, which were as
competitive as the first-team games and often a lot tougher. And so
Derek Dooley went to Sheffield Wednesday at seventeen and a half,
his local team, until a clash with an advancing goalkeeper forced
the immediate amputation of his leg in February 1953. He had not
even had a full season in the First Division.[19]

[18] S. Wagg, *The Football World* (1984), p. 104; A. Shorrocks, *Winners and
Champions* (1985), provides valuable follow-up interviews of the players, pp.
196–240.
[19] A. Hopcraft, *The Football Man* (1968), pp. 50–9.

Dooley's personal tragedy was so awful—he was so young and talented and he took the blow with such heroic, idiotic stoicism ('It's my one regret that the ball didn't finish in the net')—that a substantial sum was raised for him and he later went to work for the club. Happily it was rare to be as unfortunate as Dooley on the field, but few were able to make a good career in the game. Many were called but few were chosen. The history of the Players' Union has only intermittently been a struggle against wage and transfer controls. More central to the ordinary professional was the question of compensation for injury. This was the issue which brought the Professional Footballers' Association, founded in 1907 after several earlier false starts, into immediate conflict with the FA and the League. The PFA appealed on behalf of injured players to the courts under the terms of the Workmen's Compensation Act of 1906. When the FA protested, they received a splendid rebuff to the effect that the PFA could not be expected 'to regard seriously the opinion that a football player forfeits a common legal right on entering into a professional engagement with a football club'. The PFA urged players not to sign new contracts until this principle was accepted and several of the leading sides such as Manchester United and Newcastle United, where Colin Veitch's energetic organization and articulate socialism briefly seems to have radicalized the players, went on strike. Possibly the widening class-consciousness of militant trade unionism within the Edwardian working class, especially considering the number of players from mining origins, may also have helped encourage this flurry of 'industrial' action. Threats from the FA, however, forced 800 of the 1,200 members of the PFA to resign. A truce was eventually agreed by which players would first present any injury claims to the FA itself and a small increase in the maximum wage and a bonus system were introduced. The PFA challenged the retain-and-transfer system in the courts and lost in 1912, to which was added the indignity of needing financial help from the League to pay the costs of the case.[20]

The real weakness of any players' union lay in the difficulty of maintaining solidarity amongst its members. Competition was

[20] B. Dabscheck, 'Defensive Manchester', in R. Cashman and M. McKernan, *Sport in History* (1979), pp. 236–42; Mason, *Association Football*, pp. 111–17, gives an excellent short account of the origins of the PFA.

so intense for team-places that managers could isolate activists. The constant supply of optimistic youngsters meant that those who became bitter or critical as they got older could be quietly dropped. Hence the PFA concentrated on making small gains. It did not challenge the essentials of the system between the wars but concentrated on edging up the maximum wage and stressing the benefits of belonging to a mutual aid society for sickness or injury. There were about 2,000 members by 1939 and after 1945 the 'friendly society' dimension was further strengthened by the taking out of an expensive private insurance scheme for players, which absorbed half of the income of the Association. Anger over their failure to benefit from increased television revenue combined with the falling value of the maximum wage of £20 in relation to average industrial earnings led to a new surge of militancy in the 1950s. Professionals' self-esteem had been founded upon being at the top of the manual wages pyramid. Then there was the emergence of Jimmy Hill, a Fulham player with a grammar school education and a father in the Stock Exchange, as an articulate and shrewd spokesman for the players. Strike action to remove the maximum wage in 1960 was promised. The threat was enough this time. Public opinion, carefully managed by Hill, favoured the players and some of the top clubs, who had never liked the system, were worried about the growing tendency of the very best professionals to leave the country to play in Italy and elsewhere. So the maximum wage was scrapped but freedom of contract and mobility was harder to get. George Eastham backed by the PFA took Newcastle United to court for 'unjustifiable restraint on trade' and won the case, although significantly the logical implications of the judgement in respect of full freedom of contract for players was resisted by the Football League for nearly another twenty years.[21]

Those who think the modern footballer's life is a round of 'boutiques, blow-waves and BMWs' (as the *Sun* might put it) should read Eamon Dunphy's *Only a Game?* In a genre noted for its shoddiness and sensationalism, this playing memoir of a season with Millwall in the mid-1970s stands out as a truthful and often painful account of the player's lot. Dunphy, an Irish

---

[21] Dabscheck, 'Defensive Manchester', pp. 244–51; Wagg, *Football World*, pp. 101–20, is good on the 1950s.

international, was better off than most, but the awful uncertainty of the job, the fear of failure or injury, were always present. There was the public humiliation of being dropped from the side; the autocratic style of managers, who were themselves as afraid and insecure as their players; the refusal to let good players use their natural talent to play, forcing them through repetitive training 'systems' and naïve 'game plans'; the petty jealousies of the players, their hierarchies, and childish pranks; the fear of the new signing, who has to be included at the expense of an old friend; the view of a match from 'the inside' when you know a team-mate does not want the ball but wants it to look as if you will not give it to him. As the team faces relegation to the Third Division, Charlton offers Dunphy a job but his house is tied to Millwall. The Charlton house is

terrible. A real slum . . . And then it hit me, and I really got frightened . . . I felt really vulnerable. I've got nothing. No money, no security, no trade, no home . . . All I had to bargain with was my own little bit of skill, which really, when you compare it with a carpenter's skill, or a plumber's skill, is intangible. They can make chairs, mend the loo. But a footballer? A Second or Third Division footballer is expendable. You can be easily done without.

He felt he had to go. He would probably have been forced out anyway, as several of his friends had been. It was better to go first from choice. 'I persuaded him [the Millwall manager] that he had had eight years out of me, and I had nothing to show for it. That they weren't having to give me a testimonial, which I would be entitled to soon, and were making a profit on my sale.' He finally agreed to sell Dunphy to Charlton. Other entertainers on the wane can often fall back on a 'club circuit', musicians and dancers can sometimes coach others, but there are few openings for the ex-footballer. They cannot teach sport in schools. They may pay a high price for their few years of glory with injury problems in later life and will probably never enjoy the relative prosperity of their first working years again.[22]

There were, of course, other professional sportsmen besides cricketers and footballers. What of them? The greatest track athlete of the late nineteenth century was Walter George. He

[22] E. Dunphy, *Only a Game?* (1977), pp. 159–60.

turned professional in 1885 having won everything from the half-mile to the ten-mile AAA's events. Thirty thousand spectators turned up at Lillie Bridge in London to see him run the mile against William Cummings of Paisley and in the return match George's time of 4 min. 12.75 sec. was not beaten in Britain for forty-nine years. That his name is scarcely known today is a testament to the power of the amateur establishment to make a professional an 'unperson'. This pedestrian tradition of foot-racing for cups and prize-money survived, especially in Scotland. When Dixie Dean was on holiday in Ayr, he noticed that a professional sprint was to be held and entered it as an outsider and won; he thereby not only demonstrated the outstanding athletic abilities of top footballers (Matthews was also a fine athlete), but underlined the survival of the old pedestrian traditions at the new resorts catering for working-class holiday-makers. The Powderhall stadium in Edinburgh was the top venue for professional athletics, though competitors could not make a living by running alone. Pedestrianism remained a source of extra money for good runners, who were willing to sacrifice the more socially prestigious amateur laurels. Men did not get rich through running as they did through boxing. Next to football, boxing was probably the most important working-class spectator sport. With the establishment of the British Boxing Board of Control in 1929 boxing was freed from the private control of the gentlemen of the National Sporting Club, and despite the dominance of the United States, especially in the heavier weights, boxing remained an extremely popular professional sport. There were around a thousand registered fighters in the 1940s, but the number fell steadily in the 1950s and 1960s as working-class affluence softened inner-city boys brought up to fight out of hunger and the sheer hardness of street life. In Jimmy Wilde, the world flyweight champion from 1916, Britain produced one of the very greatest boxers of all time. He was defeated only four times in a long career, 'retiring with a fortune of £70,000, almost all of which was promptly lost for him'. Wilde was a Welshman as were two other of the great Edwardian boxers, Freddie Welsh, the lightweight champion of Britain in 1909, and Jim Driscoll, the world bantamweight champion who ended his days 'Wandering around the pubs of London, penniless, and dying at 44'.[23]

---

[23] *Observer*, 17 Aug. 1986, p. 38; N. Walsh, *Dixie Dean* (1977), p. 103; K. O. Morgan, *Rebirth of a Nation* (1982), p. 133; Prof. David Smith of University

Boxers fought an enormous number of contests by modern standards to satisfy a working-class public who wanted to see regular bouts. Wilde fought 864. Len Harvey, the leading middleweight in the inter-war years, fought 412 contests. Jack Matthews, the 'Fighting Barber' and father of Stanley, fought 350 bouts losing only nine times without winning a championship title. Jack 'Kid' Berg, who grew up in the East End ghetto, fought his way up from the streets to a world welterweight title in the tradition of oppressed racial minorities. Jewish boxers were an important part of the London sporting scene. Irish Catholics in Glasgow grew up in a similarly hostile environment. Benny Lynch, the world flyweight champion from 1935 to 1938, was their folk-hero. Born in the Gorbals, he learned boxing in a Catholic youth club and by fighting on the street-corners. He toured round the boxing-booths of the summer fairgrounds like other 'has-beens' or 'hopefuls'. The 'small halls' put on weekly programmes of fights for small purses. Paddy Reilly, a friend of Lynch's, once claimed to have had five ten-round fights in a week. Alex Farries, another Glaswegian contemporary, lost count of the number. On one occasion he went to Dundee where the promoter knocked down his purse from £4 to £2. 10s. because he had come on his motor bike rather than on the train. For this he fought a hard ten-round contest. He collapsed with a dangerous fever and inflammation when he got back to Glasgow. When Farries fought Benny Lynch for £5 at the Eldorado at Leith, the two Glaswegians cheerfully came home together on the train. In the West of Scotland, South Wales, and East London—all areas of significantly high immigration—professional boxing was followed with a fierce passion and local fighters were folk-heroes. In Belfast from 1931 to 1938 a total of 800 twice-weekly boxing-programmes were put on by 'Ma Copley', who first organized fights in the open air and then set up a boxing-hall at Chapel Fields. Threepence bought a night's boxing at 'the Nursery' as this training-ground for fighters was known. They were a tough crowd who drew fighters from quite far afield. Scotsmen, Englishmen, and Welshmen joined with local fighters like Spider Kelly, Jackie Quinn, and Rinty Monaghan to slug it out for a few pounds.[24]

College, Cardiff, is engaged on research into Welsh boxing which will be published in R. Holt (ed.), *Sport and the Working Class in Modern Britain* (forthcoming).

[24] J. Burrowes, *Benny* (1982), pp. 102–11; evocative interviews with 'The Chapelfields Fighters' were broadcast on BBC Radio 4 on 30 July 1986.

American dominance of the top weights has unduly obscured the vitality of our own fighting tradition at the lower divisions. Despite the growing protests of the medical establishment, boxing still thrives at the championship level. Black immigration, recession, and the enormous purses which television can provide have meant there remain a ready supply of men willing to risk brain damage in the ring. Public reaction to boxing is now ambivalent. As a display of complete athleticism a great boxing match is a supreme sporting event, the purest expression of skill, strength, and courage. But it is undoubtedly dangerous and often cruel, stirring not so much the boxers but the crowds who watch them to a pitch of savagery quite incompatible with the notion that boxing is 'the noble art of self-defence'. The moral opposition to boxing in the late twentieth century, which is essentially a continuation of an old Nonconformist hostility bolstered by science, is weakened by the popularity of men like Henry Cooper: 'Enry, the Londoner, the decent, gentle bruiser, who almost knocked out one of the greatest heavyweights of all time, but now prospers as a TV celebrity playing golf for charity or advertising deodorants. Boxing is certainly a business; great fortunes are made and more are kept than before. Boxers fight less and earn more. This may be accounted a kind of progress and helps to assuage the liberal moral conscience.

Wrestlers were a breed apart. They were more akin to circus performers than to more conventional professional sportsmen. *Mass Observation* made a quite careful study of this new spectator fad in Bolton in the late 1930s. A wrestling stadium was opened in 1933 by a former amateur wrestler and publican to show 'free style' wrestling from the USA with its commercial flamboyance and parodies of 'good' and 'bad' sportsmanship. Out of a sample of 300 men a third had attended wrestling. 'Thrill' was the most frequent motive for attending but 'humour' was also frequently cited—if the wrestlers went in for too much close holding choruses of 'Kiss me sergeant' and 'What blue eyes you've got' would strike up. 'Rough stuff', of the half-simulated sort that has diverted modern television audiences, was popular from the start.

Third round P-- again beats gong, rushes at B-- puts B--'s head over the rope and then lifts middle rope over part of his neck. B-- cannot get loose and seems to be choking and the crowd are on their feet yelling and waving their hands—the referee helped by both seconds manages to extricate B-- but P-- grabs him, a quick aeroplane spin, gets him with his left hand round the shoulder, right hand through his left, swings him three times round in the air and pins him with his shoulders on the floor for the count of three. Boos and Boos and one or three cheering in the 6*d*. stands.

M.C. announces first fall to P-- in 2 minutes 50 secs. of the third round.

B-- can scarcely rise, the referee is in a fit of temper, attacks P-- with stool, P-- chases him round ring—gong goes for the 4th round— P-- still has stool so B-- picks up the water bowl and with a terrific bang lands it on P--'s head. P-- drops almost unconscious. B-- jumps at him, Jack the referee drops on stomach to count but is fast between wrestlers and can't be seen and he manages to free himself, and counts 1 2 3 very quickly. Second fall to B--.

Observer asks his neighbour how he enjoyed it. 'I can't tell you proper—I can't believe my own bloody eyes.' Such were the pleasures of a night of 'dirty' wrestling.[25]

Footballers, cricketers, and boxers were the most numerous of professional sportsmen, but the best-known, especially in the late nineteenth century, were jockeys. Their own earnings were fabulous and they could make money for their followers as well. Tom Cannon was paid £15,000 simply as a retainer in the 1880s and Vamplew has calculated that the best riders in the period 1870–1914 might earn £75,000 in their careers. Most famous of all was Fred Archer. 'Crowds would block a street simply to see Archer leave a hotel and take a cab; when he married in January 1883, special trains were laid on to bring the cheering crowds to Newmarket and Cambridge.' His marriage ended tragically in the early death of his wife and a year later he shot himself. 'Hardly anything could cause a more widespread and painful sensation', wrote *The Times*, 'the news of his death has come with a sense of shock and almost personal loss to millions.' The top dozen or so jockeys would expect to ride over half the winners in a season. The profession was extremely hard to break into and to maintain a very low weight required constant vigilance and self-discipline. Archer was said to have become especially depressive when starving himself to make the required weight. Most stable-lads would have counted themselves lucky even to get a ride let

[25] T. Harrisson and C. Madge, *Britain by 'Mass Observation'*, introd. A. Calder (London, 1986), pp. 116–17.

alone to win a race. Much of this remains true today. Racing is a major source of continuity in British sport. The aristocracy has kept a tight grip on 'the sport of kings' and the British royal family have kept a close eye on the Turf—the present Queen is a fine judge of a horse. Gordon Richards, champion jockey twenty-six times between 1925 and 1952, surpassed Fred Archer's annual record of 246 winners set in 1885 with 259 in 1933 and then 269 in 1947. He got a knighthood as well as a fortune for his pains—the first professional sportsman to do so. Lester Piggott, his brilliant successor from the 1960s to the 1980s, was driven by such a desperate, obsessive need for wealth and security that he was sent to prison for persistently defrauding the Inland Revenue of its share of his millions.[26]

Tennis and golf were similarly skewed towards a handful of great competitors. From the inter-war years a small number of tennis professionals played tournaments in the United States. Most of the outstanding men who first made their name in the amateur game, turned professional—Tilden, Perry, Budge, Gonzales, Sedgman, Trabert, and then Rosewall, Hoad, and finally Rod Laver. Yet the bulk of competitive play continued to be amateur until the late 1960s. Golf employed a far larger number of professionals but these men were rarely tournament competitors. Until the 1950s there were few tournaments with substantial amounts of prize-money. Golf professionals sold equipment, gave lessons, and sometimes helped to look after the course. The 'pro' remained a servant of the club in a little 'shop' on the fringes of the premises. Those who earned their living from the game in tournament play were few and far between. Around the turn of the century there had been the great triumverate of Braid, Vardon, and Taylor but American dominance was established between the wars in the shape of Walter Hagen, who won the Open four times, and Gene Sarazen. Only one amateur could break the stranglehold of the professionals but Bobby Jones, who in 1930 took the British and American amateur and open titles in a unique Grand Slam, was an American. Henry Cotton, who won the Open in 1934 and 1937 and then again in 1948 kept up British hopes. Thereafter

---

[26] R. McKibbin, 'Working Class Gambling', *Past and Present*, Feb. 1979, p. 174; W. Vamplew, *The Turf* (1976), pp. 149–50. On jockey earnings see Vamplew, 'Playing for Pay', pp. 108–9.

Bobby Locke of South Africa and Peter Thomson of Australia dominated the British professional game alongside American entrants for the Open for twenty years after the Second World War. From their Edwardian dominance of golf and tennis, the British slipped back to the second rank. Our amateurs were simply not dedicated enough to win at a world level. It was not just a question of climate as the British sometimes liked to think. Certainly Americans and Australians could play sport for more of the year but they did so in a more positive, meritocratic context where success was admired and recognized for its own sake. Until recently social barriers both kept the working-class out of suburban sports and decreed that being a professional was a kind of elevated manual labour and not a proper or respectable career for a middle-class man. Hence our shortage of great players.[27]

2. PRESS, TELEVISION, AND PROFIT

Although professionalism was restricted and most governing sports bodies held themselves aloof from the pursuit of profit, the impression remains that sport soon became part of a 'leisure' industry catering for the needs of a new kind of urban consumer. Spectator sport in this respect seems to be a part of a wider system of entertainment, which embraced the music-hall and the cinema, the record industry, and the dance-hall. The growth of the popular press, which could bring news of the latest entertainment to the breakfast tables of the nation, clearly has played a crucial role in defining sport as part of a commercialized mass culture. But when and how did this happen? The enormous success of televised sport within the last twenty years has certainly been decisive in turning matches into 'media events' and in attracting commercial investment at unprecedented levels. But this is all quite new and it does not follow that previous generations of advertisers were as enthusiastic about sport. The progress of sport as a 'commodity' either to be sold to the media in its own right or to be used in order to sell other products was slower and more

[27] J. Arlott (ed.), *Oxford Companion to Sports and Games* (1976), pp. 537–40. The economic history of professionalism in golf and tennis remains, to my knowledge, a scholarly gap despite numerous popular biographies of professionals.

halting than might be imagined. The press have played a major part in popularizing spectator sport and sustaining interest in it, but it is misleading to think of professional football, for example, as having been created or manufactured by the media. The press reflected the living culture of the people; it could influence opinion and reinforce existing attitudes but it did not create new forms of entertainment and rarely attempted to alter the habits or loyalties of its readership. The links between sport, the media, and big business, which are now so important, have taken a long time to forge.

Sport had always been a prominent source of news in its own right. The early sporting papers such as *Bell's Life in London* existed to give news of forthcoming events and descriptions of recent ones, mostly races and prize-fights. The *Sporting Magazine* was more interested in hunting and published the literary work of 'Nimrod' and Surtees along with more conventional reporting of sports events. These papers were not so much creating a new market as servicing an established public interest. This responsiveness of the specialist press to popular tastes remained extremely important throughout the nineteenth century as modern organized sports came into being. The *Sporting Life*, which was essentially a racing-paper, had a circulation of 300,000 by the 1880s and the *Athletic News*, a weekly journal begun from Manchester in 1875, which concentrated on providing a wide range of football match reports, was soon claiming 100,000. In Scotland the *Scottish Athletic Journal* was started in 1882 coming out on Fridays for 2*d.* and was soon selling 20,000 copies. It merged six years later with the *Scottish Umpire* to form *Scottish Sport*, which appeared twice weekly at 1*d.* and claimed a circulation of 43,000. But competition was fierce and the *Scottish Referee*, costing only a halfpenny and appearing on Monday afternoons with the reports of the weekend's activities, soon put in a challenge. 'The specials', the Saturday night sporting press which reported in detail the performances of local teams, spread rapidly. There were only four such papers in the 1880s, but eighteen in the 1890s and after 1900 they were ubiquitous—'as much a part of the cultural scene as the gas-lamp and the fish-and-chip shop'. In Scotland the 'white' edition of the *Evening News* competed with the 'green' of the *Evening Citizen* and the 'pink' of the *Evening Times*. On late Saturday afternoons 'at the corner the kerb is covered with men who stand with their backs to the light, intently reading in a pink newspaper full of poetical reporting and results' noted an observer of Glasgow in 1901. The habit of reading the 'football special' died hard. Even after radio reporting of results began between the wars, the 'pink 'uns' and 'green 'uns' kept their readers. There were dialect pieces and local banter along with information on how a particular local player had performed a couple of hundred miles away. In Barnsley in the early 1950s men were even seen reading the 'green 'un' over their partner's shoulder as they mechanically steered the wife around the ballroom on a Saturday night.[28]

At first football was not so much the creature of the mass press as the source of new specialist newspapers. But the technology that permitted the almost immediate availability of match results and reports meant that sport came to occupy a larger place in the daily national press. Coverage, however, was patchy and varied. *The Times* gave prominence to cricket but thought the FA Cup Final in 1914 'of comparatively little interest except to the Lancashire working classes' (the game was between Liverpool and Burnley). Of greater interest to *The Times* was the attendance of the King at the match for the first time and the fact that a cuckoo had been heard in the vicinity of the Crystal Palace. More popular papers, however, like *Reynold's News* were starting to give football ample coverage from the mid-1880s. From ten match reports in 1882 there were twenty-five in 1886 for Association football. The *Sunday Chronicle* contained sports reports from its inception in 1885. The popular daily press in the Edwardian years began to give quite a prominent place to sport. The 'sports page' at the back of the paper established itself, though the emphasis remained on results and reports rather than background gossip and speculation about future selections. Observers of inner-city youth noted that along with smoking and clothes, talking about sport was the main amusement of lads on the street-corner. Football was their chief interest but they also followed cricket. The new literacy arising from compulsory elementary education meant that boys could read about a sport which was organized in a way that made it difficult to watch regularly. A London observer remarked that 'the fortunes of the Surrey team are followed with that breathless and extravagant interest which

[28] Mason, *Association Football*, p. 193; B. Murray, *The Old Firm* (1984), pp. 47–50; Muir, *Glasgow in 1901*, pp. 184–5; Ward and Allister, *Barnsley*, p. 3.

demands a copy of every edition of the *Star*'. In Birmingham 'the evening papers are eagerly read each night, and scores of boys who never play themselves are able to name at any time the runs made by prominent cricketers . . . and in seasons like the present, discuss readily and ably the claims of the individual members of the Australian team to be considered really worthy exponents of the game'.[29]

From the 1920s sports reporting and photography was accepted as a crucial and specialized component of popular journalism. Significantly, the *Athletic News*, which had provided splendid weekly coverage, fell from its 170,000 circulation and disappeared as an independent title in 1931. The daily national press took up the cause of sport with a vengeance. Taking their lead from the 'gee-whizzers' of American journalism, a more colourful, gossipy style of writing took over from the rather self-consciously poetic late Victorian style with its 'hapless custodians' and 'leather spheroids'. There was more team speculation and more dressing-room chat, especially in the popular Sunday papers, whose circulation rose enormously between the wars. The *People*, which boasted 'four pages of sport', sold 600,000 copies in 1924 and 4,600,000 in 1946. By 1950 it was devoting over a third of its space to sport with particular emphasis on football. The *People* even financed a year-long secret investigation of football in the early 1960s which brought to light a gambling-ring betting on the results of two or three games, which they 'fixed' by bribing players. The search for soccer stories occupied a new breed of journalist—men like Alan Hoby, the self-styled 'Man Who Knows', or the 'Man Who Knows F-- All' as he was known to some of his readers. The *News of the World* with its phenomenal eight million circulation, the *Daily Mail*, and the *Daily Express* all gave increasing space to sport. Sports writing, especially match reporting, was an 'art' in itself. Inflated language sometimes enlivened a dull game but most match reports were glib and full of clichés. Inside forwards would 'turn on a sixpence'; a centre-forward would 'rise like a salmon' and so on. The habit of reading the paper backwards even spread to the

[29] C. Andrew, 'Football Crazy', *Listener*, 10 June 1982, p. 7; Mason, *Association Football*, p. 195; R. McKibbin, 'Work and Hobbies in Britain', in J. Winter (ed.), *The Working Class in Modern Britain* (1983), p. 133.

quality press. Neville Cardus gained a devoted following for his lyrical cricket writing as well as his musical reviews for the *Manchester Guardian* between the wars. *The Times* could also be counted upon for lengthy discussion of cricket and Rugby Union, both from specialist reporters and from their readers through the institution of the Letters Page which became an important forum for influential discussion of these games. The sensationalist side of sports reporting has gone from strength to strength in the popular press since the advent of television. What happens off the pitch is the stuff of the sports pages—team rows, family rows, drink, and sex. A recent critic complained about the 'clichés, the daft, ghosted "star names" columns, the silly photos (remember Ian Botham as 'Rambo'?), the creation of heroes and villains, the concentration on the star or the result of the moment, the search for conflict, the trivialization of sporting women, the insularity (beyond Dover, forget it), the emphasis on spectating rather than participating, the dearth of analysis, the marginal treatment of those who don't quite "make it" '. The 'quality' press aside, this seems a fair verdict on the tabloids. The recent *Sunday Sport* contains little but topless models and sports gossip.[30]

Yet the power of the press within sport has until recently been severely circumscribed. Journalists could whip up public indignation but cricket and football authorities were singularly unresponsive to press influence apart from *The Times*. The educated amateur, whose organizational influence remained so strong, rarely listened to journalists. Moreover, club directors were tolerably insulated from outside pressure. They could not avoid criticism but they could usually ignore it. And a few, like J. J. Bentley, a former chairman of Manchester United, had a financial stake in the press themselves. Until the 1950s, at least, the press tended to react to events in the sporting world rather than 'create' them. The FA were brusque with Fleet Street, often hardly bothering to organize press conferences or explain themselves. When they took their stand against gambling on the football pools by refusing to release the fixture-lists in advance, they incurred the wrath of the press as well as the pools

---

[30] Inglis, *Soccer in the Dock*, ch. 11; Fishwick, *Association Football*, pp. 289-93; New Statesman, 7 Feb. 1985, p. 37.

promoters. Here Herbert Chapman stands apart. He was ahead of his time and set the pattern for the post-war development of soccer as a 'media event'. Chapman, a Yorkshireman, had not had much success as a player, but he shone as a manager, first with Huddersfield and then with Arsenal, where he had a salary of £2,000 a year and wrote a column for the *Sunday Express* into the bargain. Chapman made real efforts to shape the image of his team in the press and encouraged his players to promote themselves in public. He was usually available for comment and did not talk down to journalists. He used his generous transfer funds to the maximum advantage both to secure great players and to create a 'star' image for the club. Despite his flair and populism, he was a cautious man who took great comfort from the fact that his son had not become a footballer but was securely settled in the middle class as a solicitor. Significantly, his successor was not a football player at all but a journalist who got to know the Arsenal chairman while working as a society correspondent for the *New York Herald*. The major professional influence in his career, he later claimed, was meeting the publicity agents for Buffalo Bill's Wild West Show and seeing how the Americans managed the media. He became one of the first football commentators on radio, copying the urgent, excitable American style of the 'gee-whizzers', earning himself the nickname of 'By Jove' Allison on the way.[31]

If Allison's style was a little out of place in the sober, earnest world of Reith's BBC in the 1920s, sport itself proved an immediate success at the Corporation. In fact, broadcasting, first through radio and then even more dramatically on television, has been the single most important influence on the development of sport in this century. The number of radio licences rose from two to eight million between 1926 and 1939 with 71 per cent of all households having a wireless by the Second World War. The first sports broadcast, ironically at the suggestion of the *Daily Mail*, was of a fight between Kid Lewis and Georges Carpentier in 1922. Sport came to have an important place in the BBC canon of 'good' entertainment, though boxing did not meet with full official approval. The aim of the new Director-General was to promote sport as well as Christianity. Reith was the true successor of the

---

[31] S. Studd, *Herbert Chapman* (1981); S. Wagg, *Football World*, pp. 38–41.

Victorian headmaster, rapidly establishing a range of sporting events which the BBC in its capacity as the sole arbiter of airways deemed to be of *national* significance. A few big events joined the list of approved patriotic 'moments' like Remembrance Day—the Wembley crowd even sang 'Abide With Me'—and in Reith's words permitted the British people to be 'present equally at functions and ceremonials upon which national sentiment is consecrated'. Test cricket, Rugby internationals, the Derby, and the Cup Final were established favourites. The annual rowing contest between the two ancient universities was a great London event with many ordinary families taking sides and wearing favours but it was hardly a matter of 'national' concern until the BBC included the Boat Race in the select band of truly British events. 'Look how that's come to the fore,' remarked a Bristol listener, 'we never used to know anything about it and now there's many wouldn't miss it.' Seventy per cent of the audience panel of a BBC survey in 1939 listened to the Boat Race followed by 51 per cent for boxing, 50 per cent for soccer, and 50 per cent for cricket; soccer and boxing were predictably the favourites of the working-class respondents but the 34 per cent overall interest in Wimbledon was a clear indication that hitherto bourgeois sports were broadening their appeal.[32]

The BBC under Reith placed great emphasis on control from the centre and from above; the BBC was an openly élitist institution which 'knew best' what the public needed and suppressed regional variations and creativity. Local sporting traditions were ignored in favour of a handful of sports which were singled out as worthy of national broadcasting. Gerald Cock, head of Outside Broadcasting, led a team of technicians who increasingly brought live sport into the home. Sports commentators had what many came to consider the most enviable job in the world; they had the best seats for the best events in return for talking about what they loved anyway. This, at least, is how many people saw the job, though few understood the difficulties involved. 'It is easier to make a commentator into a temporary expert than a true expert into a commentator', wrote the *Daily Dispatch*. It was from the ranks of Oxbridge enthusiasts that these commentators were mostly drawn. George Allison has

[32] M. Pegg, *Broadcasting and Society, 1919–39* (1983), pp. 7, 22–3, 128, 214.

already been mentioned, but even better known were Howard Marshall, the Test match commentator, Freddie Grisewood, later to chair 'Any Questions', and Colonel Wakeham on rugby. Best known of all was John Snagge. Though he did other broadcasts, Snagge was particularly fond of the Boat Race, which he made his own for forty years. In 1951 'he was so excited that all he could say was "It's a desperately close race—I can't quite see from here who is ahead—it's either Oxford or Cambridge"'. Sports reporting certainly had its difficulties for the live commentator, who might be held up to ridicule for a lapse of sense or grammar in the heat of the moment. David Coleman has unwittingly given his name to this tradition of sporting gaffe published mercilessly in *Private Eye*, of which Murray Walker's 'this car is absolutely unique, except for the one behind, which is identical' must stand for the many. Maybe the commentator's lot is not such a happy one after all. Interviewing the likes of Lester Piggott or notoriously inarticulate footballers whose only comment on scoring a hat-trick is 'I'm over the moon' or 'I just hit it into the back of the net, Brian' cannot be the simplest of tasks.[33]

Commentators are a maligned lot and deserve some credit for disseminating enthusiasm for sport on a hitherto unimagined scale. This was a two-way process. Coverage of sport certainly helped popularize the otherwise earnest BBC. Manufacturers could play on the excitement of a commentary to sell their sets. 'Tense with excitement . . . thrilled. Almost seeing the game, so clearly does he hear it. Can you wonder that he shouts?' (The illustration shows a man getting out of his armchair yelling 'Shoot, Man, Shoot!') This excitement, the copy-writer continues, is brought into the home courtesy of 'the new Pye Portable . . . glorious in tone, generous in volume, comprehensive in range of reception'. Sport spread from the stands and into the home with the Cup Final as the sporting highlight of the year reaching a female audience for the first time. Writing in the *Radio Times* in 1930, the novelist Winifred Holtby, feminist and friend of Vera Brittain, recalled listening to her first football commentary:

I was excited. I had not, I have not to this day, the remotest notion of what they were all doing. But I know that I was excited. No one could

listen with cold blood and sluggish pulses to the quickening crescendo
of the roar preceding the final shout of 'Goal!' I wanted more goals. I
didn't care who shot them. I didn't know who shot them. I didn't know
who was playing or what they were playing, or where, or why. But I
wanted to feel my spine tickle and my pulses beat, and my hair stir gently
at the roots with suspense as that voice cried out from somewhere near
our drawing room curtains. 'Now he's got it. It's coming close on the
right wing. I can't see for a moment because of the crowd. Ah, there
it is now, he's got it. Jarvis has it. Jarvis has it. Goal!'

Judging by this description that breathless voice probably
belonged to none other than 'By Jove' Allison.[34]

The national dimension to sports reporting and the search for
heroes could be a source of anxiety and even distress to the more
reticent sportsman. When Jack Hobbs was approaching W. G.
Grace's record for the number of first-class centuries the massive
attention of the press actually caused him a brief loss of form.
But there was another profitable side to the coin. Despite his
shyness and natural modesty, Hobbs was willing to capitalize on
his fame. He endorsed—not without payment for some, though
not all—fountain-pens, cricket-bats and equipment, cocoa, total
abstinence, chocolate, and soft drinks. He was filmed,
interviewed, and provided with 'ghosts' who helped him to
'write' nine books, one of them a thriller called *The Test Match
Surprise* which was something of a best seller in the sixpenny
'Readers' Library' so popular in Woolworth's in the 1920s. Hobbs
did better than his soccer counterpart, Dixie Dean, whose goal-
scoring achievements were so famous for a decade from 1927.
He was used to advertise Players' cigarettes but was not even paid
a proper fee. 'Dixie'—a nickname said to derive from his swarthy
complexion and curly black hair—preferred to augment his
income by making bets with bookmakers on the basis of the
number of goals he could score in a game (one goal was evens,
two goals 5–2, and three 10–1). Sportsmen, especially footballers,
had since the 1880s been used on cigarette cards as free
advertising for a brand. Clubs were better placed than
inexperienced individuals to profit from advertising, which began
to expand the commercial potential of sport in the 1930s. The

---

[34] S. Briggs, *Those Radio Times* (1981), p. 59; Winifred Holtby, *Radio Times*,
21 Feb. 1930.

Cup finalists of 1934 promoted brands of trousers, shoe-polish, and Shredded Wheat. Manchester City gave their endorsement to a new model of radio. Yet by the standards of current advertising and sponsorship the sums involved and the use made of sport by advertisers was paltry. It was not enough to be the best in the world at your chosen sport, as Joe Davis found to his cost. Golf and tennis had an exclusive image (good for selling cars) but snooker, the most popular indoor sport, had a seedy side which discouraged advertisers. The new world snooker champion was aware of the commercial potential of his title, but was unable to persuade companies to comply with his desire to endorse their products. 'I tried eye-lotions and hair-lotions, shirtmakers and shoe-makers without eliciting the slightest flicker of interest. The only contract for endorsing a product I obtained in those days was for Churchman's cigarettes.'[35]

Television more than anything else has transformed the image of the professional sportsman or woman from the skilled artisan ('master of their craft') to the dubious cinematic status of 'star', or currently 'superstar' or 'megastar' as show-business hyperbole infects sport. Newsreel coverage of sport paved the way for this. Snappy, short news sequences certainly helped promote some of the big names but this was on a small scale in comparison with the United States where a few outstanding sportsmen became Hollywood stars. However, it was the advent of television which really transformed sportsmen. The 'TV revolution' started modestly enough with small screens and black-and-white pictures, which were not able to follow a match with the fluency, play-backs, close-ups, and other techniques that have made sport increasingly a 'televisual' phenomenon of late. Football was used as a way of encouraging working people to buy or hire televisions in the 1950s with the slogan 'When they are talking about the big match on TV will you have to remain silent?' Television offered either live coverage or by editing down the best moments presented a particularly dramatic version of events.

A series of specialist sports programmes culminated in the setting up of 'Sportsview' in 1954, a half-hour mid-week programme which interviewed personalities—Mike Hawthorn,

[35] J. Arlott, *Jack Hobbs* (1981), pp. 83–4; Walsh, *Dixie Dean*, p. 71; D. Trelford, *Snookered* (1986), p. 58.

Stirling Moss, and Danny Blanchflower featured in October 1954—as well as giving previews of top events. Peter Dimmock was the genial presenter and a powerful expansionist force in BBC sport, heading a list of commentators which included such familiar names as Harry Carpenter, Kenneth Wolstenholme, Henry Longhurst, John Arlott, Brian Johnston, Peter West, and David Coleman among others. A few, like Cliff Michelmore, went on to bigger things. But most have stayed and worn well, reassuring and fixed points in an otherwise changing landscape. The 'Beeb' has been kind to its commentators—thirty years is a long time in television—and they in turn have served it well, adjusting cleverly to the growing informality of broadcasting without ever quite forgetting the august institution in which 'they serve'. The BBC believe that no one does sport as well as they do—and they may be right.[36]

The popular press could not compete and has been pushed more and more into the 'human interest' dimension, interviewing friends and relations of players, stoking up dressing-room feuds and seizing upon the sex lives of the young, virile, and wayward. This pressure from within the media was reinforced by other social changes. Rising real incomes, especially for the young, minimal unemployment, and greater personal freedom from family and community control helped to create a 'youth culture' into which sportsmen, especially footballers, were to find an important place. George Best, a thin teenager from Belfast, whose dribbling skills made him into a star with Manchester United and the darling of the sports and gossip columns epitomized the new era. Alex James in the 1930s had not been averse to appearing at the odd night-club, but Best's moves were tracked by a posse of desperate journalists as he went from bed to boutique, from discothèque to dressing-room. Next to the Beatles and Mick Jagger he was probably the best-known teenage 'pin up'. The footballer as sex symbol was not exactly new—Dixie Dean had been the subject of female interest and cited in at least one paternity suit—but the avidity of the press for salacious gossip and the relentless pursuit of young footballers, who were suddenly rich and emotionally immature, was new. Players certainly gained in terms of rising wages, advertising, and other sources of income, but at the highest

[36] A. Briggs, *History of Broadcasting*, iv. 850–1.

level they often found there were new stresses to cope with as they were 'declassed' and lost touch with their old communities.[37]

Television has had as profound an effect on contemporary sport as the railway or the popular press had on Victorian sport. For television is not a 'neutral' provider of images or a mere facilitator, it has increasingly determined the manner in which high performance sport is played and presented to the public. In the early 1950s no more than 10 per cent of households had a television. By the late 1960s only 10 per cent did not. Not having a television was odd—the product either of extreme deprivation or self-conscious intellectualism. From the beginning sport was extremely popular with those who ran television. The reason is not hard to find. Sport was both cheap and successful. It was 'good television' and there were virtually no production costs in a sports broadcast in comparison with making a play or a documentary feature. A fee was paid to the ruling body and in the early years these were very low indeed. Huge audiences could be entertained at relatively little cost. Currently sport occupies a quarter of the BBC's own production and 17 per cent of its total output, though the fees for broadcasting have risen by as much or more than a thousandfold for certain sports like tennis and golf. Swimming is still cheap but athletics is getting more expensive. The physicality of sport, its speed and grace, along with the emotional intensity of victory and defeat are supremely visual. But this is not all. Sport has a crucial further attraction. It is 'live' entertainment at a time when more and more television is pre-recorded and packaged, and even recorded events can sustain uncertainty of outcome if the result is unknown to the viewer. An episode of the highly successful TV comedy *The Likely Lads* was based entirely on the two working-class Geordie protagonists *not* being told the result of a recorded game. Video technology has made this a frequent topic of male sporting conversation. Sport offers spontaneity which, combined with ever more sophisticated technology, allows a viewer to watch a game from many different angles, moving in for a close-up on the agonized or exultant face of the athlete, or panning back for

---

[37] R. Hoggart, *The Uses of Literacy* (1957), p. 188; Hopcraft, *The Football Man*, pp. 16–20.

a shot of the pitch, track, or the seashore during an Open golf championship. In football, rugby, or cricket the ability to stop the frame at the crucial moment or play-back a sequence, which has come recently with the development of video, has actually placed the viewer and the commentator in a better position to make a decision than the unfortunate referee or umpire.[38]

Television is the means through which the bulk of the public 'takes part' in sport. Only 14 per cent of a recent sample of the population, who declared themselves to be 'very interested in soccer', actually played the game or were members of clubs, though 98 per cent watched it on television. Football has been transformed for most of those who follow it from a Saturday afternoon activity in all weathers to a Saturday night home entertainment. Full-length games are edited down to show the highlights in a way which sometimes irritates the purist. The subtleties of the contest—running off the ball, watching an individual contest between two players rather than following the ball around through the camera lens—may be sacrificed but these failings have not deterred the audience. The football authorities have debated endlessly about the impact of these changes on their game. Clearly television is not the only reason for falling gates—affluence and a consequently greater variety of choice in entertainment, a desire to participate in physical exercise rather than watch, hooliganism, suburban family-centredness, and feminism are other factors all pulling more or less in the direction of declining live attendance. Banning TV coverage might lose important revenues without bringing back the crowds. Most probably the solution in the longer term will be a switch to the American pattern, which stresses quality over quantity. This might mean co-opting the top Scottish clubs into a 'British' premier league—still a horrifying prospect to most Scots. However things turn out the geography of football based on the Industrial Revolution seems likely to change in favour of a small 'super league' which will take high earnings from a 'live' national TV audience. In effect this is already starting to happen through

[38] G. Whannel, *Blowing the Whistle* (1983), pp. 58–63; see also E. Buscombe (ed.), *Football on Television* (1975); *Observer Magazine*, 1 Mar. 1987, p. 22.

television concentration on a few top clubs with only a brief nod in the direction of the rest.[39]

The football authorities have not been the only ones to agonize over the impact of television on sport. There have been the predictable complaints that people increasingly prefer to watch than to play, that we are producing a generation of armchair athletes. Recent social research has dismissed such speculation. Television may have made inroads on the number of live spectators but, if anything, it has encouraged a greater degree of participation in a far wider range of activities. There has been a huge expansion of golf, for example, the attractions of which were brought home to the general public through the televising of tournaments. Even Association football has grown at the grass roots with a further 2,000 clubs affiliating to the FA in the second half of the 1970s to make up a total of almost 40,000. So participation in sport is increasing although women, the old, the unskilled, and those without private transport are still under-represented. Watching on TV and taking part are not so much mutually exclusive as part of a balanced human cycle of passive and active involvement.[40]

Recently television has contributed dramatically to the rejuvenation of particular sports, most notably darts and snooker. The medium is particularly well suited to close-up shots and the viewer can make his assessment of the situation from behind the player's arm. When Joe Davis finally retired in 1964 he said 'snooker has no future'. Yet only twenty years later the Crucible Theatre in Sheffield was the focus of the attention of around twenty million viewers as Steve Davis was defeated on the final ball of the final frame by Dennis Taylor, who became the world champion in what *The Times* (won over to 'popular culture' under its antipodean ownership) declared to be a 'heart-stopping' match. Snooker has been reborn through colour television. What began as an attempt to diversify and cater for minority interests on BBC 2 turned into an extraordinary national obsession.

[39] J. Curran, 'Mass Media and Leisure', in M. Smith, S. Parker, and C. Smith, *Leisure and Society in Britain* (1973), p. 202; also Wagg, *The Football World*, pp. 131–3, 220–3.

[40] Participation levels calculated from the General Household Survey 1973 and 1977 as set out in *New Society*, 3 Sept. 1981, p. 394; for the inequalities in participation see M. Hillman and A. Whalley, *Fair Play for All* (1977).

Snooker players clash not just as players but as personalities with their own quirks, style, and personal feuds—Alex Higgins 'The Hurricane' or Jimmy White 'The Tooting Tearaway' set against the inscrutable, trance-like calmness of Steve Davis or Cliff Thorburn, or the bantering and benign Dennis Taylor and Willie Thorne; all the 'lads' are part of an immensely lucrative media 'hype' carefully planned by a professional promoter-cum-accountant. 'Whispering' Ted Lowe was suddenly a celebrity with murmured thoughts about the difficulty of 'a long pink against the nap into the top pocket'. A similar process is also taking place in darts led by an exuberant Geordie commentator with a Cambridge History degree. Rugby, in particular, has its 'characters'—Eddie Waring, a favourite with a generation of impressionists, brought the banter of the Yorkshire terraces into the commentary-box; Bill Maclaren is the embodiment of Borders rugby—firm, crackling along, supremely direct, enthusiastic and decent, a yeoman of Scotland. Appropriately enough, he is a schoolmaster and not a full-time professional commentator. Picking the select few to make the transition from a successful playing career in football to television reporting has become a minor entertainment in itself. Football now has Bob Wilson of Arsenal and Emlyn Hughes of Liverpool and on independent television there is Ian St John and Jimmy Greaves ('The Saint and Greavsie'), who have taken the art of televised sport a step further by reproducing in the studio all the mixture of jokes and outlandish memories, bets, hunches, tactical shrewdness, and affectionate 'piss-taking' that make up a friendly hour in the pub.[41]

Television, it should be remembered, can conserve and celebrate just as it can abbreviate and denature. Despite the view that television has created a 'global village' in which similar electronic images flicker before countless millions creating a common mass culture, the presentation of sport on British television differs sharply from that of the United States or of France. Each country develops its own ways of using television to promote its own tastes and values. Styles of commentary, methods of editing, programming schedules, and the interspersing of sport with other subjects all contribute to establishing national

---

[41] Trelford, *Snookered*, chs. 5–7, covers televised snooker splendidly.

styles within the framework of a common technology. In Britain, the pattern of televised sport has in many respects followed the natural preferences of the 'amateur' establishment. With the exception of the Cup Final, the independent channels have concentrated on racing and on wrestling for Saturday afternoon entertainment and do not show golf or cricket. Currently the ITV sports budget is around £14 million. 'In newspaper terms, the BBC is much more *Telegraph* and we are the *Mirror* or even the *Sun*', remarked ITV's head of sport recently. As an established 'national' institution the BBC head of sport claims 'we don't approach life from a purely business point of view'. Historically the BBC has been in a privileged position to negotiate coverage with the 'gentlemen amateurs' of the MCC, the Committee of the All-England Club, and the four rugby unions. 'I have never attempted to conceal my belief that "Wimbledon" treated us generously,' wrote the Head of Outside Broadcasts in 1952. 'I assumed it was the deliberate policy of an amateur sport towards a "public service".' From early on the government underpinned this advantage by laying down that certain 'national' events could not be contractually monopolized by either side. This had the effect of giving the BBC an effective monopoly as advertising revenue could best be maximized by providing an alternative to sport on independent television. A cricket audience was too restricted to share profitably. Despite a few celebrated deserters including former England captain Tony Greig, cricket has resisted being incorporated into a private television circus run from Australia by Kerry Packer. Mike Brearley, the subsequent England captain and a Cambridge graduate with a distinctly academic turn of mind, was revealing in his reasons for turning down the offer, which would have overturned the historical structure of international cricket: 'Money apart, Kerry Packer is not my style. England is my home. I prefer the chugging British coaster with a cargo of pig-iron to a monstrous supertanker hurriedly constructed. We put up with the buckets to catch the drips in the dressing-room at Taunton in order to enjoy the wisteria round the door of the George at Bewley.'[42]

---

[42] Brearley cited by A. Kuper, 'Gentlemen and Players', *New Society*, 9 Aug. 1984, p. 90; *Observer Magazine*, 1 Mar. 1987, p. 22; Briggs, *History of Broadcasting*, iv. 859.

Cricket, in fact, has negotiated a successful compromise with the world of broadcasting, enjoying extensive coverage, which is now used to gain lucrative 'low-key' sponsorship and advertising. Through their sponsorship of cricket, Cornhill, until recently a little-known City insurance company, turned themselves into a household name at the cost of a million pounds over five years. In 1981 Cornhill's banners appeared 7,459 times on a television service resolutely opposed to advertising. The benefit for Cornhill was its 'awareness level' (the number of people who mentioned it when asked to name an insurance company), which shot up from 2 per cent in 1977 to 17 per cent in 1981. In addition, the firm recruited cricketers for its publicity functions and was given free tickets and entertainment facilities for the Test matches. Naturally, television exposure was the overwhelming consideration for Cornhill and this was presumably also true for other sponsors, which included Schweppes, United Friendly Assurance, Commercial Union Assurance, the Prudential, Gordon's gin, Haig's whisky, Whitbread's beer, Younger's beer, Wrigley's spearmint among others. Despite the 'wisteria', cricket has come to be quietly alive to capitalism. The same has turned out to be true of show-jumping, a little-known landed pursuit before it was taken up by the BBC as a sport which might appeal to women, especially when Pat Smythe rode Flanagan to four European Championship victories between 1957 and 1963. As the standards of competition became even higher, costs shot up and sponsors came forward to support an activity with high social status and a good media profile. The BBC again found itself the unwilling accomplice of the advertisers. The unfortunate Dorian Williams, whose cultured, distinctly upper-class accent was synonymous with commentary on the sport, was required to tell the viewers that the next contestant was Harvey Smith riding 'Hitachi Music Centre'. 'Trade' had infected even gentry pursuits, though the presence of royalty in the person of Princess Anne and her husband, both competitors of international standard, kept up the social tone.[43]

The role of sponsorship and television together has brought vast amounts of new money into sport, providing high earnings

[43] Moorhouse, *Lord's*, pp. 138–41; Sandiford, 'Professionalization of Modern Cricket', pp. 274–9.

for tournament winners or top team-players. In return sportsmen and women have to make themselves available to the press and the sponsors for promotional purposes. A sea-change is taking place. Nineteenth-century amateurism has been stood on its head. Consider the following articles, which by chance appeared side by side in the *Guardian* in 1982. One concerned the transfer of Kevin Keegan from Southampton to Newcastle United. The deal involved a transfer fee plus a complicated sponsorship package, which required Keegan to advertise and do promotional work for Scottish and Newcastle Breweries. Keegan duly appeared at the press conference to extol his new club and his sponsors, despite the fact he was known not to drink the product himself. 'You don't have to sell Newcastle United to anyone. This is a great club, the only one that can beat Liverpool for the enthusiasm of its supporters', he enthused. His instant sincerity was much appreciated by all concerned. Keegan 'did the business' on the field and off. On the same page appeared a sharp rebuke to Ken Brown, an idiosyncratic professional golfer, who had committed the unforgiveable sin of refusing to give interviews to the press or television and making good his escape from a crowd of journalists by vaulting over a barrier. 'We view Brown's behaviour very seriously,' said the presiding official, 'he is doing a disservice to the PGA [Professional Golfers' Association] and to everyone concerned with the game.' The promoter of the tournament went further: 'It's time the PGA brought in a disciplinary element for this sort of behaviour. There is a lot of money to be won this week and people should earn it not only on the course but off it as well.' Brown was a 'bad sport' who was not 'playing the game', but Keegan was a 'model pro'. Such judgements were based upon a willingness to comply to the full with the turning of sports into a 'media event'. The praise of Keegan and the criticism of Brown might have surprised and distressed earlier generations of gentlemen-amateurs but it was logical in its own terms; if players wished to become rich, they had to sell themselves as well as their skill. The older code, which put the integrity of players and the game itself above money, had been abandoned. Brown was supposed to be a kind of entertainer, albeit a reluctant and irritable one, and he had to sing for his supper.[44]

Top sportsmen frequently mixed with celebrities from the 1920s onwards. Footballers sometimes appeared on a music-hall bill in the late Victorian and Edwardian years but it was not until the inter-war years that top players became 'stars'. Steve Bloomer of Derby or Billy Meredith at Manchester were famous locally rather than nationally. Dixie Dean, however, had a wider following. He was friendly not only with well-known boxers and bookies but with George Robey and with other public Merseyside figures like Bessie Braddock. Alex James of Arsenal was worshipped in London and in Scotland. In snooker Joe Davis even put on a show at the Palladium during the Second World War with Tommy Trinder, Sid Field, Arthur Askey, and Tessie O'Shea. Trinder, who became a director of Fulham, pointed the way towards a larger-scale penetration of the boardroom by entertainers. Eric Morecambe's directorship at Luton was another example. The logical culmination of the process came when the pop singer and song-writer Elton John took over the chairmanship of Watford. Pop singer Rod Stewart took inordinate pride in his brief time as a professional with Brentford and would make well-publicized appearances to support Scotland. George Best, as we saw, was closely linked to 'pop culture' and international teams began to make special records as part of a 'media package' for the World Cup. Top sportsmen liked to think of themselves as 'personalities'. Mick Channon observed that 'most famous people are "characters" ' (presumably including himself in this select group). When very successful footballers, cricketers, boxers, golfers, even amateur rugby players like Bill Beaumont and Gareth Edwards, retired from their sport they might hope to cash in somehow. They could perhaps join the growing band of pundits. There were talk shows, after-dinner speeches, and quiz programmes as well. Some of these sporting 'characters' play golf and appear with comedians such as Jimmy Tarbuck and Bruce Forsyth or actor Sean Connery for a few holes and a bit of friendly banter. Peter Allis has turned golf into a kind of harmless interview where public figures hit a few shots and chat about themselves. Substantial sums of money are raised for charity by show-biz football teams. The athletic disc jockey is a distinctively contemporary phenomenon. Ian Botham's alleged flirtation with cannabis and the occasional female admirer has occupied the popular press far more than his performances as the great all-rounder of English cricket. He inadvisedly tried to launch himself very briefly in Hollywood. He also walked from John O'Groats to Land's End for charity with celebrities doing well-publicized stints by his side. He has been endlessly harassed by the press who desperately need a story. The 'good guys' are all very well but they don't make headlines. Wimbledon has been dull without McEnroe from the gossip point of view. Cricket can be boring when Botham behaves, and snooker needs Alex Higgins even if it does not like to say so. The crazy circus rolls on and on. More coverage of more sports is supplemented by endless interviews and chat-show appearances. There seems to be no saturation point.[45]

Amidst such massive coverage there has been little television interest in what ordinary people get out of sport. Sports programmes do not see this as part of what they are supposed to be doing. Sport is high-performance stuff varied with a bit of club golf played by famous people or a marathon which involves both top athletes and the general public. The availability of less well-known sports very cheaply has attracted some interesting coverage, which brings the viewer closer to the ordinary competitor. For example the sport of crown green bowling, which was very little known outside of the north of England, has been shown to a wider public; the greens are often oddly bereft of spectators, and the northern accents of the players are plainly audible as they urge on their woods or confer solemnly as a pair over the last bowl of an important 'end'. Even these modest broadcasts show only the best of the bunch. Why are there no programmes about ordinary clubs and ordinary people? A rare exception to this unrelieved diet of excellence came recently in the shape of a programme made by unemployed men on Teesside about the place in their life of the municipal golf-course. 'For a couple of hours I feel like a man again,' said one. Another, making a joke out of his poverty, hit a good drive and sighed, 'That's gone further than I went on my holidays.' There was much of this, a few small side-bets, and plenty of mixing between the generations. The club had its blazer and badge, a captain and lady captain and an honours board. It was imitative of the suburban golf club but independent and unashamed. Television had brought

---

[45] Walsh, *Dixie Dean*, p. 103; Wagg, *The Football World*, pp. 144–8.

golf to the working class and for just a moment television gave us an idea of what it meant to them.[46]

3. HOOLIGANS

Hooliganism has been the exception to the rule that the media are only interested in victories, records, and the private life of the stars. In recent years the collective aggression displayed by groups of younger fans has caused a kind of 'moral panic' in the press. Football hooliganism has been defined as a major social problem. It has attracted not only widespread condemnation but a fair amount of sociological analysis as well with the result that there is a lively debate taking place about its origins and nature. Of particular interest to the historian is the question of continuity or discontinuity in this kind of behaviour. Did the 1960s see a sharp break in the form and content of the collective behaviour of young working-class spectators? Or is the current wave of hooliganism in British football merely a continuation of old traditions, which we now are less willing to tolerate and more anxious to report?

Serious discussion of the phenomenon began with a debate over the role of the press in reporting violent incidents at football matches. It was argued that the sensationalizing of relatively minor forms of rowdyism invented hooliganism as a 'social problem'. Young fans found a new 'hooligan' identity created for them by journalists with a vested interest in whipping up public indignation. Headlines like 'SAVAGES! ANIMALS!' or 'BIRCH 'EM' and 'SMASH THESE THUGS' encouraged the public to treat young football fans as criminals, and the fans themselves then acted out the role that had been supplied for them. Garry Whannel traced four main themes in the analysis of football hooliganism in the popular press in the 1970s: fans were 'mindless/senseless'; they were 'maniacs/lunatics'; 'foul/subhuman' (which led some fans to chant back at the police and the respectable public 'We hate humans'); finally that they were 'so-called supporters' and in a small minority, i.e. they made up only a very small percentage of the crowd and they had little interest in the game itself. Much of

[46] 'Open Space', BBC broadcast, 20 July 1984.

this analysis of the media treatment of hooliganism drew upon the work of Stanley Cohen. The new 'sociology of deviance' suggested hooligans were not abnormal young people and that the whole phenomenon—like the Mods and Rockers panic before—had been 'amplified' by the popular press in order to boost their circulation and pander to the prejudices of their readers.[47]

One of the most enduring and widespread of these prejudices, which achieved the status of a popular myth, was that 'things weren't like that in my day'. Geoffrey Pearson's recent *Hooligan: a History of Respectable Fears* gives a persuasive account of law-and-order myths, which shows that people continually locate 'the good old days' of decent behaviour at some time about twenty or thirty years in the past. Those concerned about football hooliganism today idealize the stable post-war years when it was safe to be on the terraces and one could walk the streets at night. Yet back in the 1950s there was the 'Teddy Boy' to alarm the public and to set against the allegedly poor but honest inter-war years when people could leave their doors unlocked. Between the wars the kind of juvenile gang-violence portrayed, for example, in Graham Greene's *Brighton Rock* again led to unfavourable comparisons being made with the past. In the 1920s and 1930s London had its 'Drury Lane Boys', 'Fulham Boys', 'Waterloo Road Gang', 'Chelsea Boys', and many more. Glasgow was notoriously violent. Billy Fullerton's Protestant gang from Bridgeton wreaked havoc on Catholics, especially if they incautiously made themselves easy targets by wearing a Celtic scarf. However, a closer look at the supposedly more stable Edwardian era found men like Baden-Powell and Charles Masterman deeply concerned over the problem of 'boy life'; adolescence was invented as a unique psychological stage and youth cults like the 'Ikey boys' were defined as a 'problem' requiring 'solutions' such as special 'youth clubs' and movements. And so the process went on; back into the Dickensian world of the Artful Dodger and then the violence of the eighteenth-century

[47] S. Hall, 'The Treatment of "Football Hooliganism" in the Press', in R. Ingham (ed.), *Football Hooliganism* (1978), pp. 15–37; G. Whannel, 'Football, Crowd Behaviour and the Press', in *Media, Culture and Society*, 1979 (4), esp. pp. 330–1; for 'sociology of deviance' see S. Cohen, *Folk Devils and Moral Panics* (1972), and his influential editing of *Images of Deviance* (1971).

'mob'. Each generation created its own myth of stability and fastened upon disorderly juvenile elements in its own culture to prove the thesis. Pearson sums up his argument as follows:

Across the centuries, we have seen the same rituals of territorial dominance, trials of strength, gang fights, mockery against elders and authorities, and antagonism towards 'outsiders' as typical focuses for youthful energy and aggressive mischief. Even under vastly different social conditions there are striking continuities between the violent interruptions to pre-industrial fairs and festivals, and the customary eruptions during modern Bank Holidays or the weekly carnival of misrule at contemporary football games—where the football rowdy, with his territorial edginess, mascots, emblems and choral arrangements in the 'rough music' tradition, must seem like the incarnation of the unruly apprentice, or the late Victorian 'Hooligan'.[48]

The opening sections of this book have already provided evidence of juvenile 'misrule' in pre-industrial and in modern sports. Violence of different kinds has certainly been endemic in sport and fighting between groups of players or spectators is nothing new. Territoriality was the key to urban working-class sporting loyalties and this was sometimes expressed in acts of violence. So to what extent is juvenile violence a 'constant' varying only in style and in detail over time? The notion that the media have 'amplified' football violence may have been tenable ten or twenty years ago, but the current scale of hooliganism does not appear to be much exaggerated by the media. Recently the press have, if anything, tended to understate the extent of the problem to deny hooligans 'the oxygen of publicity'. The view that hooligans actually learn how to behave from the papers and reflect back to the public the image that has been created for them is not really borne out in personal interviews. Moreover, the nature of crowd behaviour may be different from the past not just in style but in substance. The 'continuity' thesis is obviously attractive to the social historian but important reservations and unanswered questions remain. In essence the issues are these: first, given the old traditions of 'misrule' and 'gang life', how far do contemporary forms of violence in sport resemble earlier ones; second, why did football matches—the stadia, the surroundings, the routes and transport to and from the game—become the

---

[48] G. Pearson, *Hooligan* (1983), p. 202.

chosen site of hooligan behaviour? If continuity is the key to football hooliganism, then there should be some solid evidence of similar forms of violence at football matches since the formation of the Football League. If discontinuity is the case, there is the alleged distinctiveness of recent crowd behaviour and explanations of it as part of a general transformation of the urban working class since 1945 to consider.

First we need a proper idea of what it is we are seeking to explain. Who are the hooligans? This is reasonably easy to answer. Judging by surveys and by convictions they are largely white, urban, unskilled school-leavers in their teens. Married hooligans are relatively rare. What is 'hooligan' behaviour? Social psychologists have attempted to pin it down using video recordings, 'participant/observer' reports, and interviews with hooligans. What emerges is that much of the actual group aggression—the chanting, threats, charges—is symbolic and ritualized. Hooligans go through the motions of violence but relatively little damage is done either to property or to the person. The danger of injury or death arises less from fights between rival groups of fans as from the panic that actual or threatened attacks provoke amongst the general public. The tragedy at the Heysel stadium in Brussels, for example, came from the crush of spectators fleeing from the drunken charges of Liverpool fans. None of the 38 who died was murdered personally by English hooligans. The point here is not to exonerate the violent behaviour of certain Liverpool supporters but rather the reverse, i.e. to emphasize the potentially fatal risks which are being run each week in stadia where large and rowdy confrontations of young spectators take place. The Ibrox casualties of 1902, the Bolton disaster of 1946, and others were a result of overcrowding and poor facilities, but the Heysel deaths were caused by hooligans. The violence of the fans itself may be largely symbolic (though beatings and occasionally stabbings do take place), but its potential consequences in enclosed spaces present a genuine danger to public safety.[49]

It is not reasonable to suggest that hooliganism is merely inflated by the press and best treated by 'radical non-intervention'. The concentration of several thousand younger

---

[49] P. Marsh, *Aggro* (1975); E. Dunning *et al.*, *The Roots of Football Hooliganism* (1988), pp. 246–50.

fans systematically chanting abuse and taunting one another, forcibly separated by the police and each threatening to attack the other is neither an imaginary problem nor simply a product of imitative behaviour picked up from incautious media coverage. Fans dress carefully in order to identify themselves within their group. The styles change with bewildering rapidity but the way of tying a scarf or the kind of boots and socks worn carry a message about the 'hardness' of the wearer. 'Hardness' is what much of hooligan behaviour is about. When hooligans themselves are asked to define the term they usually say 'a right little hard-nut'; someone willing to get 'stuck in' when a fight breaks out. Most 'hooligans' use the word in a flattering sense to describe the 'hardest' members of their own group. Chanting is 'macho' in the sense that opposing players, supporters, and officials are often abused in sexual terms ('wankers' and 'cunts'), and some of the scornful chanting has a deliberately 'caveman' style as in 'Oxford Boys we are here / shag your women, drink your beer'—a widely favoured kind of verse freely adapted by other fans. They do not use the 'animal' terms their critics use except in the case of black players where ape-like grunting and the throwing of bananas are common. The most important feature of contemporary hooliganism is the taking and holding of 'ends'. Away supporters, especially those from clubs with 'hooligan' reputations, try to drive home supporters from their traditional end. 'That's what it is,' said a young Cardiff fan, 'that's what it's all about. You've to get in their end and take it—the away supporters have.' A young Arsenal fan made the same point after having listened rather contemptuously to a discussion by academics about working-class 'resistance' to increasing middle-class infiltration of football. 'They don't give a sod for the students and all the other wankers and pooftas that turn up', he declared. 'All the North Bank [the Highbury hooligan end] care about is their team and the other end and that's all there is to it.' Hooligans do not normally attack older or better-off supporters. They save their wrath for other working-class youths like themselves, who happen to have been born or grown up somewhere else.[50]

[50] P. Marsh, E. Rosser, and R. Harré, *The Rites of Disorder* (1978), esp. pp. 81–91; D. Robbins and P. Cohen, *Knuckle Sandwich* (1978), p. 103; J. Pratt and M. Slater, 'A Fresh Look at Football Hooliganism', *Leisure Studies* (1984), p. 204.

What evidence is there of this kind of behaviour at football matches before the First World War or in the inter-war period? There are plenty of references to violent incidents of various kinds. Football was never an entirely respectable sport and from the outset crowds swore and shouted, occasionally threw things or charged on to the pitch. There are also records of fights between individual spectators and more rarely between groups of spectators. One of the most infamous of all football riots took place in Glasgow in 1909 when a crowd of around 6,000 invaded the pitch at full time. However, in this case, the crowd was angry that extra time was not going to be played and vented their fury on the pitch and the police rather than on one another. Of course, gang fights between supporters of Celtic and Rangers were quite common, especially between the wars, as Bill Murray's study of *The Old Firm* makes clear. Something akin to the contemporary pattern of hooliganism has long existed in Glasgow as a result of Irish Catholic immigration and militant working-class Scottish Protestantism. In Glasgow fighting between fans was not just a matter for juveniles. Although youths were predominant, there was no shortage of older men willing to fight for sectarian reasons. Both Rangers' and Celtic supporters were organized into 'brake clubs' in order to travel to away matches. There were frequent rowdy incidents as these gangs of travelling supporters descended on a town for an away match, especially after the First World War when the struggle for Irish independence was at its height. The Celtic brake clubs would sing 'The Soldier's Song', 'Keep the Green Flag Flying', and 'God Save Ireland' whilst chalking slogans like 'Rebels 2, Black and Tans 0' on the sides of their carriages and vans. Rangers' supporters replied in kind, and so the blood feud went on and on—and continues to this day.[51]

Glasgow, however, was not Britain. Despite heavy Irish immigration into south Lancashire, the Midlands, and London, Orangeism was less ferocious south of the Border. Certain teams did become very loosely identified with Catholic or Protestant support in Liverpool and Manchester, but this was never a prominent feature of English football or a significant source of violence. Tony Mason, who has weighed up both the composition

[51] Murray, *The Old Firm*, esp. ch. 7, pp. 163–86.

and the behaviour of Victorian and Edwardian football crowds as carefully as the sketchy evidence permits, suggests that skilled workers were disproportionately dominant within the crowd. It seems probable that it was not until the doubling in the size of crowds between the wars that the 'rough' as opposed to the 'respectable' working class was fully represented as a proportion of the total population. Dunning and Murphy have tried to argue that violent street-gangs, whose antics led to several alarmed inquiries around the turn of the century, were likely to have been present at football matches from the outset. This is speculative but they are on firmer ground when they point out that violent incidents were underreported both by referees in their correspondence with the FA and by the press. A detailed examination of the *Leicester Mercury* from 1895 to 1914 has revealed 137 reports of violent incidents nationally as against 116 in the FA minute-books. Moreover, fifty-five of the 137 reports in the *Leicester Mercury* related to Leicester itself, which suggests that there was a good deal more trouble at local level than reached the national press or the FA. In fact, only fifteen of the *Leicester Mercury*'s 137 incidents appeared in the FA's total of 116. Conversely the *Leicester Mercury* only reported a fraction of the officially minuted FA incidents. 'Underrecording in both directions' was an important factor, as Dunning and Murphy stress. But do these totals prove that hooligan behaviour of a kind broadly comparable with the present day was widespread before the First World War?[52]

Looking more closely at the kinds of misbehaviour reported in the *Leicester Mercury*, the descriptions of crowd offences committed within Leicestershire from 1894 to 1914 do not permit any clear reconstruction of crowd behaviour. Verbal abuse and disorder was the most common category of offence followed by pitch invasions or encroachments. There were sixteen instances of physical violence or assault reported between 1895 and 1914, but these included throwing missiles at players as well as fights between spectators. Going on to the inter-war years the authors note that there was no great reduction in the number of incidents reported in the press, despite the reputation of the large crowds

[52] E. G. Dunning and P. J. Murphy, 'Working class Social Bonding and the Socio-genesis of Football Hooliganism', SSRC Report (1982), p. 43.

of those years for generally good behaviour. The bulk of reported incidents again concerned bad language and unsportsmanlike conduct. The authors conclude that the improving image of the game drew a wider and more respectable public, including more women. This runs counter to Mason's suggestion that more unskilled workers attended between the wars. There is no obvious way of resolving the question of crowd composition. Proper data was never collected at the time. One thing, however, is pretty clear. Nowhere in the vast press coverage and literature of match reports is there any reference to the growth of a violent, organized youth subculture within football. Casual, individual violence was almost certainly more common than today but 'hooliganism' in the collective and contemporary sense did not take place at football matches. It is unacceptable to deduce from the lack of prosecutions that hooligan behaviour was formerly tolerated to such a degree that the culprits were neither censured nor prosecuted. The 'argument from silence' will not do, especially in the late Victorian era. During the second half of the nineteenth century the police were increasingly active against all sorts of minor public offences such as drunken or disorderly behaviour or the playing of street games. A moralistic middle-class press or the civic or football authorities themselves would never have ignored systematic gang-violence either in football grounds or around them. The problem of 'street arabs' and juvenile gangs was very much in the mind of those who formed the Boys' Brigade, Church Lads, and the Scouts. A recent oral history of schoolchildren shows how close an eye the police kept on 'larking about'. Home Office reports on football-ground safety in 1924 did not even raise hooliganism as an item on the agenda.[53]

The picture which emerges is one where there was a good deal of casual crudity and the occasional fight between individuals or small groups but little orchestrated rowdyism or violence. Examining the reports of the Chief Constable of Birmingham between 1900 and 1940, Tony Mason notes that football does not merit inclusion as a policing problem. Perhaps most eloquent of all is the simple fact that the grounds themselves were not

---

[53] Ibid., pp. 48, 93; S. Humphries shows in *Hooligans or Rebels* (1981) that there was both a good deal of juvenile rule-breaking on the streets and an active police presence.

segregated. Large numbers of 'away' fans were uncommon except for local derbies. Even then opposing fans mixed on the same terraces without the 'taking of ends'. Accounts of watching football composed by ordinary spectators emphasize how familiar many people were to one another, the wide age-range, and the lively banter. A lifelong Manchester City fan recalled that in the 1940s 'it was a very mixed crowd. There were a lot of old blokes, and women, even some elderly women. You all stood there together. You knew everybody. You never saw 'em between games. But we always stood roughly in the same place and we knew the forty or fifty people around us 'cos they were always there. The worst hazard of standing in that crowd was someone pissing down the back of your leg.' There were occasional fights when groups of visiting supporters descended on a local pub but very little trouble at the ground itself. Moreover when there were fights, observed the chairman of the Birmingham City Supporters' Club, 'it was punch-ups among men in those days . . . when I was a lad, if I stepped out of line I got a bloody good hiding from my Dad'. Denis Brailsford, an inter-war spectator and a distinguished sports historian, recalled that he first went to football in the 1930s as part of his father's extended family of miners and their wives, who made up the core of a group that regularly went to Mansfield Town's home games. There were few visiting spectators and there was no singing or chanting. However, 'there would be swearing, there would be people coming in drunk . . . staggering from the local pubs into the ground, but they were a tiny, tiny minority and you would get the odd fight breaking out'. Brailsford quite categorically rejects the idea that group aggression was part of the spectacle in the way it has come to be since the 1960s. 'I never remember a fight with more than two people involved with the rest of us encouraging them usually, holding their coats until the police stepped in to break it up, and these scuffles normally had nothing to do with loyalty to rival teams.'[54]

[54] For a critique of Dunning and Murphy see T. Mason and J. Crump, 'Hostile and Improper Demonstrations, Football 1880–1980', in J. A. Mangan (ed.), *Proc. XI Hispa Int. Congress*, ed. J. A. Mangan (Glasgow, 1987), pp. 65–8 (1988); D. Robbins, *We Hate Humans* (1984), p. 148; Denis Brailsford talking to Tony Mason, 17 Sept. 1985, *BSSH Bulletin*, no. 5, Jan. 1986.

The structure of the crowd differed sharply from the present. This is the nub of the matter. Crowds were composed of groups of family, friends, or work-mates tending to go to the same part of the ground and recognizing those around them. There were no 'ends' where the young congregated unsupervised. Heavy drinking, spitting, and swearing rather than collective violence marked off the 'rough' from the rest—the self-controlled 'respectable' elements. How then did occasional individual violence give way to the regular and organized group aggression of the 'ends' witnessed since the 1960s? At one level the answer to this question is deceptively straightforward. Until the 1950s away support at games (except 'derbies') was limited by shortage of money, especially amongst young workers. But between 1951 and 1962 juvenile weekly wages rose by 83 per cent. Motor cycles and scooters, clothes, records, and football expenses accounted for most of the new disposable income. This in itself would hardly have been significant had it not been for a wider transformation of the adult male working class. The halving in aggregate attendance at football matches, which has taken place between the early 1950s and the early 1980s (from almost 40 million to under 20 million), is a result of the disinclination of married men to spend most Saturday afternoons watching live football. The car might need a running repair; the wife would want a 'drive' in the country or, at least, a lift to the shops. Spectator sport could be followed from home on a winter's afternoon and older men increasingly chose to do this. Thus the family, neigh-bourhood, or work-place groups of older and younger men and a sprinkling of women, which seem to have formed the basic unit of attendance between the wars and before, broke up. Juvenile hooliganism was mainly the consequence of the collapse of the controls which older family and time-served men had exerted. The composition of the crowd altered and with it went the surveillance and supervision of the young. As the age-structure changed older spectators tended to leave the terraces to take up the increasing amount of seated accommodation; the 'ends' were left to 'the lads'. As gangs of home supporters confronted rival travelling groups, the internal segregation of the ground by age was intensified. The older men, who still wanted to attend live games, learned to avoid either of the 'ends', and with falling attendances there was no difficulty in finding a relatively safe place elsewhere in the ground. So the process gained momentum. Hooliganism and segregation were mutually reinforcing.[55]

So much for the 'how' of hooliganism but what of the 'why'? Even taking an ethologist's view that young men are fighting animals who need to work off aggression harmlessly in play—a sweeping and contentious assumption—we still have to account for the specific form of football hooliganism since the 1960s. Why was group identity expressed in this rather than in some other way? What social meanings, if any, can be detected in the synchronized clapping and threats aggression? Hooligan behaviour is more elaborate than one might think. Oxford United fans, for example, were found to have a repertoire of over 250 carefully orchestrated chants ranging from 'We're gonna win the league, tra la la la' to 'You're gonna get your fuckin' heads kicked in'—the favoured greeting for visiting fans. Interpretations which see hooliganism as a conscious protest against poor urban conditions and employment prospects, though often finding favour with politicians, are facile. The contemporary hooligan phenomenon arose in the 1960s at a time of unprecedented prosperity and low unemployment and has continued through recession both in the depressed north and the relatively prosperous south. Southern hooligans in employment sing 'You'll never get a job' to northerners, especially Liverpudlians. Nor do fans see themselves as engaging in a kind of working-class resistance to the commercialization of football in any straightforward sense.[56]

Central to the phenomenon is the idea of territory and community. Hooligans often take care to evade police escorts and to slip into rival territories unobserved. Young Arsenal supporters sometimes disembark from trains south of the river and enter Chelsea territory across Wandsworth Bridge. In one sense this kind of thing has been taking place for centuries. The continuity thesis is not without some merit if carefully defined. Traditional football had been an expression of male prowess and village pride sanctioned by custom and loosely supervised by adults. Under industrialization these games and the 'bands of youth' were either

---

[55] Pratt and Slater, 'A Fresh Look at Football Hooliganism', p. 210.
[56] D. Morris, *The Soccer Tribe* (1981), p. 307; the 'trans-historical' approach is crude and unhelpful but the many photographs are valuable.

suppressed or marginalized. What Edwardian sociologists liked to call 'boy-life' existed at the informal level of the street-gang or more respectably in the 'youth club' movement. Central to the working class was the establishment of a stable urban culture segregated by sex where boys 'learned' how to be men. This kind of socialization involved, for example, finding out how to drink without getting hopelessly or degradingly drunk; how to indulge in banter and when to risk a fight. Men passed on these things to their sons and their apprentices. Although there was plenty of loutish and rough behaviour in public by groups of juveniles, there was always a counterbalancing influence within male culture. The gang rivalries of the street were kept within bounds and out of the world of adult entertainment. Since the 1950s the old solidarities of working-class culture have disappeared. So too have many of the communities themselves. Networks of neighbours have been broken up by rehousing. Sons are far less likely to follow their fathers or other male relatives into the same occupations or places of work. Football since the 1950s has come to provide a kind of surrogate community for the young; the club defines their identity and the 'end' is their territory, even if they have moved out to high-rise blocks miles away.[57]

Membership of a working-class community was something their fathers took for granted. Working men of earlier generations had less need to assert who or what they were. They inherited a firm class culture and lived within it. They were not urged by their teachers to achieve educational success or by advertisers to join a consumer society where class differences were blurred by the possession of material goods. Hooliganism is partly an assertion of 'hardness' and an attachment to local territory, which the boys see as the traditional characteristics of their class. This is what seems to have been behind the 'skinhead' or 'boot-boy' phenomenon that has been a part of football hooliganism. Shaving their heads unlike long-haired middle-class students or pop singers of the period and wearing heavy workmen's boots and braces, they seemed like a caricature of the world that their parents had left. They perpetuated the old traditions in new ways. Football

---

[57] P. Cohen, 'Subculture Conflict and Working Class Community', in S. Hall (ed.), *Culture, Media and Language* (1980), pp. 78–88, links football violence with the wider youth culture of the inner city; *Observer*, 17 Aug. 1986, p. 38.

became the single most important focus for this. Extensive community work and interviews with young Arsenal supporters in a run-down housing estate by Robbins and Cohen confirmed this impression. The boys talked nostalgically about the way fighting had been a part of their fathers' world; 'about the time old man MacIlroy, half-pissed, had taken on all the men folk of his very extended family, at his sister's wedding, and still had time to call for more beer. Young Neil told how old man Allen one day for a bet had drawn a line across a bar-room floor at the Black Horse and challenged all comers to cross it.' Would their children talk with similar nostalgia about the time their dads led 'the North Bank on a charge against the Chelsea "Shed" '?[58]

Sport presents a problem for such youths. On the one hand it offers a way of displaying hardness, on the other it is respectable, adopted as part of the official culture of 'school' or 'youth club'. In the Roundhouse, a Catholic housing estate in Liverpool, a slightly older man remarked to members of a teenage gang 'you lot are just like we was. We'd always be fighting coz we knew the older fellas had. Like yourselves, you see us lot playing for Heriots and see fellers going in hard, and say I can be just as hard.' 'The Boys', as they were known, formed their own team rather than play in established youth sides but were dismissed from the local league for fighting and violent play. In another participant/observer study of a delinquent group within a secondary school, Paul Willis noted how one boy had initially started out very well, with school reports praising his co-operative attitude and his achievements in cricket, football, and cross-country until 'his whole manner and attitude changed'. When asked to explain this the boy remarked 'my father called me an ear 'ole [a 'crawler' or conformist] once, in the second year, for playing football and coming to school'. Playing sport as opposed to watching professional football was identified with acceptance of school authority. When some boys at the school put excrement under the headmaster's chair, he contrasted the culprits unfavourably with true school sportsmen: 'Last Friday I was feeling pretty low when I found out about this lot . . . but then I went to football on Saturday, there were several lads and teachers there, playing their hearts out or giving up their time

---

[58] Robbins and Cohen, *Knuckle Sandwich*, p. 89.

just for the school, and then I thought, "Perhaps, it's not so bad after all." '[59]

Naturally this idea of sport is anathema to the hooligan. Middle-class ideals of 'playing the game' have always been alien to rough working-class culture. Deracinated urban youths have built upon this uncompromisingly physical attitude to games and turned it into a different, more aggressive, and organized subculture. Some of West Ham's most violent supporters have come from the satellite estates of north London or new towns like Harlow or Thamesmead. A young messenger-boy for the Post Office described what he thought brought youths to Highbury. 'Success isn't the most important thing, it's got most to do with where you live, which team you support, or where you used to live before you got moved out . . . you go back there, support your old team.' When a group have lost their old territory in which their traditions were established, football provides a symbolic substitute for the young in the heart of the old community. Supporting West Ham was a way of staying an East-Ender, going to the Boleyn pub beside Upton Park and 'steaming in' against rival supporters or immigrants. 'Everyone from our side of the bar used to steam round an' kick fuck out of the Pakis', remarked one hooligan approvingly. 'You get them all standin' in a mob, all talkin' that chapati language an' all that, an' you never know whether they're talkin' about you . . . It was like the black hole of Calcutta down my factory.' Crude racial abuse is widespread on the terraces. Black players have to endure endless taunts except when one scores a goal for the hooligan's team. Pakistanis have the added stigma in the eyes of the white hooligan of tending to be better off, linguistically separate, less physical, and less interested in football. Racism seems to have become one of the most dangerous and distinctive aspects of contemporary football violence in comparison to earlier forms of juvenile disorder and has begun to spread to cricket too. The National Front and other crypto-fascist fringe-groups have consciously attempted to use football as a means of spreading their ideology amongst young

[59] H. J. Parker, *The View from the Boys* (1974), p. 37; P. Willis, *Learning to Labour* (1977), pp. 67, 74.

white workers and have specifically targeted certain clubs such as West Ham and Millwall.[60]

Some of the most vicious and persistent football offenders have connections with fascist organizations, although the bulk of young supporters do not. Here it is important to make a distinction between different types of hooligan. At the apex, as it were, of the hooligan hierarchy are those in their late teens or early twenties who have a record for violence. They are a minority who are drawn to football as a means of fighting; they go seeking 'aggro' and are half-admired, half-feared by the bulk of young fans. In recent years this older element seems to have become more prominent; they are often smartly dressed and travel to games by car or on scheduled train services away from police surveillance, organized in gangs with names like the Inter-City Firm, the Main Line Service Crew, or the Anti-Personnel Firm. They plan their assaults meticulously and even have kept records to produce a league table of violence. They are a small group increasingly watched by the police and sociologically marginal to the hooligan phenomenon. It is the symbolic violence of the teenager on the terraces, which spills over into the odd affray with visiting gangs that is more typical than the premeditated violence of disturbed or habitually aggressive individuals, who see football as a kind of arena for serious assault with little risk of arrest. More extensive use of video film and exemplary sentencing may discourage the ultra-violent minority, but the assembling of large mobs of chanting and charging youngsters at the 'ends' seems to have become an established part of youth culture. Only age restrictions, which would be costly to clubs already financially hard-pressed as well as being difficult to enforce, could stop this. Stoke and Coventry have attempted to bring back families into the game with a 'Lads and Dads' programme. Watford, among other clubs, have tried a similar initiative, though re-creating 'organic' communities of spectators is beyond the scope of well-intentioned clubs.[61]

[60] G. Burn, 'Portrait of a Football Hooligan' (this article appeared in a national Sunday newspaper colour supplement in or around 1982, but despite careful checking I have not been able to find the precise reference). I. Taylor, 'On the Sports' Violence Question', in J. Hargreaves (ed.), *Sport, Culture and Ideology* (1982), provides a useful survey of theories and stresses the danger of fascist infiltration, as do Pratt and Slater, 'A Fresh Look at Football Hooliganism'.

[61] Robbins, *We Hate Humans*, pp. 107–10. Robbins provides the best account of hooliganism 'from below'; *Observer*, 2 June 1985, p. 41.

Serious as it is, the problem of hooliganism has to be kept in proportion. Only a minority of urban youth engages in such behaviour. In several African and South American states there have been far more serious incidents in which large numbers of people have been killed. In one case war was declared over a disputed game. Even in a society without any apparent 'hooligan' problem such as France there was a powerful tradition of misrule before, during, and after games, especially amongst the Rugby players of the south-west. Holland has had its violent confrontations between Amsterdam and Rotterdam teams and their fans; Borussia Dortmund's supporters' club had neo-Nazi links and the fascist Right in Italy have tried to infiltrate the 'ragazzi di stadio', such as the self-styled 'Fighters' of Juventus. American football is notoriously violent. Players in the virtually invincible Yale side around the turn of the century would dip their shirts in blood from an abattoir before a match. American football itself has been described as an exercise in 'controlled violence'. Both baseball and American football abound in 'hooligan' incidents. In 1976 at Foxboro 'one fan stole another's wheelchair, thirty were hospitalized, another stabbed. Two died of coronaries . . . and while a policeman was giving a coronary victim resuscitation, a fan relieved himself on both.' 'Mother, may I slug the umpire, may I slug him right away' was a parody of crowd behaviour at baseball games published by the *Washington Critic* in 1886. Hooliganism is more habitual and more fully developed in Britain than elsewhere, but it is not confined to Britain. Nor is violence confined to football. Rugby, whose spectators are a fairly respectable lot, turns a blind eye to fighting on the field. Slinging the odd punch is part of the game and the recent imprisonment of a prominent Welsh player for a blatant and dangerous assault was criticized by most players and supporters. In a recent 'friendly' fixture between Penygraig and Brencethin youth teams the referee himself was assaulted. His nose was broken in two places by a player he had sent off for violent play.[62]

Football hooliganism, therefore, can neither be explained in terms of simple continuities nor as an abrupt discontinuity; the

---

[62] L. Kutcher, 'The American Sport Event as Carnival', *Journal of Popular Culture*, Spring 1983, pp. 35–6; B. Rader, *American Sports* (1983), ch. 4; *Guardian*, 11 Jan. 1984, p. 22.

location and the specific forms of juvenile riotousness were new but the phenomenon itself was as old as the hills. This is why it is so perplexing. One face of the hooligan is thoroughly traditional. When young supporters chant 'We'll be running round Pompey with our willies hanging out, singing I've got a bigger one than you', or some other scatological rhyme, slightly changed to fit the time and place, they are doing nothing new. This kind of rudeness goes back to Rabelais and far beyond. The same went for the man who complained in the following terms to a local government committee for 'Better Football': 'I visited the New Stand lavatories. After two minutes I was showered with hot tea and a selection of cakes from the next door cubicle. Then a couple of Jumping Jack fireworks came over the top, one of which fell into my underpants. No sooner had I thrown it into the toilet than it exploded and I was spattered with the pan's contents. At this point I heard a gale of raucous laughter.' This suspiciously hilarious incident sounds as if it had been polished in the telling, as many hooligan incidents are. There are archetypal anecdotes which crop up again and again in one form or another. There is the one where a madcap home supporter gingerly urinates from above on opposition fans who are innocently drinking tea in what they take to be a gentle drizzle. A variant of this is the celebrated Celtic and Rangers story about a lone fan caught by the opposition and made to fetch the hot Bovril at half-time. His captors keep one of his shoes to make sure he comes back, and return it to him filled with excrement. On recounting the tale to a journalist, the victim is asked if he thinks there will ever be an end to this cycle of violence, to which he answers, 'No, as long as they keep shitting in our shoes, we'll keep pissing in their Bovril.' Antics of this kind had been the stuff of carnival throughout western Europe for centuries. In nineteenth-century Paris young revellers would melt down chocolate and smear horrified passers-by with what they took to be excrement. Examples of loose continuities could be multiplied *ad infinitum*. Fighting and joking, after all, were the main amusements of bachelors in pre-industrial Europe. An anthropologist who by chance was travelling recently on a ferry during a battle between Manchester United and West Ham fans observed a distinct similarity with the ritual warfare of tribal societies. 'They seemed to be enjoying themselves immensely, making a lot of noise, rushing dramatically up and down the stairs, spraying the fire-hoses everywhere, and throwing the occasional bottle or glass at the other side.' As they did so 'they experienced a transcendent moment of community with their mates'.[63]

So where does this leave us? Pre-industrial survival or contemporary malaise? The special circumstances of territorial displacement and the withdrawal of adult supervision, which appear to have been more pronounced in Britain than in other parts of western Europe where the family is stronger as a recreational unit, have made the problem worse here than elsewhere; this has led to the formation of the 'ends' which in turn has tended to attract a small fascist and psychotic fringe. Hooliganism is not one but several overlapping phenomena—traditional misrule, new forms of territorial aggression, youth styles both invented or reflected in the media. All this is combined with the resentment of ethnic minorities by those who see football as a way of reasserting their national pride. Chauvinism, local and national, lies at the heart of hooliganism and England fans seem to find in foreigners a convenient target for a vague resentment at Britain's diminished place in the world. Football has become a substitute for patriotism amongst the disaffected, half-educated white working-class youth of a nation which only a generation ago was respected and feared throughout the world. Street-fighting and village brawls at football matches were so much a part of 'traditional' society that we tend to forget how relatively civilized modern social life has become. There are manifest continuities between the rites of violence in contemporary Britain and earlier periods. But the *specific forms* of hooliganism *are* new; football crowds were not segregated by age before the 1960s; youth did not congregate around parts of football clubs as their territory—they had a larger territory and community which they shared with their older male relatives. When there were fights at football matches there was no dramatic media coverage. All of these features have combined to create the contemporary problem; hooliganism exemplifies to perfection the difficulty of disentangling what is new from what is old in social history.

[63] Pratt and Slater, 'A Fresh Look at Football Hooliganism', p. 205; *Private Eye*, 10 Jan. 1986, citing *Croydon Advertiser*, 2 Nov. 1985; Marsh, Rosser, and Harré, *Rites of Disorder*, p. 72; 'Geoff's wicked act', *Guardian*, 18 Aug. 1986, p. 18.

6
Conclusion

IN 1965 a Sports Council was set up to advise the government on future policy on sport and physical education. This was a novel step and came from the advice of the Wolfenden Committee which reported in 1960 on 'Sport and the Community'. Wolfenden was commissioned not by the state but by the Central Council of Physical Recreation (CCPR), which had been set up in 1935 as a co-ordinating body for the many voluntary associations involved in the running of sport. Alongside the CCPR there was the National Playing Fields Association formed in 1925 to increase urban playing space; there was also some limited provision of physical training facilities for the unemployed in the 1930s by the National Council for Social Service. But all of these organizational initiatives stopped well short of full-blooded state intervention. Even the Physical Training and Recreation Act of 1937, which made funds available to promote fitness amidst rumours of war and the realities of domestic rearmament, was exceedingly modest in scope with a meagre two-million-pound budget in comparison with the vast sums spent on 'Kraft durch Freude' by the Third Reich and Mussolini's 'Dopolavoro' programme. The small-state tradition of the Victorians was strong and resilient. There was a very restricted physical education 'establishment' in the form of specialist colleges for teacher-training. These institutions were concerned mainly with gymnastics and confined largely to women until after the Second World War. Games were not even made compulsory in state schools until 1944 despite the importance of athleticism in private education. The ideology of amateurism discouraged the notion that sport was an appropriate sphere of state activity. The government even declined an invitation to take part in an UNESCO conference on 'The Place of Sport in Education' in 1954. It was not that sport was unimportant. On the contrary, sport was a characteristic, almost a birthright of Britons everywhere.

But its virtues would be sapped if it was 'nationalized'. Sport was the true province of private persons in private clubs and tampering with this smacked of an authoritarianism foreign to all that Britons—Labour, Liberal, and Tory—held most dear.

The full story of how this attitude has gradually changed cannot be told here. My purpose has been to account for the rise and consolidation of amateurism rather than to catalogue its contemporary decline. Pressure to increase state involvement came from various directions. There was the huge extension of state activity in other areas of social life that came about as a result of the 'warfare means welfare' principle of the 1940s. If sport was 'a good thing', then the state should provide for it within the framework of the welfare state along with health and education. The limits of what had formerly been considered the proper role of the state had changed. Additionally the growing importance of the media, especially radio and television, highlighted the relatively poor performance of British sportsmen and women at an international level. Britain only won one gold medal in the 1952 Olympics and that was in an equestrian event. The Soviet Union had entered international sport with a vengeance, throwing the weight of a massive state machine against West European and American dominance of athletics. Cold War influences filtered through gradually and merged with a growing concern about the effects of increased leisure and affluence on the young, especially the problem of delinquency. 'It is easy to ridicule the "that's not cricket old boy" attitude,' remarked Wolfenden, 'but in its deeper (and usually inarticulate) significance it still provides something like the foundations of an ethical standard which may not be highly intellectual but does have a considerable influence on the day-to-day behaviour of millions of people.' It took a Labour Government less inhibited than the Tories with their informal links to the amateur élite to bring sport within the ambit of the welfare state by setting up the Sports Council.[1]

The consequences of state intervention since 1964 have been usefully summarized in a recent report of the Sports Council on 'The Impact of the Sport For All Policy, 1966–84'. The efforts of the state have mainly gone into providing better facilities for

[1] J. Hargreaves, *Sport, Power and Culture* (1986), p. 183.

sport, especially in inner cities. This rather belated official intervention has not met with much success. ' "Sport For All" has done little to overcome the inequalities present at the start of the campaign', conclude the report's authors. Sports centres with excellent pitches and pools have been built but they have either been under used or more often patronized by groups who already had a high participation ratio, especially adult male car-owners. The unskilled, women, the older members of community, and rough youths on the delinquent fringe have been conspicuous by their absence. This is not the place to enter into a debate about contemporary sports policy. The point is rather to stress the limits of state action. The mere provision of facilities is not enough. As this book has insisted over and over again, sport is to do with attitudes and values not just with exercise. Peter McIntosh, the co-author of this report and a pioneer in the historical study of sport in modern Britain, concludes that the state via the Sports Council should 'base both research and promotion on enjoyment rather than social function'. Commitment to sport has to be freely given; it has to be fun; it cannot be foisted on to the poor or the wayward from above because it is good for them.[2]

This brings us back to a central theme of *Sport and the British*: the extraordinary degree to which it has been promoted privately without politicians, employers, or trade unionists taking a significant part except as enthusiastic individual sportsmen. People have created their own kinds of pleasure through sport and there has been no powerful institutional 'push' of the kind that came, for example, from the French Church after 1905 or the German Social Democratic Party of the Wilhelmine era. Britain even lagged behind the United States in the provision of industrial recreation facilities. Muscular Christians and middle-class moralists in a private capacity certainly boosted the cause of games. But their ideals had only limited influence on the way games were played and understood by the mass of manual workers. This leads naturally to another key point: whatever social or political meanings are attached to sport by different groups, participation remains intensely sociable and largely organized around the institution of the individual 'club'—a

[2] P. C. McIntosh and V. Charlton, *The Impact of the 'Sport for All' Policy, 1966-1984* (1986), pp. 190–3.

neglected social creation of the Victorians. Conviviality has been at the heart of sport. The fierce rivalries of teams and top competitors has masked the warmth of participating together in a team or standing on the terraces cheering on your side. Sport is more about making friends, building communities, and sharing experiences than keeping fit. There may be hostility to rivals but there is also the deep sense of solidarity and identity that comes from fierce loyalties to a place or a people.

This sociability has been largely male. Female participation in sport has been negligible until recently. Men have kept women out of sport except as helpers for those aspects of club life like dances and teas which were not segregated. When Frankenberg went to carry out anthropological research in a village on the Welsh borders in the early 1950s he found that the village football team provided 'a symbol of village unity and cohesion against the outside world' and had 'a central place in village social activity'. The team had a supporters' club in which local women were represented. Conflict arose when their wishes over the use of club funds towards a Coronation carnival were ignored by the men. The women demanded their 'gifts' of time and interest to the club be reciprocated by the donation of time and money by the players for the collective life of the community. Female *social* participation may have been more widespread than has been realized. Women have certainly been socially active in middle-class sports like tennis and golf, which also have a significant element of active female participation. But in sport as a whole they have been mostly conspicuous by their absence. In swimming—the single most popular physical recreation after walking—the importance of teaching children to swim has drawn in some women and competitive swimming is a very important sport for girls. As the social secretary of a swimming-club remarked, 'you start off by just coming down to watch . . . and gradually you start to get involved'. She had to admit that she found swimming 'a bit boring really' but there was the possibility of shared recreation. 'We were always very interested in the dances'—the links between sport, dances, and courtship is a world of its own which would repay further study. Female involvement may have been at the fringes, though what took place in this 'marginal' area may turn out to have been more important than long-forgotten events on the field of play. However, the social integration element, though unduly neglected, should not be pressed too hard, especially amongst urban workers. Observers of a mining community in the 1950s noted that 'husband and wife live separate and in a sense secret lives . . . it is a point of honour among men to keep some time for drinking and attending sporting events with their mates'. After a year or two of marriage 'men return once more to the company of their mates'. In modern Britain sport has been one of the ways that men have kept themselves apart, defined their own territory, and indulged their enthusiasms. What the Edwardians called 'boy-life' had its own kind of 'clubbable' logic whether amongst the 'Old Boys' of the Long Room or on the terraces of Old Trafford.[3]

The pattern of male involvement, however, has depended primarily on social class with important regional and national variations. The way changing class structures and urban experience have moulded sport has been the central concern of the book. Chapter 1 examined the nature and decline of traditional forms of sport. Old-established festive customs, in which sports mixed with eating, dancing, and drinking according to the traditions of the Church and agricultural practice, were gradually eroded. Different activities declined at different times and in different ways. Animal sports were put down by crusading urban and evangelical pressure. The creation of a private association to prosecute offenders and chivvy local and central government into action was a pioneering effort in Victorian middle-class moral interference in the lives of the poor. Yet the prohibition of cock-fighting and animal-baiting was only politically possible because of the tacit consent of the landed élite, who had already largely deserted these activities for more exclusive and civilized ones. Disgust at cruel sports came to be a distinguishing feature of British life. Even a vocal minority of skilled manual workers supported the ban. The same applied to traditional football except that in this case legislation merely banned the game from the public highway. Football, however, had lost much of its rumbustiousness before it was outlawed from the streets. Still, the continuities were as important as the changes. Cricket and

---

[3] R. Frankenberg, *Village on the Border* (1957), pp. 51, 100; Dennis, Henriques, and Slaughter, *Coal is our Life*, cited in R. Frankenberg, *Communities in Britain* (1966), pp. 125–6; P. Hoggett and J. Bishop, *Organising around Enthusiasms* (1986), p. 114.

horse-racing prospered, drawing good crowds and plenty of money. Prize-fighting remained popular, though technically illegal, until the 1880s. Increasingly publicans took over the task of providing facilities for sports which had once been enjoyed on the streets or on common land. Sporting grounds were opened alongside pubs, and by the mid-nineteenth century, there were plenty of independent commercial grounds where 'pedestrian' events were held. Although the Highways Act of 1835 steadily drove pedestrianism off the roads, it did not drive it out of existence. Athletics was a popular sport before the age of the Oxbridge blue and village cricket was thriving when county cricket was still unknown.

There was no leisure vacuum in early Victorian Britain. Rather there had been a subtle unravelling of what had once been a more integrated pattern of recreation. First, the withdrawal of the gentry and later their large tenants from rural life coincided with growing criticism and interference from an increasingly powerful middle class. Second, the combined forces of civilized distaste gradually had an effect on the working-class élite whilst the actual times and spaces for the old sports both in town and country were ever more restricted. By no means all of the old sports were abandoned, but they were more or less confined either to the margins of community life or to the remoter parts of the nation. This was particularly evident as far as the young were concerned. The special place that they had enjoyed in traditional sports was much reduced. Either they joined in with their adult workmates or they played children's games in the streets. Ancient games did survive amongst the young and continued to be enjoyed into the middle of this century, but their songs and rhymes, and the old chasing, throwing, and racing games were increasingly regarded as puerile. Adults would have been thought foolish to take part in what were now only infantile amusements. The enthusiasm of the common people for the old sports was weakened to such an extent that there was a genuine receptiveness on the part of the mass of the population to the revised forms of play that were being nurtured amongst the privileged in the mid-Victorian public schools.

There were two sides of middle-class sport. The first was the code of amateurism as embodied in public school games; the second was the emergence of suburban recreation. Amateurism provided a bridge between the old world of aristocratic values and the new one of bourgeois exertion and competitiveness. Fair play embodied a new philosophy that was probably more pervasive and influential than the more widely known 'work-ethic' and 'call to seriousness' amongst the Victorians. The dynamism and distinctiveness of the new private educational system with its unprecedented cult of games is perhaps the best-known aspect of the social history of sport. 'Athleticism', as it was sometimes called, was a kind of moral code or system of ideas. Public school sport and the 'old-boy' network helped foster a sense of solidarity rather than social division between landed wealth, the new industrial élites, and the liberal professions. Yet sport did not bind the whole of the bourgeoisie and the aristocracy together. The middle classes were split between the northern industrial element, which tolerated professionalism and took directorships of Football League and Rugby League clubs, and the bankers, brokers, doctors, lawyers, civil servants, and schoolmasters who formed the bulk of the amateur establishment in southern England. That amateurism was both a code of ethics and a system of status was borne out by the fact that 'amateur' was often used in conjunction with 'gentleman'. The two went hand in hand until the later nineteenth century.

One way of defining the middle classes is to try to understand how they kept themselves morally distinct from the lower orders. An alternative perspective comes from looking at what they did rather than what they said. In practice, the force of amateur values was slowly eroded. Nationalism, the media, and market forces were partly responsible. But changing middle-class manners and values were also important. There was a shift towards a more casual, private, and hedonistic style of life. The late Victorian and Edwardian period offered low taxes, cheap servant labour, and reasonable returns of capital whilst the retail price index fell by around 10 per cent between the wars. By 1939 there were two million private cars and taxation was no more than 10 per cent for a man on £500 a year. 'You need money in this England,' as Priestley said, 'but you do not need much money.' Suburban commuters, who increasingly formed the bulk of the middle-aged middle classes, were often rather hazy about 'the games ethic' and confined the ideal of amateurism to rugby, cricket, or athletics. Amateurism waned as a set of values for living. Golf had rules of 'etiquette' rather than an ethic of fair play and public service. Being middle class was becoming more a matter of consumption than of belief. Any family could join in provided they had the money and were not Jewish—racism thrived tolerably well in meritocratic suburbia where Jews sometimes had to form their own clubs. What better forum for conspicuous consumption than the locker-room or the golf club car-park? Whilst paying lip service to the sporting values of the public schools, suburban man was busy with less physically and morally taxing forms of exercise. The mould of cheerful materialism was starting to take shape.[4]

The amateur ideal prospered in its purest form in the Empire. 'Athleticism' provided a crucial, distinctive element in the British 'imperial idea'. A flair for games and a talent for government went hand in hand. The British were a superior race, blessed with exceptional energy, toughness, and qualities of leadership, which they refined in their play and used throughout the world to promote the rule of law, the Christian religion, and the 'rational' use of economic resources. This 'civilizing mission' was both a 'burden' and a 'duty' as well as being a source of pleasurable employment and riches. Such was the self-image of Empire, which spread out from the public schools and into the public mind with the growth of the popular press and the introduction of compulsory primary education. Banner headlines and patriotic textbooks told the British they were 'an imperial race'—a message pictorially reinforced on biscuit-tins, sauce-bottles, and cigarette-cards. Youth movements were fiercely loyal to Crown and colonies, especially the 'Boy Scouts', which their founder, Baden-Powell, at first had wished to name the 'Imperial Scouts'. Then there was the elaborate and explicitly imperial ceremonial that surrounded the monarch in life and in death. This helped pave the way for the full-blooded domestication of the idea of Empire at the popular imperial exhibitions held first at Wembley and later in Glasgow between the wars. All this helped provide a favourable climate for imperial sport—Test matches, rugby tours, and ultimately the institution of the Empire Games itself. Whilst sport offered an acceptable outlet for Dominion nationalism it also proved a useful tool for incorporating indigenous rulers into the

---

[4] Priestley cited in J. Stevenson, *British Society 1914–45* (1984), pp. 117, 130.

running of the Empire, especially in India. Even with decolonization and the cutting of formal colonial ties, a sport like cricket in the West Indies has consolidated good relations.

Coexisting—sometimes uneasily—with imperialism there was domestic nationalism. Sport has helped to give the English a coherent national culture no less than it has the Irish, the Welsh, or the Scots. It also spread English values through the Empire which became hopelessly confused with 'Britishness'. For it was the English élite, formed in those new institutions of national culture, the public schools, who ran the show. Despite strong parochial and provincial loyalties, the pull of sport as part of a national culture in England grew stronger between the wars. And this in turn fed the flames of a wider imperial culture of British sports. Since the 1960s the problem of South Africa, which goes beyond the scope of the present survey, has placed far greater strains on Commonwealth sporting links than ever before. Yet they continue, still surprisingly vigorous, though how long the Commonwealth Games can survive boycotts of the kind mounted at Edinburgh in 1986 is much less certain. Historically sport has broadly been a cohesive force in imperial relations. Only the nationalist Irish explicitly exempted themselves from the interplay of national identity and shared sentiments through games. The Irish enforced a 'Ban' on British sports in the sense that those who wished to play Gaelic football or hurling under the aegis of the Gaelic Athletic Association could not also play football or cricket. The Welsh and Scots adopted a different tactic which was more in keeping with their less explicitly political expression of nationality. Rugby in South Wales and football in central Scotland reflected a new sense of working-class cultural nationalism which was distinct from the bardic celebrations in Wales and the romanticism of readers of Sir Walter Scott and nostalgic expatriates.

Nationalism was only one element in the working-class sporting tradition. The range and richness of sport as a component of popular culture has been overlooked by those who take a 'diffusionist' view, concentrating on how middle-class games and values were passed on to industrial workers via muscular Christians and social reformers. Two major points emerged in our analysis of popular participation. First, there was no effective imposition of middle-class games on urban workers in the name of 'social control' or 'rational recreation'; second, a distinct and introverted tradition of sport grew up combining old-established popular traditions within a more systematic national framework. While there was no shortage of articulate individuals with the *intention* of improving the lower orders through their play, the impact of churches, youth movements, and employers was largely restricted to the provision of facilities and routine organization. Ideologically they did not get very far. Such ventures never formed more than a significant minority of the total number of clubs, most of which were based on street or neighbourhood groups set up and run by ordinary working people. These clubs did not necessarily take their sport in the spirit of fair play. Fierce local loyalties and rivalries were the life-blood of the amateur football leagues just as they had been in parish recreations a century before, and this carried over into commercial spectator sport, which offered a new kind of community life and identity. As industrial communities became established on a grander scale with second, third, and fourth generation residents, there was a need to express territoriality in new ways.

This tension between change and continuity is the key to understanding the inner meaning as opposed to the outward form of working-class sport. Hence the attachment to gambling. Here the traditions of the gentry and the common people met in joint rejection of the middle-class sporting morality that outlawed betting in the name of decency and 'character'. Horse-racing, a sport that had largely remained in the hands of the aristocracy and which was the object of criticism from bourgeois ideologues and socialists alike, grew rapidly in popularity. Rationality, so dear to the reforming heart, ironically found its fullest expression in the picking of winners after careful perusal of 'the sporting intelligence'. Calculating the draws on the coupon, the odds on a dog, the speed of a bird might draw upon reserves of numeracy and judgement, but this did not betoken the triumph of a 'scientific world-view'. Record-breaking and the alleged mania for quantification cannot properly explain the appeal of sport. A new precision was certainly present and this was important for the dedicated few. But statistics were not at the heart of the thing except for the occasional schoolboy or zealot. Nor, on the other hand, was violence. Edwardian working-class sport as a whole was less violent than it had been a half-century before.

Even ratting contests and prize-fights seemed to lose their appeal in the last quarter of the century. The tradition of gambling that had been associated with brutal sports came to be centred on horse-racing and later football. Boxing, or football for that matter, was still pretty rough and the crowds could be crude and rowdy, but the overall impression was of a more orderly world. Popular recreation was more 'rational' in a bureaucratic sense and it was more respectable than before, but its pleasures remained deeply traditional: drinking and betting, chaffing your mates and cheering on the standard-bearers of your real or adopted territory.

This, at least, was the way things were until the third quarter of this century. Since the Second World War Britain's industrial and imperial heyday has passed and with it a peculiarly British way of playing. Most dramatic has been the demise of the amateur. The MCC abolished the distinction between gentlemen and players in the early 1960s. Henceforth there would only be 'cricketers'. Wimbledon followed suit a little later by opening up competition to professional tennis players. Amateurism was scrapped at the same moment that the imperial structure it had helped to sustain was itself wound up. Simultaneously the status of the professional improved as players began to assert themselves not as 'club servants' or 'skilled workmen' but as entertainers who should be paid in accordance with their market value. Footballers successfully abolished the imposition of the maximum wage, though the retain-and-transfer system took longer to scrap. British sport began for the first time to embrace commercialism, although the process was cautious and gradual. The Football League, for example, has only accepted shirt advertising and full commercial sponsorship in the last few years. The Amateur Athletic Association have clung to their name despite condoning the principle that athletes be paid—often very large sums—provided it is done through the setting up of 'trust funds'. Behind these profound changes lies the impact of television combined with a shift in the values of the organizing élite. Media coverage now offers the possibility of enormously increased revenue from advertising either directly or indirectly through named sponsors. The idea of 'the game for the game's sake' that underpinned athleticism as a moral code has come to seem strangely antiquated. Gentlemanly distaste for 'trade' is as out of place in sport as it is in the Conservative Party of Mrs Thatcher.

Alongside the late entry of capitalism into sport, which is bringing Britain closer to the commercialism of the Tour de France or the Superbowl—both of which significantly have begun to attract British audiences in sizeable numbers in the later 1980s—there lie two pressing issues: the decline of live audiences for sport and the rise of a hooligan subculture. The old crowd controls at football matches have gone as working men increasingly stay at home to watch sport, leaving the stadium— or the unseated 'ends' at least—as an arena for the young. Football has become the focus for a new kind of identity for working-class male youth and it is quite possible that other forms of sport— cricket for instance—will be similarly used. Fierce loyalties to a professional club—often located outside an adolescent's immediate territory as is the case with many Manchester United or Liverpool supporters attracted by playing success, glamour, and television coverage—create new juvenile communities, who briefly suspend hostilities at internationals in the cause of English chauvinism.

No wonder George Orwell had no respect for sport. By chance the writing of this book began in 1984 amidst a flood of neo-Orwellian speculation about nuclear war, the ecology of the planet, information technology, the North–South dialogue, and the dangers of television. Then, as abruptly as it had pitched camp, the caravan moved on. Gratefully or guiltily, we plunged back into the present with its reassuring calendar of events from Wembley to Wimbledon, from Lord's to Twickenham, from Ascot to 'The Open'. The apocalyptic stock-taking was put aside for some future anniversary or crisis. Sport resumed its place at the centre of male culture providing familiar landmarks for private lives, giving a kind of chronology or structure to the year. There is no escaping sport. Each year the time devoted to it and the importance attached to it, especially on television, seems to increase. The cult of sport sometimes seems to take on the quality of an Orwellian nightmare. Will the next millennium see man obsessed by athletic entertainment to the exclusion of other kinds of culture? Will the state promote sport as a safe, numbing kind of nationalistic cocoon for healthy, obedient citizens? If the past is anything to go by—and what better measure do we have?— this will not happen. Sport may be taken too seriously; high-performance spectator sport is arguably too central to our lives already. But the friendliness and common sense of ordinary players, the humour, excitement, and the fun it affords offer reasonable grounds for hope. These values will mediate the impact of mass culture. The relationship between the two will determine the shape of British sport in the future.

APPENDIX

SOME OBSERVATIONS ON SOCIAL HISTORY AND THE SOCIOLOGY OF SPORT

SOCIOLOGISTS frequently complain that historians lack a conceptual framework for their research, whilst historians tend to feel social theorists require them to compress the diversity of the past into artificially rigid categories and dispense with empirical verification of their theories. In truth both disciplines need each other, and distinguished authorities in both areas have recently emphasized the interdependence of sociology and history in the identification and pursuit of common problems in social science. The purpose of this short appendix, however, is not to hold forth about the elusive goal of interdisciplinary research nor to set out a sociology of sport. I simply wish to make more explicit the reasons for the thematic approach I have taken and to spell out the organizing concepts implicit in this study.[1]

History crudely weighted down with the apparatus of theory and couched in specialist language spoils the enjoyment of a subject without enhancing our understanding of it. Clarity must be a precondition of explanation. Hence I have avoided the formal vocabulary of much recent sociological research into sport with its 'negotiation of hegemonic values', 'commodification of athletic products', and 'cultural reification' amongst other highly abstract formulations. It seems particularly ironic that studies of phenomena that are by definition popular tend to be carried on in terms that even highly educated non-specialists have great difficulty in following. Few stay the course and the gap between the new theorists of sport and the ordinary historian can seem unbridgeable. Take the following sentence from a new journal which has published theoretical work on sport: 'Massification as the negation of publics designates that moral inter-subjectivity as a process of need expression and sublimation is replaced by corporatized, desublimating modes.' Most historians of sport would dismiss such writing out of hand as pretentious and incomprehensible. Such a reaction is quite understandable, and often sensible. Yet hacking through the thickets of jargon, there are some good

---

[1] For example, P. Burke, *Sociology and History* (1980), and P. Abrams, 'History, Sociology and Historical Sociology', *Past and Present*, May 1980, which summarizes his more extensive *Historical Sociology* (1982).

358 *Appendix*

things to be found. The author of the excruciating sentence quoted above may have a serious point to make about the way sport historically has dramatized deeply shared community values. Nowadays, he argues, the power of big business and the media has turned moral 'heroes' into paid 'stars'. Of course, such interesting ideas remain nothing more than assertions unless proper historical evidence for them can be produced. This is why the theorists and the historians should get together. We should be trying to talk to each other and we are not doing so. This is a further reason for my making explicit what limited theoretical borrowing I have done in the writing of this book.[2]

The first hurdle for the historian seeking assistance from the body of work loosely termed the 'sociology of sport' is the lack of any degree of consensus about what the subject entails or the guiding principles of analysis. Social scientists express little surprise about this. As there is no broad agreement on anything in sociology, why should sport be any different? 'The defining characteristic of sociology ought to be the special tension between a critical attitude to the broad frameworks available and an imaginative approach to the sheer data', as a recent practitioner aptly puts its. But the non-specialist expecting consensus may find all this perplexing at first, and some give up at this stage. There is a tendency for some historians to expect 'sociology' to hand them ready-made concepts 'off the shelf' that they can cheerfully take back and apply uncritically to their evidence. When they find that sociologists quite reasonably disagree profoundly about what it is they are trying to explain and how they should go about it, the historian retreats into the 'facts' and constructs his 'stories' based frequently upon the sequence of what seem to be significant events in a chosen individual activity. Such 'selection' of themes is based upon previous work in the area, existing evidence, and more or less shrewd 'hunches' about where to go next. However, though some fine work has been produced in this fashion, the criteria of 'significance' remain hard to pin down. Why do we focus on one set of themes rather than others? How do we pick out and define the problems we want to solve? This is without doubt the major obstacle for anyone writing a general history.[3]

The preoccupation of much contemporary research on sport has been of a fairly limited empirical kind—a positivistic sociology of who plays what. Whilst such data is clearly relevant to recreation management, which has emerged as a distinct specialism in recent years, relatively little of this kind of work has been done historically. More of this basic work is needed in history where problems of collecting data are often very

---

[2] J. Alt, 'Sport and Cultural Reification', *Theory, Culture and Society*, 1983 (3), pp. 99, 102.
[3] J. Eldridge, *Recent British Sociology* (1980), p. 36.

serious. What do we do after we have found out, for example, how many men/women, young/old, rich/poor individuals engage in certain sports? A simple explanation of patterns in terms of access to facilities or the resources required does not take us far. Why, for example, is Rugby Union a popular game in Wales and a middle-class one in England? The answer to such questions cannot come from mere reference to facilities. The social structure of Welsh rugby needs to be set in the context of a new kind of 'Welshness' that grew out of the impact of economic growth and immigration upon pre-existing cultural traditions. Additionally this 'Welshness' of rugby has to be set against a kind of 'Englishness' based upon the triumph of a code of amateurism nurtured in the social élite. Hence an apparently simple question takes us straight into the heart of a complex debate about the class structure of Britain and the relations between different historical components of the state. Awareness of the nature of the problem comes both from a historical understanding of the national structure of Great Britain and from a theoretical standpoint that sees sport not just as a straightforward physical activity but as a social process through which cultural meanings are produced.[4]

This leads us into the thick of sociological argument. Until quite recently the sociology of sport tended to see organized physical activity as unproblematic. Sport was a natural human phenomenon, the specific forms of which were determined by the 'modernity' of the context in which it took place, i.e. by the levels of industrialization and urbanization and by the accompanying degree of bureaucratic control and regulation. The trouble with such 'modernization' theories of sport is precisely that they do not account for the distinctiveness of sports within and between different classes and nations. 'Modernization' sees sport as a natural activity which has simply been adjusted to fit the changing demands of space and time in a new world of factory and clerical labour. 'Traditional' society with its agricultural rhythms and religious holidays gave way to 'modern' industrial society, and sport accordingly became time-conscious, codified, and nationally administered. The appropriateness of a game like Association football to urban life in the late Victorian city is a useful point to make. We must not throw out the baby with the bath water. 'Modernization' must not be swept aside just because it is simple. The trouble is that such an explanation does not take us very far in understanding why certain groups of people preferred one activity to another and why quite culturally specific meanings were attached to

---

[4] P. McIntosh and V. Charlton, *The Impact of the 'Sport For All' Policy, 1966–84* (1986), summarizes research on patterns of participation and stresses the need for more work on the perception of sport 'from below' rather than the provision of facilities 'from above'.

sports in different places and at different times. To assume all sports are essentially similar in their significance just because they mainly take place in industrial cities is deeply misleading. It is not so much that a 'traditional/modern' typology of sport is wrong in itself but that it simply does not tackle the most interesting questions. It is precisely the differences between England and Ireland or France and America, for example, or between working-class and middle-class forms which prompt our curiosity. The crux of the matter for historian and sociologist alike is the perception of sport and the varying cultural meanings that are attached to games—sometimes to the same game—by different social groups or by different forces within the state that command our attention. This is what sets the serious study of sport apart from the enthusiast's unthinking and happy absorption in it. On the basis of my previous research on France and as I progressed with research for this book, the tension between fairly obvious changes in the material context of sport—hours of work, rates of pay, communications, urban densities, and so on—and the power of 'traditional' aspects of sport (especially its role in sustaining various forms of male community) emerged as the central theme. In other words, beneath the apparently simple transformation of sport into a 'modern' activity lay a whole range of arresting ideas about the role of sport which were positively obscured by the assumption that sport could be reduced to a kind of automatic response to the forces of industrialization.[5]

If the historian wishes to go beyond 'modernization' an approach which accepts the plurality of sport is vital. This is harder to find in the realm of social theory than one might imagine. Theorists are by the very nature of their purpose generally concerned with the inner coherence of a body of ideas. Whether the resulting theory corresponds to the diversity of the subject it seeks to explain is another matter. When it comes to sport 'the problem' is usually perceived to be establishing the 'essence' of sport. This involves defining some of the chief characteristics either a priori or by examining what those activities held to be sports have in common. Of the latter kind we have assertions about the 'religious' nature of sport, its transcendence of utility, and the personal growth it is held to promote. As a radical alternative there is one Marxist view of sport which concentrates on the extension of capital into leisure (the 'commodification' thesis). There is a neo-Marxist theory, which combines Marx and Freud to assert that sport is in essence a way of repressing the potentially liberating forces of the libido—of sexual energy—into alienated forms of exercise which emphasize the worklike and competitive. For followers of J.-M. Brohm, for example, sport is a

[5] For a critique of 'modernization' see T. Judt, 'A Clown in Regal Purple', *History Workshop Journal*, Spring 1979, pp. 66–92.

ceaseless and absurd struggle for records at the expense of more sensible and sociable impulses. Another 'essentialist' position is put forward by Allen Guttman in a thoughtful book which seeks to rebut the neo-Marxist argument. In *From Ritual to Record* he suggests that the key distinguishing feature of modern sport is the expression of Weberian rationality, the triumph of the scientific and bureaucratic world-view. The Protestant ethic has triumphed as sport has become a matter of keeping records of performance and constantly trying to improve upon them. Finally, mention must be made of the important contribution of Norbert Elias and his disciple Eric Dunning, who insist that sport must be seen as part of a wider 'civilizing process' involving the gradual internalizing of standards of self-control and gentility percolating down the social structure over centuries. Like Guttman, Elias and Dunning have gone to some pains to attempt to prove their case historically. Indeed historical change is built into their theory, although to the historian their impressive work still seems to be a little 'one-dimensional', lacking context; it involves 'reading off' changes in the past as part of a linear 'developmental sociology'.[6]

My purpose is not to elaborate upon such ideas or to evaluate them. It is simply to highlight a few of the many theories put forward to explain sport and to indicate the difficulty facing anyone seeking to draw upon theory to explain the general development of sport over time. The person who attempts a synthesis soon realizes that sport may be a single word but it is not a single thing; this is the nub of the matter. There is casual play, organized participation, and full professionalism; there are team-games and individual ones. Perhaps we should pay rather more attention to the warnings of Wittgenstein and his followers over the use of words. Social theorists want to give precise meanings to words. If we can define sport, runs the argument, then perhaps we can explain it. Any right definition presupposes that the phenomenon can be reduced to the kind of manageable proportions required for the isolating of its 'essence'. But language is just not like this. Words are not used in a forensic fashion. Language is social and changing; meanings depend upon the context in which words are used and there is no reason to suppose a common core of meaning can be attached to a single word.[7]

---

[6] For a broad hegemonic survey see J. Hargreaves (ed.), *Sport, Culture and Ideology* (1982), chs. 1 and 2; J.-M. Brohm, *Sport: A Prison of Measured Time* (1978) asserts the displacement of libido view; the most convenient introduction to Elias and Dunning is E. Dunning (ed.), *The Sociology of Sport* (1971), and their recent *Quest for Excitement* (1986). I have made use of the 'civilizing process' but I cannot accept it as an all-embracing and unifying principle.

[7] J. M. Hoberman, *Sport and Political Ideology* (1984) surveys the different uses made of sport by conflicting ideologies; see also T. Mason, *Sport in Britain* (1988), ch. 3, 'Theory and Opinion'. I am grateful to Dr G. Kitching, who is currently working on Wittgenstein and the social sciences, for bringing the relevance of his work to my attention.

Hence the recent difficulty of the Sports Council in getting any
agreement about what constituted 'sport' and their weary, anodyne
formulation to the effect that it should involve 'an acceptable balance
of physical effort and skill'. Most of those questioned thought sport
should have a competitive element but this view was not universally
accepted. 'Physical recreations' are often also played as 'sports' and referred
to as such. Swimming and fishing are two of the most popular 'sports'
in Britain even though most are content to splash around the pool or
sit peacefully by the canal without catching much. Some people even
thought gardening and cooking were 'sports' as both required physical
skill and can be competitive. This clearly is going a bit far, but common
sense requires us to admit that when a person says 'I like sport' it can mean
'I like fierce competition', 'I like a jog round the park', or 'being part
of a big crowd', or 'watching athletes of all kinds on television'. Sport,
therefore, is *not* reducible to a single essence. The writer of a historical
synthesis is not out to champion one theory or another. What may seem
conceptually confused and unacceptable to the theorist may be
appropriate and right for the historian drawing on different theories to
illuminate different aspects of what is in reality not a single phenomenon
but a set of loosely related activities shifting their forms and meanings
over time. Eclecticism is justified provided it is reasoned and critical.
There are certainly aspects of high-performance sport, which in recent
years have been turned into 'commodities', though the history of sport
as a business belies facile generalizations about the origins of this in the
nineteenth century—at least as far as Britain is concerned. Similarly, the
drive for scientific rationality casts light on the reorganization of sport
into national structures but tells us little or nothing about the attitudes
of those who participated in or watched the activities thus administered.
The social historian wants to know how most participants and spectators
responded most of the time, and this may have little to do with any
alleged 'essence'.[8]

It is at this point that the value of what may be termed the 'cultural
Marxist' approach becomes evident. Instead of looking at sport in terms
of 'surplus value' or 'alienation', sport is seen as one of a range of
processes through which the values of a dominant class are passed on
to the bulk of the working population. The importance of this is that
it does not impute any inherent values to sport but instead concentrates
on the use made of it. Sport is seen as part of a process through which
a consensus is reached about existing economic and political
arrangements. This position derives from the work of Gramsci on
'hegemony' and, though useful, has several important pitfalls for the

[8] For a variety of contemporary definitions of sport see 'What is Sport?',
Observer, 22 Aug. 1982, p. 18.

unwary. First, of course, it *assumes* that there is a body of unreconciled and potentially hostile opinion which will destroy the state if it is not assimilated into the dominant culture. Secondly, it seems to suggest a preponderant role for the state, which may have made sense in Mussolini's Italy, but works less well in the context of nineteenth-century liberalism, especially the 'small government' variety of which Britain was the supreme exemplar. Thirdly, and most importantly, if crudely handled the idea of hegemony simply degenerates into a bland proposition about the manipulation of the masses by controlling cliques. Vulgar 'social control' models assume that popular culture is a blank book upon which the ruling class can write what they wish. The British school of 'cultural' Marxism have been shrewdly aware of such dangers. E. P. Thompson set out in uncompromising terms the power of the working class to 'create itself' and produce a political culture of 'resistance'. Raymond Williams has refined the theoretical tools to create a model of cultural change in which there is a permanent dialogue between imposed values and autonomous, self-generating ones. Richard Gruneau in *Class, Sports and Social Development* has recently attempted to synthesize this line of thinking with specific relation to sport by setting a case-study of the development of Canadian sport alongside a more lengthy and highly sophisticated theoretical discussion.[9]

Sport, Power and Culture by John Hargreaves is an important recent attempt to present a coherent theoretical account of the growth of sport in modern Britain in terms of what he calls 'the hegemonic project'. He interprets nineteenth-century sport as the conquest of bourgeois values embodied in the ideology of amateurism. This helped to create a unified élite of birth and wealth. Alongside this process there was also a 'philanthropic strategy' which transmitted these hegemonic values to the working class so as to reinforce the separation of the more skilled and articulate elements from the rest. Here the argument obviously links up with the much wider debate about both 'social control' and the emergence of a 'labour aristocracy' in Victorian Britain. Hence sport both solidified 'the ruling class' and split the working class. The theoretical neatness of this account, however, leads to problems when dealing with the complex historical reality—problems which cannot be properly resolved in the hundred or so pages of a single book which also provides a detailed analysis of what has taken place in British sport in the late twentieth century. As these issues—the ideology of amateurism, the

[9] S. Hall, D. Hobson, A. Lowe, and P. Willis (eds.), *Culture, Media and Language* (1980); Hall surveys the growth of this body of thought through the work of the Centre for Contemporary Cultural Studies whose publications, especially *Working Class Culture* (1979), debate these issues thoroughly; R. Gruneau, *Class, Sports and Social Development* (1983).

doctrine and practice of 'rational recreation', the 'relative cultural autonomy' of sport—have been examined in some detail in the text, especially in Chapters 2 and 3, I do not propose to go over the historical evidence again here. For the moment I simply want to state a number of reservations about the use of 'hegemony' as a tool of analysis. The first is simply that there is a danger of thinking of 'hegemony' as unproblematic whereas in fact it is a strongly contested concept both within the Marxist tradition and without. Hargreaves certainly takes account of this—if anything his 'history' is too packed with abstract formulation elaborately qualified at the expense of concrete historical examples—but there is a real danger of others simply taking a 'hegemonic' approach as a convenient 'catch-all' concept and applying it crudely. A convincing account can only be provided by a wealth of detailed evidence. The claims for sport as a tool for the moral leadership by the bourgeoisie of a divided working class needs to be treated with great caution. Which sports? When? How? The agencies of hegemony have to be made clear. As the debate over Victorian 'social control' revealed, it is not enough to show that there were individuals with the *intention* of exercising control over the workers. It has to be established that some kind of moral influence was in fact exercised. The hegemonic argument cleverly accepts that such control was only partially and incompletely achieved, and in fact interprets this cultural independence as 'resistance', thereby providing further proof of the strength of the concept. We are presented with a closed system of thought which can account for all manner of conflicting interests and responses. Yet sport did not unite the middle and upper classes in any straightforward way. Despite the manifest importance of amateurism, northern business men were paradoxically excluded from a 'bourgeois' amateur consensus (as, for example, the Northern Union in rugby revealed). Furthermore, it could easily be argued that the public school ideal of 'fair play' was not so much a 'bourgeois' doctrine as an adaptation of older aristocratic traditions of honour and style which created the ideal of 'effortless superiority'. The extent of working-class incorporation into the ideology of amateurism appears to have been fairly restricted. Working-class sportsmen seem to have been more or less indifferent to amateur values, though the game of cricket in its MCC-dominated county form did embody an unquestioned subordination of the professional to the amateur which could be construed as 'hegemonic', i.e. involving manual workers freely accepting the moral leadership of the ruling élite. My point is not that hegemony is valueless but that it needs to be carefully confined to precise contexts within sport rather than used as blanket 'explanation'.[10]

[10] John Hargreaves, *Sport, Power and Culture* (1986).

The 'cultural' approach fits well into the established pattern of British social history which has taken the relationship between classes and levels of class-consciousness as a central issue for discussion. The attack on old sports by middle-class reformers, the emergence of amateurism as a new kind of élite ideology, and, most importantly, the attempt to impose 'rational recreation' on the workers all relate to the wider definition and implementation of a theoretically dominant bourgeois culture. Even those who had no ideological axe to grind have found themselves caught up in such discussion. For my own part I have tried to do justice to the undoubted activism of middle-class reformers whilst stressing their failure to dominate the working class. Fair play, rationality, and amateurism on the one side were more than compensated by partisanship and professionalism on the other. Here I follow Gareth Stedman-Jones in his analysis of the self-sufficient and inward-looking culture of the London working class in the later nineteenth century, especially his view of the cultural significance of the music-hall. I have stressed the 'relative autonomy' of working-class culture. For it seems to me that one can address these problems without having to accept the full implications of their premisses, i.e. the intention to control can be accepted without believing that success was crucial for the stability of the state. Like Molière's 'bourgeois gentilhomme' social historians have found themselves talking 'prose' (i.e. in this case discussing class relations in a 'hegemonic' sense) without realizing it. Theoretical formulations have served mainly to make explicit a concept of which historians were already implicitly aware.[11]

In trying to understand what constituted the popular culture of sport the role of shared masculine and community values has proved very important. For there was no 'socialist' culture of resistance to control expressed through sport but rather a fierce commitment to locality, a pride in belonging to a neighbourhood, or a wider sense of a specific regional or urban identity. Here a feminist-derived awareness of sport as a means of constantly re-creating and sustaining male identity becomes important. I developed the theme of sport as a male institution in earlier work on France and subsequent feminist writing has reinforced my belief that sport, both spectator and participant, has been central to the maintenance of male sociability in all classes. The degree to which sport carries class meanings is more difficult to establish than the obvious cult of masculinity—hardness, strength, courage, and durability alongside physical skill—that is promoted through sport. A 'cultural Marxist' view of working-class sport, which neglects the role of sport as a source of

---

[11] G. Stedman-Jones, 'Working Class Culture and Working Class Politics in London, 1870–1900', reprinted in *Languages of Class* (1983), which also contains the important 'Class Expression versus Social Control?'

sexual identity will be inevitably incomplete. Trying to understand the watching of professional football in terms of whether or not the game offered a compensation for loss of skill at work or conversely a reinforcement of the idea of 'work-rate' and specialization of functions may be interesting, but it is inevitably speculative and inconclusive. However, the celebration of a distinctive brand of popular 'masculinity' is pretty obvious and incontestable. This may be contrasted with the more refined 'manliness' of the gentleman-amateur, which gave the same prominence to physical prowess but overlaid it with moral considerations of 'uprightness' and gallantry towards women. Class and gender values meshed together to create socially distinctive ways of playing and watching.[12]

This brings me to a final and related consideration: the role of sport as a source of sociability and a new kind of identity both at the level of the street and of the city. The links between popular sports and fairs, holidays, and feasts is a frequent theme of research into traditional recreation, and the historian is naturally struck by what became of the communal character of sport in a heavily industrial and urban context. This, in theoretical terms, ties in with the concern of Durkheim and his followers over the social consequences of the division of labour. Durkheim believed that there was a real danger of isolation and disintegration of collective life in the city. Solidarity was under attack. 'A whole series of secondary groups near enough to individuals to attract them strongly in their sphere of social action and drag them, in this way, into the torrent of social life' were needed. Durkheim's own solution was a return to a kind of guild sociability which would provide institutions where men could gather 'principally for the pleasure of living together, for finding outside of oneself distractions from fatigue and boredom, to create an intimacy less restrained than the family and less extensive than the city'. A more settled and supportive network of groups did in fact emerge within the mature industrial city in the late nineteenth century. The kind of 'Gemeinschaft/Gesellschaft' division raised by Tönnies between intimate communities and mass society turned out to be more of a problem in theory than in practice. The social life of workers was not impoverished. Obviously sport was only one way of sustaining collective life; by stressing 'solidarity' I do not mean to propose a crudely functionalist view of sport but rather to suggest that within the broad class cultures of sport the role of locality and the power of regional identity were extremely powerful. While we should not forget that sport was always a minority activity even at the spectator level, it did have

---

[12] D. Whitson, 'Structure, Agency and the Sociology of Sport Debates', *Theory, Culture and Society*, 1986 (1); see also the related contributions of Dunning and of Jennifer Hargreaves in the same issue.

an important place in pub and shop-floor gossip amongst men in general—a point I have developed in more detail elsewhere. For the present I wish simply to stress the convergence between classic problems in the sociology of the city and the sense of belonging that came from membership of a football or cricket team or for that matter turning up each week to watch 'your' team with a group of workmates, kin, or neighbours.[13]

Sport as a 'tool for conviviality' and a source of cultural continuity between generations and within classes concludes this brief review of some of the concepts that have informed *Sport and the British*. Historians are pulled in different directions by the evidence to hand—in my case this was frequently determined by the choice of approach that other historians of sport have made—and the more rigorous and abstract propositions of theorists. The first requirement of the historian is to try to construct an account which acquires a 'cumulative plausibility'. But smuggled into any general interpretation there will be also a fair degree of subjectivity in the choice of organizing ideas. I have played down the role, for example, of the 'rationality' of sport, of the significance of setting down rules and keeping records, in favour of looking at the kinds of emotional bonds sport creates between people. Here my own experience of playing sport and my early memories of watching professional football have unavoidably influenced me. If I had ever raised my performance above the run-of-the-mill I might have had more interest in the competitive rather than the social, the high-performance sportsman rather than the ordinary athlete or spectator. This brings us back to a basic distinction between psychological and sociological theories of sport. This book has been concerned with the social meanings of sport but it also broadly accepts that sport is 'natural' in the general sense that people simply enjoy playing or watching it. Sport provides immediate pleasurable sensations—Caillois called it a sense of the 'vertiginous'— which will always have to be balanced against the historical significance of organized play at a particular moment in the past. It is the tension between timeless impulses and historical time, between the need to play and to be sociable on the one hand and the structure into which such needs have been incorporated on the other, that underlies any enterprise of this kind. There has to be fun, friendship, spontaneity, and thrills, but equally there is the sense of social change, the role of sport in the construction of class and national identities. Both aspects are real and my purpose has been to try to keep them in balance.

[13] E. Durkheim, *The Division of Labour* (1964), pp. 12, 28. There are some inspiring passages on sociability in Fred Inglis, *The Name of the Game* (1977). R. Holt, 'Working Class Football and the City', *BJSH*, May 1986.

BIBLIOGRAPHY

ABRAMS, P., 'History, Sociology and Historical Sociology', *Past and Present*, **87**, May 1980.
—— *Historical Sociology* (London, 1982).
ALLAN, G. A., *A Sociology of Friendship and Kinship* (London, 1979).
ALLISON, L., 'Batsman and Bowler: The Key Relation in Victorian England', *JSH*, **7**, Summer 1980.
—— *The Condition of England: Essays and Impressions* (London, 1981).
ALT, J., 'Sport and Cultural Reification: From Ritual to Mass Sport', *Theory, Culture and Society*, **1**, 1983, no. 3.
ANDERSON, R. D., 'Sport in the Scottish Universities, 1860–1939', *IJHS*, **4**, Sept. 1987.
ANCHOR, R., 'History and Play: Johan Huizinga and his Critics', *History and Theory*, **17**, 1978, no. 1.
ANDREW, C., 'Football Crazy', *Listener*, 10 June 1982.
ARCHER, R. and BOUILLON, A., *The South African Game: Sport and Racism* (London, 1982).
ARLOTT, J., 'Sport', in S. Nowell-Smith (ed.), *Edwardian England 1901–14* (London, 1964).
—— *Jack Hobbs: Profile of the Master* (London, 1981).
—— (ed.), *Oxford Companion to Sports and Games* (Oxford, 1976).
ASHPLANT, T. G., 'London Working Men's Clubs, 1875–1914', in S. and E. Yeo (eds.), *Popular Culture and Class Conflict*.
ATKINSON, P., 'Strong Minds and Weak Bodies: Sports, Gymnastics and the Medicalization of Women's Education', *BJSH*, **2**, May 1985.
BAILEY, P., *Leisure and Class in Victorian England* (London, 1978).
BAKER, W., 'The Making of a Working Class Football Culture in Victorian England', *Journal of Social History*, **13**, Winter 1979.
—— *Sports in the Western World* (New Jersey, 1982).
—— 'The State of British Sport History', *JSH*, **10**, Spring 1983.
BALE, J., *The Development of Soccer as a Participant and Spectator Sport: The Geographical Aspects* (Sports Council/SSRC, 1979).
—— *Sport and Place: A Geography of Sport in England, Scotland and Wales* (London, 1982).
BELL, Lady (Florence), *At the Works: A Study of a Manufacturing Town*, introd. A. V. John (London, 1985 edn.).
BELL, R. R., *Worlds of Friendship* (London, 1981).
BILSBOROUGH, P., 'The Development of Sport in Glasgow, 1850–1914', M.Litt. thesis (Stirling, 1983).

BIRLEY, D., 'Sportsmen and the Deadly Game', *BJSH*, **3**, Dec. 1986.

BLANCH, M. D., 'Nation, Empire and the Birmingham Working Class, 1899–1914', Ph.D. thesis (Birmingham, 1975).

BOURDIEU, P., 'Sports, classes sociales et sub-cultures', in *Sports et sociétés contemporaines: VIIIᵉ symposium du ICSS* (Paris, 1983).

BOURNE, J. M., *Patronage and Society in Nineteenth Century England* (Cambridge, 1986).

BOVILL, E. W., *The England of Nimrod and Surtees* (London, 1959).

BOWEN, R., *Cricket: A History of its Growth and Development throughout the World* (London, 1970).

BRAGG, M., *Speak for England* (London, 1976).

BRAILSFORD, D., *Sport and Society: From Elizabeth to Anne* (London, 1969).

—— 'Sporting Days in Eighteenth Century England', *JSH*, **9**, Winter, 1982.

—— 'The Locations of Eighteenth Century Spectator Sport', in *Proceedings of the Conference 'Geographical Perspectives on Sport', University of Birmingham, 7 July 1983*.

—— 'Religion and Sport in Eighteenth Century England', *BJSH*, **1**, Sept. 1984.

—— 'Morals and Maulers: The Ethics of Early Pugilism', *JSH*, **12**, Summer 1985.

—— 'Notes on the Geography of Regency Pugilism', Geography and Sports Studies Conference, West London Institute of Higher Education, 1985 (unpub.).

—— 'In Conversation with Tony Mason', *BSSH Bulletin*, Jan. 1986.

—— *Bareknuckles: a social history of prize-fighting* (Cambridge, 1988).

BRAIN, R., *Friends and Lovers* (London, 1976).

BRIGGS, A., *Victorian People* (London, 1965 edn.).

—— *The History of Broadcasting*, ii (Oxford, 1965) and iv (Oxford, 1979).

—— 'The View from Badminton', in A. Briggs (ed.), *Essays in the History of Publishing: Longman 1724–1974* (London, 1974).

BRIGGS, S., *Those Radio Times* (London, 1981).

BROHM, J.-M., *Sport: A Prison of Measured Time* (London, 1978).

BROOKES, C., *English Cricket: The Game and its Players through the Ages* (London, 1978).

BURKE, P., *Popular Culture in Early Modern Europe* (London, 1979).
Sociology and History (London, 1980).

BURROWES, J., *Benny: The Life and Times of a Fighting Legend* (Edinburgh, 1982).

BURTON, R. D. E., 'Cricket, Carnival and Street Culture in the Caribbean', *BJSH*, **2**, Sept. 1985.

BUSCOMBE, E. (ed.), *Football on Television* (London, 1975).

BUTLER, B., *The Giant Killers* (London, 1982).

CAILLOIS, R., *Man, Play and Games* (London, 1962).

CAMPLIN, J., *The Rise of the Plutocrats* (London, 1978).

CANNADINE, D., 'The Context, Performance and Meaning of Ritual: The British Monarchy and the "Invention of Tradition", c.1820–1977', in Hobsbawm and Ranger, *The Invention of Tradition*.

CARDUS, N., *Cardus on Cricket*, introd. R. Hart-Davis (London, 1977 edn.).

—— *The Roses Matches, 1919–39* (London, 1982 edn.).

CARR, R., *English Fox Hunting* (London, 1976).

CASHMAN, R., 'The Phenomenon of Indian Cricket', in Cashman and McKernan, *Sport in History*.

—— F. R. Spofforth, "The Demon" (1853–1926): 'An Anglo-Australian Hero', in Proceedings of the Fourth Annual Conference of the BSSH, 1986 (privately circulated).

—— and MCKERNAN, M., *Sport in History: The Making of Modern Sporting History* (Queensland, 1979).

—— *Sport: Money, Morality and the Media* (New South Wales, 1982).

CASHMORE, E., *Black Sportsmen* (London, 1982).

Cassell's Complete Book of Sports and Pastimes (London, 1893).

Centre for Contemporary Cultural Studies, *Fads and Fashions* (Sports Council/SSRC, 1980).

CHANDLER, T. J. L., 'The Emergence of Athleticism: Social Control or Mutual Adaptation?', in *Proceedings of the XI HISPA International Congress*, ed. J. A. Mangan (Glasgow, 1987); for a revised version see *IJHS*, **5**, Dec. 1988.

CHANDOS, J., *Boys Together: English Public Schools, 1800–1864* (Oxford, 1984).

CHESNEY, K., *The Victorian Underworld* (London, 1972).

CLARK, J. C. D., *English Society 1688–1832: Ideology, Social Structure and Political Practice during the Ancient Regime* (Cambridge, 1985).

CLARK, P., *The English Alehouse: A Social History 1200–1830* (London, 1983).

CLARKE, J., and CRITCHER, C., *The Devil Makes Work: Leisure in Capitalist Britain* (London, 1985).

CLAYRE, A., *Work and Play: Ideas and Experience of Work and Leisure* (London, 1974).

COBB, R., *Still Life: Sketches from a Tunbridge Wells Childhood* (London, 1984).

COHEN, P., 'Subcultural Conflict and Working Class Community', in Hall *et al.* (eds.), *Culture, Media and Language*.

COHEN, S. (ed.), *Images of Deviance* (London, 1971).

—— *Folk Devils and Moral Panics* (London, 1972).

COHN, B. S., 'Representing Authority in Victorian India', in Hobsbawm and Ranger, *The Invention of Tradition*.

COLLS, R., and DODD, P. (eds.), *Englishness: Politics and Culture 1880–1920* (London, 1986).

CRAMPSEY, BOB, *The Scottish Footballer* (Edinburgh, 1978).

CRAMPSEY, BOB, *Mr. Stein: A Biography of Jock Stein CBE, 1922–85* (Edinburgh, 1986).

CRITCHER, C., 'Football since the War', in J. Clarke, C. Critcher, and R. Johnson (eds.), *Working Class Culture: Studies in Theory and History* (London, 1979).

CROSSLEY, C., 'Travail, loisir et vie communautaire en Angleterre au XIXe siècle: Le Cas de Bournville', in A. Daumard (ed.), *Oisiveté et loisirs dans les sociétés occidentales au XIXe siècle* (Abbeville, 1983).

CRUMP, J., 'The Amusements of the People: The Provision of Recreation in Leicester, 1850–1914', Ph.D. thesis (Warwick University, 1985).

—— and MASON, T., 'Hostile and Improper Demonstrations: Incidence of Football Crowd Disorder 1886–1914' *Proceedings of XI HISPA International Congress*, ed. J. A. Mangan (Glasgow, 1987).

CUDDON, J. A., *The Macmillan Dictionary of Sport and Games* (London, 1980).

CUNNINGHAM, H., *Leisure in the Industrial Revolution* (London, 1980).

CUNNINGTON, P., and MARSFIELD, A., *English Costumes for Sports and Outdoor Recreation* (London, 1969).

DABSCHECK, B., 'Defensive Manchester: A History of the PFA', in Cashman and McKernan, *Sport in History*.

DALY, J. A., 'Sport, Class and Community in Colonial Australia', in *Proceedings of the XI HISPA International Congress*, ed. J. A. Mangan (Glasgow, 1987).

DELANEY, T., *The Roots of Rugby League* (Keighley, 1984).

DELVES, M. A., 'Popular Recreation and Social Conflict in Derby 1800–1850', in S. and E. Yeo (eds.), *Popular Culture and Class Conflict*.

DE SELINCOURT, H., *The Cricket Match*, introd. Benny Green (Oxford, 1980).

DOBBS, B., *The Edwardians at Play: Sports 1890–1914* (London, 1973).

DODD, C., *The Oxford and Cambridge Boat Race* (London, 1983).

DOWN, M., *Archie: A Biography of A. C. MacLaren* (London, 1981).

DUNNING, E., *Soccer: the Social Origins of the Sport and its Development as a Spectacle and a Profession* (Sports Council/SSRC, 1979).

—— (ed.), *The Sociology of Sport: A Selection of Readings* (London, 1971).

—— Sport as a male preserve: notes on the social sources of masculine identity and its transformations, *Theory, Culture and Society*, **3**, 1986, no. 1.

—— and MURPHY, P, J,, 'Working Class Social Bonding and the Sociogenesis of Football Hooliganism', SSRC Report (1982).

—— and SHEARD, K., *Barbarians, Gentlemen and Players: A Sociological Study of the Development of Rugby* (Oxford, 1979).

—— MURPHY, P., and WILLIAMS, T. *The Roots of Football Hooliganism: an historical and sociological study* (London, 1988).

DUNPHY, E., *Only a Game?*, ed. P. Ball (London, 1977).

DURKHEIM, E., *The Division of Labour* (New York, 1964 edn.).

DYER, K. F., *Catching up the Men* (London, 1982).

ELDRIDGE, J., *Recent British Sociology* (London, 1980).

ELIAS, N., *The Civilising Process*, i. *The History of Manners*, trans. E. Jephcott (Oxford, 1978).

—— and DUNNING, E., 'Folk Football in Medieval and Early Modern Britain', in Dunning (ed.), *The Sociology of Sport*.

—— and DUNNING, E., *Quest for Excitement: sport and leisure in the civilising process* (Oxford, 1986).

EVERTON, C., *The Story of Billiards and Snooker* (London, 1979).

FISHWICK, N., 'Association Football and English Social Life, 1910–1950', D.Phil. thesis (Oxford, 1984).

FLETCHER, S., *Women First: The Female Tradition in English Physical Education 1880–1980* (London, 1984).

FORD, J., *Prizefighting: The Age of Regency Boximania* (Newton Abbot, 1971).

—— *This Sporting Land* (London, 1977).

FRANKENBERG, R., *Village on the Border: A Study of Religion, Politics and Football in a North Wales Community* (London, 1957).

—— *Communities in Britain* (London, 1966).

GARVIN, T., *The Evolution of Irish Nationalist Politics* (Dublin, 1981).

GASH, N., *Aristocracy and People: Britain 1815–1865* (London, 1979).

GEERTZ, C., 'Deep Play: Notes on a Balinese Cockfight', *Daedalus*, **101**, Winter 1972.

GIDDENS, A., *Capitalism and Modern Social Theory* (Cambridge, 1971).

GILLIS, J. R., *Youth and History: Tradition and Change in European Age Relations, 1770 to the Present* (London, 1981 edn.).

GOLBY, J., 'Bourgeois Hegemony? The Popular Culture of Mid Nineteenth Century Britain', *Social History Society Newsletter*, **13**, Autumn 1981.

——and PURDUE, A. W., *The Civilisation of the Crowd: Popular Culture in England 1750–1900* (London, 1984).

GRACE, W. G., *'W.G.': Cricketing Reminiscences and Personal Recollections*, introd. E. W. Swanton (London, 1980 edn.).

GRAYSON, E., *Corinthian Casuals and Cricketers* (Havant, Hants., 1983 edn.).

GREEN, G., *Soccer, the World Game* (London, 1953).

—— *There's Only One United* (London, 1978).

GREEN, P., 'A Hundred Years of Tennis', *Times Literary Supplement*, 1 July 1977.

GREENE, D., 'Michael Cusack and the Rise of the GAA', in C. C. O'Brien, *The Shaping of Modern Ireland* (London, 1960).

GRUNEAU, R., *Class, Sports and Social Development* (Amherst, 1983).

GUTTMAN, A., *From Ritual to Record: The Nature of Modern Sports* (New York, 1978).

—— 'English Sports Spectators: The Restoration to the Early Nineteenth Century', *JSH*, **12**, Summer 1985.

GUTTMAN, A., *Sports Spectators* (New York, 1986).

HALEY, B., *The Healthy Body in Victorian Culture* (Cambridge, Mass., 1978).

HALL, S., 'The Treatment of "Football Hooliganism" in the Press', in Ingham (ed.), *Football Hooliganism*.

—— and JEFFERSON, T., *Resistance through Rituals: Youth Sub-cultures in Post-war Britain* (London, 1976).

—— HOBSON, D., LOWE, A., and WILLIS, P. (eds.), *Culture, Media and Language* (London, 1980).

HALLADAY, E., 'Of Pride and Prejudice: The Amateur Question in English Nineteenth Century Rowing', *IJHS*, **4,** May 1987.

HARDING, J., *Football Wizard: The Story of Billy Meredith* (Derby, 1985).

HARGREAVES, JENNIFER, ' "Playing like Gentlemen while Behaving like Ladies": Contradictory Features of the Formative Years of Women's Sport', *BJSH*, **2,** May 1985.

—— 'Where's the Virtue? Where's the Grace?' A discussion of the social production of gender through sport, *Theory, Culture and Society*, vol. 3, no. 1, 1986.

—— (ed.), *Sport, Culture and Ideology* (London, 1982).

HARGREAVES, JOHN, *Sport, Power and Culture: A Social and Historical Analysis of Popular Sports in Britain* (Cambridge, 1986).

HARRIS, H. A., *Sport in Britain* (London, 1975).

HARRISON, B., 'Religion and Recreation in Nineteenth Century England', *Past and Present*, no. 38, Dec. 1967.

—— 'Animals and the State in Nineteenth Century England', *English Historical Review*, **88,** Oct. 1973.

HARRISSON, T., and MADGE, C., *Britain by 'Mass Observation'*, introd. A. Calder (London, 1986 edn.).

HAY, R., 'Soccer and Social Control in Scotland 1873–1978', in Cashman and McKernan, *Sport: Money, Morality and the Media*.

HILL, J., ' "First Class" Cricket and the Leagues', *IJHS*, **4,** May 1987.

HILLMAN, M., and WHALLEY, A., *Fair Play for All: A Study of Access to Sport and Informal Recreation* (London, 1977).

HOBERMAN, J. M., *Sport and Political Ideology* (London, 1984).

HOBSBAWM, E., *Worlds of Labour· Further Studies in the History of Labour* (London, 1984).

—— and RANGER, T. (eds.), *The Invention of Tradition* (Cambridge, 1983).

HOGGART, R., *The Uses of Literacy* (London, 1957).

HOGGETT, P., and BISHOP, J., *Organising around Enthusiasms: Mutual aid in Leisure* (London, 1986).

HOLT, A., 'Hikers and Ramblers: Surviving a Thirties' Fashion', *IJHS*,**4,** May 1987.

HOLT, R., *Sport and Society in Modern France* (London, 1981).

—— 'Working Class Football and the City: The Problem of Continuity', *BJSH*, **4,** May 1986.

HOPCRAFT, A., *The Football Man: People and Passions in Soccer* (London, 1968).

HOPKINS, E., 'Working Hours and Conditions during the Industrial Revolution: A Re-appraisal', *Economic History Review*, **35,** Feb. 1982.

HOPKINSON, M. A., *The Irish Civil War* (Dublin, 1988).

HOPKINSON, T. (ed.), *Picture Post, 1938–50: An Anthology* (London, 1970).

HORGAN, T., *Cork's Hurling Story: from 1890 to the Present Time* (Dublin, 1977).

HOWKINS, A., 'The Taming of Whitsun', in S. and E. Yeo (eds.), *Popular Culture and Class Conflict*.

—— and LOWERSON, J., *Trends in Leisure, 1919–39*, a review for the Sports Council and the SSRC (London, 1979).

HUIZINGA, J., *Homo Ludens: A Study of the Play Element in Culture*, introd. G. Steiner (London, 1970).

HUMBER, R. D., *Game Cock and Countryman* (London, 1966).

HUMPHRIES, S., *Hooligans or Rebels? An Oral History of Working Class Childhood and Youth, 1889–1939* (Oxford, 1981).

HUTCHINSON, J., *The Football Industry* (Glasgow, 1982).

HYAM, R., *Britain's Imperial Century, 1815–1914* (London, 1976).

IBBOTSON, D., and DELLOR, R., *A Hundred Years of the Ashes* (London, 1982).

INGHAM, R. (ed.), *Football Hooliganism: The Wider Context* (London, 1978).

INGLIS, F., *The Name of the Game: Sport and Society* (London, 1977).

INGLIS, K. S., 'Imperial Cricket: Test Matches between England and Australia, 1877–1900', in Cashman and McKernan, *Sport in History*.

INGLIS, S., *Soccer in the Dock: A History of British Football Scandals 1900–1965* (London, 1985).

—— *The Football Grounds of England and Wales* (London, 1985).

ITZKOWITZ, D. C., *Peculiar Privilege: A Social History of English Fox Hunting 1753–1885* (London, 1977).

JACKSON, B., *Working Class Community* (London, 1972).

JAMES, C. L. R., *Beyond a Boundary* (London, 1963).

JARVIE, G., 'Dependency, Cultural Identity and Sporting Landlords', in Proceedings of the Third Annual Conference of the BSSH, June–July 1985 (privately circulated).

JENKINS, R., *The Thistle and the Rose*, introd. Cairns Craig (Edinburgh, 1983 edn.).

JONES, S. G., 'The Economic Aspects of Association Football in England, 1918–39', *BJSH*, **1,** Dec. 1984.

—— 'Sports, Politics and the Labour Movement: The British Workers' Sports Federation, 1923–35', *BJSH*,**2,** Sept. 1985.

JONES, S. G., *Workers at Play: A Social and Economic History of Leisure 1918–1939* (London, 1986).

JOYCE, P., *Work, Society and Politics: The Culture of the Factory in Late Victorian England* (London, 1980).

JUDT, T., 'A Clown in Regal Purple: Social History and the Historians', *History Workshop Journal*, no. 7, Spring 1979.

KIRCHNER, R., *Fair Play: The Games of Merrie England*, trans. R. N. Bradley (London, 1928).

KIRK-GREENE, A. H. M., 'Imperial Sidelight or Spotlight? Sport and His Excellency in the British Empire', in *Proceedings of the XI HISPA International Congress*, ed. J. A. Mangan (Glasgow, 1987).

KITSON CLARK, G., *The Making of Victorian England* (London, 1962).

KNOX, W., *Scottish Labour Leaders, 1918–39* (Edinburgh, 1984).

KORR, C., 'West Ham United and the Beginning of Professional Football in East London, 1895–1914', *Journal of Contemporary History*, **13**, Apr. 1978.

—— 'The Men at the Top: The Board of Directors of West Ham United Football Club', in Vamplew (ed.), *Economic History of Leisure*.

—— *West Ham United* (London, 1986).

KUPER, A., 'Gentlemen and Players', *New Society*, 9 Aug. 1984.

KUTCHER, L., 'The American Sport Event as Carnival', *Journal of Popular Culture*, **16**, Spring 1983.

KYNASTON, D., *Bobby Abel: Professional Batsman* (London, 1982).

LAWTON, TOMMY, *Football is My Business* (London, 1946).

LE QUESNE, L., *The Bodyline Controversy* (London, 1983).

LIDKE, V. L., *The Alternative Culture: Socialist Labor in Imperial Germany* (New York, 1985).

LLOYD, A., *The Great Prize Fight* (London, 1977).

LOVESEY, P., *The Official Centenary History of the Amateur Athletic Association* (London, 1979).

LOWERSON, J., 'English Middle Class Sport', in Aspects of the Social History of Nineteenth Century Sport: Proceedings of the Inaugural Conference of the BSSH, 1982 (privately circulated).

—— 'Joint-stock Companies, Capital Formation and Suburban Leisure in England, 1880–1914', in Vamplew (ed.), *Economic History of Leisure*.

—— 'Sport and the Victorian Sunday: The Beginnings of Middle Class Apostasy', *BJSH*, **1**, Sept. 1984.

——'Brothers of the Angle. Match Fishing 1850–1914', paper delivered to the Society for the Study of Labour History, 24 Nov. 1984 (abstract in *Bulletin of the Society for the Study of Labour History*, no. 50, Spring 1985).

—— and MYERSCOUGH, J., *Time to Spare in Victorian England* (London, 1977).

LUKES, S., *Emile Durkheim: His Life and Work, a Historical and Critical Study* (London, 1975).

MacAloon, J. J., *This Great Symbol: Pierre de Coubertin and the Origins of the Modern Olympic Games* (Chicago, 1981).

McCarra, K., *Scottish Football: a Pictorial History from 1867 to the Present* (Glasgow, 1984).

McCrone, K. E., 'Play Up! Play Up! and Play the Game! Sport at the Late Victorian Girls' Public School', *Journal of British Studies*, **23**, Spring 1984.

—— 'The "Lady Blue": Sport at the Oxbridge Women's Colleges from their Foundation to 1914', *BJSH*, **3**, Sept. 1986.

—— *Sport and the Physical Emancipation of English Women* (London, 1988).

MacDonagh, O., Mandle, W. F., and Travers, P., *Irish Culture and Irish Nationalism* (London, 1983).

McIntosh, P. C., *Sport in Society* (London, 1963).

—— *Physical Education in England since 1800* (London, 1968 edn.).

—— *Fairplay: Ethics in Sport and Education* (London, 1979).

—— 'The History of Sport and Other Disciplines', in Aspects of the Social History of Nineteenth Century Sport: Proceedings of the Inaugural Conference of the BSSH, 1982 (privately circulated).

—— and Charlton, V., *The Impact of the 'Sport for All' Policy, 1966-1984* (Sports Council, London, 1986).

Mackenzie, J. (ed.), *Cycling* (Oxford, 1981).

Mackenzie, J. M., 'Hunting and the Imperial Élite', in Proceedings of the Fourth Annual Conference of the BSSH, 1986 (privately circulated).

—— (ed.), *Imperialism and Popular Culture* (Manchester, 1986).

McKibbin, R., 'Working Class Gambling in Britain 1880-1939', *Past and Present*, no. 82, Feb. 1979.

—— 'Work and Hobbies in Britain, 1850-1950', in J. Winter (ed.), *The Working Class in Modern Britain* (Cambridge, 1983).

McNair, D., and Parry, N., *Readings in the History of Physical Education* (Ahrensburg bei Hamburg, 1981).

Maguire, J., 'Images of Manliness and Competing Ways of Living in Late Victorian and Edwardian Britain', *BJSH*, **3**, Dec. 1986.

Malcolm, E., 'Popular Recreation in Nineteenth Century Ireland', in MacDonagh *et al.*, *Irish Culture and Irish Nationalism*.

Malcolmson, R. W., *Popular Recreations in English Society 1700-1850* (Cambridge, 1979 edn.).

—— 'Sports in Society: A Historical Perspective', *BJSH*, May 1984.

Mandle, W. F., 'The Professional Cricketer in England in the Nineteenth Century', *Labour History*, Canberra, **23**, Nov. 1972.

—— 'Games People Played: Cricket and Football in England and Victoria in the Late Nineteenth Century', *Historical Studies*, **15**, Apr. 1972.

—— 'Cricket and Australian Nationalism in the Nineteenth Century', *Journal of the Royal Australian Historical Society*, Dec. 1973.

MANDLE, W. F., 'The IRB and the Beginnings of the Gaelic Athletic Association', *Irish Historical Studies*, **20**, Sept. 1977.

—— 'Sport as Politics: The Gaelic Athletic Association 1884–1916', in Cashman and McKernan, *Sport in History*.

—— 'W. G. Grace as a Victorian Hero', *Historical Studies*, **19**, Apr. 1980.

—— 'The GAA and Popular Culture', in MacDonagh *et al.*, *Irish Culture and Irish Nationalism*.

MANGAN, J. A., *Athleticism in the Victorian and Edwardian Public School* (Cambridge, 1981).

—— 'Gentlemen Galore: Imperial Education for Tropical Africa: Lugard the Ideologist', *Immigrants and Minorities*, July 1982, vol. 1.

—— 'Social Darwinism, Sport and English Upper Class Education', in Aspects of the Social History of Nineteenth Century Sport: Proceedings of the Inaugural Conference of the BSSH, 1982 (privately circulated).

—— 'Imitating their Betters and Disassociating from their Inferiors: Grammar Schools and the Games Ethic in the Late Nineteenth and Early Twentieth Centuries', History of Education Society: Annual Conference (Dec. 1982).

—— ' "Oars and the Man": Pleasure and Purpose in Victorian and Edwardian Cambridge', *BJSH*, Dec. 1984, vol. 1.

—— 'Imperial Reproduction: A Case Study of Canada', in Proceedings of the Third Annual Conference of the BSSH, June–July 1985 (privately circulated).

—— *The Games Ethic and Imperialism* (London, 1986).

—— (ed.), *Pleasure, Profit and Proselytism: British Culture and Sport at Home and Abroad, 1700–1914* (London, 1988).

—— and PARK, R. J. (eds.), *From 'Fair Sex' to Feminism: Sport and the Socialization of Women in the Industrial and Post-industrial Eras* (London, 1987).

MARLOW, J. E., 'Popular Culture, Pugilism and Pickwick', *Journal of Popular Culture*, **15**, Spring 1982.

MARRUS, M. R., *The Emergence of Leisure* (London, 1974).

MARSH, P., *Aggro: The Illusion of Violence* (London, 1975).

—— ROSSER, E., and HARRÉ, R., *The Rules of Disorder* (London, 1978).

MASON, R., *Ashes in the Mouth: The Story of the Bodyline Tour 1932–3* (London, 1984).

MASON, T., *Association Football and English Society* (Brighton, 1980).

—— *The Blues and the Reds: A History of Liverpool and Everton Football Clubs* (Lancashire and Cheshire Historical Society, 1985).

—— *Sport in Britain* (London, 1988).

'Mass Observation', *The Pub and the People*, introd. G. Smith (London, 1987 edn.).

MATTHEWS, G. R., 'The Controversial Olympic Games of 1908 as viewed by The New York Times and the Times of London', *JSH*, **7**, Summer, 1980.

MATTHEWS, STANLEY, *Feet First* (London, 1948).

MEACHAM, S., *A Life Apart: The English Working Class 1890-1914* (London, 1977).

MEHIGAN, P. D., *Vintage Carbery*, ed. S. Kilfeather (Dublin, 1984).

MELLER, H., *Leisure and the Changing City, 1870-1914* (London, 1976).

METCALFE, A., 'Organised Sport in the Mining Communities of South Northumberland, 1880-1889', *Victorian Studies*, **25**, Summer 1982.

MIDWINTER, E., *W. G. Grace: His Life and Times* (London, 1981).

MOLYNEUX, D. D., 'The Development of Physical Recreation in the Birmingham District, 1871-1892', MA thesis (Birmingham, 1957).

MOORE, K., 'Sport, Politics and Imperialism: The Evolution of the Concept of the British Empire Games from 1891-1930', in Proceedings of the Fourth Annual Conference of the BSSH, 1986 (privately circulated).

—— 'The Concept of the British Empire Games: An Analysis of its Origin and Evolution from 1891 to 1930', Ph.D. thesis (University of Queensland, 1986).

MOORHOUSE, G., *Lord's* (London, 1983).

MOORHOUSE, H. F., 'Scotland against England: Football and Popular Culture', *IJHS*, **4**, Sept. 1987.

MORGAN, K. O., *Rebirth of a Nation: Wales 1880-1980* (Oxford, 1982).

MORGAN, P., 'From a Death to a View: The Hunt for the Welsh Past in the Romantic Period', in Hobsbawm and Ranger, *The Invention of Tradition*.

MORRAH, P., *Alfred Mynn and the Cricketers of His Time* (London, 1986).

MORRIS, D., *The Soccer Tribe* (London, 1981).

MORRIS, J., *The Oxford Book of Oxford* (Oxford, 1978).

MOTT, J., 'Miners, Weavers and Pigeon Racing', in Smith, Parker, and Smith (eds.), *Leisure and Society in Britain*.

MOYNIHAN, J., *The Soccer Syndrome: From the Primeval Forties*, introd. B. Glanville (London, 1987 edn.).

MUIR, J. H., *Glasgow in 1901* (Glasgow, 1901).

MÜLLER, N., and RÜHL, J. K. *The Olympic Scientific Congress 1984 Official Report* (Niedernhausen, 1985).

MURRAY, BILL, 'The Scottish Catholic Community and the Celtic Football Club', *Proceedings of the BSSH*, Sept. 1983.

—— *The Old Firm: Sectarianism, Sport and Society in Scotland* (Glasgow, 1984).

OBELKEVICH, J., *Religion and Rural Society: South Lindsey, 1825-1875* (Oxford, 1976).

O'CROHAN, THOMAS, *The Islandman* (Oxford, 1978).

ONSLOW, R., *The Squire: George Alexander Baird, Gentleman Rider 1861-1893* (London, 1980).

OPIE, I. and P., *Children's Games in Street and Playground* (Oxford, 1984 edn.).

PARK, R. B., 'British Sports and Pastimes in San Francisco 1848-1900', *BJSH*, **1**, Dec. 1984.

PARKER, H. J., *The View from the Boys: A Sociology of Downtown Adolescents* (London, 1974).

PARKER, S., *Work and Leisure: Trends and Prospects* (Sports Council/SSRC, 1979).

PARKINSON, M., and HALL, W., *Football Classified: An Anthology of Soccer* (London, 1973).

PEARSON, G., *Hooligan: A History of Respectable Fears* (London, 1983).

PEGG, M., *Broadcasting and Society, 1919-39* (London, 1983).

PHILLIPS, S. K., 'Primitive methodist Confrontation with Popular Sports', in Cashman and McKernan, *Sport: Money, Morality and the Media*.

PINTER, H., 'Arthur Wellard, 1901-1980', in M. Meyer (ed.), *Summer Days: Writers on Cricket* (London, 1981).

PLOMER, W. (ed.), *Kilvert's Diary* (one-vol. selected edn., London, 1964).

PLUMB, J. H., *The Commercialisation of Leisure*. Stenton Lecture, University of Reading (Reading, 1973).

PONTING, K. G., 'Lawn Tennis: The Formative Years, 1880-1914', in Vamplew (ed.), *Economic History of Leisure*.

PRATT, J., and SLATER, M., 'A Fresh Look at Football Hooliganism', *Leisure Studies*, **3**, May 1984.

PRIESTLEY, J. B., *The Good Companions* (London, 1929).

—— *English Journey* (London, 1934).

QUIGLY, I., *The Heirs of Tom Brown* (London, 1982).

RADER, B., 'Modern Sports: In Search of Interpretations', *Journal of Social History*, **13**, Winter 1979.

—— *American Sports: From the Age of Folk Games to the Age of Spectators* (Englewood Cliffs, NJ, 1983).

RANGER, T., 'The Invention of Tradition in Colonial Africa', in Hobsbawm and Ranger, *The Invention of Tradition*.

REARDON, R., with BUXTON, P., *Ray Reardon* (London, 1982).

REASON, J., and JAMES, C., *The World of Rugby: A History of Rugby Union Football* (London, 1979).

REDFERN, A., 'Crewe: Leisure in a Railway Town', in Walvin and Walton, *Leisure in Britain*.

REDMOND, G., *The Sporting Scots of Nineteenth Century Canada* (Toronto, 1982).

—— 'Moral Tales for Manly Boys: Christian Sport in Children's Literature, 1783-1857', in Proceedings of the First Annual Conference of the BSSH, Sept. 1983 (privately circulated).

REES, R., 'The Development of Physical Recreation in Liverpool during the Nineteenth Century', MA thesis (Liverpool, 1968).

REID, D. A., 'The Decline of Saint Monday, 1766-1876', *Past and Present*, no. 71, May 1976.

—— 'Interpreting the Festival Calendar: Wakes and Fairs as Carnivals', in Storch (ed.), *Popular Culture and Custom*.

—— 'Labour, Leisure and Politics in Birmingham, c.1800–1875', Ph.D. thesis (Birmingham, 1985).

RIGAUER, B., *Sport and Work*, trans. A. Guttman (New York, 1981).

ROBBINS, D., 'Sport and Youth Culture', in Hargreaves (ed.), *Sport, Culture and Ideology*.

—— *We Hate Humans* (London, 1984).

—— and COHEN, P., *Knuckle Sandwich: Growing up in the Working Class City* (London, 1978).

ROBBINS, K., *Nineteenth Century Britain: integration and diversity* (Oxford, 1988).

ROLLEN, J., *Soccer at War, 1939–1945* (London, 1985).

ROSS, A., *Ranji: Prince of Cricketers* (London, 1983).

—— (ed.), *The Penguin Cricketer's Companion* (London, 1981).

ROSSELLI, J., 'The Self-Image of Effeteness: Physical Education and Nationalism in Nineteenth Century Bengal', *Past and Present*, no. 86, Feb. 1980.

ROTHMAN, B., *The 1932 Kinder Trespass* (Altrincham, 1982).

RUBINSTEIN, D., 'Cycling in the 1890's', *Victorian Studies*, 21, Autumn 1977.

—— 'Sport and the Sociologist 1890–1914', *BJSH*, May 1984.

RÜHL, J. K., 'Religion and Amusements in Sixteenth and Seventeenth Century England', *BJSH*, 1, Sept. 1984.

RULE, J. G., 'Methodism, Popular Beliefs and Village Culture in Cornwall, 1800–1850', in Storch (ed.), *Popular Culture and Custom*.

SANDIFORD, K. A., 'English Cricket Crowds during the Victorian age', *JSH*, 4, Winter 1982.

—— 'The Professionalization of Modern Cricket', *BJSH*, 2, Dec. 1985.

—— 'Cricket and the Barbadian Society', *Canadian Journal of History*, 21, Dec. 1986.

—— and STODDART, B., 'The Élite Schools and Cricket in Barbados: A Study in Colonial Continuity', *IJHS*, 4, Dec. 1987.

SASSOON, S., *Memoirs of a Fox-hunting Man* (London, 1960 edn.).

SCANNELL, V., *Sporting Literature: An Anthology* (Oxford, 1987).

SETH-SMITH, M., WILLET, P., MORTIMER, R., LAWRENCE, J., *The History of Steeplechasing* (London, 1966).

SHILS, E., *Tradition* (London, 1982).

SHIPLEY, S., 'Tom Causer of Bermondsey: A Boxer Hero of the 1890's', *History Workshop Journal*, no. 15, Spring 1983.

—— 'Two Faces of Boxing', abstract in *Bulletin of the Society for the Study of Labour History*, no. 50, Spring 1985.

SHORROCKS, A., *Winners and Champions: The Story of Manchester United's 1948 FA Cup and 1952 Championship Winning Teams* (London, 1985).

SISSONS, R., and STODDART, B., *Cricket and Empire: The 1932 Bodyline Tour of Australia* (London, 1984).

SMITH, D., and WILLIAMS, G., *Fields of Praise: The Official History of the Welsh Rugby Union 1881-1981* (Cardiff, 1980).

SMITH, M., PARKER, S., and SMITH, C. (eds.), *Leisure and Society in Britain* (London, 1973).

SMOUT, T. C., *A Century of the Scottish People* (London, 1986).

SPEAKE, M., 'The Social Anatomy of Participation in Sport in Lancaster in Early Victorian England', in *Proceedings of the XI HISPA International Congress*, ed. J. A. Mangan (Glasgow, 1987).

STACEY, M., *Tradition and Change: A Study of Banbury* (Oxford, 1970 edn.).

STEARNS, P., *Lives of Labour* (London, 1975).

—— *Be a Man! Males in Modern Society* (New York, 1979).

—— 'The Effort at Continuity in Working Class Culture', *Journal of Modern History*, **52**, Dec. 1980.

STEDMAN-JONES, G., 'Working Class Culture and Working Class Politics in London, 1870-1900', *Journal of Social History*, **7**, Summer 1974.

—— 'Class Expression versus Social Control? A Critique of Recent Trends in the Social History of "Leisure" ', *History Workshop Journal*, no. 4, Autumn 1977.

—— *Outcast London: A Study in the Relationship between Classes in Victorian Society* (London, 1984 edn.).

STEVENSON, J., *British Society 1914-45* (London, 1984).

STEWART, G. J., 'The British Reaction to the Conquest of Everest', *JSH*, **7**, Spring 1980.

STODDART, B., 'Cricket's Imperial Crisis: The 1932 MCC Tour of Australia', in Cashman and McKernan, *Sport in History*.

—— 'Sport, Cultural Imperialism and Colonial Response in the British Empire: A Framework for Analysis', in Proceedings of the Fourth Annual Conference of the BSSH, 1986 (privately circulated).

STORCH, R. D. (ed.), *Popular Culture and Custom in Nineteenth Century England* (London, 1982).

STOREY, D., *This Sporting Life* (London, 1962).

STRUTT, J., *The Sports and Pastimes of the People of England* (1903 edn.), reissued with a preface by N. and R. McWhirter (London, 1969).

STUDD, S., *Herbert Chapman: Footballer Emperor: A Study in the Origins of Modern Soccer* (London, 1981).

SUGDEN, J., and BAIRNER, A., 'Northern Ireland: Sport in a Divided Society', in L. Allison (ed.), *The Politics of Sport* (Manchester, 1986).

SURTEES, R. S., *Mr Sponge's Sporting Tour* (Oxford, 1982 edn.).

TALBOT, M., *Women and Leisure* (Sports Council/SSRC, 1979).

TAYLOR, I., 'On the Sports' Violence Question: Soccer Hooliganism Revisited', in Hargreaves (ed.), *Sport, Culture and Ideology*.

THOMAS, K. V., 'Work and Leisure in Pre-industrial Society', *Past and Present*, no. 29, Dec. 1964.

—— *Rule and Misrule in the Schools of Early Modern England*. Stenton Lecture, University of Reading (Reading, 1975).

—— *Man and the Natural World* (London, 1983).

THOMPSON, E. P., 'Time, Work Discipline and Industrial Capitalism', *Past and Present*, no. 38, Dec. 1967.

THOMPSON, F. M. L., *English Landed Society in the Nineteenth Century* (London, 1963).

THOMSON, A. A., *Hirst and Rhodes* (London, 1986 edn.).

THOMSON, I., 'The Acceptance of a National Policy for Physical Recreation in Scotland, 1872–1908', Ph.D. thesis (University of Stirling, 1976).

THORBURN, A. M. C., *The Scottish Rugby Union: The Official History* (Edinburgh, 1985).

TIFFIN, H., 'Cricket, Literature and the Politics of Decolonisation: The Case of C. L. R. James', in Cashman and McKernan, *Sport: Money, Morality and the Media*.

TISCHLER, S., *Footballers and Businessmen* (New York, 1981).

TOMLINSON, A., *Leisure and the Role of Clubs and Voluntary Groups* (Sports Council/SSRC, 1979).

TRANTER, N. L., 'Popular Sports and the Industrial Revolution in Scotland: The Evidence of the Statistical Accounts', *IJHS*, **14,** May 1987.

—— 'The Social and Occupational Structure of Organised Sport in Central Scotland during the Nineteenth Century', *IJHS*, **4,** Dec. 1987.

TRELFORD, D., *Snookered* (London, 1986).

TREVOR-ROPER, H., 'The Invention of Tradition: The Highland Tradition in Scotland', in Hobsbawm and Ranger, *The Invention of Tradition*.

VAMPLEW, W., *The Turf: A Social and Economic History of Horse Racing* (London, 1976).

—— 'The Sport of Kings and Commoners: The Commercialisation of British Horse Racing in the Nineteenth Century', in Cashman and McKernan, *Sport in History*.

—— 'Ungentlemanly Conduct: The Control of Soccer Crowd Behaviour, 1888–1914', in T. C. Smout (ed.), *The Search for Wealth and Stability* (London, 1979).

—— 'Playing for Pay: the Earnings of Professional Sportsmen in England 1870–1914', in Cashman and McKernan, *Sport: Money, Morality and the Media*.

—— 'The Economics of a Sports Industry: Scottish Gate Money Football, 1890–1914', *Economic History Review*, **35,** Nov. 1982.

—— 'Profit or Utility Maximisation? Analysis of English County Cricket before 1914', in Vamplew (ed.), *Economic History of Leisure*.

—— (ed.), *The Economic History of Leisure: Papers Presented at the Eighth International Economic History Congress, Budapest, August 1982* (Flinders University of South Australia, 1983).

VEBLEN, T., *The Theory of the Leisure Class: An Economic Study of Institutions*, introd. C. Wright-Mills (London, 1970).

VEITCH, C., ' "Play Up! Play Up! and Win the War!" Football, the Nation and the First World War', *Journal of Contemporary History*, **20**, July 1985.

WAGG, S., *The Football World: A Contemporary Social History* (London, 1984).

WALKER, H., 'The Popularisation of the Outdoor Movement', *BJSH*, **2**, Sept. 1985.

WALLER, P. J., *Town, City and Nation: England 1850–1914* (Oxford, 1983).

WALSH, N., *Dixie Dean* (Newton Abbot, 1977).

WALTON, J. K., and POOLE, R., 'The Lancashire Wakes', in Storch (ed.), *Popular Culture and Custom*.

—— and WALVIN, J., *Leisure in Britain 1780–1939* (Manchester, 1983).

WALVIN, J., *The People's Game: A Social History of British Football* (London, 1975).

—— *Leisure and Society, 1830–1950* (London, 1978).

—— *A Child's World: A Social History of English Childhood, 1800–1914* (London, 1982).

—— *Football and the Decline of Britain* (London, 1986).

WARD, A., and ALLISTER, I., *Barnsley: A Study in Football* (Barton-under-Needwood, Staffs., 1981).

WARNER, Sir Pelham, *Lord's 1787–1945* (London, 1946).

WATERS, C., 'Social Reformers, Socialists and the Opposition to the Commercialisation of Leisure in Late Victorian Britain', in Vamplew (ed.), *Economic History of Leisure*.

WATSON, R., and GRAY, M., *The Penguin Book of the Bicycle* (London, 1978).

WAUGH, A., *The Loom of Youth* (London, 1955 edn.).

WEEKS, J., *Sex, Politics and Society: The Regulation of Sexuality since 1800* (London, 1981).

WERTHEIMER, E., *Portrait of the Labour Party* (London, 1929).

WHANNEL, G., 'Football, Crowd Behaviour and the Press', *Media, Culture and Society*, **1**, 1979, no. 4.

—— *Blowing the Whistle: The Politics of Sport* (London, 1983).

WHITSON, D., 'Factors in the Survival of Local Games against the Inroads of Metropolitan Culture: A Scottish Case Study, in *Proceedings of the 5th Canadian Symposium on the History of Sport, Toronto, Sept. 1982*.

—— 'Structure, Agency and the Sociology of Sport Debates', *Theory, Culture and Society*, **3**, 1986, no. 1.

WIENER, M. J., *English Culture and the Decline of the Industrial Spirit* (Cambridge, 1981).

WILKINSON, D. G., 'Association Football in Brighton before 1920', MA thesis (Sussex, 1971).

WILLIAMS, G., 'From Grand Slam to Great Slump: Economy, Society and Rugby Football in Wales during the Depression', *Welsh History Review*, **11,** June 1983.

—— 'How Amateur was my Valley?: Professional Sport and Amateur Identity in Wales 1890-1914', *BJSH*, **2,** Dec. 1985.

—— 'From Popular Culture to Public Cliché: Image and Identity in Wales', in Mangan (ed.), *Pleasure, Profit and Proselytism.*

WILLIAMS, M., *The Way to Lord's: Cricketing Letters to The Times* (London, 1984).

WILLIAMS, R., *The Long Revolution* (London, 1961).

—— *The Country and the City* (London, 1973).

WILLIAMS, W. M., *Gosforth: The Sociology of an English Village* (London, 1956).

WILLIS, P., *Learning to Labour: How Working Class Kids Get Working Class Jobs* (London, 1977).

WILLMOTT, P., *Adolescent Boys of East London* (London, 1969).

WRIGHT, T., *Some Habits and Customs of the Working Classes, by a Journeyman Engineer* (1867; New York, 1967 edn.).

——*The Great Unwashed, by 'The Journeyman Engineer', 1868* (London, 1970 edn.).

WYNN JONES, M., *The Derby* (London, 1979).

YEO, S., *Religion and Voluntary Association in Crisis* (London, 1976).

——and YEO, E. (eds.), *Popular Culture and Class Conflict, 1590-1914: Explorations in the History of Labour and Leisure* (Brighton, 1981).

YOUNG, M., and WILLMOTT, P., *The Symmetrical Family* (London, 1973).

YOUNG, P., *A History of British Football* (London, 1968).

INDEX

Abel, Bobby 289–90
Abrahams, Harold 275
Africa 207–8, 210–11, 219
 see also imperialism; South Africa
agricultural revolution 48–50, 54
Aikman-Smith, James 111
Aintree 57, 64
Alcock, C. W. 107
Allen, 'Gubby' 113
Allis, Peter 324
Allison, George 311, 314
Almond, Hely Hutchison 81
 see also Loretto
Alverstone, Richard Everard
 Webster, 1st Viscount 111
amateurism 4–5, 74, 96–9, 102,
 104–5, 116–17, 120–1, 174,
 205–7, 220, 248–9, 281, 321,
 344–6, 349–50
 see also class; fair play; middle
 classes; public schools
animals, attitudes to 32
 see also bull-baiting, cockfighting,
 cruelty, hunting
anti-Semitism 133, 351
Archer, Fred 304
archery 72
Arlott, John 10, 316
Arnold, Matthew 95
Arnold, Thomas 1, 75, 82
Arsenal FC 175, 256, 336, 338–9
Astley-Cooper, J. 224
Aston Villa FC 138, 293
athletics:
 Amateur Athletic Association
 109–11, 275–6
 four-minute mile 279
 Ireland 244–5
 pedestrianism 38, 62, 103–4,
 184–5, 300–1, 348–9
 women 129–30
 see also amateurism;
 Commonwealth Games;
 Olympic Games
Australia 203, 207, 229–36
 see also cricket

Baden-Powell, Robert Stephenson
 Smyth, 1st Baron 205, 327
badminton 125, 211
Baird, George Alexander ('The
 Squire') 64–6
Baldwin, Stanley 268, 269
Balfour, Arthur James 125, 269
Bannister, Roger 278
Barnes, S. F. 176
Barnsley FC 168, 175, 295–6
Barson, Frank 295
Baxter, Jim 260
Beale, Dorothea 121
bear-baiting 30
Beauclerk, Revd Lord Frederick
 27, 103
Beaumont, Bill 324
Belfast, boxing in 302
Bell, Lady (Florence) 183–4
Bennett, Arnold 285
Berg, Jack 'Kid' 302
Bergman-Osterberg, Martina 118–19
Best, George, 245, 316, 324
billiards 190–1, 211, 215
Birkenhead, F. E. Smith, 1st Earl of
 269
Birmingham 42, 125, 150–1, 175,
 178, 333
Blackburn 115, 167
Blackheath RFC 116
Blair, A. S. 111
Bloomer, Steve 163, 324
Boat Race 23, 75–6, 83, 96, 312–13
 see also Cambridge; Oxford;
 rowing
bodyline series 233–6
 see also Australia; cricket
Bolton FC 297
 crowd disaster of 1946: 287, 329
Botham, Ian 310, 324–5
bowls 28, 72, 158, 193
 crown green 157, 189–90, 325
 and miners 63–4, 156
boxing 147, 149, 276, 301–3
 pugilism 20–2, 62, 64–5, 180,
 182